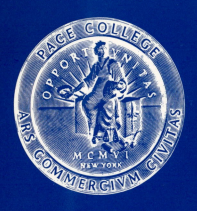

LIVERPOOL AND
MERSEYSIDE

LIVERPOOL AND MERSEYSIDE

Essays in the economic and social history
of the port and its hinterland

Edited by

J. R. HARRIS

AUGUSTUS M. KELLEY PUBLISHERS
New York 1969

First published in 1969 by
FRANK CASS AND COMPANY LIMITED
67 Great Russell Street, London W.C.1.

Published in the United States by
Augustus M. Kelley, Publishers
New York, New York 10010

SBN 7146 1314 2

Library of Congress Catalog Card No. 68–21449

Printed in Great Britain

Contributors

B. L. Anderson, Lecturer in Economic History, University of Manchester.

D. E. Baines, Lecturer in Economic History, London School of Economics and Political Science.

T. C. Barker, Professor of Economic and Social History, University of Kent at Canterbury.

R. Bean, Lecturer in Economics, University of Liverpool.

P. N. Davies, Lecturer in Economic History, University of Liverpool.

J. R. Harris, Senior Lecturer in Economic History, University of Liverpool.

F. Neal, Principal Lecturer in Economics, Mid-Essex Technical College.

G. W. Oxley, Archivist, City and County of Kingston upon Hull.

B. H. Tolley, Lecturer in Education, University of Nottingham.

D. M. Williams, Lecturer in Economic History, University of Leicester.

Contents

Maps

Introduction

THE STUDY of regional history has a perennial importance to the economic and social historian. Admittedly, in the immediate post-war era there were occasionally those to be met with who hinted that its value might be declining, that diminishing returns might be setting in. Many of the regions which were most interesting from an industrial point of view already had notable works of scholarship devoted to them—for example, the studies of Scotland by Hamilton, of North Wales by Dodd, and of the Midlands by Court. It seemed reasonable to ask if this work need be done over again, if it were necessary that every other region which had undergone marked economic development need be similarly surveyed, and if a proliferation of such surveys would add much to our understanding. But the more closely the origins of economic growth are examined, the more interesting the study becomes. On the one hand the theoretical study of economic growth has given the economic historian a new box of tools with which to tackle the job, and even if at first he may tend to blunt or twist them in an attempt to do more than they are capable of, the range of work he can successfully undertake has certainly been much extended. Moreover, it is increasingly realised that it is only after an intensive study of many aspects of pre-industrial and industrialising society that can we be at all confident of identifying the seeds of growth; in addition to more conventional economic factors the historian will now look for such things as the level of technological knowhow at any period and the means of disseminating it, educational patterns and standards, social mobility and those influences in the political and social atmosphere which permit and encourage, or hinder and discourage, economic enterprise. The more aspects of life we need to look into, the more complex the tasks of investigation and interpretation become, and the more difficult does it become to cover all these factors on a national scale so as to make valid generalisations about them.

The task however, though formidable, is not so unmanageable or insuperable when tackled on a regional basis. Perhaps even here the day is passing when the solitary scholar could make a broad survey entirely based upon personal research; the day of carefully planned team studies, conducted with a continuous exchange of findings and ideas, may be soon upon us. But whether individual or team work prevails broadly-based research can build up a more complete, and hence a more satisfying, picture of the historical growth of a regional economy than of the national one, and the best hope we have of a reliable national picture comes from the assembly of a number of regional ones. There are many regional record sources containing most important evidence which are still seriously under-investigated. Though voluminous they can be searched and analysed thoroughly by scholars of sufficient energy and resource; among such records there immediately come to mind parish registers, wills, legal proceedings (especially where geographically limited in their coverage as in the case of Quarter Sessions and Palatinate courts), shipping registers, port books, poor law papers.

The examination of local sources can provoke questions, which when asked and answered in terms of one area, demand to be posed in other comparable regions, and perhaps nationally. Many years ago when investigating the Old Poor Law in a very limited area of Lancashire I met with some firm information, and many hints, that the Workhouse Test Act of 1723 was of much greater practical importance than it was generally deemed to have been; subsequent much wider research by Mr. Oxley, some of which appears in this book, indicates that this was generally true of South Lancashire. It would be well worth the while of Poor Law historians elsewhere to examine whether this applies in other regions. If it does, we have to further modify our ideas on workhouse policy under the Old Poor Law; if it does not, we realise that Lancashire is marked out from other parts of the country in this important aspect of the administration of the poor.

Other evidence from the same study suggested to me that the activity of the small investor was much greater in the century after the Restoration than had ever been suggested by historians of the period; Mr. Anderson's recent investigation of Lancashire sources for the middle of the eighteenth century (which has included the examination of 6000 wills) has shown how extensive this investment was. In these pages he confines himself to the part played by the lawyers in making the local capital market an efficient one. His findings prove that too much attention has in the past been focused on the large lenders and the large borrowing institutions, whereas it would appear that in South Lancashire virtually all classes were active lenders or borrowers, or both. How far was this a particular characteristic of South Lancashire? How far back did it go? A preliminary examination of my own* would indicate that the same pattern can

*This survey, which is not yet complete, will cover Liverpool and its environs over the last two decades of the seventeenth century.

be clearly discerned at the end of the seventeenth century—but was it already active long before? Was there a simple and smooth transition from a period when borrowing was largely for expenditure on land and its improvement (or for the temporary or long-term relief of improvident or unsuccessful landholders) to one where a large proportion of the borrowing was for ventures in industry or foreign trade? The pattern so far revealed shows not only that investment habits spread far down the scale but also that men with only a small personal estate and a modest range of household goods can be found to have had a surprisingly large part, even sometimes a majority, of that estate lent out on mortgage, bond, or note of hand. Was this situation unique to Lancashire? Is it paralleled in other regions of rapid economic growth? How far can it explain that growth?

These are merely examples of the questions which are provoked by a close study of regional sources. There are, as we have seen, occasions when the historian is struck by theories or interpretations which have gained current attention in the field of modern economic and social theory at a national or international level, and is stimulated to try them out on historical evidence to see if they can explain the riddles of the past. Quite as frequently, however, the investigation of regional sources will show the people of past periods exhibiting patterns of behaviour which have been previously unobserved, or which have been observed only in random instances, without an understanding of their wider significance. Patterns established in one region can then be searched for in others until we know whether it is an interesting regional variant or a factor of national significance which we have discerned. Where, as in the case of Merseyside, we have under examination an area of particularly rapid economic development it becomes especially interesting to see if patterns newly discovered there have their parallels in other regions of marked expansion.

It is hardly necessary to defend Merseyside as a region with an economic and social history of great interest. Beginning with the early transatlantic voyages of the Restoration period the growth of Liverpool was swift, often furious. Her population multiplied about fifteen times during the eighteenth century and about ten times during the nineteenth. For the benefit of Liverpool merchants the first commercial dock in the outports was begun in 1709 and the first English canal of the Industrial Revolution in 1755. The eighteenth century saw Liverpool rise to predominance in the most miserable of trades, that in African slaves, and in its last years a similar dominance was achieved in the trade with the U.S.A. As Mr. Tolley shows, the political disruptions which blocked and hampered trade with the United States, culminating in war in 1812–14, had unusual significance for Liverpool and gave rise to a strong local reaction. To study nineteenth-century Liverpool is virtually to study the international economy in microcosm; throughout the century she was the main outlet for British manufacturers and a main centre of import of many principal commodities, principally raw cotton and timber, and her trade covered the globe. Early in the century her shipping, as Mr. Neal shows, was growing relatively much faster than the national total, and Liverpool shipowners led the way in the development of the steam liner trades in the late nineteenth century. Dr. Davies is able to illustrate this for us by examining the development of the African Steam Ship Company, which came to form part of Elder Dempsters, and was a stepping stone to commercial power of one of Liverpool's greatest tycoons, Sir Alfred Lewis Jones.

Behind all this commercial development there was a great deal of misery and degradation. Liverpool was the first great staging post of the Irish migration, but also itself a main centre of absorption, notorious for overcrowding, for cellar dwelling, for the low expectancy of life of its slum districts. Labour questions were complicated by the bitter divisions between Protestants and Catholics, which were exacerbated by fanatics on either side, while the employment of many of the working classes, that of the dockers especially, was dangerously dependent on the fluctuations in the level of activity on the waterfront. The hardness and precariousness of life in nineteenth-century Liverpool meant that by the early twentieth century the local labour movement showed its resilience and solidarity in bitter strikes, and those qualities (as Mr. Baines and Mr. Bean show) later influenced its participation in the General Strike of 1926, from which local labour emerged having displayed better organising power and greater efficiency than its national leadership.

This very incomplete catalogue is sufficient to show that the economic and social history of modern Liverpool is full of interesting subjects for the historian. Perhaps one of the most fascinating puzzles for future social historians will be the way in which the city came to impose its image on the international world of entertainment and 'pop' culture in the 1960s. Yet, to take the economic aspect alone, we have (among others) omitted all the topics relating to the provision of docks and of transport facilities to the hinterland, and, within that hinterland, the growth of industrial towns with close regional ties with Liverpool—Birkenhead, St. Helens, Warrington, Widnes, Runcorn.

This book can attempt to deal with only a few of these themes. The collection has been made with several ideas in mind. In 1965 there had been completed, or were nearing completion, several pieces of research by young scholars associated with the Department of Economics at Liverpool, where over the last two decades Professor F. E. Hyde had strongly encouraged research into regional economic history. I had been privileged to teach many of them as undergraduates and had been able to take a keen interest in their later research. In the cases of Mr. Oxley, Mr. Anderson, Mr. Tolley and Mr. Neal, their postgraduate studies had been under my own supervision. While the diverse topics of research reflected the individual interests of the scholars concerned they were all closely linked to Liverpool and its region. These were not the only common features. For instance, the studies of Mr. Tolley, Mr. Neal and Mr. Williams were good examples of the way in which careful quantification, based on statistics of some reliability can result in positive statements about economic trends. On each of the studies they undertook, even where ignorance had not formerly prevailed, there had been only unsatisfactory surmise, based upon facts which were possibly untypical. To obtain reliable statistical trends of Liverpool's trade during the period of dispute and war with U.S.A., or to elucidate the cotton trade and shipping activities of Liverpool in the early nineteenth century, is not to pursue a subject of a limited local importance, but to make a major study of a main sector of the national economy with important international effects.

It seemed worth while and appropriate to bring together some of the work of these younger scholars which focused on the Merseyside region, and to do so at a length which would give readers an opportunity of judging the quality of their work, rather than in the unsatisfying fragments which seem increasingly common in symposia. While the volume was still being planned I was delighted to be given the opportunity to include two further essays which fitted in very happily with our regional theme. The first, by Professor T. C. Barker and the late F. A. Bailey, was welcome because of my close associations with both authors, particularly Professor Barker, and because it helped to perpetuate Bailey's memory; all who recall his services to historical pursuits in Lancashire and Cheshire will be glad, I am sure, that some of his unpublished research has seen the light. The collaboration of the two authors had achieved a most valuable synthesis of regional and metropolitan research material, and remarkably illustrated the importance for technology in general of a most interesting regional development, the extreme division of labour in the specialised domestic manufacture of watch parts, and the associated development of early, but quite sophisticated, machine tools. The second essay, by D. E. Baines and R. Bean, on the

General Strike on Merseyside, strengthened the social history content of the volume, provided a topic from the twentieth century, and gave me the welcome opportunity of publishing the latest research of two friends and departmental colleagues. Finally, I have included a revised version of an earlier essay of my own, partly to represent that most significant aspect of Merseyside history which is concerned with the inland transport facilities of the port, partly to produce an example of the conflict of interest and opinion in the eighteenth century, and partly because I felt it would gain from the company it was in.

It is not, I am told, unknown for editors of intended symposia to find themselves exasperated by delayed or by unpublishable manuscript, or even by the situation where some of those who have promised essays never put pen to paper at all. It has been my good luck to have a group of collaborators who were understanding, helpful, and punctual, so that the manuscript reached the publisher only a few months later than our first, very optimistic, estimate. For their politeness and patience under editorial prodding I am very grateful. Mr. Frank Cass has been encouraging and tolerant—what more can one ask of one's publisher?—while his assistant, Mrs. Patricia Lawrence, has managed to reduce those production problems which are often made to seem so mountainous to minimal proportions, and her friendly efficiency has made the task much less daunting. Mr. B. L. Anderson and my colleagues P. L. Cottrell, J. H. Porter and P. N. Davies have helped me with proofs. My secretary, Mrs. Jean Girling, has spotted my errors, repaired my omissions and made light of a variety of difficult tasks. I can only trust that an enterprise in which I have been instrumental in involving many others, and in which they have given me such willing co-operation, will prove to have been worth their efforts.

J. R. HARRIS

October, 1967

CHAPTER ONE

The Seventeenth-Century Origins of Watchmaking in South-West Lancashire

F. A. BAILEY AND T. C. BARKER*

I

THE PUBLISHED histories of British watchmaking, written mainly by connoisseurs and technical specialists, notably Britten and Baillie,[1] have been based chiefly upon the evidence of the watches themselves, eked out by such biographical information as could be gleaned about the men whose names or initials appeared upon them. There are obvious dangers in this particular form of approach, for, as a writer explained more than two centuries ago:

> 'At the first Appearance of Watches they were but rude to what they are now; they were began and ended by one Man, who was called a Watch-Maker; but of late Years the Watch-Maker properly so called, scarce makes any thing belonging to a Watch, he only employs the different Tradesmen among whom the Art is divided, and puts the several Pieces of the Movement together and adjusts and finishes it. . . . The Watch-Maker puts his Name upon the Plate, and is esteemed the Maker, though he has not made in his Shop the smallest Wheel belonging to it.'[2]

Perhaps we may doubt whether, even in the very early days to which the writer refers at the beginning of the quotation, one man made the whole watch. It seems unlikely that any one craftsman could

* I began to collaborate with F. A. Bailey, Senior History Master at Prescot Grammar School, in his researches on this subject four years before his sudden and tragic death in 1955. When I joined him, he had already amassed a great deal of information not only from Prescot sources, of which he had an unrivalled knowledge, but also from others in the area. Our collaboration was extremely happy and would have resulted in a book about the watchmaking industry long before now. That this present chapter is the only published result of our researches yet to appear, is due mainly to the loss of the senior member of the partnership and partly to my having become involved in other commitments. I hope, however, to produce the book as a joint work in due course. I would like to acknowledge the help we received from the late Professor D. S. Torrens, Dr. W. H. Chaloner, Mr. B. C. Jones and Mr. R. Sharpe France (T. C. B.).

1

produce specially-tempered steel springs, steel pinions, brass wheels, frames and dials and the often elaborate and costly cases, though there was probably no division of labour in the manufacture of movements at the outset. Even then, therefore, the name on the dial did not truly represent all the makers of the various parts: some of the work was almost certainly sub-contracted. Later, as the writer rightly emphasises, the 'watchmaker' though himself usually a trained man, spent all his time organising the actual manufacturers and selling the finished product. His name on the watch face vouched for its quality and fulfilled the function of a present-day trade-mark. No doubt these were the great business men in the trade; but to write the history of the actual manufacturing of watch parts in terms of these names alone is almost as misleading as it would be today to try to write the history of the hosiery or shirt industry in terms of the owners of the trade mark 'St. Michael'.

So long as watches remained articles of luxury, the main market for them was in London. But since the price of labour, the main item in watchmaking costs,[3] was higher in London than elsewhere, it was obviously advantageous for as much of the manufacturing as possible to be done in these lower-cost areas. It has long been known from printed sources that south-west Lancashire had developed into the main manufacturing centre by the later eighteenth century. Thomas Hatton, for instance, dedicated his *Introduction to the Mechanical Part of Clock and Watch Work* (1773) to Lord Stanley, whose family lived 'in the centre of the whole support of this great branch of trade'[4] and Thomas Pennant, passing through Prescot in the same year, noted that the district produced 'the best and almost all the watch-movements used in England'.[5] Although Francis Buckley's useful list of Liverpool horologists, compiled mainly from directories, poll books, wills and newspaper references, shows that watchmakers were already at work in the area at the end of the seventeenth century,[6] there has not so far been any serious attempt to discover what light the local manuscript sources shed on the subject.

II

The beginnings of watchmaking on the continent date from the year 1500 or soon afterwards. The use of the spring instead of weights as a driving mechanism for clocks made possible smaller clocks, and at the beginning of the sixteenth century Peter Henlein of Nuremburg is said to have produced the first portable spring-driven timekeeper small enough to be carried about on the person. The early watches were poor timekeepers and possessed only an hour hand; they were, nevertheless, expensive luxuries which could be afforded only by the well-to-do.[7]

The French soon learned the watchmaker's craft and, according to John Carte, who served his time as a watchmaker not later than the 1680s, the success of the French 'set the English on work and kindled in them a spirit of emulation, if possible to outdoe them: but this required time'.[8] The first English-made watches seem to date from the end of the sixteenth century. Although watchmaking grew out of clockmaking—the first English watchmakers, like Bartholomew Newsam, were primarily clockmakers—and although there remained close links between the two, watchmaking soon developed into a separate craft. Clockmaking was by origin blacksmiths' work. It had grown up in the fourteenth and fifteenth centuries when all the moving parts of clocks were made of iron. Although brass came to be used for the making of wheels, frames and dials of domestic (but not public) clocks after about 1550,[9] clockmaking was by then already well established as a form of smiths' work. It was no accident that the London Clockmakers' Company grew out of the Blacksmiths' Company.[10] Watchmaking, on the other hand—apart from the manufacture of the steel springs, arbors and pinions—was precision bench work calling for file, cutter and vice, not forge and anvil. Perhaps this explains why clockmakers were as widely spread geographically as smiths themselves, whereas watchmakers were much more localised.

The earliest known British watchmakers—or, at least, those whose names or initials appeared on watch faces—were London men. Carte, however, goes out of his way to select for special mention one of them who flourished in the 1620s called 'Mr. Aspinwell' whom he describes as 'an ingenious workman'.[11] This was probably Thomas Aspinwall, one of whose watches Britten illustrates and dates about 1605.[12] Nobody has yet identified this early pioneer. He was, however, almost certainly Thomas Aspinwall of Toxteth Park, just south of Liverpool, who died in 1624. The inventory of his goods, made for probate purposes, consists mainly of household and agricultural items typical of a yeoman farmer; but it concludes with the interesting entry: 'In the Worke Lofte—Tooles: watch worke and watch stuffe etc', valued at £10. At the time of his death he owed £180 and had £165 owing to him, including £3 10s. 0d. 'for a watch' from a Mr. Hyde, and 'an old det for a watch' and 20s. 'for a Larum' from a Mr. Stanley.[13]

The deer park at Toxteth had been disparked by the fourth Earl

B

of Derby in 1591 and divided into about twenty small farms for letting. As an extra-parochial area, it was a place which had obvious attractions for puritans. Thomas Aspinwall's eldest brother, Edward (1568–1633), probably the Edward Aspinwall of Lancashire who had matriculated at Oxford (Brasenose College) in 1585,[14] was already living there in 1596[15] and Thomas Aspinwall seems to have joined him soon afterwards. As the sons of William Aspinwall of Aspinwall in the township of Scarisbrick, they were not without means, and Edward Aspinwall left property not only in Scarisbrick but also in other parts of Lancashire.[16] Under his leadership the little puritan community at Toxteth Park attained some distinction, for it educated the eminent New England divine, Richard Mather,[17] and was the birthplace of the brilliant astronomer, Jeremiah Horrocks (educated at Emmanuel College, Cambridge), who was the first person to predict the transit of Venus.[18] He was the son of James Horrocks who had married the Aspinwalls' sister, Mary, in 1615. He is described as a watchmaker in his brother's will, drawn up in 1631.[19] Perhaps he was engaged in the Aspinwall business, and he may have managed it for a time, for Thomas Aspinwall's son, Samuel, who eventually took it over, was a minor at the time of his father's death.

It is difficult to know how to interpret this evidence of early watch-making at Toxteth Park, for it is so slender. What, for instance, was the scale of operations? Were Aspinwall and Horrocks developing a growing trade in a new industry or was Aspinwall's claim to recognition solely that he was 'an ingenious workman' who produced a few watches which, by the standards of the day, were of unusually good quality? If the former was true, then it is reasonable to suppose that a number of other men were already being employed in the area; if the latter—and the value of tools and materials in Aspinwall's work-loft when he died would make it more likely—then the Toxteth Park venture represents merely the very beginnings of something that was only to grow to national significance later.

Another question worth asking is whether there were others who, like Aspinwall and Horrocks, were trying their luck in the new craft. This we cannot answer with any conviction. But perhaps it may be significant that, of the only three other Lancashire watchmakers we have been able to trace in the 1620s and 1630s, one, Samuel Midgley, who was admitted to the freedom of Liverpool on 4 January 1636/7,[20] was the son of Ellen Aspinwall who had married Isaac Midgley in 1609, and the second, William Aspinall [sic], who is mentioned in the Manchester parish registers on 13 November 1628,[21] may have been Edward Aspinwall's son of that name. Only

James Gregson, who appears on the roll of the Preston Guild (celebrated at twenty-year intervals) in 1622 and again in 1642 had no clear connexion with the Aspinwalls.[22]

The most difficult question of all—why watchmaking should start two hundred miles away from the main market—is even more puzzling and perplexing in the present state of our knowledge, for the local records shed no light at all on this. It is worth noting, however, that there was already quite close contact between Lancashire and London. Adam Martindale,[23] for instance, who was born in the area at this time, remarks upon the numbers of people who fled from London to friends in Lancashire to escape the plague in 1625. His sister, who went to live in London soon afterwards, was supplied from home with 'country provisions such as bacon, cheeses, pots of butter etc.' It was by no means unusual for Lancashire people to have relatives in the capital. The Aspinwalls, for instance, had a brother-in-law, James Fletcher, who was a London haberdasher.[24] There was no lack of communication between Lancashire and London.

But, even granted this, why should south-west Lancashire have witnessed these early beginnings rather than other regions equally well, or perhaps better, situated? It is possible that investigation into other local records—at Coventry, for instance[25]—may reveal that there were stirrings elsewhere at the beginning of the seventeenth century. If so, it will make Lancashire's early start the less remarkable. Perhaps we need to look no further than the technical and entrepreneurial ability of one well-connected man living in the area where there was already a tradition of metal-working skill. (Matthew Gregson's hoary old explanation of the beginnings of Lancashire watchmaking in terms of the unemployed armourers of Halton Castle[26] is helpful in reminding us of this latter point, if of nothing else.) The makers of watch parts depended upon metal-working specialists for the production of their tools and, as we shall see presently, these toolmakers were very resourceful in developing mechanical aids for watchmaking. That the new craft should make its appearance in a small but obviously rather remarkable puritan community, will also, no doubt, be taken into account by those who hold that there is a link between dissent and the rise of capitalism.

III

Whatever may have been the status of Lancashire watchmaking in Thomas Aspinwall's time, there can be no doubt that his son, Samuel, greatly extended the family business during the forty years or so that he was in charge of it. When he died in 1672 he left watch-making materials worth, not £10 as his father had done, but £797 11s. 0d, and had owing to him, not £165, but £959 11s. 0d. In all, his goods and chattels were valued at £2,258 13s. 6d. He had evidently built up a thriving trade with London, for he owned premises there, which he left to one of his sons, Josiah. A hint of the scale on which he operated is contained in a passage in his will by which he gave to 'all watchmakers masters that have wrought under me each a pair of gloves and . . . all other watchmakers hereabouts Ribands'.[27] Here was a great man in the trade by national, as well as by local, standards.

The spread of Lancashire watchmaking begins to be reflected by this time in Liverpool, Wigan and Preston sources. The registers of St. Nicholas's, Liverpool, happen by good fortune to list occupations for a period during the later seventeenth century.[28] Twelve watchmakers are included during the 1670s: Joshua Cobham, Thomas Darbyshire, Henry Higginson, John Hoult, John Litherland, Joseph Pryor, John Storey, James and William Winstanley, James, John and Robert Whitfield. This source is of particular interest because it contains the first clear evidence that watch cases and springs were being made in the area, Cobham being described as a case-maker, Hoult as a spring-maker, and the Winstanleys as watch-smiths, a description which is made clear when William Winstanley also appears on another occasion in the register as a spring-maker. At Wigan the earliest known watchmaker, Roger Darbyshire, applied for the freedom of the borough in 1662 and explained that, although his home was at nearby Pemberton, he had for some time owned a watchmaking business in Wigan itself. At least five other craftsmen are known to have worked in or around the town between 1670 and 1700: Evan Hilton, John Billinge of Billinge, Oliver Platt, John Lowe of Ashton-in-Makerfield and Thomas Martin.[29] At Preston, the Guild Roll for 1682 includes the names of eight watchmakers: Richard Bolton, John Gregson, William Houghton, Robert Maire, Henry Mitton, Job Pemberton, Richard Houghton of Grimsargh and Robert Moore.[30] There are other references to watchmakers at this time in the records of Aigburth, Childwall, Halewood, Huyton, Prescot and West Derby, as well as of Toxteth itself. The industry was already firmly established in the area.

The growth of watchmaking owed much to the support it gained from the local toolmakers, and Lancashire's reputation for tools, as well as for watch parts, seems to have been established in the seventeenth, rather than in the eighteenth, century. At first these were limited to small tools such as pliers, nippers and files; but the local

makers seem to have shown considerable resourcefulness in inventing machines which not only saved labour but also performed the
various watchmaking operations more accurately than was possible
by hand. Carte, who possessed intimate practical knowledge of the
watchmaking industry from the 1680s, drew attention to

> 'the peculiar improvement the English have made in their En-
> gines and Tooles for the working-part whereby their Works are
> performed with the more quickness and exactness. They have
> invented that Curious Engine for the Cutting the Teeth of a
> Wheel, whereby that part of the work is done with an exactness
> which farr exceeds what can be performed by hand: Then there
> is an Engine for equalling the Ballance wheel: Likewise the En-
> gine for cutting the turnes of the Fusie: And lastly the Instrument
> for drawing of the steel pinion wier: All which ingenious inven-
> tions were first conceived and made at *Leverpool* in *Lancashire* in
> *England*.'[31]

Of these inventions, the wheel-cutting machine was the most important. It was no novelty in 1675, for a writer in that year advised
anyone buying a watch to be sure that the wheels in it were machine-
and not hand-cut.[32] A reference in the diary of the celebrated Robert
Hooke, on 16 August 1672, to a meeting between him and a 'Lancashire watchmaker's son about wheel-cutting engine'[33] has until
now been interpreted as meaning that Hooke in fact invented this
particular machine;[34] but in the light of our new information he
may well have been consulting the Lancashire watchmaker's son,
perhaps Josiah Aspinwall who, as we know, was living in London at
that date and was the son of the leading Lancashire watchmaker of
his day.

Of the origins of machines for equalling the balance wheel and for
cutting the turns of the fusee, nothing is known; but one or two early
references to pinion wire drawing are worth while recalling. When
an Englishman named Blackey (or Blakey) obtained permission to
draw pinion wire in France in 1744, he stated that the English had
then enjoyed a monopoly of the process for over forty years.[35]
According to Aikin, in his account of the Prescot area, published in
1795, 'the drawing of pinion wire originated here, which is carried
as far as fifty drawings, and the wire is completely adapted to every
size of pinions to drive the wheels of watches, admirable for truth and
fitness for the purpose, but left for the workmen to harden'.[36] A
local tradition, recalled nearly a century later, credited the invention to William Houghton who, it is said, first carried on the process
at Halebank, near Prescot.[37] Certainly a Mr. Houghton – not fur-

ther identified – reported to the Royal Society in March 1680 on his wire-drawing experiments; but this man seems to have been chiefly interested at the time in discovering a substitute for steel rods for drawing purposes and there is no evidence that he was concerned with *pinion* wire.[38] As Aikin indicated, the pinion wire-drawing process was a lengthy one, the slit steel rods having to be first of all roughly rounded by swaging between tools, then drawn in a round-holed drawplate, next passed through a plate with polygonal holes and finally drawn into pinion section by progressive stages, gradually deepening the grooves. The early pinions consisted of six or fewer leaves.

The later seventeenth century, of course, also witnessed important improvements in watchmaking itself as well as in the manufacture of particular watch parts and with some of these developments Lancashire men were associated. They do not, however, appear to have been connected in any way with the most important one, the invention of the balance spring, which greatly improved the time-keeping of watches and made possible the introduction of the minute hand. The conflicting claims of Hooke and Huygens to the invention are well known. Christian Huygens's communication to the Royal Society in February 1675 brought a strong reaction from Dr. Robert Hooke, who claimed that he had demonstrated the same principle to the Society a few years earlier, a claim which would seem to be justified.[39] A few weeks later Thomas Tompion, a London craftsman working under Hooke's instructions, made the famous balance-spring watch which was presented to the king. This gave Tompion enormous publicity and from relative obscurity he quickly became the most celebrated 'watchmaker'—i.e. watch dealer—in the country. 'Is yours Aspenwolds? [Aspinwalls]' asks a character in Shadwell's play, *The Lancashire Witches* (1681), who is discussing the behaviour of his watch with a friend. 'No', comes the reply, 'Tompions'.

Although Tompion has been studied by a number of writers, none of them has yet satisfactorily explained how a man trained as a blacksmith was able to become overnight a highly successful watchmaker. The first thirty years of his life are very obscure. It is not even known when he arrived in London from (presumably) Northill, near Biggleswade, where he had been born, the son of a blacksmith, in 1639. Mr. Symonds in his *Life*[40] is even of the opinion that his arrival may not have been until 1671 when he was admitted a brother of the Clockmakers' Company. (He became a freeman by redemption three years later.) He was then a 'great clockmaker', that is to say a man who specialised in large turret, or church, iron clocks.[41] His first task for Hooke, undertaken in 1674, was to make, not a watch, but a quadrant of hammered iron and brass to be shown at the Royal Society. Indeed, it was not until Hooke himself had given him practical advice upon the techniques of watchmaking that Tompion was able to make his celebrated watch in the following year—which, not surprisingly, took him from 10 April to 28 July, much to Hooke's growing irritation. On the strength of the fame which this brought him, he was able to move his premises to a fine situation at the corner of Water Lane and Fleet Street. But how much help did he need to achieve the scale of production that his new-found fame now demanded? Like other London 'watch-makers' whose names appeared upon the face of their products, he must have been above all a good organiser of other workmen. And, in the light of what we now know about Lancashire's role in the watch industry by this time, is it too much to suppose that some of the watch parts and some of the tools he used for finishing may have come from Lancashire? Indeed, is tempting to see Tompion taking over from the Aspinwalls and, perhaps, employing many of the Lancashire craftsmen whom they had employed, for after Samuel Aspinwall's death in 1672 the drive seems to have gone out of their business.[41]

Tompion was certainly associated with Edward Barlow (1639–1719), the Lancashire recusant priest whose inventive genius in the field of watchmaking contemporaries ranked second only to that of Hooke. His place in the *Dictionary of National Biography* is well deserved. Edward Booth, the son of Richard and Jane Booth, was born in the township of Woolston in Warrington parish and was baptised at Warrington parish church on 15 December 1639.[42] According to a contemporary, Charles Dodd, who knew him well, he later assumed the name of Barlow in tribute to his godfather, Ambrose Barlow, a Benedictine monk who was executed at Lancaster in 1641.[43] He was sent to the English College at Lisbon where he was ordained priest, and came back to England 'on the mission', spending some time with Lord Langdale in Yorkshire before returning to his native Lancashire, where he resided with the Houghton family at Park Hall in the parish of Charnock Richard, near Chorley. According to Dodd,

'He was master of the Latin and Greek languages, and had a competent knowledge of the Hebrew, before he went abroad: and 'tis thought the age he lived in could not show a person better qualified by nature for the mathematical sciences; tho' he read not many books of that kind: the whole system of natural causes seeming to be lodged within him from his first use of reason. He has often told me that at his first perusing Euclid, that author was easy to him as a newspaper'.

He took an interest in watchwork, an interest no doubt generated by the watchmaking activity of the area.

Barlow was the first man to invent a clock which would, on the pulling of a string, strike the hour, quarter and minute at any time of the day or night. This invention, said to have been made about the middle of the 1670s, was

'talked of among the London Artists, [who] set their heads to work; who presently contrived several ways to effect such a performance. And hence arose the divers ways of Repeating work, which so early might be observed to be about the Town, every man almost practising according to his own Invention'.[44]

Although Barlow made no attempt to patent this first invention for the manufacture of repeating clocks, he did try to take out a patent in 1686/8 after he had devised a means of applying his invention to watches.[45] According to William Derham's book, published in 1696, for which both Hooke and Tompion supplied information, Barlow at this juncture

'set Mr. Tompion, the famous Artist, to work upon it: who accordingly made a Piece according to his directions.

Mr. Quare (a very ingenious Watchmaker in London) had for some years before been thinking of the like Invention: but not bringing it to perfection, he laid by the thoughts of it, until the talk of Mr. Barlow's Patent revived his former thoughts; which he then brought to effect. This being known among the Watchmakers, they all pressed him to endeavour to hinder Mr. Barlow's Patent. And accordingly applications were made at Court, and a Watch of each Invention produced before the King and Council. The King, upon tryal of each of them, was pleased to give the preference to Mr. Quare's: of which notice was given soon after in the Gazette.

The difference between these two Inventions was, Mr. Barlow's was made to Repeat by pushing in two pieces on each side the Watch-box: one of which Repeated the Hour, the other the Quarter. Mr. Quare's was made to Repeat by a Pin that struck out near the Pendant; which being thrust in (as now 'Tis done by thrusting in the Pendant) did Repeat both the Hour and the Quarter, with the same thrust'.[46]

The Privy Council register shows that Barlow's patent was in fact challenged by the Clockmaker's Company, not by Quare. Both parties attended on 2 March 1687/8, each represented by learned counsel. The patent was refused on the grounds that several clock-makers [sic] were already making 'pulling clocks and watches'.[47] Barlow had obviously lost his case by delaying the patenting of his original clockmaking invention of the 1670s; but the whole affair shows that the Londoners were well aware of his work.

Tompion's own position in this patent application was a little curious. Presumably as a loyal member of the Clockmakers' Company, he would have been on the side of the Company; yet, if we are to believe Derham's account (for which as we have seen, he himself supplied information), he made the specimen watch for Barlow. There is also the further puzzle of why Barlow employed Tompion at all rather than someone nearer home. Possibly he may have seen advantages in putting the work in to the hands of the most celebrated 'watchmaker' of the day.

Tompion was also involved with Barlow in the application for another patent, in 1695, this time a successful one.[48] In the specifi-cation Barlow is referred to by his original name and place of birth—Edward Booth of Wulstan [sic], gentleman—and Tompion is de-scribed as a clockmaker. A third signatory to the application was William Houghton of Chorley, gentleman, who, presumably, had a financial stake in the invention. As we have already noticed, he was the owner of Park Hall where Barlow lived. The invention was for an alternative to the verge escapement, employing 'a new sort of teeth made like tenterhooks'. It is difficult to estimate the practical value of the discovery. It seems to have been the earliest known attempt to devise what came to be known as a cylinder escapement, de-signed to effect for the balance-spring watch the greater freedom which the recently discovered anchor escapement had given to the pendulum clock. It does not appear to have been put into produc-tion, however, until further modifications had been introduced by Tompion's partner and successor, George Graham. But, again, it does draw attention to Lancashire's interest in watchmaking and to its link with the London trade.

IV

It is quite clear that the beginnings of Lancashire watchmaking go back much earlier than used to be supposed. It was, in fact, a crea-tion of the seventeenth century, not of the eighteenth. By 1700 it al-ready employed many skilled craftsmen, was supported by a resourceful toolmaking industry and had close ties with London, the main market. The foundations had been laid which were to be built upon later by John Wyke and others. The area already had its own case and spring makers, but the sources so far discovered do not reveal the extent to which specialisation has developed in the manufacture of particular watch parts. It may be relevant to note, however, that a writer in 1701, in the course of urging the advantages of the division of labour, cites watch manufacture in support of his arguments.[49] Even if the idea came to him from looking at the complexities of a watch itself rather than from any first-hand knowledge of watchmaking, it must also have occurred to others within the trade.

These seventeenth-century developments may not be without relevance to the great events of the later eighteenth. The early growth of watchmaking in south-west Lancashire no doubt made its contribution to the changing economic climate and growingly acquisitive outlook which were among the preconditions of take-off. The outworkers on their small farms who made watch parts helped to generate wealth. Their employers gained business skill. A branch of precision engineering was developed. Inventiveness was encouraged. New machines, like that for cutting wheels, increased productivity. The great unknown is the extent to which these developments in Lancashire were spontaneous and the extent to which they were induced from London. No doubt to the rich London 'watchmaker' Lancashire was, so to speak, colonial territory, to be exploited for its cheap labour. (This applied to textiles, too, of course.) But the evidence such as it is—the Aspinwalls' early start; the resourcefulness in the inventing of machines; Barlow's contribution to the development of the watches themselves—would suggest that Lancashire was exploiting the opportunities of a new industry rather than just being harnessed to London's order of things.

When to watchmaking are added the other metal trades which, we know, were already flourishing in the area, it does not seem too extravagant to claim that in the seventeenth century the economy of south-west Lancashire was already developing in a different direction from that of the east of the county. The outworkers around Blackburn, Bolton and Rochdale continued to concentrate on textiles; those near Liverpool, Warrington and Wigan were already moving away from textiles. One wonders how much Lancashire stood to gain from this divergence. Did the knowledge and skills acquired in mechanical engineering in south-west Lancashire later come in useful for machine-building in the textile districts? The Clockmakers' Company in 1814 was at pains to point out that 'the national advantages derived from the perfection to which the Art of Clock and Watchmaking has been carried in this Country . . . extend to every branch of manufacture in which machinery is used'.[50] It seems to have been the clockmakers, rather than the watchmakers, however, who were chiefly in demand in the factories. Indeed, mechanics in the early cotton spinning mills were generally known as clockmakers.[51] Prescot and Warrington might produce excellent watchmakers and toolmakers, accustomed to using the same sort of implements as the cotton machine makers, but, complained a leading Manchester cotton manufacturer in 1824, they were too specialised. 'They have almost as much to learn as if they had never learnt any working in metal at all.'[52] Evidence such as this does not seem to support the view that east Lancashire gained direct and immediate technical help in the Industrial Revolution period from the earlier watch-making developments elsewhere in the county. Yet it might still have gained indirect advantages over a longer period. It seems unlikely that work of greater precision, made possible by the invention of new machine tools, failed to have some ultimate influence upon the nations' mechanical engineering standards— Wyke helped Watt, for instance[53]—or upon its supply of skilled labour. To this extent these developments in watchmaking may have had consequences far beyond the industry and the area.

(1) F. J. Britten, *Old Clocks and Watches and Their Makers* (1889; 6th ed. 1932); G. H. Baillie, *Watches: Their History, Decoration and Mechanism* (1929); *Watchmakers and Clockmakers of the World* (1929; 2nd ed. 1947); *Clocks and Watches: an Historical Bibliography* (1951).

(2) R. Campbell, *The London Tradesman* (1747), pp. 250, 252.

(3) See, for instance, the memorial from the Clockmaker's Company to the Treasury, 8 February 1832, in *A Statement of the Various Proceedings . . . of the Clockmakers' Company* (1832), pp. 63–4.

(4) Hatton, *op. cit.*, p. iv.

(5) Thomas Pennant, *A Tour from Downing to Alston Moor* (1801), p. 21. See also W. J. Roberts and H. C. Pidgeon, 'Biographical Sketch of Mr. John Wyke, With Some Remarks on the Arts and Manufactures of Liverpool from 1760 to 1780', *Transactions of the Lancashire & Cheshire Historic Society*, Vol. 6 (1854), and James Hoult, 'Prescot Watch-making in the Eighteenth Century', *ibid.*, Vol. 77 (1925).

(6) Guildhall Library, MS. 2921.

(7) F. A. B. Ward, *Time Measurement* (Science Museum Publication, H.M.S.O. 1949), pp. 28–9; Abbott Payson Usher, *A History of Mechanical Inventions* (revised ed., Cambridge Mass. 1962), ch. xii.

(8) Bodleian Library, MS. 10709, fo. 34. Carte's account was written c. 1708.

(9) Ward, *op cit.*, p. 23.

(10) Samuel Elliott Atkins and William Henry Overall, *Some Account of the Worshipful Company of Clockmakers of the City of London* (privately printed 1881), pp. 1–23.

(11) Carte MS., fo. 34.

(12) Britten, *op. cit.*, pp. 114 and 370. When Britten wrote, the watch was in the Evan Roberts Collection but this has since been broken up and we have not been able to trace its present whereabouts.

(13) Will and inventory of Thomas Aspinwall at the Lancashire Record Office.

(14) Joseph Foster, *Alumni Oxonienses, 1500–1714* (Oxford n.d.), p. 37.

(15) Lancashire Record Office, Molyneux Papers DDM/50/2–6.

(16) The main facts about the Aspinwalls will be found in *The Aspinwall and Aspinall Families of Lancashire A.D. 1189–1923, A Collection of Family Records brought together by Henry Oswald Aspinall, M.I.E.E.* (Exeter 1923). The author (p. 10) cites *Familiae Minorum Gentium* (Harleian Society, vol. 38 (1895), Lathom pedigree) for the statement that *Edward* Aspinwall was the 'first watchmaker in England', but this statement does not appear in Dugdale's original pedigree of 1665 (*The Visitation of the County Palatine of Lancaster*, ed. F. R. Raines, Chetham Society (1872), p. 177).

(17) Horace E. Mather, *Lineage of the Rev. Richard Mather* (Hartford, Conn. 1890), pp. 41–2, for particular reference to Edward Aspinwall. Mather was also educated at Brasenose College, Oxford.

(18) Arundell Blount Whatton, *Memoir of the Life and Labours of the Rev. Jeremiah Horrocks* (1859), pp. 1–5, 49–50; See also S. B. Gaythorpe, 'Jeremiah Horrocks: Date of Birth, Parentage and Family Associations', *Transactions of the Lancashire & Cheshire Historic Society*, Vol. 106 (1955) pp. 23–33.

(19) The will of Christopher Horrocks, proved 15 February 1638/9, is at the Lancashire Record Office.

(20) Liverpool Record Office, Town Books.

(21) *The Registers of the Cathedral Church of Manchester: Burials 1616–1653*, Lancashire Parish Register Society, Vol. 56 (1919), p. 432.

(22) Lancashire Record Society, Vol. 9, pp. 90, 98.

(23) *The Life of Adam Martindale* (Chetham Society, Vol. IV, O.S. 1845), pp. 6, 10.

(24) *The Aspinwall and Aspinall Families*, p. 15.

(25) Carte's master, Samuel Watson, was in the business in Coventry in the later seventeenth century, but this is the earliest reference to watchmaking there that we have come across. Mr. John Prest's otherwise most valuable *Industrial Revolution in Coventry* (Oxford, 1960) confesses that 'nothing seems to be known about the early history of the [watchmaking] trade, except that it had been introduced by the beginning of the nineteenth century' (p. 81).

(26) Matthew Gregson, *Portfolio of Fragments Relative to the History and Antiquities, Topography and Genealogies of the County Palatine and Duchy of Lancaster* (ed. John Harland, Manchester 1869), p. 181.

(27) The will, proved in October, 1672, and the inventory are at the Lancashire Record Office.

(28) *The Earliest Registers of the Parish of Liverpool (St. Nicholas's Church) 1660–1704*, Lancashire Parish Register Society, Vol. 35 (1909).

(29) Arthur John Hawkes, *The Clockmakers and Watchmakers of Wigan 1650–1850* (Wigan, 1950), pp. 16 *seq.*

(30) Lancashire Record Society, Vol. 9, pp. 160 *seq.*

(31) Carte MS, fo. 44.

(32) *J. S. Clock-maker, Horological Dialogues. In Three Parts. Shewing the Nature, Use and Right Managing of Clocks and Watches* (1675), p. 28.

(33) *The Diary of Robert Hooke* (ed. Henry W. Robinson and Walter Adams), p. 5.

(34) *Ibid.*, p. 5 n.

(35) *Histoire de l'Academie Royale des Sciences.* Année MDCCXLIV, p. 61. A William Blakey had become director of an 'iron and steel manufactory' at Harfleur, which was later moved to St. Germain near Versailles. John Law was then (1718) attracting British watchmakers to France (P.R.O., S.P. 35/25/52).

(36) J. Aikin, *Description of the Country from Thirty to Forty Miles Round Manchester* (1795), p. 311.

(37) *The Lancashire Watch Company: Its Rise and Progress* (Prescot, 1893). Houghton is a common Lancashire name and, as will be seen elsewhere in this chapter, a William Houghton was making watches in the Preston area at this time and William Houghton of Park Hall near Chorley was associated with Barlow in his patent of 1695.

(38) Thomas Birch, *History of the Royal Society* (1756), Vol. 4, pp. 20–1.

(39) *Philosophical Transactions of the Royal Society,* Vol. X, pp. 272–3; Birch, *op. cit.*, p. 190; Sir Henry Lyons, *The Royal Society* (Cambridge, 1944), p. 88.

(40) R. W. Symonds, *Thomas Tompion, His Life and Work* (1951), p. 14. The other facts in this paragraph have been taken from this source. See also A. J. Nixseaman, *First Production, Tompion's Great Clock* (Biggleswade, 1953).

(41) Josiah Aspinwall, described as watchmaker of St. Martin-in-the-Fields, died in 1679. His will, proved on 30 September 1679, is at Somerset House, but there is no inventory.

(42) *The Parish Registers of Warrington 1591–1653,* Lancashire Parish Register Society, Vol. 70 (1933), p. 238.

(43) *The Church History of England from the Year 1500 to the Year 1688* (Brussels, 1742), Vol. III, pp. 280–1, upon which the rest of this paragraph is based. For Dodd's Lancashire connexions, see Joseph Gillow, *A Literary and Biographical History or Biographical Dictionary of English Catholics* (n.d.), Vol. V, pp. 549–50.

(44) William Derham, *The Artificial Clock Maker* (1696), p. 106.

(45) P.R.O., S.P. 44/71, p. 289. Petition dated 26 August 1686.

(46) Derham, *op. cit.*, pp. 107–8.

(47) Atkins and Overall, *op. cit.*, pp. 243–4.

(48) British Patent number 344 of 1695.

(49) *Considerations on the East-India Trade* (1701) in J. R. McCulloch (ed.), *Early English Tracts on Commerce* (1856; reprinted Cambridge 1952), pp. 591–2.

(50) Petition of the Clockmakers' Company to the House of Commons, 4 May 1814, in *A Statement of the Various Proceedings . . . of the Clockmakers' Company* (1832), p. 11.

(51) G. W. Daniels, 'Industrial Lancashire Prior and Subsequent to the Invention of the Mule', *Journal of the Textile Institute,* Vol. XVIII, p. 82.

(52) Evidence of Peter Ewart to the Select Committee of the House of Commons on Artizans and Machinery, 23 March 1824, published in its Fourth Report (1824).

(53) An account, dated 5 December 1767, rendered by Wyke to Watt (now in the possession of Major Gibson-Watt), was displayed at the Lunar Society Bicentenary Exhibition in Birmingham. Wyke later made engine counters for Watt. (See [Eric Robinson], Exhibition Catalogue, Birmingham Museum and Art Gallery, [1966], p. 41.)

CHAPTER TWO

The Permanent Poor in South-West Lancashire under the Old Poor Law

G. W. OXLEY

I

THIS STUDY is based on the Old Poor Law records of the parishes and townships of West Derby Hundred, an administrative unit containing a wide variety of geographic and economic environments. Liverpool,[1] the chief town of the Hundred, was only a small port in the early seventeenth century, but its great expansion began with the development of trade with America during the Restoration period.[2] A modern estimate puts its population at only 1000 during the decade 1663–73,[3] but it had reached nearly a quarter of a million by 1841.[4] Next in size and importance to Liverpool were the towns of Wigan and Warrington. The former was situated in the coalmining area but transport difficulties and the rigid enforcement of borough regulations delayed its economic development until the late eighteenth century, when it rose to new heights of prosperity.[5] Warrington grew up where the main road to the north crossed the Mersey, and this favoured position contributed much to its commercial and industrial development.[6] The district round Liverpool and the plain to the north of the town were chiefly agricultural. The rural area was served by the market town of Ormskirk which also had a small watch- and clockmaking industry.[7] The highly subdivided trade of watch-part making was very important in Prescot, a small town on the south-western extremity of the coalfield.[8] Other metal trades using local coal also developed in the Hundred. Nailmaking was carried on in widely scattered forges in the vicinity of Wigan and Atherton. Wigan also had bellfounders and brass and pewter workers, though these were moving into a period of decline. At Ashton there were nail, lock, and hinge makers, and in Warrington pins, locks, wire and tools were made and copper smelting and copper and brass manufacture flourished during most of the eighteenth century.[9] Textile manufacture, both linen and cotton, was to be found in most parts of the Hundred but was most important in the district around Leigh and Wigan.[10]

The improvement of transport was stimulated by these activities, particularly by the need to move coal from the pits to the consumers. First came turnpike roads and river navigations, then canals, and later railways.[11] It is significant that St. Helens, which developed from a hamlet to a considerable industrial town during this period, was at the terminus of the Sankey Canal, the first industrial canal in England.[12] Another newcomer among the towns of the Hundred was Southport, which developed during the latter part of the period to serve the needs of those seeking the medical and recreational benefits of sea bathing.[13]

Many contrasts developed in West Derby Hundred during the period when the Old Poor Law was in force: contrasts between town and country, between the colliery and the metal-worker's shop, between the weaver's cottage and the huge cotton mill. Whatever the environment, it was changing; in some periods and places change was fairly slow, in others it was very rapid. In this study we shall seek to isolate for examination that section of the population which, in this changing region, was forced to become permanently dependent upon public assistance, to analyse the circumstances which brought this about and to examine the ways in which relief was given.

During the whole of the Old Poor Law period the obligation to relieve was derived from the great Poor Law of 1601, which established the necessary administrative machinery and defined the main classes of poor and forms of relief. The essence was that each parish was made responsible for its own poor: two, three or four substantial householders were to be appointed annually as overseers of the poor to act in conjunction with the churchwardens, who were *ex officio* overseers. Their first task was to help those who could to achieve independence by 'setting to work the children of all such whose parents shall not . . . be thought able to keep and maintain their children', by binding poor children apprentice at the expense of the parish, and by setting adults to work on materials purchased with public funds. To 'the Lame, Impotent, Old, Blind, and such other among them being poor and not able to work' the overseers were to give relief. The money for these purposes was to be raised by a levy on the occupiers of lands and houses within the parish.[14]

The majority of the acts passed during the next two centuries to explain, amend, and extend this law were concerned with the administrative machinery and the prevention of fraud and abuse and are not relevant to this study. However, the first, and perhaps the most important, of them must be mentioned because it dealt with a problem which had arisen in Lancashire and other northern counties. When framing the 1601 Act its compilers had in mind the parishes

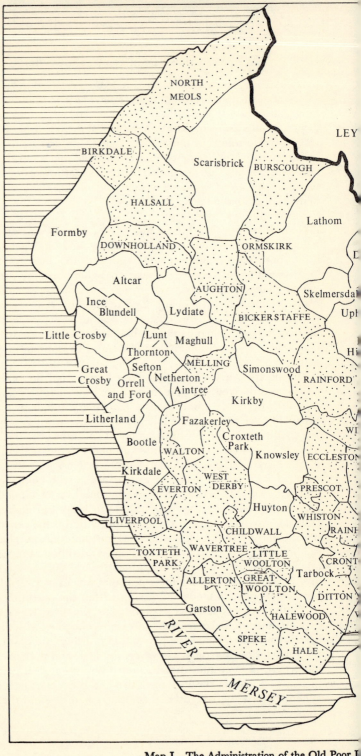

Map I The Administration of the Old Poor I

HUNDRED

SALFORD

HUNDRED

Haigh

Orrell

WIGAN

PEMBERTON   Ince

Winstanley   HINDLEY   ATHERTON

d   TYLDESLEY
WITH
SHAKERLEY

llinge   Abram   WESTLEIGH
ower End   ASHTON

BEDFORD

GOLBORNE   PENNINGTON
LOWTON   Astley

HAYDOCK

PARR   Kenyon

NEWTON

Southworth

WINWICK   CULCHETH

BURTONWOOD   Houghton   Rixton
with
Glazebrook

BOLD   POULTON
WITH   Woolston
FEARNHEAD   with
GREAT   Martinscroft
SANKEY   WARRINGTON

Penketh

CUERDLEY

C H E S H I R E

0   Miles   5

st Derby Hundred and its Townships (*referring to Chapter Two*) of southern and midland England, ignoring the fact that far larger parishes were common in the north. When a parish like Prescot, the most extensive in West Derby Hundred, contained fifteen townships, each similar in size to a southern parish, it was evidently in the spirit of the 1601 Act to make the township responsible for its own poor in districts where parishes were large. This was done in 1662 by the Act which introduced the concept of settlement to the Poor Law.[15] Some parishes in West Derby Hundred had anticipated this reform, others were tardy in implementing it, but by 1700 the law and reality were one.[16]

The most important addition to the relief provisions of the Poor Law between 1601 and 1834 was enacted in 1723. It empowered parishes and townships to spend money from the poor rate fund on the establishment of workhouses.[17] Some had done so without waiting for statutory powers when, in some cases as early as the 1630s, they had realised that their obligation to set the poor to work could be more economically and efficiently fulfilled if they established institutions where the work could be carried on under close supervision.[18] According to Sir Josiah Child most of these early workhouse experiments were unsuccessful.[19]

Before 1723 those seeking to establish workhouses were faced with two main problems. Firstly, expenditure of public money for this purpose was not sanctioned by law, which meant that a minority of hostile ratepayers could prevent the establishment, or procure the premature closure, of a workhouse. Secondly, many parishes were too small to support a workhouse alone but unions of parishes, without any legal backing, stood as little chance of success as did the workhouse itself. Several parishes, following the example set by those of Bristol in 1696,[20] obtained local acts which empowered the establishment of workhouses and gave unions a permanency which could be secured in no other way.

This procedure was expensive and beyond the means of the smaller parishes and groups of parishes, which continued to found workhouses without legislative aid.[21] It was for their benefit that a clause permitting the establishment of workhouses and the formation of unions was inserted in the Act of 1723. Parishes could only make use of these powers when the ratepayers had signified their consent but, once the workhouse was open, the overseers were empowered to deny relief to those who refused to enter it.[22] By simplifying the legal position this Act removed some of the difficulties facing parishes which wished to form unions and establish workhouses, but to neither could it give the permanency offered by a local Act. Even so, the evidence from West Derby Hundred shows that it did stimulate the foundation of what became stable and long-lived unions.[23]

During the decades after 1723 various writers brought to light scandals and inefficiences to be found in workhouses established under this Act. Many of them offered schemes for the correction of these evils but only the plan put forward by Thomas Gilbert proved acceptable to Parliament. Placed on the statute book as the second permissive workhouse act in 1782 it contained step by step instructions for the formation of a union and the management of a workhouse and a formulary and a set of workhouse rules to promote the standardisation which Gilbert sought.[24] After this date parishes intending to open workhouses could choose between the rigid formulae of Gilbert's Act and the greater freedom offered by the 1723 Act.

Although a considerable quantity of Poor Law records from the townships of West Derby Hundred have survived it is only rarely that they supply information about the circumstances of paupers and of applicants for relief. From among these records two groups stand out as being particularly useful in this context. One relates to the early seventeenth century, the other to the early nineteenth, thus making possible a comparision between the circumstances which would entitle a person to relief at the beginning and towards the end of the period in which the Old Poor Law operated.

For the early years information is to be found in the petitions presented to Quarter Sessions by those seeking relief. Filed with them is a document headed 'A list of pensioners in Prescot Parish relieved by Quarter Sessions order'.[25] It listed fourteen people and added two 'relieved without an order'. Evidently most people had to obtain a court order before the overseers would relieve them. This implies that we can turn to the records of Quarter Sessions to discover the reasons why relief was sought and get some understanding of the circumstances in which it was given or refused. The Prescot document also shows that a minority of claims were recognised without an order. Gradually this practice gained ground and the petitions had already ceased to present a reliable picture of poverty when, in 1691, local magistrates were given the task of hearing those who had been refused relief by the overseers and Quarter Sessions was made a final court of appeal.[26] The early relief petitions are of exceptional interest because they come from persons suffering from those fundamental forms of poverty which were the first to be recognised as deserving relief and which, as will be shown below, remained a significant charge on the rates during the whole of the Old Poor Law period.

The cause of poverty mentioned most often in the petitions of the 1620s and 1630s was old age. Typical of many were those of Thomas Twiss (1627) and John Scath (1628). Twiss sought weekly relief because he was over eighty years old and 'not able to work nor go abroad to receive alms of well-disposed people',[27] while Scath was only seventy-two and could still work, but he could not earn enough to keep himself and his wife. She was eight years older and 'like to famish for want of food' because she could not 'go forth out of doors to receive relief of her neighbours'. The churchwardens were to allow them twenty shillings a year.[28]

Many elderly petitioners stressed their inability to go out and beg, thus basing their claims to relief on grounds of infirmity as well as old age. This was certainly true of Anne Read a poor, blind, lame, ninety-seven year old widow of Ditton. She had been accustomed 'to seek relief among her neighbours' but in 1628 she petitioned to have it from Prescot parish, where she had been born and lived all her life.[29] Gilbert Walsh, an Ormskirk carpenter, had a similar problem. In 1633 he reported that he had earned his living and brought up nine children but that he could no longer practise his craft being 'dim of sight' and seventy-four years old. His wife had been bed-ridden for three-and-a-half years and these calamities had caused his 'former gotten goods' to be spent. The magistrates referred his case to the churchwardens and overseers.[30]

Sometimes the nature of the infirmity which accompanied old age was specified. Thus John Mason of Ashton was troubled by his wounds and lameness acquired during his service in Ireland as a soldier.[31] William Gill, a webster of Ormskirk, had been independent and brought up seven children, but in 1631 he was injured in a fall. For over a year he depended upon his neighbours but then at the age of ninety he sought and obtained parochial relief.[32] It was not uncommon for petitioners to stress that they had been hardworking and independent for many years. Ninety-seven year old William Glover of Cronton, who had 'laboured all his life at his calling as a husbandman', requested and obtained relief in 1631 because he was unable to work 'by reason of his old age or otherwise by the Judgements of God'.[33]

Lunatics were included among the impotent poor at an early date. Perhaps on account of their complete incapacity they appear to have been particularly expensive to maintain. In 1627 the churchwardens and overseers of Prescot were ordered to collect no less than fifty shillings a year for Elizabeth Wyke, a seventy-five year old idiot.[34]

Lameness was a common impediment to work and consequently a

frequent reason for seeking relief. Agnes Wood had been lame for four years when in 1629 she petitioned for relief from Wigan parish.[35] Isabell Debell had been so for twelve years and was maintained by her neighbours until, in 1633, they 'begin to be weary of the burden' and sought parochial relief for her.[36] Sometimes lameness was a result of an industrial accident. John Smith of Ashton had an allowance until 1632 because his legs had been broken in a fall of marl,[37] and in 1635 Thomas Houghton of Eccleston sought relief having been lamed by an accident in a sawpit.[38]

Children comprised the last of the main groups of relief-petitioners in this early period. Generally the petitions gave few details, but most child paupers were either bastards or orphans. In 1633 an exceptionally informative petition was presented on behalf of the children of Thomas Hunt, a Prescot collier. He maintained them by his labour and for the last year he had lacked the assistance of his wife, she having died. One day he was 'in a cole pitt going to work [and he] was suddenly by a fire in the said pitt burn'd'. A week later he died leaving five orphans all under five years of age. The churchwardens and overseers were ordered to provide for them.[39] The Mawdesley children of Ormskirk became dependent upon the parish in the same year but for a different reason. Their father, Thomas, had been born in Ormskirk and lived there all his life but 'through loss of goods and badness of times' he had got into debt. As his troubles crowded in upon him, the death of his wife proved the last straw. He deserted his children and by the time they were found one was already dead and the other two were in 'need of relief according to the statute'.[40] Parentless children were usually relieved by boarding out. Sometimes townships were tardy in paying their maintenance or 'table wages', and foster parents had to petition Quarter Sessions for an order to the overseers to honour their obligations, as did Thomas Barret of Prescot in 1633.[41]

In the late 1630s a new class of poor became frequent petitioners. They were widows and deserted wives with young children whom they were unable to maintain. One such was Ellen Rothwell of Winwick, whose 'late dec'd husband' had left her with seven small children. While she was fit she had been at great pains to 'maintain and educate them that they might be big enough to be put forth apprentices' but by 1636 she had become 'weak, impotent and poor' and was unable to clothe her children and bind them apprentices and the churchwardens and overseers were ordered to provide for her.[42] Similar orders were made in 1638 for Widow Elizabeth Lyon of Windle who had no means of supporting her seven children, three of whom were under eight years of age,[43] and in 1639 for

Mary Greave, a widow of Ormskirk, who had three children.[44] In 1638 relief was ordered for a wife and six children, some of them disabled. The father, Richard Crosse, had gone to London leaving a destitute family and heavy debts.[45]

Little is known about the ways in which the poor were relieved in the early seventeenth century because the magistrates usually ordered the 'churchwardens and overseers to provide' leaving the method of doing so to their discretion. When the petitioners were in permanent necessity some form of continuous allowance was required. It is no doubt significant that when the Prescot paupers were listed in 1641 they were described as 'pensioners'.[46] Occasional references in the petitions confirm that a regular cash payment was the usual form of relief. At first an annual sum was specified. Richard Hitchmough, an aged labourer of Prescot was allowed thirty shillings a year in 1634[47] and in 1640 John Spencer of Prescot petitioned for the resumption of a similar allowance which the overseers had paid for four years and then withheld.[48] New relief orders made in this year specified weekly allowances. Thus Elizabeth Heapie of Down-holland whose husband had deserted her and was thought to be dead was allowed two shillings a week for herself and her four young children,[49] and Dorothy Crosse of Ormskirk, perhaps the wife of the absconding Richard Crosse, mentioned above, was allowed eightpence a week for her infirm son.[50] These examples all show that in the early seventeenth century poor relief was granted in West Derby Hundred in general accordance with the statute. The poor were 'Lame, Impotent, Old, Blind'. The only able-bodied to be relieved were the widows, whose needs were self-evident.

II

The most valuable information about the nature of poverty in the early nineteenth century is to be found in the surveys of the poor which were taken in certain townships. Two of these will be examined in detail. One was taken in Ashton and Haydock in 1815[51] and the other in Bedford in 1836.[52]

Apparently the Ashton and Haydock 'Census of the Poor' was taken by a committee formed to distribute charitable relief during a period of exceptional distress. The enquirers' terms of reference were:

'1. Where according to the average earnings of a family each person shall have an income of above four shillings a week no account shall be taken of that family.

'2. Wherever different families live in the same house and keep only one common purse they shall be considered one family, when they keep separate purses they shall be considered as separate families.

'3. Particular pains shall be taken to ascertain accurately the weekly income of each family: when the income has been fluctuating it shall be taken upon the average of the last quarter of a year.'

The investigators were issued with printed forms which specified what information was to be recorded. First came the name of the householder with his address and place of settlement. Then followed ages, occupations, employers and earnings of all members of the family. For unemployed persons, other than young children, the name of their last employer was given, and for the sick the nature of their illness.

Thirty-eight families settled and resident in Haydock came within the terms of reference but only six were on township relief. The census also revealed two families receiving relief from Haydock but resident in Ashton. Twenty-six Haydock families were entirely dependent upon their earnings from labour and two more on income from this source and from lodgers. Twenty of these families were headed by men and seventeen of them had an income of between two and four shillings per head per week. In sharp contrast, six of the eight families headed by women had under one shilling per head per week. These figures amply demonstrate the impoverishment which could be brought by the death or desertion of the main breadwinner. Seven families, all headed by men, had their incomes augmented by Friendly Society benefits. One of these was also receiving poor relief and in all its income came to three shillings per head per week, more than that received by many independent families. It may be that its circumstances had undergone improvement which had not yet come to the notice of the overseer, or that the township wished to encourage Friendly Societies by not imposing too rigid a means test on their members when in distress.

Of the families on relief three contained elderly people and three more were headed by women. These factors alone were enough to justify relief. Of the two families which were headed by men, one has already been discussed and the other was that of a hinge maker. His wages were very low compared to those of colliers, waggoners and even labourers and he had a family of nine to support. Even with relief the family income was under two shillings per head per week.

The paupers of Ashton were much the same. The census covered thirty-four families which were settled there, resident in Ashton or

Haydock, and already on township relief. Twelve consisted of old people and seven were headed by women. The elderly were the best off of all the pauper classes, perhaps because their deserts were unquestioned, but it is interesting that this township was relieving fifteen families headed by men for no obvious reason but that the father's earnings were insufficient for the support of their families.

This census of the poor has one major defect: it was only concerned with families whose average income was under four shillings per head per week. This information must be set against returns from the overseers to Parliament which show that in the years 1812–14 these townships were relieving far more people than were mentioned in the census.[53] Information in the annual reports issued by Ashton overseers in the years 1806–11 supports the testimony of the returns. They show that the majority of the paupers were living in the township, so the discrepancy cannot be explained by non-resident relief.[54] There is no clear reason why some families should have had relief taking them above four shillings per head per week while others were independent yet poorer. Some of these discrepancies can perhaps be explained by the character of the families involved. Other families may have suffered rapid changes of fortune during the economic difficulties of 1815, and there may have been some who escaped the notice of a census based on households because they were lodging with, but not dependent upon, families not poor enough as a whole to qualify for inclusion in the census. The discrepancy cannot be adequately explained but the conclusions drawn from the census may be borne in mind for comparison with those produced by an examination of the Bedford survey of the poor.

This was carried out in 1836 by the Select Vestry. It recorded the names, ages and incomes of every member of every family which was, or sought to be, on permanent relief. From this information a picture similar to that drawn from the Ashton and Haydock census can be built up, and once again the families can be grouped into those consisting of old people, those headed by women, and those headed by men. The male heads of household were chiefly hand-loom weavers whose earnings were insufficient for the support of their dependents. The survey recorded the ways in which these various classes were relieved. The old people were all relieved with pensions though a few were also given an allowance for rent. The families were helped in various ways, the type of relief being adapted to the specific needs of each one. It could take the form of a pension, a weekly payment to the landlord for rent, the use of a cottage owned or rented by the township, relief from paying parish rates or any combination of these. The survey also contained families whose allowances were reduced or stopped or to whom the Select Vestry refused to grant anything. Clearly it was only willing to aid the really destitute.

There are noticeable similarities between the kinds of people eligible for relief in the early seventeenth and the early nineteenth centuries. The widows and the elderly remained prominent and marginal notes show that infirmity continued to be an important subsidiary ground for claiming relief. Nevertheless, a change of a more subtle character had occurred, for the surveys of the poor suggest that the claims of these classes were readily recognised and that they did not have to fall into the extremes of poverty described in the early petitions before relief was forthcoming.

The greatest contrast between the forms of pauperism in the early seventeenth and the early nineteenth centuries was the relief of able-bodied men in employment in the later period. This practice was caused by these men's inability to maintain their families with the low wages which they received. It became widespread during the early nineteenth century and was later given the name 'Speenhamland System'. In some places the relief was given to the men themselves to augment the family incomes. Elsewhere it was, nominally at least, given to those children who would otherwise be destitute.

The process by which this form of relief came into being is obscure, but it is possible that the need for it was recognised in the 1601 Act which provided for the setting to work of children whose parents were unable to maintain them, without specifying that such parents had to be unemployed or infirm. Even if it was not the legislators' intention, this clause could clearly be construed to authorise relief to the able-bodied in employment who could not support all their children, if given in the form of work for those children.[55] The payment of weekly doles imposed less of a burden on overseers than the provision of work, and Miss Hampson found that in early seventeenth-century Cambridgeshire monetary relief was being given to fully employed labourers.[56] This practice was widespread by 1697 when John Locke compiled his well-known scheme for the relief of the poor because, even if he minimised in saying that 'a man and his wife in health may be able by their ordinary labour to maintain themselves and two children', there can be little doubt that having numerous children brought many families into dependence on public assistance.[57]

There is evidence that such families had been accepted as eligible for relief in West Derby Hundred as early as the mid-seventeenth century. In 1654 the inhabitants of Whiston petitioned Quarter Sessions to revoke the relief orders which had been granted to certain persons, among whom was one Humphrey Lyon, a pipemaker. Both he and his children were able to work. The mention of children may indicate that relief had been granted at an earlier date when they were dependent and the father unable to support them.[58] The accounts of the overseers of Tyldesley with Shackerley for the year 1703 seemingly reveal another early case of relief to the able-bodied in employment. In that year the township was paying the rents of eleven families or individuals, yet only three of these appear in the pension list. The others may have had their income reduced by sickness or unemployment but is also possible that some were 'Speenhamland' type cases. [59]

The payment of paupers' rents was a regular branch of poor relief during the eighteenth and early nineteenth centuries, because even if the recipients were undeserving it could be difficult to avoid this payment. When a family was careless or unfortunate and, as a result, unwilling or unable to save up and pay the rent at the end of the year the landlord's only means of redress was the distress and sale of the defaulter's chattels. When this happened the family might well be forced on to the parish devoid of both home and belongings. Overseers would naturally seek to avert this expensive situation by paying the rent, but in so doing they set a dangerous precedent, discouraging thrift among the poor and encouraging landlords to resort more speedily to distress. A letter written to the overseers of Atherton in 1807 by Thomas Leigh, a St. Helens landlord, reveals the attitude of his class:

'I am under the necessity of writing to you concerning James Stock's rent, as it was due on old May day and I cannot see any probability of his paying it himself for his wife is now big with child and near her time therefore I would have you take it into consideration before I come over which will be in the course of a week or two for perhaps it would be better to pay it than me to distress him and throw them entirely upon your expense and by so doing you will greatly oblige your Humble Servant.'[60]

It seems in fact that the townships were blackmailed into paying what was the main, and may perhaps have been the only, form of relief given to fully employed able-bodied men during the eighteenth century.

A parliamentary enquiry of 1777 asked all overseers to state how much their parishes had spent during the previous year on the rents of workhouses and cottages for the poor. The townships of West Derby Hundred spent widely varying proportions of their total relief expenditure in this way, if only because some owned and others rented their workhouses.[61] Most spent between 10 and 20 per cent on housing but how much went to the aged, impotent and widows and how much to ordinary families which simply could not make ends meet it is impossible to say. One of the most interesting features is the low proportions of their total relief expenditure which the three towns Liverpool (1·0 per cent), Warrington (none) and Wigan (3·87 per cent) spent on rents. The first two owned their workhouses, which like that at Wigan, were large and may have been able to house an exceptionally high proportion of the poor. It is possible that these towns, with the most to gain by so doing, were already resisting pressure brought to bear on them by landlords. Some other townships sought to follow this example. In 1821, its first year of office, the Ormskirk Select Vestry announced that in future it would pay no rents. Later reports do not indicate whether it succeeded in adhering to this resolution.[62] In 1836 the Bedford Select Vestry applied a strict test to those seeking rent relief and families allowed relief in this way had to be in just as poor circumstances as those relieved in other ways. Rent relief was therefore a form of relief to the able-bodied in employment which it was often difficult to refuse, and which could get out of hand, but which could be brought under control by careful and close supervision.

It has often been suggested[63] that one of the most important antecedents of Speenhamland was a clause in Gilbert's Act which empowered the Guardians, who were entrusted with the management of the poor in parishes which adopted this Act, to find work for the unemployed and make up their wages out of the rates if they were insufficient.[64] This clearly resembled the roundsman system under which the unemployed worked for all the ratepayers in turn at subsidised wages, but it only applied in those parishes which adopted the whole Act; and in 1797, two years after the Speenhamland decision, Sir F. M. Eden reported that few Gilbert Unions had been formed.[65] This statute may well have been legalising an existing practice and it seems more probable that Speenhamland developed out of the various long-standing practices which have been described in the Lancashire examples rather than from this one Act.

It was the bread crises of 1795[66] which produced the Speenhamland decision and the difficulties of later years which perpetuated the scales then promulgated. Prices remained high and there were further crisis years. In the south population was expanding faster than opportunity for employment, and, after 1815 demobilisation increased the competition for jobs while the spread of threshing machines eliminated much winter employment and made agricultural work more seasonal than ever. In Lancashire hinge-makers and nailmakers such as those in Ashton and Haydock were swiftly hit by depressions and the position of the handloom weavers deteriorated steadily with the rapid spread of power-looms in the mid 1820s.[67]

The various practices which later came to be called the Speenhamland System were of great interest ot the Royal Commission on the Poor Laws and they featured prominently in the queries it sent out to overseers. The replies from West Derby Hundred indicate the extent to which relief was paid to fully employed, able-bodied men. Selected country townships were asked whether they did so. Walton,[68] Much Woolton[69] and West Derby[70] replied with a curt 'None'. It was unnecessary in the vicinity of prosperous Liverpool. North Meols occasionally relieved weavers or others with large families, Burscough[72] gave aid to the unemployed and to non-resident weavers and Halsall[73] sometimes, and 'in peculiar circumstances', assisted widowers. Newton[74] bracketed all the questions relating to able-bodied relief and stated that 'The system alluded to . . . is not practised in this part of the country'. The towns were asked to describe exactly what sort of people were being given out-door relief. Toxteth Park[75] and Everton[76] gave brief, unhelpful replies, but those from Liverpool[77] and Ormskirk[78] and Prescot were of greater substance. Prescot's may be quoted as an example:

> 'There are generally more in Winter than in Summer: at present about 108 individuals and heads of families; about 45 aged to whom 1/6d. to 2/- allowed. The rest chiefly widows with families. A woman with three children would probably be allowed about 1/- a head, and we should endeavour to put them in the way of getting a living. A few sick and cripples. No able-bodied persons now on the book.'[79]

By contrast Wigan replied that 'about 370 individuals some with families at the present time are receiving relief out of the workhouse. About two-thirds are aged people: the remainder consist of widows, cripples and men with large families, unable to maintain them by their industry. Usually weavers with three small children.' This township gave no regular relief to bricklayers, stonemasons, joiners or other mechanics, labourers, or servants but it did accept applications from weavers and spinners with three children under nine years of age.[80] Handloom weavers with large families were also relieved in Warrington, but their numbers were declining as those who could obtained other employment.[81]

The evidence from the Royal Commission's returns confirms that revealed by the study of individual townships: the bulk of the poor were aged, infirm, or widows and handlooom weavers were the only major group which it was necessary to relieve while in full employment. This situation was observed by Assistant Commissioner Henderson who was in the County making his own observations on behalf of the Commissioners at about the same time as the overseers were answering their queries. He reported that:

'The Poor-Rates have been greatly augmented by the transition from hand to power loom weaving.

'The depression of Wages, and the difficulty of obtaining employment, especially for the older weavers, whose habits are fixed has led to a general practice in the weaving district of making an allowance to able-bodied weavers with more than two children under ten years of age. There is no fixed scale for this allowance but the practice is to make up the earnings of the family to 2/- or, in some places 1/6d. a head'.

He realised

'the danger of perpetuating such wretchedness by a system of bounties in the shape of parish allowances. Handloom weaving in its coarser branches is completely superseded as a profitable employment, and ought to be abandoned with all possible dispatch. It is gratifying to observe that the number of weavers is diminishing (though in various degrees) in all the large towns; that few young men are now brought up to weaving, few looms are made and nothing is more common than to see a solitary weaver working amidst vacant looms, which have been deserted for other occupations.'

Knowing the Commissioners' interest in the payment of relief to able-bodied men in employment he observed that

'This course certainly is an approximation to the payment of wages out of the Poor Rate; but there are some material distinctions between the case of the weaver and the case of the agricultural labourer. The agricultural roundsman has no spur to exertion, nor interest to please the farmer who is his master only for a day, consequently his habit of industry is relaxed and destroyed; on the other hand, as the weaver always works by the piece, and as the current rate of wages is well known it is easy to calculate what he might earn if industrious, and the parish allowance is apportioned accordingly; so that if he is indolent, he suffers for it; if he is industrious he reaps the benefits of his exertions; and the fact unquestionably is that the weavers are stimulated beyond their powers under the allowance system.'

In another passage their conditions were described in greater detail:

'The weavers receiving parochial relief are in a state of great destitution; their houses are bare of furniture; their children half clad; their food chiefly potatoes, oatmeal porridge and milk, with the addition of oatcakes. . . . Butter, beer and meat are luxuries beyond their reach.'[82]

The case of the handloom weavers as it may be reconstructed from township records, overseers' returns and the eye-witness description of Henderson is an important and interesting example of relief to the able-bodied in full employment. It shows that from the same roots could grow not only the Speenhamland system of the south with its many abuses and evils but also an essential means of alleviating human need and suffering brought about by technological change.

III

The Bedford survey of the poor listed eight people who formed a class of their own: the inmates of the workhouse. Among them were two children, two sick people and an idiot. Why did this, and many other, townships relieve a small proportion of their poor in this specialised manner? In seeking an answer to this question it is necessary to survey the development and organisation of the workhouses of West Derby Hundred, noting particularly any indications of what they were expected to achieve and how the overseers set about attaining those ends.

It has already been pointed out that the workhouse movement in West Derby Hundred did not begin until after the Statute of 1723 had been passed. In fact this Act directly stimulated the establishment of workhouses. In 1723 the Liverpool Vestry ordered the overseers to pursue 'the new Act of Parliament passed this Session' and before the year was out a Special Vestry was held to finalise the arrangements for opening a workhouse.[83] Windle and Parr bought 'The Act of Parliament relating to the House' when they were establishing their workhouse in 1732,[84] and the first of the proposed articles of Prescot I Workhouse was to be a recital of '9 K.G.I'.[85] The movement took a few years to get off the ground but workhouses became widespread during the 1730s.

It is impossible to say how many workhouses there were in West Derby Hundred at any one time because so much important source material has failed to survive.[86] Even so a general picture of the way the provisions of the 1723 Act were put into practice can be built up from the documents which are available. The most important single-township workhouses were those in the larger towns, Liverpool, Warrington and Wigan. Small, one-township workhouses are those most likely to evade the searches of an enquirer and few of them have come to light. But, if the evidence available reflects the true position it seems that they were tried in the early years but had generally died out by 1776 when each township made a return to Parliament indicating whether it had a workhouse. Most of those reported are known from other sources to have been union houses and few of the remainder were small enough to have been used by a single township.

The union workhouse was the main feature of the workhouse system in this Hundred. The townships of the north-western district of the Hundred were served by two workhouses situated in Ormskirk. They counted among their members almost every township in the region for a period of more than a century. The townships in Childwall and Warrington parishes and the southern parts of Prescot and Winwick parishes showed no such uniformity. There were several workhouses in this area but apparently none except Culcheth had a period of existence comparable with that of the Ormskirk workhouses. The townships of this region had no consistent policy but chopped and changed from one workhouse to another, not even confining themselves to the local ones but sending their paupers farther afield to institutions in Brindle (Leyland Hundred), Aspull (Salford Hundred, near Wigan), and to Grappenhall, Kinderton, and Middlewich in Cheshire. The third section of the Hundred, the central and north-eastern area, might be termed the industrial district. In the eighteenth century the situation was what might be expected of an area situated between the Merseyside and the Ormskirk areas. On the one hand there were townships like Lowton which pursued as inconsistent a policy as its southern neighbours, while on the other there were stable unions like those of Pemberton and Pennington. Doubtless owing to the increasing population which industrialisation brought, the workhouse accommodation of this area was expanded in the late eighteenth and early nineteenth centuries in a way not to be found in the other two districts. Newton and Windle workhouses were opened in 1793, Tyldesley Bank about the same time, Atherton in 1812 and Lowton in 1817, Hindley and Sutton had their own workhouses in 1837 though the former had been a member of Aspull workhouse in 1804 and Sutton a member of Newton in 1806.[87]

The union workhouses were all organised on similar lines. The main arrangements were worked out when they were being planned, and laid down in the articles of agreement. Naturally the most important question was that of finance. Workhouse expenditure could be classified under four heads: the cost of the house; the cost of furniture, equipment and utensils; the feeding and clothing of the paupers; and transactions relating to their employment. The individual township's share of these costs could be calculated either by dividing the total cost by the number of townships in the union or as a proportion of the cost based on the number of paupers they actually had in the house. In practice it was usual to use each of these methods where appropriate. The cost of the house, whether rent or purchase price, and of its contents, usually termed 'utensils' in the workhouse bills, were shared equally by each of the member townships. Food, clothing, medical attention and any other expenditure specific to a particular pauper were paid for by his own township, food costs being calculated on a per-head-per-week basis. The earnings of individual paupers were credited to their own townships, and though nothing was said about the cost of materials this was no doubt deducted from the earnings before they were set down in the bills.[88]

With member townships spread over a wide area it was impractical for the overseers to supervise the day-to-day running of the workhouse. Their task was to direct general policy through the medium of their monthly account-settling meetings. In some unions each township appointed a representative to meet with his colleagues for this purpose. The indenture of union signed by the members of Aughton Street workhouse in Ormskirk provided for the appointment of inspectors by each township, but their duties were not specified.[89] When the first Prescot Workhouse was being planned each prospective member township appointed a trustee and these men formed a committee which brought the project to fruition, and having done so, supervised its operation.[90]

The day-to-day administration was entrusted to a governor. The names of nearly a hundred governors and governesses of workhouses in West Derby Hundred are known, but for the most part this is the full extent of knowledge about them. Very few examples of career governors have been found. Apparently there was only one, Hamnet Caldwell, governor at Pennington from 1765, or earlier, until 1769,[91] and at Warrington from 1769 until 1780.[92] Workhouse governing was still a fairly new profession in the middle of the eighteenth century and many of those who joined it left after only a short stay. Evidently it did not take long for them to tire of their new occupation or for their employers to find them unsatisfactory. Those who were successful usually stayed at one workhouse for considerable periods. There was little incentive to move as most workhouses were about the same size and promotion opportunities were therefore few.

Which paupers were selected for indoor rather than outdoor relief? The answer to this question is crucial to any understanding of workhouse policy but it is far from easy. Information is provided by lists of workhouse inmates, by the records of how vestries dealt with individual applicants for relief and by statements of general policy by overseers and vestries.

A remarkable feature about several of the lists of workhouse inmates was the high proportion of children among them. This was the case in the workhouses at Warrington (1757),[93] Moor Street in Ormskirk (1832),[94] Much Woolton (1832),[95] and Atherton (1837).[96] Others, such as Liverpool (1794)[97] and 1832)[98] and Wigan (1832)[99] had a higher proportion of elderly inmates. Children were particularly suitable for workhouse maintenance, especially if considerations of efficiency and economy were paramount. Among their number were orphans and children who shared their poverty with unmarried, deserted or widowed mothers. In the workhouse the children could be taught to read and write, and as they grew older set to work under the supervision of a few adults while their mothers were busy with the domestic tasks of the house or with gainful employment. Thus the time and energies of both children and mothers could be most efficiently used to the benefit of themselves and the ratepayers.

The principles applied by Ormskirk and North Meols in selecting adult paupers for workhouse relief were enunciated in 1832. The Rev. T. J. Horton, Vicar of Ormskirk, wrote that his township used the workhouse solely as 'an asylum for aged, infirm and otherwise helpless persons'.[100] The Select Vestry, of which Horton was a member, stated its policy with more detail in its report of 1821:

'As far as this Township is concerned, none but houseless and impotent have been placed within its walls and that in all their views they have looked to it rather as a comfortable asylum for those really distressed and without comfort of a home than for the Idle and Disorderly. These remarks appear to the Select Vestry the more necessary because it is too much the custom with other townships to make workhouses a receptacle for the idle and refractory Paupers and a lying-in hospital for Bastardy Delinquents'.[101]

North Meols was evidently one of these offending townships for its assistant overseer reported that:

'The alternative of the workhouse has often been offered to good

D

for nothing fellows; they think it a prison and refuse to go. We avoid sending old and infirm people, because it would grieve them'.[102]

Both of these townships were members of the Moor Street Workhouse in Ormskirk[103] and the governor must have had considerable difficulty running an institution intended to satisfy such contradictory purposes.

North Meols was pursuing the traditional workhouse test envisaged in the 1723 Act when it authorised overseers to refuse relief to applicants who would not enter the workhouse. At first most townships seem to have applied the test by sending all their pensioners to the workhouse. Two townships which certainly did this were Bickerstaffe, a member of the Aughton Street Workhouse in Ormskirk, and Parr, which shared a Workhouse at Moss Bank in Windle with that township. After a few years the pension lists reappeared in their overseers' accounts.[104] The needs of many of the poor were unquestionable and the test was reserved for borderline cases. In 1755 the Prescot authorities told two applicants that they could only obtain relief by entering the Workhouse and informed another that though her outdoor pension could not be raised she might enter the Workhouse.[105] The Burtonwood Vestry pursued a similar policy. When it made arrangements for the relief of eight widows in 1770 five were offered a choice between a pension and the Workhouse.[106]

As time went on it was realised that the workhouse was not the best way to relieve short-term distress and statutes which authorised magistrates to order temporary relief to persons who had refused to enter the workhouse were passed in 1795 and 1815.[107] Vestries and overseers continued to use the powers that remained. In 1805 Rainford Vestry ordered Ellen Spencer to the workhouse rather than give her the house she petitioned for; in 1806 it gave Mary Justice a choice between the workhouse and a pension of two shillings a week; and in 1824 it issued a general order that all young persons applying for relief were to be sent to the workhouse.[108] The reaction of one relief applicant on being offered the workhouse was recorded in the Lowton Vestry Minutes in 1826. He said that 'he will rather list for a soldier than come into the House'.[109] This makes it clear that the workhouse was still an effective deterrent, keeping off the township books people who could maintain themselves if they tried.

There remained a minority who were willing to enter the workhouse rather than seek work for themselves, and it was the task of the governors to change their minds for them. William Hardman faced this problem when he was appointed Governor of Liverpool Workhouse in 1804. Evidently the previous administration had been lax and 'The House was in a most disorderly state'. There were only five weaving looms, and 'no other employment for the paupers beyond the necessary business of the House'. Hardman managed to reduce the population of the House by exacting from each person able to work a reasonable portion of labour daily. The task imposed was picking oakum, work which was not unwholesome or straining, but tiresome, and thus very well suited to a workhouse test system.[110] The greatest threat to this policy was a slow decline in the initial enthusiasm, allowing slackness and inefficiency to creep in. This clearly happened in Liverpool, for though Hardman remained governor one of the first tasks of the Select Vestry, appointed in 1821, was to repeat the policy adopted in 1804: 'The introduction into the Workhouse of a regular system of labour, by means of different workshops, has relieved the Parish from many thriftless paupers, who have preferred seeking a livelihood out of doors rather than submit to the stated labour within the House'.[111] The workhouse test was a useful part of the old Poor Law system but constant effort was needed if it was to remain effective.

The records show that Ormskirk Select Vestry was not exaggerating when it spoke of townships using the workhouse solely as a 'Hospital for Bastardy Delinquents'. Parr was a member of Newton Workhouse between March 1802 and August 1804, but the only time it had any poor there was in April 1803. During that month Alice Holland was in for nineteen days and Ruth Holland for thirteen. The bill for the month contained as special items three shillings for the midwife and the cost of tea, sugar and beer.[122]

Equally, Ormskirk Township was not unique in using the workhouse as a home for the aged and infirm. In the Liverpool Workhouse in 1795:

'The old people, in particular are provided with lodging, in a most judicious manner: each apartment consists of three small rooms, in which are 1 fireplace and 4 beds, and is inhabited by 8 or 10 persons. These apartments are furnished with beds, chairs, and other little articles of domestic use that the inmates may possess, who being thus detached from the rest of the poor, may consider themselves as comfortably lodged as in a secluded cottage; and thus enjoy in some degree (even in a workhouse), the comforts of a private fireside. The most infirm live on the ground floors; others are distributed through two upper stories'.[113]

At this date Liverpool Workhouse had about a thousand inmates, while most others had fewer than a hundred.[114] It was thus able to carry out the various specialised tasks for which workhouses existed in different parts of the one institution. Elsewhere the need to fulfil justified, but often conflicting, objectives on a limited scale must often have reduced the efficiency with which this was done.

The term workhouse implies that one of its objects was to obtain from the inmates a contribution to their maintenance by means of work. The provision of employment in workhouses is, therefore, an aspect of their administration which must be looked at in detail. A list of all the inmates of Liverpool Workhouse, showing how they were employed, was compiled on 25 March 1794.[115] It dealt with 1197 persons including paid staff such as the Governor and, perhaps, the school teachers and some of those who supervised the work. About half this population was non-productive: to be precise there were 524 'lunatics, idiots, sick, lame, infirm, very old and very young'. A 'family' (as workhouse populations were usually called) as large as this required a considerable number of people to carry out the domestic chores. There were three house servants, five hall and stair cleaners, two cooks and six servants, two salters, ten washerwomen, a milk mistress, a bread cutter, ten kneaders of bread, a brewer, and a few others. Some of the non-productive inmates had to be looked after by others. Thus there were fourteen 'Nurses for lying-in women, and for the sick, infirm, venereal, fever and lunatic wards', six 'nurses and servants for infants' and four people described as 'Keeper of Lock' (venereal hospital) 'and servants'. A gardener, his assistant, and two swineherds contributed to the economy of the house in the sphere of food production.

This activity was of greater importance in those workhouses which had more land. The township of Parr, as a member of Newton Workhouse, had to pay for digging and sinking a well, marling, ploughing and loading dung. This was heavy labour, unsuitable for many paupers, who no doubt came into their own with the sowing, planting and harvesting which had to be carried out after 'seeds, cabbage plants, and potato setts' had been bought.[116] Costeth House[117] had land on which oats, barley and potatoes were grown, and the regular sale of calves seems to indicate the presence of a herd of cows.[118] This institution was replaced by the second Prescot Workhouse which had a garden cultivated by the paupers. It supplied the house with potatoes for three months and produced vegetables for sale.[119] Pigs were a convenient form of livestock requiring little space. They were kept at Newton in 1801, Atherton in 1812, and Moor Street (Ormskirk) in 1834.

The majority of the working inmates of Liverpool Workhouse in 1794 were engaged in textile and clothing work. There were 266 cotton pickers, 102 spinners, 3 weavers, 4 boy weavers, 51 knitters and seamstresses, and 11 tailors. This group no doubt had a dual function, saving money by making and mending clothing for the Workhouse inmates and earning it by producing goods for sale. Textile working was the commonest form of profitable employment used in workhouses. Bills for the purchase or repair of spinning wheels, looms, cards, spindles, bobbins, and many other things required for this occupation appear continually in workhouse and overseers' accounts.[121] The cost of equipment rose as inventors devised more complex machines. In 1787 Parr paid 2s. 8d. for a cotton wheel,[122] but in 1800 for a tenth share of a carding engine costing three pounds.[123] At the reorganisation of Pennington Workhouse in 1782 the equipment to be provided for the paupers was specified. Each township in the union had to provide two pairs of looms and a spinning jenny. They were to remain the property of the township and were to be taken away, together with any materials bought for use with them, when not required. One or two carding engines were to be bought at joint expense for the use of all the inmates.[124] Most paupers worked with cotton, often woven on a linen warp to make fustian.[125] An exception to this rule occurred in the early days of Warrington Workhouse, where the men wove silk, the children wound it and the women made lace. References to hemp and flax in 1731 show that diversification was taking place.[126] By 1797 there had been a decline in the quality of the products. Hair was spun for hair cloth and sail warp was wound.[127] This change was no doubt imposed by the lack of skill and unreliability of pauper labour.

The survey of Liverpool Workhouse mentioned several craftsmen. They were probably elderly or disabled in some way and not able to earn an independent living though still able to do some work and contribute to the economy of the House. Thus two smiths were 'making nails for sale and own use'. It is likely that the craftsmen were also teaching their skill to younger inmates, for the smiths, coffin-makers, joiners and shoemakers all had groups of boys enumerated with them. Nail-making was common around Leigh,[128] and it is likely that the smithy at Pennington Workhouse was for this purpose.[129] The monthly bills of Atherton Workhouse regularly included 'nailers' earnings.[130] When townships such as Prescot[131] and Warrington[132] found they had to admit able-bodied men to the workhouse they employed them, usefully if not profitably, in repairing the roads.

The 1794 survey of Liverpool Workhouse only reveals the presence of children by occasional references to boys and it is probable that most of them were included in the totals for cotton operatives. Nine years later special work was provided for children in the form of a pin manufactory which provoked strong criticism from James Neild, a correspondent of the *Gentleman's Magazine*. He complained that many of the children in the Workhouse had sore eyes and that, through working eighteen hours a day, they had no opportunity to learn to read. It is not known how long this work was continued but in Manchester Workhouse it was stopped as a result of Neild's criticisms. This same writer also reported that other children in Liverpool Workhouse were 'tolerably well' taught to read.[133] In fact it seems to have been general for the younger workhouse children to be given the rudiments of literacy. For instance, there is a note in one of the Warrington Workhouse account books that the schoolmaster began the school there in 1749.[134] Nearly a century later, in 1836, a new plan was adopted, the township subscribing two pounds a year to the National School so that the workhouse children could be taught there.[135] In 1746 the Prescot overseers spent fourpence on books for the children in the Workhouse.[136]

The financial aspect of work in workhouses can be dealt with briefly. In 1803 Parliament obtained from all overseers returns of the amounts spent in setting the poor to work and what their earnings had been. Many townships which had paupers in workhouses gave no reply to either of these questions; some only reported earnings and others indicated vast losses or profits.[137] These facts are hardly surprising, as union houses usually only accounted for earnings. It is clear that the townships had little concern for the financial aspects of workhouse employment. Their attitude was no doubt well summed up by the Liverpool respondent to the 1832 enquiry:

'Profit has never been contemplated in the employment of paupers in the Workhouse, indeed it is obvious that in such a changeable population profit would be absorbed in the loss occasioned by spoiled work, particularly by children. The main and desired objects are the providing of work so as to prevent the adult and able-bodied pauper from eating the bread of idleness, and to bring up children to habits of industry, and prepare them to be apprenticed.'[138]

If the objects of the workhouses were to be attained, life within its walls had to be regulated and the paupers subjected to some measure of discipline. The codes of rules drawn up for this purpose provide an illuminating picture of the daily life a workhouse inmate was expected to lead. Three sets of rules used in the workhouses of West Derby Hundred are known. The first was drawn up by Warrington

Vestry in 1729,[139] the second was laid down in Gilbert's Act in 1782[140] and introduced into Liverpool Workhouse in 1814[141] under the provisions of an act of 1810[142] and the third was made for Lowton Workhouse, probably about the time of its opening in 1817. This was a Gilbert workhouse and these rules appear to be based on the Statute but they are much fuller and do not agree with their model in all respects.[143]

Many rules were concerned with general discipline. The Lowton paupers were to obey the governor and governess in all reasonable commands and demean themselves orderly and peaceably, with decency and cleanliness. All the codes prohibited swearing and, while Lowton and the Gilbert rules forbade bringing spirituous liquors into the House, Warrington made provision for the punishment of drunken inmates. Movement in and out of the building was carefully controlled by both Lowton and Warrington. The former vetoed going into or out of the inner yard without permission and provided that persons allowed out of the House who did not return on time must obtain a new order placing them in the House. If they were found in a room other than the one where they worked they were liable to punishment. In Warrington the poor were only allowed to become inmates if they obtained a 'licence signed by two Justices of the Peace' or an 'Order of the Committee'. Once inside they were to be distinguished by a badge sewn on their shoulder and must obtain permission if they wished to go out. They were not allowed to beg from those who visited the House, but a box was to be set up and any money found in it was to be spent on the 'sick and diseased in the House'.

Gilbert's Act imposed on the governor the duty of preventing wastage of fire and candles. The Warrington rules were more specific. There were to be no fires in summer except for 'dressing victuals' and 'washing and ironing linen'. In winter other fires, with an allowance of one peck of coal a day, were allowed if 'absolutely necessary for sick and lying-in women'. A century later a more lenient attitude seems to have prevailed; Lowton simply ordered that all fires be extinguished by ten o'clock in summer and by nine o'clock in winter. Cleanliness, both of buildings and of people, was demanded in general terms by Gilbert and the other two codes laid down the routines by which it was to be achieved.

The hours of work in Lowton Workhouse differed markedly from those laid down in Gilbert's Act. The latter specified the hours from six in the morning to six at night from Lady Day to Michaelmas, and from eight to four for the rest of the year. Lowton altered this to six to seven-thirty in summer and seven to eight-thirty in winter. The

Warrington Workhouse rules of 1729 show a greater leniency, reflecting, perhaps, the more easy-going attitude of the pre-factory era. It was laid down that each person should work 'so many hours as the master shall appoint according to their age and ability', but it may well be that the hours for all were shorter than in Lowton. Work did not begin until after breakfast, which itself followed prayers at seven o'clock in summer and at eight in winter.

Both Lowton and Warrington encouraged good work by offering rewards. The latter specified that all those who observed the rules of work were entitled to a penny in the shilling of their earnings. Those who did 'other necessary business in the House' were to have 'such encouragement money as in the judgement of the Master and Committee they shall deserve'. In 1765 or thereabouts a detailed scale of rewards was issued:

'Bounties allowed to be . . .	
Anyone who earns 4/- in one fortnight	4d.
The spinners for every 1/-	1d.
The overseers of the spinners per week	3d.
bread cutter per fortnight	2d.
cooks per fortnight	1/-
schoolmistress per week	2d.
chambermaids per week	2d.'[144]

Bounties were still being paid in the early nineteenth century. They usually amounted to over £20 a year in the 1820s but dropped below £10 in the 1830s.[145] Lowton was slightly more generous, allowing one eighth of their earnings to those who did no wilful damage and executed their work to the best of their ability.

The religious needs of the paupers were catered for. Lowton, following Gilbert, ordered that all adults attend divine service every Sunday and added that all children were to go to Lowton Sunday School. Warrington enjoined the participation of all 'able poor' in two Sunday services at 'the Parish Church or some other Place of Religious Worship'. In addition, prayers were to be said daily before breakfast and supper and those not attending were debarred from the ensuing meal.

The Gilbert rules dealt with some matters not mentioned in the other codes. They regulated the burial of the dead, required the governors to keep inventories of the goods and materials in the House and directed that, when the rooms were being allocated to the inmates, the best should be given to 'Persons who, having been creditable Housekeepers, are reduced by misfortune, in Preference to those who are become poor by Vice and Idleness'.

The rules were enforced by various punishments. In Warrington most offences led to corporal punishment for those under twelve and loss of meals for those over that age, but in the case of theft the culprits were to be prosecuted at public expense. The Gilbert rules ordered punishment by alteration of diet and by confinement. Lowton had a dungeon for this purpose but it added to the Gilbert penalties distinction of dress, corporal punishment, the prosecution of thieves and loss of gratuities. The latter was used extensively. The inmates had to pay for breakages for which they were responsible and some offences carried fines, part of which went to the informer. In Pennington Workhouse all who neglected or spoiled their work, misbehaved in the House or committed any other misdemeanour were liable to corporal punishment and a post was erected where they were to be 'corrected in reason' at the discretion of the governor.[146]

These sets of workhouse rules, with their common emphasis on similar subjects show a considerable consensus of opinion about workhouses in West Derby Hundred during the century after 1723, and the value attached to them is demonstrated by the long lives of some workhouses and by the continued adherence to the idea of the union workhouse. Within this framework experience taught various lessons, and the townships came to use these common institutions for widely differing purposes. Success is difficult to measure, but the very continuity of the system points to its having obvious value, even if conflicting objectives sometimes reduced its efficiency.

IV

Superficially the two aspects of poor relief in south-west Lancashire, which have been discussed above, appear to be much the same as their counterparts in other parts of England. The pensioning of the aged and the widowed, the payment of relief to the able-bodied in employment, and the provision of institutional relief by means of the workhouse, were all described more than thirty years ago by Leonard, Marshall and the Webbs,[147] but the evidence from West Derby Hundred suggests that in the traditional view the emphasis is sometimes misplaced.

The importance of the aged and widows as the chief recipients of poor relief is not always stressed sufficiently: the records say little about them because their eligibility for relief was unquestioned. Generally there was no need to record their circumstances either as the basis for a means test or in order to justify their pensions to the ratepayers, yet an assessment of the relative importance of these and other forms of poverty, both in terms of expenditure and in terms of numbers of people, is essential if phenomena such as the rise in relief expenditure are to be understood.

Another aspect of poor relief which can be illuminated by information of this sort is the Speenhamland System. Recent work has shown that it was neither as widespread or as systematic as was at one time supposed.[148] If, as has been suggested, Speenhamland was the result of slow evolution rather than of specific stimuli such as Gilbert's Act, when was relief first given to the able-bodied in employment and under what circumstances? Did the payment of rents play as important a part in this evolution in other parts of the country as it seems to have done in Lancashire? In Bedford near Leigh, the hand-loom weavers certainly made as great demands on the public purse as did the aged and the widows, but around Liverpool and in the country districts where weavers were fewer, Speenhamland practices were unknown. It may well be that this system was the wrong solution to the difficulties facing the southern agricultural labourer in the first quarter of the nineteenth century, but relief to the able-bodied in employment certainly served a useful purpose in Lancashire, where the problem was limited in extent and temporary in nature but none the less serious for those involved.

Workhouses were to be found in all parts of the country, and those in West Derby Hundred were put to all the uses ascribed to them by the Webbs: 'a Device for Profitably Employing Pauper Labour', 'a Means of Applying the Test by Regimen', 'an Asylum for the Impotent', and 'a Place of Specialised Institutional Treatment'.[149] But the Webbs' discussion of the 1723 Act brings out one of the most significant differences between West Derby Hundred and the country as a whole. They summarised their conclusions thus:

'The results of the 1723 Act, which authorised the establishment of workhouses by one or more parishes, had, after the first flush of apparent success, not been such as to lead to its adoption in rural districts, where the defects of management under parish officers, or the horrors of the farming system, outweighed the advantages of the workhouse itself.'[150]

Yet in south-west Lancashire a system of union workhouses was introduced in the 1730s in accordance with the 1723 Act, and this form of organisation remained in general use for the ensuing century. The reason for this success is not immediately apparent, but it is noticeable that for the management of their work-

THE PERMANENT POOR IN S.W. LANCASHIRE

houses the overseers of West Derby Hundred chose a compromise between the two methods, direct management and contracting, to which the Webbs attributed the failure of most workhouses founded under this Act. The employment of governors, who were paid a salary for their own maintenance, and charged the townships the actual cost of maintaining the poor, avoided the worst evils of the other two systems. The governors lost their main incentive to mal-treat the poor and the overseers were relieved of the burden of day-to-day administration. They retained the task of supervising the gover-nor to prevent extravagance and the misappropriation of funds. This system was not perfect, but it worked.

One result of the general use of union workhouses in West Derby Hundred was that workhouse relief was probably more widely available there than in many other counties. Where the one-parish workhouse was the accepted type, a parish had to decide whether it had sufficient need of a workhouse to make the experiment worthwhile. Many rural parishes had to answer this question in the negative, and others which did establish workhouses soon found that they should not have done so and brought the experiment to a close. In south-west Lancashire, on the other hand, a township could re-main a member of a workhouse union by contributing its share to the general costs, only sending the occasional pauper to it when there was someone for whom this form of relief seemed appropriate. The evidence is far from complete, but it does seem that most of the townships in the Hundred joined a workhouse union in the second quarter of the eighteenth century and remained members of one or other of them until the end of the Old Poor Law period.[151]

By demonstrating that, while the main features of Poor Law administration in West Derby Hundred were similar to those else-where, there were some significant differences, both in the problems facing the overseers and in the ways in which they tackled them, this study has shown that our knowledge of the Old Poor Law is far from complete and that much more detailed research is needed before it will be possible to make reliable generalisations about it.

(1) The map on pp. 18–19 shows the places mentioned in the text.

(2) F. A. Bailey, 'The Modern Period' in W. Smith, *A Scientific Survey of Mersey-side* (1953), p. 237.

(3) R. Lawton, 'The Genesis of Population', *ibid.*, p. 120.

(4) *Victoria County History of Lancashire* [hereafter *V.C.H. Lancs.*] (1906–14), Vol. II, p. 348.

(5) F. Walker, *Historical Geography of Southwest Lancashire before the Industrial Revolution*, Chetham Society, Vol. 103 (1949), p. 131.

(6) J. Aikin, *A Description of the Country from Thirty to Forty Miles around Manchester* (1795), p. 301.

(7) F. H. Cheetham, 'Notes on some Ormskirk Watch and Clock Makers', *Transactions of the Antiquarian Society of Lancashire and Cheshire* (*T.A.S.L.C.*), Vol. LI (1936), pp. 1–10.

(8) J. Hoult, 'Prescot Watchmaking in the XVIII Century', *Transactions of the Historic Society of Lancashire and Cheshire* (*T.H.S.L.C.*), Vol. 79 (1928), pp. 39–53.

(9) T. S. Ashton, *An Eighteenth Century Industrialist* (1939), *passim;* J. J. Bagley, *A History of Lancashire* (1956), pp. 54–55; G. H. Tupling, 'The Early Metal Trades and the Beginnings of Engineering in Lancashire', *T.A.S.L.C.*, Vol. LXI (1949), pp. 16–25.

(10) Aikin, *op. cit.*, pp. 294, 297.

(11) E.g. the Prescot to Liverpool and Warrington to Wigan Turnpikes authorised in 1726, the Sankey Canal opened in 1757, the Leeds–Liverpool Canal opened in 1774, the canal from Leigh to Worsley opened in 1795, the Liverpool to Manchester, Wigan to Warrington and St. Helens to Runcorn Railways, all in operation before the passage of the Poor Law Amendment Act in 1834.

(12) T. C. Barker and J. R. Harris, *A Merseyside Town in the Industrial Revolution, St. Helens, 1750–1900* (1954), pp. 75–89, 108–19; Aikin, *op. cit.*, pp. 312–3.

(13) F. A. Bailey, *A History of Southport* (1959), pp. 29–58.

(14) 43 Eliz. I, c. 2.

(15) 13 & 14 Car. II, c. 12, s. 21.

(16) G. W. Oxley, 'The Administration of the Old Poor Law in the West Derby Hundred of Lancashire, 1601–1837', M.A. Thesis, University of Liverpool (1966), pp. 28–34.

(17) 9 Geo. I, c. 7, s. 4.

(18) E. M. Leonard, *The Early History of English Poor Relief* (1965), pp. 225–27.

(19) R. Burn, *History of the Poor Laws* (1764), p. 174.

(20) E. Butcher, 'Bristol Corporation of the Poor 1696–1834', *The Bristol Record Society*, Vol. III (1932), pp. 1–5.

(21) E.g. several parishes in Bucks., S. and B. Webb, *English Poor Law History*, Part I *The Old Poor Law* (1953), p. 243; Eaton Socon, Beds., F. G. Emmison, 'The Relief of the Poor at Eton Socon', *Bedfordshire Historical Record Society Publications*, Vol. 15 (1933), p. 20; Barking, Essex, J. E. Oxley, *Barking Vestry Minutes* (1955), p. 108.

(22) 9 Geo. I, c. 7, s. 4.

(23) See below, p. 31.

(24) 22 Geo. III, c. 83.

(25) Lancashire Record Office (L.R.O.), QSB/1/250/38.

(26) 3 Wm. & Mary, c. 11, s. 11.

(27) L.R.O., QSB/1/30/41.

(28) L.R.O., QSB/1/42/64.

(29) L.R.O., QSB/1/38/65.

(30) L.R.O., QSB/1/118/56.

(31) L.R.O., QSB/1/110/70.

(32) L.R.O., QSB/1/118/51.

(33) L.R.O., QSB/1/86/66.

(34) L.R.O., QSB/1/30/34.

(35) L.R.O., QSB/1/62/55.

(36) L.R.O., QSB/1/110/76.

(37) L.R.O., QSB/1/118/48.

(38) L.R.O., QSB/1/158/48.

(39) L.R.O., QSB/1/122/53.

(40) L.R.O., QSB/1/130/162.
(41) L.R.O., QSB/1/146/58.
(42) L.R.O., QSB/1/178/72.
(43) L.R.O., QSB/1/198/45.
(44) L.R.O., QSB/1/218/43.
(45) L.R.O., QSB/1/202/77.
(46) L.R.O., QSB/1/250/38; see above, p. 19.
(47) L.R.O., QSB/1/142/40.
(48) L.R.O., QSO/230/58.
(49) L.R.O., QSB/1/230/36.
(50) L.R.O., QSO/230/54.
(51) Warrington Public Library (W.P.L.), MS. 748–50.
(52) Leigh Public Library, Bedford Township Book.
(53) *Parliamentary Papers* (1818), Vol. XIX, p. 219.
(54) W.P.L., PS. 14.
(55) See above p. 17.
(56) E. M. Hampson, *The Treatment of Poverty in Cambridgeshire, 1597–1834* (1934), p. 48.
(57) H. Fox Bourne, *The Life of John Locke* (1886), Vol. II, p. 384.
(58) L.R.O., QSP/259/12.
(59) L.R.O., QSP/916/26.
(60) L.R.O., PR/1930/1.
(61) *Parliamentary Papers*, First Series, Vol. 9, pp. 379–81.
(62) L.R.O., PR/2815/1.
(63) G. Nicholls, *History of the English Poor Law* (1904), pp. 89–90; Webbs, *op. cit.*, pp. 171–72.
(64) 22 Geo. III, c. 83, s. 32.
(65) Sir F. M. Eden, *The State of the Poor* (1797), Vol. I, p. 366.
(66) W. Stern, 'The Bread Crisis in Britain, 1795–6', *Economica*, Vol. XXX (1964), pp. 168–87.
(67) D. Bythell, 'Handloom Weavers in the English Cotton Industry during the Industrial Revolution: Some Problems', *Economic History Review*, Vol. XVII (1964–65), p. 348.
(68) The Royal Commission on the Poor Laws, *Report* (1834) [hereafter P.L.C.], Ap. Bb, p. 278.
(69) *Ibid.*, p. 278.
(70) *Ibid.*, p. 271.
(71) *Ibid.*, p. 275
(72) *Ibid.*, p. 270.
(73) *Ibid.*, p. 273.
(74) *Ibid.*, p. 276.
(75) P.L.C., Ap. B2g, p. 75.
(76) *Ibid.*, p. 64.
(77) *Ibid.*, pp. 66–7.
(78) *Ibid.*, p. 70.
(79) *Ibid.*, p. 72.
(80) P.L.C., Ap., B2g and h, p. 77.
(81) P.L.C., Ap. B2h, p. 77.
(82) P.L.C., Ap. A. pp. 909–10.
(83) H. Peet, *Liverpool Vestry Minutes* (1912–15), Vol. I, pp. 83–89.
(84) St. Helens Public Library (S.H.L.), Parr Township Papers, 355.
(85) The Library, King's College Cambridge, Prescot Township Papers, (K.C.L.), PC/2/31.

(86) The following list includes all the workhouses for which there is any evidence. In some cases this evidence is very dubious: these are marked (D). The existence of any workhouse should not be assumed without consulting the detailed discussion of relevant problems in G. W. Oxley, *op. cit.*, 425–47.

Allerton, 1776 (D); Ashton, 1732–1819; Atherton, the Town's House, 1732–36; Atherton Workhouse, 1813–37; Aughton, 1776 (D); Aughton Street (Ormskirk)' 1732–37; Bedford, 1833; Bold, 1734–1837; Childwall, 1776 (D); Costeth House' (see below, n. 117) 1751–80; Cronton, 1770–90 (D); Cuerdley, 1776 (D); Culˉcheth, 1731–1837; Ditton, 1776 (D); Eccleston, 1776 (D); Golbourne, 1837; Grea Sankey, 1776 (D); Hale, 1776 (D); Halewood, 1776–1837; Hindley, 1837ˀ Huyton, 1732; Liverpool, 1723–1837, Lowton, 1817–37, Melling, 1776 (D); Moor Street (Ormskirk), 1732–1837; Moss Bank (Windle), 1732–43; Newton, 1793–1837; Parr, 1750–59; Pemberton, 1731–1837; Poulton with Fearnhead 1740–54; Prescot, 1732–50, 1811–37; Rainford, 1776 (D); Speke, 1742–76; Sutton, 1732–1837; Tyldesley Bank House of Industry, 1798–1808; Warrington, 1728–1837; Wavertree, 1776 (D); West Derby, 1731–1834; Widnes, 1770–92; Wigan, 1734–1837; Windle, 1793–1837; Woolton, Great, 1834–37.

(87) G. W. Oxley, *op. cit.*, pp. 288–90, 425–71.
(88) *Ibid.*, pp. 292–94.
(89) L.R.O., PR/445.
(90) K.C.L., PC/2/31.
(91) L.R.O., PR/1681/8.
(92) W.P.L., MS. 131.
(93) W.P.L., MS. 127.
(94) P.L.C., Ap. B2g. 70.
(95) P.L.C., Ap. B1b. 278.
(96) L.R.O., PR/1755.
(97) Peet. *op. cit.*, Vol. I, p. 334.
(98) P.L.C., Ap. B2g, 67.
(99) *Ibid.*, p. 77.
(100) P.L.C., Ap. B2g, 70.
(101) L.R.O., PR/2815/1.
(102) P.L.C., Ap. B1d, p. 275.
(103) G. W. Oxley, *op. cit.*, pp. 436–7.
(104) L.R.O., PR/445, 417; S.H L , 352, 04204. L.B; T. C. Barker and J. R. Harris, *op. cit.*, pp. 133–4.
(105) K.C.L., PC/2/198;PC/3/40.
(106) L.R.O., PR/2720/2.
(107) 36 Geo. III, c. 23; 55 Geo. III, c. 137.
(108) L.R.O., PR/2509.
(109) L.R.O., PR/349.
(110) P.L.C., Ap. A, pp. 914–15.
(111) Peet, *op. cit.*, Vol. II, p. 143.
(112) S.H.L., 362. 51. L.B.
(113) Sir F. M. Eden, *op. cit.*, p. 329.
(114) Peet, *op. cit.*, Vol. I, p. 334; G. W. Oxley, *op. cit.*, pp. 425–447.
(115) Peet, *op. cit.*, Vol. I, p. 334.
(116) S.H.L., 362. 51. L.B.
(117) Situated in Sutton (J. R. Harris, 'The Hughes Papers. Lancashire Social Life, 1780–1825', *T.H.S.L.C.* Vol. 103 (1951), p. 115) and rented from the Prescot Almshouses Trustees (K.C.L., PC/2/31) for use as a workhouse by the Townships of Prescot and Whiston (K.C.L., PC/2/194).
(118) K.C.L., PC/2/227, 179, 112, 189, 168.

(119) *P.L.C.*, Ap. B2g, p. 72.

(120) S.H.L., 362. 51. L.B.; L.R.O., PR/1681/10; British Museum, Add. MS. 36876.

(121) S.H.L., Parr Papers, Workhouse Bills; K.C.L., PC/2/25; L.R.O., PR/1681/10.

(122) S.H.L., Parr Papers, Workhouse Bills.

(123) S.H.L., 362, 51 L.B.

(124) L.R.O., PR/1743.

(125) *Ibid.*

(126) W.P.L., MS. 104.

(127) Eden, *op. cit.*, Vol. II, p. 370.

(128) *V.C.H. Lancs.* Vol. III, p. 435.

(129) L.R.O., PR/1681/7/479, 533, 583.

(130) L.R.O., PR/1681/21.

(131) P.L.C., Ap. B2g, 72.

(132) *Ibid.*, p. 77.

(133) *Gentleman's Magazine*, 73, Vol. II, (1803), pp. 1104–05.

(134) W.P.L., MS. 127.

(135) W.P.L., MS. 775.

(136) K.C.L., PC/2/40.

(137) *Parliamentary Papers* 1803–04, Vol. XIII, pp. 248–51.

(138) P.L.C., Ap. B2g, pp. 66–67.

(139) W.P.L., MS. 105.

(140) 22 Geo. III, c. 83; s. 34 and Schedule.

(141) Peet, *op. cit.*, Vol. II, p. 83.

(142) 50 Geo. III, c. 50, s.1 permitted non-Gilbert workhouses to use these rules.

(143) L.R.O., PR/407/8.

(144) W.P.L., MS. 110.

(145) W.P.L., PS. 25.

(146) L.R.O., PR/1743.

(147) The relief of the aged poor is discussed in Leonard, *op. cit.*, pp. 207–15 but it is difficult to find a specific discussion of this group or of widows by either the Webbs or Marshall. They are not mentioned in the Webbs' subject index but there is mention of them in Webbs, *op. cit.*, pp. 150–60 and Marshall, *The English Poor in the Eighteenth Century*, pp. 93–105. Workhouses are described in Leonard, *op. cit.*, pp. 225–27; Marshall, *op. cit.*, pp. 125–60 and Webbs, *op. cit.*, pp. 233–64. The Speenhamland System is described in Webbs, *op. cit.*, pp. 172–96.

(148) M. Blaug, 'The Myth of the Old Poor Law and the Making of the New', *Journal of Economic History*, Vol. XXXIII (1963), pp. 151–84, and 'The Poor Law Report Re-examined', *ibid.*, Vol. XXIV (1964), pp. 229–45.

(149) Webbs, *op. cit.*, pp. xxv–xxvi.

(150) *Ibid.*, p. 125.

(151) G. W. Oxley, *op. cit.*, pp. 448–57.

CHAPTER THREE

The Attorney and the Early Capital Market in Lancashire

B. L. ANDERSON

I

IT IS some twenty years since the question of the supply of capital in the English economy of the eighteenth century was first seen as crucial for explaining the origins of the Industrial Revolution.[1] Earlier writers were most concerned with the formation of capital and emphasised the fact that the threshold of entry into industrial activity was normally quite low for the entrepreneurs of that period.[2] But little attention was given, outside of banking, to the distribution of capital, and the self-financing habits of individual businessmen tended to be interpreted as a sufficient explanation of sustained, industrial capital formation taking place in an environment of capital scarcity.[3] Subsequent research, while reiterating the importance of non-industrial capital in the growth process, has so far failed to throw much light on the nature and effectiveness of the capital market in the eighteenth century.[4] As one writer has remarked, 'Very little has been written in any organised way on the development of the capital-market in the early stages of industrialization. . . . Financial intermediaries other than the banks are largely ignored . . . and about the local markets in which long-term capital was provided through solicitors and other intermediaries in the early days of industrialization we are also very much in ignorance'.[5] The same writer also makes the important point that if, as is often assumed, the landed classes were not directly concerned with investment themselves then it is even more important to know in what ways savings might be transferred to entrepreneurs in industry and trade.

Through the seventeenth and eighteenth centuries a growing number of instances show that the legal profession was concerning itself with financial intermediacy and, when taken together, these suggest that a capital market was coming into being in England, outside of London and apart from the growth of the national debt. The financial activities of the lawyers developed over a long period but even as early as the fifteenth century they were showing a peculiar capacity for acting as a bridge between the merchants and the nobility and the most outstanding among them were on a par with the greatest London merchants.[6] By the early seventeenth century the country attorney was also able to channel landed profits into trade by way of legal fees, as was the case with Thomas Stampe of Lincoln's Inn, sometime recorder of Wallingford, who invested in the Guinea trade.[7] At the same time the diary of Walter Powell of Monmouth shows that he was managing his clients' estates as well as making short- and long-term loans. Money-lending formed a considerable part of the practice of James Casen, a seventeenth-century Norfolk attorney, while at the turn of the eighteenth century Joseph Hunt of Stratford-upon-Avon combined scrivening with estate management. In fact, wherever the activities of such men have been investigated this financial intermediacy seems to be an almost invariable part of their work, and some of them must have operated on a considerable scale. In the early years of the eighteenth century Peniston Lamb of Nottingham amassed a fortune of £100,000 and at the middle of the century John Cooper of Salisbury became very prosperous as a money-scrivening attorney. Even later in the century the financial expertise of the attorney was in demand and the notebook of Robert Lowe records some thirty borrowing transactions in Nottinghamshire between 1781 and 1800.[8] By this time, however, the attorney was exploiting new investment opportunities. For example, in the 1790s Robert Alcock of Halifax was dealing in the shares of the Rochdale Canal Company and Robert Hobbes of Stratford-upon-Avon was involved in arranging transfers of shares in the Birmingham and Warwick Canal Company in the first years of the nineteenth century.[9]

II

The century after the Restoration saw significant developments taking place in the organisation and practice of the legal profession in England. Whereas previously the attorney, as an officer of the court, had performed a function similar to that of the modern common law clerk, almost wholly concerned with procedure, by the late seventeenth century he was beginning to encroach on the numerous activities which traditionally belonged to 'counsel'. The aspirations of the country attorney to interpose himself between the pedestrian practice of procedure and the high flights of advocacy had met with considerable success by the eighteenth century and he had come to play an important part in the affairs of the local community. The

E

influence of law was finding its way into so much of economic life at this time, the demand for legal experience and techniques had increased to such an extent after the Civil War, that the attorney came to occupy a pivotal position in local affairs and his social status was moving perceptibly nearer the ranks of the rural gentry and the urban élite. In town and borough attorneys were to be found performing the duties upon which municipal government depended. They filled the offices of clerks of the peace, town and corporation clerks, and came to monopolise the stewardships of the manorial courts, which introduced them to the circles of landed society.[10] Their involvement in local government administration meant that they could be extremely influential in local politics, particularly as election agents.[11]

The progress of these developments tended to be, if anything, more rapid in those areas farthest removed from London which were beginning to show signs of facing the Home Counties on new and improved economic terms. Throughout this period provincial society was demanding men of versatile talent to grapple with its emergent problems of administration and business and the country attorney seems to have been best equipped to deal with them.[12] In Lancashire, for example, where the number of barristers was relatively small and professional monopoly less effective, the attorney found it easier to take on more of the work of advising clients, handling straightforward conveyancing and arranging mortgages. It is the financial activities of the attorney with which this essay is chiefly concerned, for in Lancashire, at least, there is evidence that he was making a singular contribution to the economic life of the eighteenth century.

The concern of attorneys with financial matters no doubt emanates from their involvement with the large amount of real estate dealings made necessary by the long and complex processes of land sale and recovery following the Civil War.[13] Such business brought them the acquaintance of merchant and county families, which not only enhanced the social prestige of attorneys, but also led to many of them accumulating fortunes comparable with those of their clients. The key factor in the great volume of real estate business which passed through the hands of the Restoration lawyers was the practice of 'entailing' estates. This legal technique had been in existence as early as the thirteenth century, but it was not until the seventeenth century that entails were perfected with the help of a trust protected by the court of Chancery, when it was widely used by landowners during the Civil War to safeguard their estates.[14] The principal advantage gained from this 'strict settlement' was the possibility of mortgage without the loss of rights of redemption and the implications of this legal breakthrough for the owners and holders of land were decisive for the development of the mortgage in its modern form. By the middle decades of the seventeenth century the process by which large amounts of land in institutional and private hands were sold on an open market had almost run its course.[15] In the late seventeenth and eighteenth centuries the characteristic feature of the land market was the relatively low level of sales, partly as a result of decreasing social mobility and increasing tendencies towards consolidation of ownership among the landed classes, and partly because of the reassertion of legal restrictions on alienation which, incidentally but most importantly, offered the alternative of the mortgage as a method of raising long-term loans on the security of land.[16]

After the Restoration the mortgage market grew rapidly and became part of the process by which eighteenth-century landowners made indebtedness the normal condition of real estate management. At the same time this growing volume of mortgage business gave attorneys numerous opportunities to employ their various techniques in order to make land into a security for debt, opportunities which were quickly seized upon and frequently exploited to the limit as the corresponding increase in litigation during this period shows. Arranging mortgages and drawing up the necessary documents, whether the funds so raised were to be used for commercial or industrial investment, for agricultural improvement, or for personal consumption, had to be carried out by the legal profession, for although it was not until 1804 that outsiders were prevented from practising conveyancing this function had been monopolised by the profession during the course of the eighteenth century. Conveyancing embraced not only the business of transferring or mortgaging property but all the work of the Conveyancing Room which included the business of trusts and consequently the need to become acquainted with clients' financial affairs and advise on loans and investments.[17] In addition, many lawyers undertook the provision of personal loans at interest, either on their own account or as intermediaries; nevertheless, the mortgage remained the most typical form of their security dealings in the eighteenth century. It was not the academicians or the lawyers of Parliament and the bureaucracies who were important in this context, but rather the provincial 'men of business', most of them trained in provincial practice, who had knowledge of the whole range of local problems. These attorneys came to dominate the county mortgage market in the eighteenth century through their intimate knowledge of local society and their ability to tap reservoirs of savings in order to accommodate an increasing demand for loanable funds. It was these attorneys of whom Johnson spoke when he asked: 'What is their reputation but an instrument of getting money?'[18]

In this way the provincial capital market of the eighteenth century was based on the mortgage market at the centre of which stood the money-scrivening attorney, characterised as much by his familiarity with business practice and local affairs as by his knowledge of the law. It would be incorrect to suppose that the careers of all or even most country lawyers indicate a class of successful financial entrepreneurs at this period and the modest achievements of a majority would barely justify the conclusion that they were the most significant organ of local finance. Yet in Lancashire, as presumably elsewhere, the names of a large number of attorneys and scriveners occur so frequently and in such contexts that it is certain their financial activity was ubiquitous.[19] Future research might well show that the number of attorneys and others who rose to first rank in this field bears comparison with the number of successful industrial entrepreneurs in the eighteenth century. In any event, the following evidence on the nature of the attorney's activities lends some support to the proposition that he functioned as an intermediary for inter-personal lending and that his practice was, in all important respects, a capital market.

III

Isaac Greene of Childwall Hall (1678–1749) is one of the most outstanding examples of a successful lawyer in Lancashire. Descended from an old yeoman family, his father Edward Greene entered business as a mercer in Liverpool in the late seventeenth century and prospered sufficiently to apprentice his only son Isaac to Daniel Lawton, a Prescot attorney, in whose large practice he gained his early experience. Isaac Greene's association with Edward Blundell, a Prescot barrister, was the first step towards personal success, for it enabled him to take over the work of the Molyneux family's legal affairs from Blundell, around which he built up a substantial practice of his own.[20] Greene's clientele varied considerably in terms of social status but most of his business appears to have been done with people requiring a mortgage in order to make or repay loans. For example, when one of the local gentry, Thomas Worthington of Coppull, needed to settle his debts he mortgaged certain lands in his possession to Thomas Lydiate of Lydiate for £700. Later the mortgage was transferred to Richard Bristow, a London goldsmith, and

Isaac Greene, both of whom were acting for clients, the former for one Thomas Kemp of London and the latter for two local gentlemen, William Haydock and Thomas Banks.[21] This association of a Lancashire lawyer with a London goldsmith is an interesting illustration of the opportunities for collusion in the organisation of loans which existed at the time. Greene's expertise made him invaluable as a trustee and the small but ambitious yeoman anxious to safeguard the gains of a lifetime was among those who sought the attorney's services. Such a man was Thomas Moss who by the time of his death, had acquired the 'Ship' inn and other property in Prescot together with Hayes House in Whiston, and who held the office of Bailiff-Serjeant of Widnes by purchase. As one of the trustees administering the Moss estate Greene was charged with placing the residue out at interest.[22]

It is to be expected that Greene drew most of his clients from local landed society but his interests did not end there for it appears that he was also involved in financing local industry. The site of one of the earliest glasshouses in Lancashire, the Sutton Glasshouse estate, had been mortgaged by the founder-owner John Leafe I to a London physician named Dr. Palmer, presumably for the purpose of financing its early growth. Under John Leafe II the estate was reconveyed on payment of £100 to Joshua Palmer of the Middle Temple, son of the original mortgagee, and Greene was called in to manage the affair. The fact that Greene's own land adjoined the Leafe property and that he possessed the coal rights of the manor of Eltonhead in which it stood gave him a vested interest in the transaction and makes it possible that he was personally involved in the financial affairs of this glassmaking family.[23]

Business of this sort is a sufficient explanation of Isaac Greene's success, a measure of which can be gained from his acquisition of land over the years. At the age of forty he had made himself the owner by purchase of the manors of Childwall, Much and Little Woolton, West Derby, Wavertree, Everton and Eltonhead, as well as considerable lands in Rainhill, Whiston, Sutton, Windle, Hardshaw, Thornton, Sefton and Lunt, where it is known he was an energetic improver, figuring prominently in local enclosure agreements. Greene's marriage into the ancient family of Ireland of Hale brought him that manor, and when in 1751 his estate was estimated at £60,000, this probably only referred to the personalty. At his death Greene's estate was inherited jointly by his two daughters, Ireland and Mary, who divided the properties between them in 1751. Ireland Greene took Hale, her mother's portion, and later married into the Blackburne family who dominated the salt trade of the Mersey in the eighteenth century. Mary Greene received the remainder of her father's estate and in 1757 married Bamber Gascoyne whose eldest son of the same name was to be a Member of Parliament for Liverpool in the period 1780–96. The latter's only daughter Frances Mary Gascoyne eventually married Lord Salisbury.[24] It is an interesting reflection of the openness of English society in the eighteenth century that the provincial attorney Isaac Greene, son of a mercer, was in his lifetime able to establish strong professional links with merchant and county gentry and to bring together what were later to become the Lancashire estates of the Marquess of Salisbury.

In many respects the contemporary career of John Plumbe of Wavertree Hall (1670–1763) shows marked similarities to that of Isaac Greene. Plumbe also came originally from a yeoman family, his grandfather Thomas Plumbe was a small freeholder in Cuerdley and had purchased more land in Whiston in 1646. After the Restoration Plumbe's father enlarged his patrimony further and was able to bequeath to his eldest surviving son a messuage, tenement and land in Whiston, and another tenanted holding in Prescot.[25] From these modest beginnings John Plumbe went on to accumulate substantial landed property through inheritance and by purchase; at the same time he built himself an extremely successful legal practice and even adventured in trade. As with Isaac Greene, Plumbe gained some of his early experience in the stewardship of a manorial court, namely that of Nicholas Blundell of Crosby: Blundell's journal and disbursement books reveal the steady growth of Plumbe's influence in the affairs of that family in the early decades of the eighteenth century.[26] He also used his family connexions to further his professional interest and one incident shows something of the character of the attorney at this period. His uncle Oliver Lyme of Prescot, decribed as being 'afflicted with many indispositions of the body and singularly with great infirmities in his eyes', engaged Plumbe, 'an attorney at law and man of business', to manage his concerns and negotiate his transactions. John Plumbe's relations with his uncle, a noticeably litigious character, were far from being satisfactory, however, and disputes continued to arise between them until, finally, in May 1710 Lyme took his grievances to arbitration. He was awarded £100 per annum for four years, £48 per annum for life, and an immediate payment of £300, but Plumbe soon began to find legal loopholes in the bonds he had been required to give and, by June 1712, he had ceased making payments.[27] This example is significant not so much because of its hint at sharp practice on the part of an attorney, a professional defect which linked his name with a string of malodorous adjectives, but because it is typical of the sort of situation in which he developed his aptitudes for management and trusteeship.

Fortunately, the nature and scope of Plumbe's financial activities as an attorney-landowner can be described more fully from a series of account books which, though incomplete, range from 1697 to 1757 and show the part played by a financial intermediary in accommodating many people, drawn from all social levels, with loans and investments both large and small.[28] For more than half a century Plumbe was involved in short- and long-term lending, both on his own account and for others, usually at the official and generally accepted rate of 5 per cent interest. Sometimes, however, he appears to have charged no interest at all on very short loans made to people of small means. On 22 December 1699 he lent £20 to one Richard Mercer which was repaid to him on 25 January the following year. It seems likely that the money was borrowed for seasonal expenditure and the fact that no interest was charged may be attributed to seasonal goodwill.

Plumbe appears to have been chiefly engaged in taking in and putting out at interest much larger sums of money, frequently on mortgages of long duration. Deposits with him did not usually lie idle for long before being taken up, and the evidence suggests that the local market for funds was in a buoyant condition. Typical of the way in which Plumbe organised his activities is the example of Mrs. Elizabeth Prescott, a widow of Liverpool, who deposited £50 with him on 12 July 1701. The whole of this deposit could not be put at interest for some months and, in the interval, Plumbe financed his carrying of it by fragmenting it into a number of small short-term loans: his practice was to maintain throughout the interpersonal character of a transaction, so that each individual deposit found a particular taker, and perhaps because of this joint-investment through him was quite common. One such fragment of Mrs. Prescott's deposit, a mere £3, was borrowed by John Seacome, a Liverpool gentleman, who repaid it on 29 November 1701; this loan was obviously 'called in' because on the same day Plumbe mentioned that he had been able to find a mortgage for the money. The sum needed was £60, however, and Mrs. Prescott made up the difference of £10 before the whole was placed out on mortgage with a certain William Hardy of Fazakerley. On 12 December 1701 Plumbe wrote: '. . . Paid Mr. Lawton's man for Wm. Hardy, the money I rec'd of Mrs. Prescott for which I took a mortgage to her from him—£60'. This mention of Mr. Lawton refers to Daniel Lawton, a Prescot attorney with an adjoining practice, and indicates that Plumbe had in fact found a contact among the clients of the Prescot attorney, which implies that he was not simply an intermediary in his own area but was also in communication with attorneys operating elsewhere. Another instance occurs on 21 June 1703 when he records the receipt of £100 from Alderman Houghton of Liverpool who was delivering the sum for the Rev. Richard Richmond, incumbent of Walton parish: Plumbe sent Richmond's deposit to Joseph Lancaster, a Warrington attorney, to be put out in that area. Lawyers Radcliffe and Horwich from elsewhere in the county are also mentioned in similar contexts, while Isaac Greene, as well as Daniel Lawton, had dealings with him on a number of occasions: indeed Plumbe was receiving funds from as far away as Rochdale, while in Ireland he had a business rendezvous at the Exchange tavern in Dublin where he made payments for Liverpool merchants trading to that port.

The personal details of most of Plumbe's clients have proved difficult to trace and remain largely unknown, nor is any indication given in his accounts and memoranda of how loans were used by recipients. Among the most noteworthy of his clients were Madame Sarah Clayton and Thomas Cobham, two important mine owners on the coalfield, and the Rev. Richard Richmond who, in July 1716, made £500 over to Plumbe as an annuity fund for his family. The prospect of an annuity was a powerful incentive to long-term lending in the eighteenth century, and provided a substantial proportion of the capital needed to finance mortgages. Two other important names appear in the memoranda for 1750, John Chadwick of Birkacre, the charcoal ironmaster, and John Okill of Liverpool, the timber merchant and shipbuilder, but again no details of their affairs are given. Plumbe's dealings with such prominent individuals did not prevent him from finding a use for almost anybody's savings, however small; on 17 March 1739, for instance, he put £5 out at interest to a certain William Payne of Prescot for one of his servants. Great or small, there is no evidence that any of his clients were dissatisfied with the service he provided, in fact the same Mrs. Prescott mentioned above subsequently became a consistent depositor with Plumbe, to the extent of almost £500 between 1702 and 1712, when her son Ralph Prescott, a linen draper, became a client and began to make deposits.

The money-scrivening activities of John Plumbe not only provide information about debt-management but also offer a useful insight into the private structure of debt in the eighteenth century. The surviving accounts are set out below and show, at irregular intervals, the details of Plumbe's security holdings at year's end. It cannot be assumed that these represent a complete picture of his security holdings in the years for which they are available, or that all the securities listed are his alone and not held by him for others, while the breaks in continuity mean that very short-term business does not appear. What does emerge clearly is that, in general, mortgages were numerically fewer than bonds, promissory notes, etc., but of greater proportional value and duration, and that the 5 per cent interest charged remained constant over the whole period with the exception of the particularly reliable or long-standing client who was charged 4½ per cent. The occasional cash breakdown which occurs, particularly that for 1737, shows an interesting resemblance between Plumbe's 'budore' and the vault of any small, provincial banker at this period. The final table shows the result of an attempt to gather a number of scattered figures together and to present them as an incomplete series of annual accounts, showing receipts, disbursements and cash balances. Another category, showing cash held besides the annual balance, has been construed as representing a fluctuating reserve which gives some slight indication that Plumbe's liquidity ratio was 'normally' high and increasing up to 1740, and low and declining thereafter: possibly no such ratio existed in fact, and if it did it was by no means sacred, but it may be significant that when Plumbe purchased some land in 1733 he paid for it by realising two bond debts rather than by reducing his cash reserves. This may possibly reflect changing investment opportunities over the period, but equally it could be explained in terms of the necessity to guard against a bad security or to realise investments made through him at short notice.

The occupations and domiciles of only a few of Plumbe's debtors have been discovered, nevertheless it is clear that much of his business was done with the local landed classes; for the rest, a number of his clients are identifiable as merchants and master craftsmen, usually engaged in watchmaking and the pottery manufacture. The largest and longest mortgage loan mentioned was made to James Brettargh of Prescot—one of those country gentry whose family had seen better days—in August 1748 when, on his own account, Plumbe lent an initial sum of £1,658 7s. 0d. on a mortgage of the Brettargh family property called the Holt estate in Little Woolton: by January 1756 the principal to carry interest had risen to £2,190. The reason for the mortgage is to be found in the fact that Brettargh's widow was in receipt of a £40 annuity from the Holt estate when she made her will in 1758.[29] The soundness of the investment can be gauged from the fact that as late as 1789 Plumbe's daughter Elizabeth Smarley was able to bequeath all the interest money on the Brettargh mortgage to her grandchildren.[30]

THE SECURITIES OF JOHN PLUMBE

Outstanding at the end of 1732

		£	s	d.
30 May 1712	Case & Huddleston's bond	10	0	0
15 March 1720	remainder of John Winstanley's bond	9	5	7
Pd. 4 April 1724	Humphrey Topping's bond	5	0	0
2 December 1724	remainder of J. Pemberton's note	4	0	0
27 June 1726	Mr. Haskayne's bond	40	0	0
1 May 1728	David Hall's contract	17	0	0
5 March 1728	Barton's bond	100	0	0
Pd. 13 March 1730	Mr. Radcliffe's bond	200	0	0
16 March 1730	Mr. A. Radcliffe's note	50	16	7
Pd. 7 March 1731	Mr. Lawton's bond	90	0	0
20 August 1731	remainder of Mr. Plumbton's bond	13	10	0
Pd. 18 March 1731	John Leadbetter's bond	70	0	0
Pd. 24 August 1731	Robert Taylor's bond in my son's hands	10	0	0
Pd. 10 November 1732	Mr. Caryl Hawarden's bond	30	0	0
28 December 1732	Mr. Payn's note & warr't acc't	20	0	0
	BONDS AND NOTES, etc.	739	12	2
30 November 1726	Robert Barnes' mortgage	45	0	0
18 June 1730	Richard Lonsdale's security	12	0	0
1 July 1731	John Hales' mortgage	46	0	0
1 July 1731	Daniel Jenkinson's mortgage (3)	215	0	0
	MORTGAGES, etc.	318	0	0
	CASH IN HAND	230	11	8
	TOTAL	1,288	3	10

'Memo. May 1733—I took in Mr. Radcliffe's and Mr. Lawton's [attorneys] to pay towards my purchase of Halsall's in Aughton —£280.'

*   *   *

Outstanding at the end of 1737

	£	s.	d.
Samuel Bolton's assignment in sec's	30	0	0
Richard Kingsley's bond	20	0	0
Mr. Paine's warr't acc't for sec. of	20	0	0
Henry Watkinson's bond[32]	35	0	0
John Grayston's bond[33]	10	0	0
Mrs. Kelsall's note for £10 and John Balmer's £3	13	0	0
William Fairclough's note	2	0	0
Randle Brownsword's note	1	7	0
John Morecroft's note	3	0	0
John Part's note	0	10	0
Other old securities not to be depended on	21	0	0
	154	17	0
CASH NOW BY ME	369	0	0
TOTAL	523	17	0

	£	s.	d.
In guineas in my Budore 260	273	0	0
more in my pocket 6	6	6	0
more 5 moidurs at 27s. each	6	15	0
Silver in the Budore	70	0	0
more in my pocket		12	0
more in a bag	8	0	0
more in silver for market money abt.	4	7	0
	369	0	0

* * *

Outstanding at the end of 1739

	£	s.	d.
Worthington's bond	50	0	0
Watkinson	35	0	0
Payne's bond	15	0	0
Grayston	18	0	0
Kelsall	10	0	0
Balmer	8	0	0
Glover's bond	10	0	0
Robert Plumbe	5	0	0
	151	0	0
CASH BY ME	645	14	0

	£	s.	d.
In guineas by me 571½	600	1	6
Portugal Gold	20	2	0
In Silver about	25	10	6
	645	14	0
TOTAL	796	14	0

* * *

Outstanding at the end of 1740

	£	s.	d.
Henry Watkinson	35	0	0
Mr. Ince	60	0	0
Mr. Glover	10	0	0
Robert Gore	10	0	0
Robert Plumbe's note	5	0	0
Lonsdale's note	2	5	0
	122	5	0

Debts desperate since last year

	£	s.	d.
Worthington	50	0	0
Payne	15	0	0
Grayston	10	0	0
	75	0	0
TOTAL	197	0	0

* * *

Outstanding at the end of 1747

	£	s.	d.
June 1737 Henry Watkinson's security	35	0	0
6 December 1742 Ralph Balshaw's bond	10	0	0
10 August 1743 Mr. Pritchard's bond	300	0	0
Roger Horrocks' warr't acc't remains with int.	10	0	0
1 August 1748 Mr. Brettargh's mortgage and bond	1,658	7	0
16 December 1746 William Penketh's bond	200	0	0
MORTGAGES AND BONDS	2,213	7	0
Robert Marshe's remains due besides int.	5	13	6
John Fazakerley's ,, ,, ,, ,,	54	0	0
Charles Tong's ,, ,, ,, ,,	29	2	0
John Goor's note desperate	6	4	0
Richard Page	1	0	0
PROMISSORY NOTES	95	19	6
Nicholas Fearns on balance besides int.	21	7	6
James Bolton—poor	13	0	0
Mr. Paine's security—dead at London	20	0	0
Josiah & John Worthington's bond	50	0	0
OTHER SEC.'S LOST OR DESPERATE	104	7	6
CASH IN HAND	209	2	3
TOTAL	2,622	16	3

*   *   *

Outstanding at the end of 1748

6 December 1742 Ralph Balshaw's bond	10	0	0
10 August 1743 Mr. Pritchard	300	0	0
Roger Horrock's' bond	3	3	0
16 December 1746 Mr. Penketh's bond	200	0	0
1 August 1748 Mr. Brettargh's mortgage	1,658	7	0
Arrears of Rent from tenants clear	252	18	7
Others subject to Taxes	597	18	10
and several securities desperate			
	3,122	7	5

*   *   *

Outstanding at the end of 1750

	£	s.	d.
Balshaw	10	0	0
Pritchard	300	0	0
Penketh	200	0	0
17 April 1749 more by note from Forbes	260	0	0
20 June 1749 Mr Clare's bond assigned	30	0	0
Robert Okill's bill	19	11	0
1 August 1748 Mr. Brettargh's mortgage	1,658	7	0
	2,477	18	0
CASH IN HAND	264	6	0
TOTAL	2,742	4	0

	Principal	Interest		
Outstanding at the end of 1756	£	£	s.	d.
William Penketh	200	10	0	0
Mr. Brettargh's mortgage	2,020	101	0	0
20 September 1751 Robert & Thomas Barton	30	1	10	0
Joseph Finney's mortgage	100	5	0	0
Thomas Aspinwall's bond	20	1	0	0
Mr. Crosby's bond @ £4 10s. p.c.	600	27	0	0
Thomas Brownbill's bond	100	5	0	0
Thomas Topping	100	5	0	0
Thomas Appleton	200	10	0	0
John Fogg	100	5	0	0
John Webster	100	5	0	0
Robert Fogg with suretys	100	5	0	0
some with other suretys	150	7	10	0
William Simpson's mortgage & bond	600	30	0	0
Thomas Tipping's mortgage	100	5	0	0
James Farrer's bond	50	2	10	0
Daniel Mackneal	500	25	0	0
December 1755 Peter Gerrard	100	5	0	0
	5,170	255	10	0
2 February 1756 John Livesley's bond	300	15	0	0

31 January 1756 Brettargh settled account to carry
int. from this day is to be £2,190

Cash   £448 18 8

*   *   *

Outstanding at the end of 1757	£	s.	d.
James Brettargh's mortgage (the Holt estate in Little Woolton)	2,190	0	0
9 June 1752 Joseph Finney's mortgage[34] (messuage and other buildings in Thomas St.)	100	0	0
27 March 1754 William Simpson's mortgage (several houses on Liverpool Common)	600	0	0
27 December 1754 Thomas Tipping's mortgage (ground in Liverpool and gave bond for)	100	0	0
MORTGAGES	2,990	0	0
16 December 1746 William Penketh	200	0	0
20 September 1751 Robert Barton	30	0	0
17 July 1752 Thomas Aspinwall	20	0	0
3 May 1753 Mr. Crosby	600	0	0
3 August 1753 Thomas Topping	100	0	0
26 November 1753 Thomas Appleton	200	0	0
18 July 1754 John Fogg	100	0	0
3 August 1754 John Webster	100	0	0
6 October 1754 Robert Fogg	100	0	0
3 March 1755 James Farrer	50	0	0
20 October 1755 Daniel Mackneal	500	0	0
9 December 1755 Peter Gerrard	100	0	0
2 February 1756 J. Livesley (and another for £200 not included)[35]	300	0	0
30 October 1756 D. Kenyon	300	0	0
BONDS	2,700	0	0
CASH	460	0	0
TOTAL	6,150	0	0

RECONSTRUCTED ANNUAL ACCOUNTS OF JOHN PLUMBE 1729–57[36]

Year	Receipts			Disbursements			Ann. Balance			Cash Besides Ann. Balance		
	£	s.	d.	£	s.	d.	£	s.	d.	£	s.	d.
1729	581	5	11	630	1	5½	—48	15	6			
1730												
1731												
1732	437	13	4	399	6	2	+ 38	7	2	192	4	6
1733												
1734												
1735												
1736	405	7	8	378	9	10	+ 26	17	10			
1737	409	13	7	336	16	9	+ 72	16	10	369	0	0
1738												
1739	455	3	6	293	12	5	+160	11	1	645	14	0
1740	542	3	1	1,061	7	9	—519	4	8	144	10	0*
1748	3,942	15	3	752	1	4	+3,190	13	11	66	16	0
1749												
1750	4,780	7	4	528	12	1½	+4,251	15	2½	264	6	0
1751												
1752												
1753												
1754												
1755												
1756										448	18	8
1757										460	0	0

N.B. Receipts increase more than seven-fold over 1740–48.

The money-scrivening activities of John Plumbe represent his most important, but not his only, excursion into business affairs. He was also involved in an oyster fishery concern with his brother-in-law Thomas Townley of Royle and William Hesketh of Means, near Poulton-le-Fylde. In the early years of the eighteenth century a patent had been applied for by Robert Davys of Chester and Thomas Townley who maintained that they had been at some expense in searching several areas of the sea between the mouth of the Ribble and the Piel of Fouldrey for an oyster bed below the low-water mark. By 1729 Plumbe was actively involved and accountable for a quarter part of the concern, another quarter part being taken by Townley and a half share by Hesketh, but the venture does not appear to have been particularly successful.[37] Plumbe was also eminent in the more orthodox practice of the law and as an attorney he frequently represented the Liverpool Common Council and many prominent private individuals in lawsuits. Yet he was also a considerable landowner and his professional achievements must, in some

measure, be attributed to the social repute gained from the possession of land: all his business activities were ultimately founded upon
landed wealth and cannot be considered in isolation from his position as a rentier.[38]

In the eighteenth century a shrewd attorney and man of affairs
was peculiarly well placed for accumulating substantial landed
property from the nucleus of a modest patrimony and the fortunes
of John Plumbe cannot have been untypical. By 1720, with the
deaths of his elder brothers William (d. 1719) and Thomas (d.
1712), he had inherited the family property in Whiston, Prescot
and Cuerdley. At that date he was already resident at Wavertree
Hall, whose manor he had purchased together with those of Aughton and Uplitherland. In 1694 he had married Sarah, the daughter
of Peter Marsh, niece and coheir of James Vernon of Vernon Hall,
West Derby, which increased his landed wealth still further. From
these areas Plumbe expanded his landownership at the expense of
older declining families, his Liverpool property being acquired
chiefly from the Moore family and his lands in Aughton and
Scarisbrick from the Heskeths. It is significant that Plumbe's final
purchase of such estates was usually preceded by a period of heavy
mortgage lending on his part to secure the financial dependence of
the family concerned. In the case of the Heskeths, for instance,
Plumbe lent Alexander Hesketh of Aughton no less than £2,400
from 1715 until he finally purchased the manorial rights of Aughton
and Uplitherland in 1718. Over the same period Hesketh's Ormskirk property and his lands in Scarisbrick, Aspinwall, Tarleton and
Snape were mortgaged to Plumbe.[39] Prior to 1715 the Hesketh
estate had been mortgaged to and recovered from Richard Legh of
Lyme, a Cheshire squire, and when the Heskeths went down to
Plumbe it was not without a struggle.[40]

Rents were undoubtedly Plumbe's major source of income, certainly some of the bond and note debts recorded among his securities were for interest-bearing rent arrears, and there is evidence that
he possessed a number of characteristics associated with the progressive 'gentleman' farmer of the period. Just occasionally he was
willing to accept payment of rent in kind, but more usually he allowed credit for work done in marling etc.; similarly, if a tenant improved the property, Plumbe would not pay him for the improvements or reduce his rent, but instead would give credit on rents due.
In this way he appears to have subsidised his tenants and sometimes
rent arrears were very heavy, as with James Marsh who farmed the
Aughton Hall estate and parts of the demesne in Aughton and Scarisbrick at a rent of £105 per annum. Marsh owed Plumbe £306

18s. 4d. for rent on 1 January 1747/8, and he himself was sub-letting to at least five other tenants.[41]

What little is known of the attorneys Greene and Plumbe as land-owners would appear to lend support to the view that in the century following the Restoration many landed estates were units of ownership rather than production, and that the professional classes were among the most important of what new entrants there were into the upper levels of landed society.[42] Neither belonged to established landed families of high repute in the county and both may well be typical of those who acquired land at the expense of the declining sections of the squirearchy, and who, as gentlemen farmers, were not by any means exclusively involved in agriculture. In the case of a landowning attorney his rent income was likely to be supplemented from money-scrivening rather than, as happened in other cases elsewhere, from lucrative army posts and government pensions. Scrivening, like banking, was a technique rather than a full-time occupation in the eighteenth century and, even within the legal profession itself, quite different sorts of men might practise it. Greene and Plumbe both pursued their careers in the environment of landed society and eventually joined its ranks themselves, but there were others whose landed links were much less apparent and who exhibit rather different traits.

IV

Daniel Lawton and Edward Deane were two attorneys who operated large practices in south-west Lancashire during the first half of the eighteenth century. They merit attention, in particular, because both carried on their activities from Prescot, a town that was well endowed with attorneys at this period, a fact that may, to some extent, account for its importance as a financial centre. Before the navigation of the Sankey Brook Prescot stood on the main line of supply of coal to Liverpool, and the accounts, memoranda, etc., of Lawton and Deane give some notion of the wide scope of activities that were open to financial intermediaries on the edge of a developing coalfield, ranging as they do from the handling of bankruptcy cases and business partnerships to attending to apprenticeship indentures and local Poor Law matters.[43] A number of the small coal-mining partnerships which abounded on the Lancashire coalfield before the monopoly movement of the 1750s appear among the clientele of Lawton and Deane. In September 1751 articles were drawn up between Robert Gwyllym and Robert Roper, the executors of Cobham and Makin, one of the most important partnerships, for carrying on their coalmining business in Sutton.[44] Similarly, in the summer of 1753 a partnership agreement was drawn up between a certain Mr. Barton of Poulton-le-Fylde and three local men, John Halliwell, William Lomax and John Shepherd, for working Barton's coal-pits in Blackrod.[45] Although clear instances of direct financing are difficult to isolate in such cases it is certain that Edward Deane and the Lawton brothers, Daniel and William, were deeply involved in the legal and financial affairs of many of them. In 1749 one or other of them advised Nicholas Cross, a Mr. Fisher, Samuel Smith, a Mr. Rowe and others, all part-owners of a ship and its insurance policy, about the mortgages which encumbered the vessel and drew up a Chancery petition for them.[46] Again, in 1752 they assigned the share of John Chorley of Prescot in a sailcloth-making concern called Messrs. Matthews, Leather and Chorley, to a certain William Webster.[47]

This kind of work enabled the attorney to delve deep into the private business affairs of a large number of people with the result that he gained a rare and intimate knowledge of the financial position of individuals while at the same time cultivating those personal contacts so essential, for instance, when raising a mortgage loan. In November 1750 Thomas Golden of Hardshaw, being indebted to the daughters of Isaac Greene on a mortgage, engaged Deane to raise a sum of money with which to pay it off. After consulting Alexander Leigh, the Wigan attorney, best known for his financing of the Douglas Navigation, and the Greene sisters' own attorney, Mr. Taylor, Deane eventually managed to obtain a loan from Nicholas Fazakerley, the famous Preston lawyer. In the course of negotiating this loan a dispute arose over the time taken to get the money and the rate of interest to be charged, but after an inspection of the securities was made Deane managed to raise £900 from Fazakerley with Golden's Hardshaw estates as collateral.[48] One of the Prescot attorneys' most important clients was John Wyke, the celebrated watchmaker and toolmaker of that town, who was to become one of Liverpool's earliest bankers, building up a flourishing business there after 1758. In June 1745 Deane obtained a £200 mortgage for Wyke on property the latter had only recently acquired in Prescot: a certain Mr. Garnett of Farnworth supplied the loan and before its arrival Deane personally met Wyke's occasions for money.[49] The same Mr. Garnett was not always so fortunate in his lending for he is mentioned as being one of sixteen creditors involved in bankruptcy proceedings against Henry Marsh, a local businessman, in 1749–51; Marsh owed Garnett £100 on mortgage.[50] It is interesting to note that another of Marsh's creditors was a Mr. Plumbe of

F

Bolton-le-Moors who was being represented by his relative the Rev. Thomas Plumbe of Aughton, the second son of William Plumbe, attorney, and grandson of John Plumbe discussed above.[51]

The Prescot lawyers also had connexions with Henry Wiswall of Ormskirk, a scrivening attorney who practised throughout the first half of the eighteenth century and who appears to have often had an excess of deposits over loans. As early as 1709 Wiswall is described as 'one that is much concerned in the letting out of moneys upon securitys' and in that year a Liverpool slater, Gabriel Westhead, son of a glovemaker of Lathom, borrowed £14 from him on the security of a leasehold tenement in Lathom worth £8 per annum. The money which Westhead received had been put out at interest with Wiswall by a Prescot tobacconist named Thomas Taylor. In 1749 James Tyrer, a Liverpool merchant, borrowed £142 from Wiswall on land security and Daniel Lawton acted as intermediary for the loan. When Tyrer needed more money to pay off his creditors Lawton transferred the mortgage from Wiswall to Thomas Barron, another more substantial Prescot lawyer. Barron paid Tyrer £142 and interest for Wiswall and accepted an assignment of the mortgage for securing a further £180.[52]

Because almost anyone with the necessary personal credit and connexions was able to arrange mortgages and make loans in the eighteenth century, the attorney was wont to associate with all manner of people in his search for clients. For example, Thomas Taylor of Manchester, the Greene sisters' attorney, was assisted by his uncle Thomas Hulme, the parish clerk of Salford, who appears to have concerned himself with attracting local savings, while Taylor found securities on which loans could be made. An entry in Hulme's memorandum book for 4 February 1783 reads: 'I now am Dr. to Mrs. Smith twenty pounds which I will endeavour to put out to Interest for Her with my Hundred pounds as soon as Mr. Taylor can find proper security.'[53] The association of Hulme and Taylor brought them a varied business: at the same time as he is lending £300 on mortgage to a John Makinson of Blackburn, Hulme is also making shorter loans: for instance, on 20 April 1782 he lends £100 to a Thomas Gates of Norbury which is to be repaid on 2 February 1783 with £3 18s. 0d. interest. On at least one occasion Thomas Taylor is found going to London to collect a debt and this may account for his representing the Greene sisters in the affair concerning Thomas Golden's mortgage, mentioned above, since at that time they resided there. The collecting of debts, often for trivial amounts, was an important part of the everyday business of a country attorney in the eighteenth century, an age when the problem of small debts was very acute. One of the legacies of Elizabeth Arnold, a Liverpool widow, was a debt for £2 9s. 0d. owed by 'a man in London and which Mr. Statham (attorney) is imployed to recover'.[54] Debt recovery could adversely affect relations with clients as is shown by one experience of the Prescot attorneys in the case of a sum of money placed out with them by the executors of one Mary Tarleton in the name of her grandson William Simkin of Great Sankey. When Simkin wanted the money at his coming of age in 1750 the lawyers had some difficulty in calling the loan in; the penalty for delay was a smaller percentage, to judge from the complaint of one of them when settling the accounts: 'But now I think myself ill used in having no allowance for managing the money for 10 yrs. together, tho' I was to have had it @ 4 p.c., for there was risk which they refused to consider.'[55]

The extent to which the legal profession in the eighteenth century concerned itself with financial matters naturally varied a good deal: with some their activities resemble those of a financial entrepreneur rather than an attorney, while in many cases local government and administration occupied a large part of their professional careers. Henry Brown of Liverpool (1745/6–1822), for example, was almost entirely concerned with municipal affairs.[56] Nicholas Fazakerley of Prescot, whose career covered a period rather earlier in the century was, on the other hand, able to combine civic and financial business: a recorder of Preston, he was also deeply implicated in managing the affairs of the Lancashire recusants; he was a celebrated money-lender and is traditionally supposed to have left a large fortune. The money-scrivener and financial intermediary was most commonly found among this latter type of attorney who flourished particularly in the first half of the century and who, by virtue of the very range of his activities, was always something of an interloper. Consequently, such men had no monopoly of activities which lay on the margins of law and finance; indeed many of them were probably no different from a seventeenth-century conveyancer like Sir Orlando Bridgeman, who attained power and wealth while remaining outside the legal profession.[57] These 'merchants of capital' could thus appear in many guises by the eighteenth century, though that of the scrivening attorney was the most characteristic.

It is the quite distinct function which such men performed and the special ability they showed in the management of loanable funds that is significant, representing an important element in financial communications that was often instrumental in releasing funds from tightly-knit personal groups and channelling them to investment opportunities within the county and beyond. In this way, for example, a Liverpool widow, Elizabeth Sharples, was placing large sums of money out at interest through an intermediary named Edward Veal of Wingheays, near Poulton-le-Fylde. Some of those who borrowed the money are mentioned as being in arrears over interest payments; they were John Wesby of the Burn, who owed £150 on bond, Robert Hoole of Kirkham, who owed £20 on bond, and Thomas Roe, a Poulton attorney, who owed £100 on bond.[58] This sort of investment from centres of wealth to outlying areas where funds were less plentiful went on side by side with the investment of capital seeking more intensive utilisation in areas of rapid growth, though the latter type probably became increasingly important as the century proceeded. An early instance of this was the £260 belonging to a Preston spinster, Susanna Doughty, who heard that Thomas Ball of Ormskirk, later of Liverpool, attorney, 'was a person very much made use of by several persons for the placing out their moneys at interest, and that he would be a very proper person to be employed in putting out the money, having the character and reputation of a very careful, substantial honest man'.[59] Some of her money was lent to Richard Norris of Speke, a mayor of Liverpool, and may well have helped finance the famous slave-trade voyage of the *Blessing* in 1699.

V

The functions associated here with the attorney appear, at first sight, to be very close to those of his contemporary the country banker. Both professions may be said to have consisted of specialists in techniques already practised in combination with other activities by a variety of people: just as it is difficult to estimate the numerical importance of financial intermediaries who came from many walks of life, and whose activities are often difficult to disentangle from the normal business of merchants, tradesmen, country gentry or professional men, so it would be unwise to attach too much significance to the number of bankers, properly so called, at the end of the century.[60] The attorney and the banker, however, while both provided valuable financial services in the emergent capital market of the eighteenth century, came from essentially different moulds.

There appears to be no evidence to suggest that anyone in England before the seventeenth century regularly performed that dual function, which is fundamental to modern banking, of borrowing from some people in order to lend to others at a profit. There were thus no English counterparts of the Venetian 'campsores', for in

England the Jews, and the Lombards after them, were merely lending their own capital. Banking as opposed to money-lending was first carried on in this country by the scriveners and goldsmiths: the scriveners were clerks who took care of the legal minutiae of conveyances, bonds and other transactions, and who were thus able to arrange borrowing and lending.[61] Although the scriveners were probably among the very first bankers the chief instrument of modern banking was introduced by the goldsmiths when, just prior to the Civil War, the London merchants began to deposit money with them; a new departure, this may be attributed, on the one hand, to a decline of the trade in plate and, on the other, to an increasing need for financial security on the part of the merchants.

After the Civil War the goldsmiths began to act not merely as depositaries paying interest but also as agents for making payments to third parties, and soon a cheque system was effectively in being, arising out of a special use of the bill of exchange which was already in existence. It is, of course, difficult to distinguish between banking and broking aspects of the financial structure at this period and in the activities of the goldsmith it is possible to find much that is characteristic of both banking practice and financial intermediacy. Similarly with the scriveners who were probably the first to perform the basic banking functions, yet who later became more important as agents for loanable funds and advisers on investment portfolios. Thus at first both practised two functions together which gradually grew apart, and which would now be considered as separate. Nevertheless, it is possible to distinguish different emphases in the work of each of them and, at the risk of oversimplification, the deposit and remittance activities of the seventeenth-century goldsmith stand in a direct line of precedence with the banking of the eighteenth century, while the financial agency and brokerage business of his contemporary the scrivener were wholly, or in part, taken over and extended by the money-scrivening attorney of the eighteenth century.

In practice, of course, these two functions took some considerable time to disentangle themselves from the corpus of financial work, indeed the process of clarification had not been completed by the time the joint-stock banks and an institutionalised capital market came to serve the very different economy of nineteenth-century Britain. Thus the kind of services which the banking specialists were providing towards the end of the eighteenth century were not in themselves new but rather an integration of existing techniques in response to an urgent need arising in the first phase of industrialisation. The provision of a local means of payment and facilities for the transfer of payments were among the most pressing problems confronting the early entrepreneurs; it is not surprising, therefore, that the country bankers were typically engaged in note-issuing, discounting and remittance activities and were rarely to be found consistently channelling savings to the points of investment demand, even in the short run. As a result, deposit banking cannot have amounted to very much in eighteenth-century England, and this situation appears to have prevailed until the advent of joint-stock banks after 1826. The precocity of the Scottish banks at this period is shown by their more favourable attitude towards granting loans, particularly their 'cash-credit' facility;[62] yet Scottish industry does not appear to have benefited from a greater degree of financial freedom than existed elsewhere. By contrast, London's private bankers, particularly the old-established ones in the West End who came to serve the landed interest, were greatly involved in the market for government securities: the same was true of the City bankers, whose mercantile links were much stronger and who carried out most of the London agency business when country banking expanded after 1750.[63] It is significant that the younger firms created in the banking boom of 1769–73 and afterwards were the ones who took most of the agency business, yet for much of the century it seems that the private bankers of the capital were the willing tools of public finance.

The Lancashire banks, when they appeared, were part of the response to a general acceleration of industrial and commercial activity which involved, in particular, an increased demand for discounting facilities. Note-issue was never very important in Lancashire and even Bank of England notes came into use much later than elsewhere; in part this can be attributed to the widespread mistrust of note-issues, but probably more important was the fact that there was no great need for them. Bills of exchange, coin and, later, banker's drafts were much the most popular means of payment, and it was in these that the Lancashire bankers specialised. The draft was the only new instrument which they brought to bear on the monetary situation in the county and this never became popular, reissue being almost always in the form of bills, so that in the early years of the nineteenth century its importance was small.[64] Coin and bills of exchange had, of course, long been provided before the arrival of the banks, together with discounting facilities in Lancashire and London, so that there is no reason to suppose that they radically altered, rather than merely supplemented, existing facilities.[65] What is more, it seems unlikely that the banks fitted easily into the credit and currency system of Lancashire, for even during the crisis of 1793 it was the Corporation of Liverpool, not its bankers, who finally resorted to a note-issue.[66] It is also worth noticing that the mercantile communities of Lancashire, and not its bankers as such, rallied to defend the bill of exchange system when it was threatened.[67]

The timing of the appearance of banking in Lancashire and the origins of the early bankers illustrate the type of individual who stood nearest to the specialist and the functions he was most concerned with during the century. In Liverpool, for example, banking grew out of the needs of local commerce and most of the city's early bankers were merchants such as William Clarke, engaged in the linen trade, the first banker to appear in a Liverpool Directory.[68] John Wyke, acknowledged to have been the first banker in Liverpool, was a merchant middleman, and a watch and machine toolmaker. Similarly, a number of Manchester's earliest bankers were traders, in particular tea dealers such as John Jones, the son of a nonconformist minister. The first Manchester bank, founded in December 1771, was launched by Edward Byrom, son of a physician, William Allen, son of a tradesman, Roger Sedgwick, another physician's son, and Edward Place, son of a clergyman.[69] The professional middle-class element was marked from the beginning in banking as shown, for example, by the number of attorneys who moved into it during the course of the century. The fact that bankers usually only made specific practices which had previously been grafted on to the main body of a business, should not be taken to apply only to merchants and traders who, no doubt, were in the forefront of the eighteenth-century credit expansion and, therefore, among those most likely to specialise in banking. Although very little is known about the progress of credit in the internal economy of the period it was almost certainly as crucial, in its way, as the growth of credit in foreign trade. Hence, attorney-bankers such as George Tyndale, a partner in the Exchange Bank of Bristol, and Charles Henry Hunt, the Town Clerk of Stratford-upon-Avon who founded a bank there in 1790, are significant not so much for themselves as for the tradition of which they were the last exponents, and which finally petered out in 1890 when the last solicitor-banker, Joseph Dickinson of Alston, sold out to the Carlisle City and District Banking Company.[70]

It has been suggested that one reason why banks were not founded in greater numbers outside of London was because attorneys were offering some banking services to provincial society throughout the greater part of the eighteenth century.[71] The evidence examined here suggests that this was in fact the case and that country banking was essentially a response to the phenomenal increase in the demand for payments facilities, consequent upon population growth and industrialisation, with which existing arrangements were inadequate to cope.

The real importance of the scrivening attorney, however, lies not in his ability to apply rudimentary banking principles before the spread of country banking but in his role of broker for negotiating secured loans. The English banking system was largely a response to industrialisation rather than a causal factor, the banks were capital-servicing rather than capital-forming institutions, and if the problem of how long-term capital requirements were met in the eighteenth century is to be solved more attention needs to be focused on the working of the mortgage market with which the scrivening attorney was intimately connected. An important link in continuity between the scrivener and the attorney in the seventeenth century seems to have been the former's uncertain hold on conveyancing business which was more and more taken over by the ascendant attorneys.[72] The evolution of easy mortgaging by the end of the seventeenth century gave the attorney an immense opportunity to build on the art of the scrivener and subsequently 'by most of the scriveners becoming attorneys, and most of the attorneys practising as scriveners, the business of the two professions became united in the same persons'.[73] There was never any conflict of interest between banking and financial intermediacy during the eighteenth century, for their respective spheres, if they sometimes overlapped, were basically distinct. On the contrary, they must frequently have complemented one another; indeed, Thomas Hulme of Salford, mentioned above in connexion with scrivening, was at the same time investing in the Manchester bank of Scholes and Cundall and mentions receiving a dividend of £418 3s. 6d. on his own account, plus £354 12s. 5d. on account of Edward Kenyon, an Altrincham attorney. In this way the early country banks may have provided yet another investment outlet for local savings managed by financial intermediaries.

The part played by rural-based savings in financing the early stages of the Industrial Revolution, in particular capital raised on real security, has been given scant consideration to date, yet it is now clear that money-scrivening attorneys, among others, were able to effectively mobilise such resources fully a century or more before the industrial and technological changes of the later eighteenth century. The business interests of the London firm of scriveners, Sir Robert Clayton and John Morris, between 1650 and 1700, for example, extended over the south-east and Midland counties.[74] The Lancashire attorneys practised mainly between 1700 and 1760, their interests appear to have been confined to the county and, significantly, they did much more mortgage business than the London concern and their clientele was more varied. Much remains to be done before all the implications of the money-scrivening attorney's important position in the financial life of the eighteenth century can be known. Many more detailed studies of his activities need to be undertaken before his significance as compared with other contemporary channels of finance can be appreciated. Finally, it would be useful to know how widespread were the business connexions of the attorney, outside of his purely scrivening activities, and what, if any, were his contributions to entrepreneurship.

(1) T. S. Ashton, *The Industrial Revolution 1760–1830* (1948), p. 11.

(2) H. Heaton, 'Financing the Industrial Revolution', *Bulletin of Business History*, Vol. XI (1937).

(3) M. M. Postan, 'Recent Trends in the Accumulation of Capital', *Economic History Review*, Vol. VI (1935).

(4) S. Pollard, 'Fixed Capital in the Industrial Revolution in Britain', *Journal of Economic History*, Vol. XXIV (1964).

(5) A. K. Cairncross, 'Capital Formation in the Take-off', in W. W. Rostow ed., *The Economics of Take-off into Sustained Growth* (1963).

(6) Sylvia Thrupp, *The Merchant Class of Medieval London 1300–1500* (1948), p. 263.

(7) A. Harding, *A Social History of English Law* (1966), p. 208.

(8) M. Birks, *Gentlemen of the Law* (1960), pp. 181–205.

(9) *Ibid.*, and my 'Aspects of Capital and Credit in Lancashire during the Eighteenth Century' (University of Liverpool M.A. thesis, 1966), p. 176.

(10) S. & B. Webb, *English Local Government: The Parish and the County* (1906), *passim*.

(11) M. Cox, 'Sir Roger Bradshaigh and the Electoral Management of Wigan, 1695–1747', *Bulletin of the John Rylands Library*, Vol. 37 (1954).

(12) R. Robson, *The Attorney in Eighteenth Century England* (1959) p. vi.

(13) H. J. Habakkuk, 'Landowners and the Civil War', *Economic History Review*, Vol. XVIII (1965).

(14) G. A. Grove and J. F. Garner, ed., *Hargreaves on Land Law* (1963), pp. 64–66.

(15) L. Stone, 'Social Mobility in England, 1500–1700', *Past and Present*, Vol. 33 (1966).

(16) H. J. Habakkuk, 'The English Land Market in the Eighteenth Century', in J. S. Bromley and E. H. Kossmann, ed., *Britain and the Netherlands* (1959), Vol. II.

(17) E. B. V. Christian, *Solicitors: An Outline of their History* (1925), p. 129.

(18) Quoted in R. Robson, *op. cit.*, p. 53.

(19) *Vide* my M.A. thesis *op. cit.*, appendix 1.

(20) R. Stewart Brown, *Isaac Greene: A Lancashire Lawyer of the Eighteenth Century* (1921).

(21) Indenture of Assignment, 1 April 1710, Misc. Deeds, 37, Blainscough, Captain Case Deeds, Wigan Public Library.

(22) Will of Thomas Moss of Prescot, yeoman, 1730, *Lancashire and Cheshire Record Society*, Vol. 22 (1890).

(23.) 'An Abstract of the Title to the Glasshouse Estate in Sutton . . .' 920MD155; also Glasshouse Sutton (1675–99), 1762, 1920SAL681; both in Liverpool Record Office.

(24) Salisbury Mss. 920SAL18/1, Liverpool Record Office.

(25) For the early history of the family *vide* 'Genealogical Memoranda Relating to the Families of Plumbe and Tempest' (1898), 920PLU, Liverpool Record Office.

(26) 920MD74–5, Liverpool Record Office.

(27) Lancs. Chancery Petition, P.L.6.52/7 (1712), P.R.O.

(28) Plumbe-Tempest Deeds and Papers, 920PLU9, Liverpool Record Office.

(29) Will of Ann Brettargh of Prescot, widow, 1788, *Lancashire and Cheshire Record Society*, Vol. 44 (1902).

(30) Will of Elizabeth Smarley of Liverpool, widow, 1789, *ibid.*

(31) Daniel Jenkinson of Liverpool, innkeeper.

(32) Henry Watkinson of Halsall, husbandman.

(33) John Grays[t]on of Liverpool, mariner and later shipbuilder.

(34) Joseph Finney of Liverpool, watchmaker.

(35) John Livesley of Liverpool, pottery manufacturer.

(36) The trend of the accounts is indicative of the prevailing situation in agriculture (*vide* G. E. Mingay, 'The Agricultural Depression 1730–50', *Economic History Review*, Vol. VIII (1956).) Most of the data relating to the 1740s is missing but it would seem that 1739–40 was a major turning-point in Plumbe's career: during the thirties a growing concern with 'desperate debts' is evident and, at the same time, a strengthening of his liquidity position. It is clear that Plumbe began deficit spending in 1740 but whether on investments, on subsidies, or on both is not known. The most remarkable feature of the 1740s, however, was the complete change in the order of magnitude between 1740 and 1748, particularly with regard to receipts; in the absence of further evidence it is impossible to be certain but such a change indicates something more than merely recovery to a pre-depression level of income.

(37) 'Papers of an Oyster and General Fishery off the Fylde . . . 1727–50', 920PLU14, Liverpool Record Office.

(38) Similarly with Isaac Greene, *vide* G. E. Mingay, *English Landed Society in the Eighteenth Century* (1963), pp. 92–93 and 104.

(39) Plumbe-Tempest Deeds and Papers, 920PLU A2/3–15 and A1/35–42, Liverpool Record Office.

(40) 'Papers of legal actions between J. P. Plumbe and the Hesketh family in defence of his title . . . 1724–44', 920PLU10, Liverpool Record Office.

(41) John Plumbe's Account Book, 1748, 920PLU9, *loc. cit.*

(42) H. J. Habakkuk, 'English Landownership 1680–1740', *Economic History Reveiw*, Vol. X (1939–40).

(43) The Account Book of a Prescot Attorney, 1745–52, in possession of Dr. J. R. Harris.

(44) *Ibid.*, p. 140.

(45) *Ibid.*, p. 141.

(46) *Ibid.*, p. 35.

(47) *Ibid.*, p. 57.

(48) *Ibid.*, pp. 105–06.

(49) *Ibid.*, loose leaf insert. For Wyke see above, pp. 12, 65.

(50) *Ibid.*, p. 26.

(51) *Ibid.*, p. 36.

(52) *Ibid.*, pp. 39, 45–46, 221–22.

(53) Memorandum Book with will of Thomas Hulme of Salford, 1786.

(54) Will of Elizabeth Arnold of Liverpool, widow, 1786, *loc. cit.*

(55) The Prescot Attorney's Account Book, p. 66.

(56) G. T. Shaw, 'Henry Brown: A Liverpool Attorney of the Eighteenth Century', *Transactions of the Lancashire & Cheshire Historic Society*, Vol. 16 (1900).

(57) A. W. B. Simpson, *An Introduction to the History of the Land Law*, (1961), p. 217.

(58) Will of Elizabeth Sharples of Liverpool, widow, 1731.

(59) Lancaster Chancery petition, P.L.6.48/6 (1701), P.R.O.

(60) L. S. Pressnell, *Country Banking in the Industrial Revolution*, (1956), p. 12.

(61) H. C. Gutteridge, 'The Origin and Historical development of the Profession of Notaries Public in England', *Cambridge Legal Essays* (1926), pp. 123–33. Also M. Beloff, 'Humphrey Shalcrosse and the Great Civil War', *English Historical Review*, Vol. LIV (1939).

(62) For comparisons, *vide* R. Cameron, 'Banking in the Early Stages of Industrialization', *Scandinavian Economic History Review*, Vol. XI (1963).

(63) D. M. Joslin, 'London Private Bankers 1720–1785', *Economic History Review*, Vol. VII (1954).

(64) T. S. Ashton, 'The Bill of Exchange and Private Banks in Lancashire, 1790–1830', *Economic History Review*, Vol. XV (1945).

(65) L. S. Pressnell, *op. cit.*, p. 177.

(66) F. E. Hyde and Sheila Marriner, 'The Port of Liverpool and the Crisis of 1793', *Economica*, Vol. XVIII (1951).

(67) S. G. Checkland, 'The Lancashire Bill System and its Liverpool Protagonists, 1810–27', *Economica*, Vol. XXI (1954).

(68) J. Hughes, *Liverpool Banks and Bankers, 1760–1837* (1906), pp. 56–59.

(69) L. H. Grindon, *Manchester Banks and Bankers* (1878), pp. 23–31.

(70) L. S. Pressnell, *op. cit.*, p. 44.

(71) M. Birks, *op. cit.*, p. 186.

(72) A. Harding, *op. cit.*, p. 179.

(73) E. B. V. Christian, *op. cit.*, p. 122.

(74) D. C. Coleman, 'London Scriveners and the Estate Market in the Later Seventeenth Century', *Economic History Review*, Vol. IV (1951).

CHAPTER FOUR

Early Liverpool Canal Controversies

J. R. HARRIS*

'NO TOWNS have derived greater advantages from canals perhaps than Manchester and Liverpool,' wrote a contemporary of the canal age,[1] and the significance of Liverpool as a canal terminal is too obvious to need labouring. What is often overlooked is the way in which early canal building gave Liverpool a rapid linkage with its immediate hinterland and connected it advantageously with the more commercially successful parts of the growing national canal system at a very timely stage of its development. Liverpool, in other words, was profiting greatly from its canal facilities before canals had appeared at all in most other regions; those radiating from the port were predominantly the creation of that first period of canal investment which culminated in the boom of 1767–72.[2] This paper seeks to do three things: to amplify the early history of the Mersey-side canal system, and thus continue the narrative so far pieced together by Professor T. C. Barker and the writer;[3] to outline the various competing schemes dangled before the public between 1769 and 1772, including the almost forgotten project of the Liverpool–Wigan Canal; and, finally, to emphasise the preoccupation of the citizens of Liverpool, from the highest rank to the lowest, with the question of coal supply. Other more general reasons must not be neglected—the favourable nature of the flat Lancashire and Cheshire plains for canal building, and the previous experience won with the Mersey–Irwell, Douglas, and Weaver river navigations—but contemporary documents would show that the encouragement of canal building round Liverpool came principally from the intense demand for coal there, and from the welcome and patronage extended to such schemes by the Common Council of Liverpool.

The Sankey Navigation had been welcomed by the Common Council, and largely financed by its members. While the scheme

* The present paper is a revised version of one which appeared in the *Journal of Transport History*, Vol. II, 1955–56, and I am grateful to its editors, and to Leicester University Press, for allowing me to reprint it. I would also like to express my thanks to Mr. Gordon Benzie for his assistance in planning the original version of the accompanying map, and to Miss P. J. Treasure for revising it for this volume, to Mr. R. W. G. Bryant, Dr. W. H. Chaloner, Mr. C. Hadfield, and Prof. S. B. Saul for advice and comment, and to the staff of the Liverpool and Lancashire Record Offices.

enlisted public support by promising the town an improved fuel supply, the main intention of the principal promotor, John Ashton, was obviously to supply his Dungeon saltworks with coal. Another 'undertaker' was John Blackburne, owner of the Liverpool salthouse, while the canal, by opening into the Mersey opposite the mouth of the Weaver, was clearly designed to supply coal to the Cheshire salt boilers also.[4] John Holt is explicit on this point, assigning 'the want of coal to the saltworks', together with the badness of the roads serving them, as the 'great motives' for the building of this, the first canal of the Industrial Revolution.[5]

To the salt boilers and to other Liverpool industrial consumers,[6] who would be prepared to hold considerable stocks of coal, the Sankey was no doubt a reasonably efficient communication; the householders of Liverpool, however, did not find it satisfactory as a source of domestic fuel. It is true that it proved more efficient than the former method of carting from Prescot and St. Helens, and that its first effect was to put many of the carters out of business.[7] But the price of its coal rose from 7s. at the opening of the canal in 1757 to 8s. 6d. four years later,[8] the quality of the dearer grades of coal deteriorated, and there were complaints of bad measure at the proprietors' coal yards in Liverpool. The dealers were also reluctant to sell in the small quantities which the ordinary householders desired[10] —a point on which the Duke of Bridgewater deferred to his poorer customers in Manchester and (later) at Liverpool.[11] In the early sixties the coal supply of Liverpool in fact passed through the hands of a very limited group; not only was the means of transport the Sankey Canal, with its handful of proprietors, but the St. Helens coalfield was very much in the power of the great woman coal owner, Sarah Clayton, and her nephew, Jonathan Case.[12] The canal, moreover, had many technical defects, the greatest being its joining the Mersey in the tideway, leaving onward transit to Liverpool at the mercy of wind and current. The proprietors, too, did not keep the canal in the best repair, and were slow in connecting it to the new mining district of Ravenhead outside St. Helens, which was not reached till 1773.[14] Some measures were indeed taken to placate the Liverpool public, canal dues on coal were reduced from 10d. to 7d. a ton, and precautions taken to prevent coal being sold short-measure or in inferior qualities under the names of superior grades. But, nevertheless, great annoyance was felt, and vitriolic correspondence appeared in the Liverpool newspapers.

The Sankey canal scheme did not end the interest of either the Corporation or the public of Liverpool in transport improvement; if anything its very deficiencies spurred them to greater efforts. In

1764 the Common Council sent for Brindley to recommend a method of cleaning out their docks,[16] and in 1765 (once they had satisfied themselves that it was for 'the encouragement and promotion of trade') they contributed handsomely to the preliminary costs of the Trent and Mersey scheme, wrote to the M.P.s of the neighbouring counties in its favour, and assured the undertakers that they would give them 'all the interest and assistance they can'.[17] In the following year Liverpool was offered a scheme far in advance of its time—that of a combined canal aqueduct and road bridge over the Mersey at Runcorn. An immediate opposition from both Warrington and Liverpool, attacking it because of its possible interference with the navigation of the Mersey, suppressed the plan for the time being.[18] These various endeavours for transport improvement show that the canal fever of the late sixties and early seventies in Liverpool was but the climax of a long period of intense interest in improving the local communications system, and that the Common Council was favourable not simply to local schemes, but also to those of wider application, and appreciated to the full the possibility of extending the economic hinterland of Liverpool by inland navigations.

The Leeds & Liverpool scheme dominates the next phase in Liverpool canal history, which is now concerned with the controversies it excited and the rival schemes it inspired. While the Corporation and townspeople took a keen interest in the progress of the Bridgewater and Trent and Mersey canals the evidence is clear that the controversy about the Leeds project aroused their feelings much more and that they expressed a more immediate concern in it. A scheme of this nature was first mentioned in 1764, and by 1766 a meeting had been held in Bradford to raise subscriptions for surveying. John Hustler, a Bradford merchant, was the leading promoter, while John Longbottom, a pupil of Smeaton's and a native of Halifax, was the engineer who first suggested the scheme.[19] For a time the Leeds & Liverpool project had to contend with opposition from a rival plan to achieve east–west navigation by connecting the Calder and Mersey–Irwell navigations by a canal from Manchester to Sowerby Bridge. This, however, was shelved,[20] and a subsequent scheme for a York to Preston canal was short-lived.

Obviously such a canal as the Leeds & Liverpool could not be carried out without Lancashire participation and assistance. As soon as Longbottom had surveyed a line down the Ribble valley, and then through the Ormskirk district to Liverpool, 'a committee of 14 gentlemen, of the said County of York, was appointed in order to obtain surveys and estimates for the prosecution of the said plan,

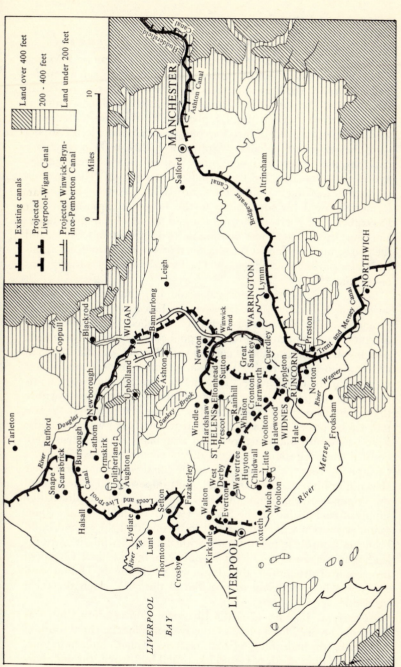

Map II   South Lancashire and its Water Transport in the Eighteenth Century (*referring to Chapters Three and Four*)

and to meet and confer with the gentlemen of Lancashire'.[21] Nevertheless, even before this conference was held at Preston on 1 March 1768, the first hint of possible dissension had already been given, for on 25 February the Yorkshire subscribers resolved to call in none of their subscriptions until the Lancashire men had paid in as much as had been raised in Yorkshire. Longbottom's survey was not adopted without question, and in fact a second survey was made. Liverpool Corporation, which had already subscribed £200 for the preliminary expenses, now agreed to pay another £50 towards the fresh survey, and seems to have insisted that Brindley be employed. The new survey was in fact made by Brindley and Robert Whitworth, and the former reported his conclusions to the Liverpool promoters on 9 December 1768.[22] His report (which had already been given to the Yorkshire subscribers) was favourable to Longbottom's route, and the two committees met at Burnley ten days later to arrange an application for parliamentary powers. The formal taking of subscriptions now began.[23]

Before parliamentary approval could be obtained, however, a serious rift had taken place between the Lancashire and Yorkshire promoters. The Yorkshire subscribers, for their part, wanted the speediest communication with Liverpool consistent with cheapness. This involved omitting direct contact with Burnley and Blackburn in order to shorten the route. At the same time considerations of cost meant that the canal made a long detour through Burscough on its way into Liverpool, because a longer route on the level was cheaper than a short one with locks, and this deviation meant that Wigan, too, was by-passed. These features were naturally not welcome to the East Lancashire manufacturers and merchants whose towns were omitted from the route, nor were they acceptable to the citizens of Liverpool. From their point of view the canal would not serve their Lancashire hinterland so well, and, most important, the omission of the Wigan coalfield meant that it would not furnish an alternative supply of coal to that of the Sankey Canal. To the East Lancashire manufacturers it was cold comfort to be told that they could build branches from their towns to join with the canal, while it was misleading to suggest to the Liverpool public, as one Leeds & Liverpool propagandist attempted, that Lathom, Newborough, Dalton, and Skelmersdale were likely to provide all the coal which the town needed.[24]

As early as January 1769 the Liverpool Conversation Club was debating the need for a more southerly course for the canal south of Ormskirk, 'through mines of coal, quarries of flag, slate, limestone, etc., rather than north of Ormskirk, round by the sea, through barren land etc.' If this were not feasible, then some members thought it could be joined at an unspecified point with the Sankey Canal, and thence connected with the Trent & Mersey, which it was proposed to carry over the Mersey at Runcorn Gap by means of an aqueduct. While the junction with the Sankey was no doubt suggested by some interested proprietor or coal owner, the project of carrying the Trent and Mersey Canal over the latter river was, we have seen, already under discussion, and Brindley had been consulted upon it. So interested were the attenders at the Conversation Club that they advocated a survey.[25]

At a meeting of the Leeds Canal proprietors in Yorkshire on 14 June 1769 the Lancashire opposition was found to be so serious that Longbottom was sent off to see Brindley, 'some of the Lancashire gentlemen being so warm for almost an entire alteration of the proposed canal through that county . . . we earnestly desire you will as expeditiously as possible settle with him the proper means of satisfying them how far it is eligible by a view of it or otherwise'.[26]

The line Brindley was required to check was one surveyed on behalf of the Liverpool subscribers by John Eyes and Richard Melling, two Lancashire surveyors of some repute. Whitworth seems to have done the detailed work for Brindley, and claimed to find a major error in the Lancashire surveyors' level near Burnley. Hustler seized on this with some relief: 'It is worth considering the impropriety of employing people so incapable the undertaking, or placing the least dependence upon their reports.'[27] However, the Liverpool promoters initiated yet another survey, this time by the Liverpool surveyor P. P. Burdett. At this stage there was a distinct danger that the promoters on either side of the Pennines might break into mutually incompatible groups. Hustler smoothed matters over for the time being by agreeing that the Lancashire surveys should be completed, and the two lines then be examined by Brindley.

At the end of 1769 the Liverpool subscribers met at the Golden Lion in Dale Street to consider the Burdett route.[28] They informed the Yorkshiremen that they could not fall in with Longbottom's scheme, 'having considered the impossibility that a committee of gentlemen in Yorkshire, be they ever so attentive, should be able to carry into execution a line of such an extent, and likewise being apprehensive that two committees might be impeded by a difference of opinion'. They would therefore make themselves fully responsible for the canal on the Lancashire side, 'and this is to be understood as a total cessation of all connections and a withdrawing of our subscriptions'. Eighty-two signatures were appended.[29] But the meeting of Leeds & Liverpool proprietors at Burnley a few days later rejected

G

Burdett's plan, adopted Longbottom's and decided to press on with the application to Parliament for the necessary Act.[30] The affairs of the canal had now reached a crisis. However, fresh deputations were sent to the Liverpool promoters and to the Corporation of Liverpool, matters were somehow smoothed over, and many of the Liverpool dissentients again entered the fold, their only known gain from their opposition being the declaration that the Lancashire end from Liverpool would be proceeded with as fast as the Yorkshire one, a stipulation which, it might be thought, could have been obtained with much less fuss. Strangely enough, it seems to have been Burdett's more southerly line, or an approximation to it, which was in fact built, after the long break in the construction of the central stretch of the canal between 1777 and 1790. The reasons advanced for giving the preference to the Longbottom line can scarcely have been convincing; while it may in fact have been the cheaper to build, its 'admitting of a more easy communication with the northern parts of Lancashire and with Westmorland'[31] meant that it was taking the route which would bring less traffic. The reasons for the collapse of the Liverpool opposition must remain obscure, but it is possible that one consideration leading the Leeds & Liverpool proprietors to close their ranks may have been the emergence of a new scheme of canal communication based on Liverpool.

By May 1770 the Leeds & Liverpool Canal Bill had become law,[32] and by November work was proceeding on the Newborough to Liverpool section.[33] But in September the support of the Liverpool public had been sought for another scheme. This was to carry a canal over the Mersey as had already been suggested, but, in this case, to join it to a branch starting near Duke Street in Liverpool, passing round the east side of the town, and connecting with the Leeds & Liverpool Canal at North Ladies Walk. The section between the Mersey aqueduct and Duke Street could be built through Appleton and Cronton and the Tarbock coal mines, and then enter Liverpool by Halewood and Toxteth. Once this was completed, it was suggested that an extension could be made to the coal district of Whiston and Prescot, with possibilities of further development through Ashton-in-Makerfield towards Bolton, Bury, Rochdale and Halifax. This, its promoters said, would be a better scheme than that originally proposed of making a low-level branch from Runcorn to Liverpool, which could not have been connected with the Leeds & Liverpool and could not have been easily taken into the Whiston area, nor thence, if so desired, connected with a wide area of South Lancashire.[34]

The Liverpool Canal thus seems to have been something of a

composite scheme, joining together various plans already broached. It would incorporate a footbridge as part of the aqueduct, and would enable passengers to get from Cheshire to Lancashire far more easily, and indeed passenger tolls would largely recoup the cost of the bridge's construction. It would carry the Trent and Mersey Canal across the Mersey, as had already been proposed. It would thus join two great canals, that and the Leeds & Liverpool, and vessels could pass from one to the other. The course of the canal behind Liverpool would mean that there would be plenty of space for building and warehousing upon it and the Corporation could take the opportunity to establish the town markets in this relatively unoccupied district. The town's acute water shortage for industrial and other purposes could be relieved by building this virtual reservoir at its back and at a higher level. Last, but not least, it would be easy to extend the Runcorn end of the canal so as to communicate with the coalfield. As time went on it was this last part of the plan which aroused the greatest enthusiasm and altered the original idea almost out of recognition.

A week after this original advertisement in the newspapers, the projectors hastened to point out that their present subscription was only for the purposes of a survey, but that such subscriptions would establish a preference for any eventual share issue if the plan was found 'eligible and advantageous'.[35] The next week it was announced that the promoters of the scheme to join the two great canals 'and for a branch out of ditto to Prescott, Bolton, &c.' had met with such encouragement that there was to be a subscribers' meeting at Pontack's coffee house on 23 October. A president and committee would be chosen for the ensuing month to carry forward the plans and estimate the cost of the canal.[36]

When the meeting was reported an interesting addition had been made to the project, for the branch was approved of as running to 'Prescot, Wigan, Bolton, &c.'; there had clearly been pressure to put the Wigan coalfield on the route. Surveyors had been appointed to work out the canal's course, and three of the committee (of twenty) had been deputed to wait upon the Duke of Bridgewater to 'know his pleasure respecting their design of going over at Runcorn to join his Canal'.[37]

Whether unexpected difficulties were met, or whether the support shown by the subscription books was insufficient, is not clear, but the Liverpool press is silent upon the subject for nearly ten months. It was not until 16 August 1771 that a general meeting of those interested in the new canal 'from Liverpool to Wigan, &c.' was advertised for the 21st of the month.[38] A writer a few weeks later welcomed the new interest shown in the project: 'the same laudable zeal for the public good seems reviving amongst us. . . . From what I have heard and understand of the present scheme for joining the Staffordshire [i.e. Trent & Mersey] and Leeds Canals, it seems to be founded on the most generous principles, calculated for the general good of the country, and the trade of this port; on this account alone it merits the protection of the public, and therefore it may be hoped that no *selfish* principles or *private* views can wish the least opposition to its success.'[39] Obviously the new canal was expected to arouse antagonism.

Preliminary plans were by this time available to the public, and a letter to *Gore's Advertiser* the following week gave details of the route. Starting from Park Mills on the south side of Liverpool, it would run 'under Sion Hill and Mount Pleasant, above the Infirmary, to the Loggerheads, through Everton Vale and Kirkdale on the south of Walton, [West] Derby and Huyton, through the principal coal mines in Whiston, under Cronton to Appleton, upon one level from thence to fall down by locks to the Runcorn Gap'. The junction with the Leeds canal would be by a branch 'from the Loggerheads to the North Ladies Walk', and this could be connected with the Mersey either by locks down to the river from 'the north end of the town' or by wagon ways. The idea of taking the canal through Prescot and Knowsley had now gone, and instead a short branch was suggested to the Prescot collieries. The inland course of the canal was also somewhat revised: 'from Appleton the same level will carry the canal south of Farnworth and Bold, cross the Sankey Brook by an aqueduct near Penkford Bridge north of Newton, near Ashton by Lowton School thro' the coal mines near Hedge Green, Bamfurlong &c., by Platt Bridge to near Bosden Bridge, there to join the intended canal from Kendal, Lancaster, Preston and Chorley, to his Grace the Duke of Bridgewater's canal at Worsley.'[40] This branch would serve the Haigh and Arley collieries. From Bosden Bridge the canal could be branched to Wigan, and thence by a few locks to the Douglas Navigation. Thereabouts a junction could easily be made with the Leeds canal. This arm of the projected canal would open up about thirty miles of waterway into the mining and manufacturing district of south Lancashire; its southward sweep would complement the northward sweep of the Leeds canal and would greatly assist in opening up the Liverpool hinterland. Once again, as in the previous year, the advantages of the Runcorn bridge and the immediate communication it would open up with the growing canal system of Cheshire and the Midlands were rehearsed, as well as those of the canal in the vicinity of Liverpool.

Towards the end of this long letter the likely source of opposition emerged, and an attempt was made to placate the Sankey proprietors. When their vessels were detained by wind or tide in the Mersey, they could send on their coal to Liverpool by the new canal, 'with certainty and expedition, at as small a charge as coming down the river, and receive their full tonnage as at present'. They could also make a branch through the northern part of modern St. Helens to join the new canal at some unspecified point, and thence bring their coal to Liverpool along a lockless and cheaper navigation.[41]

The Liverpool South Canal scheme seems to have fallen on more attentive ears than it had done a year before, probably because of the efforts made to turn it into a coal-carrying waterway, for it must soon have become apparent in Liverpool that the Newborough section of the Leeds canal would do little or nothing to break the Sankey coal monopoly. Subscription books for the Liverpool Canal were again opened, and it was further announced that it would not only pass near Wigan but also near Chorley, to join the Leeds Canal near Cuerdon.[42]

It is at this point that canal matters come to occupy a prominent place in the Liverpool newspapers over a period of some months. While the Lancaster Canal, planned to join the Leeds & Liverpool, was being brought to public attention, Hustler was writing to the Liverpool press to give a rosy picture of the progress of the Leeds & Liverpool, suggesting that it would only take a few years to complete, and that it would not exceed, and might even be cheaper than, the estimate.[43] In both suppositions time was to prove him grotesquely wrong. Some of the correspondence in the newspapers of the time is quaint rather than informative, but on 1 November 1771 a letter from one 'Candidus' not only provides valuable information, but firmly ties the canal politics of Liverpool to the coal issue. Opening with the generalisation that 'such is the depravity of human inclination, so great the influence of private interest, that few public designs escape the malignity of opposition, from some selfish principles, or private views', the writer made a hard-hitting attack on the Sankey proprietors. He outlined the technical deficiencies of their canal, its disadvantages in falling into the tideway, and the fact that coal prices had risen rather than fallen during the period of its operation.

His chief target was a scheme for an opposition branch which the Sankey proprietors were now advancing, which was to run from Winwick Pond on their canal, through Newton, Lowton, Abram, and Golborne to Bryn Moss in Ashton, and thence by branches to Ince and Pemberton. This scheme was designed, as was the

Liverpool Canal, to tap the coalfields south of Wigan, but 'Candidus' did not find it equally acceptable. Though the Sankey proprietors proposed making the new branch into a sort of ship canal so that vessels of 80 to 100 tons could reach Wigan, it would still open into the Mersey tideway with all its disadvantages, 'so that the poor inhabitants of Liverpool may still starve in winter, with joyful expectations of having larger morsels in summer'. The Sankey party claimed that with this extension their canal could itself fulfil all Liverpool's needs, but there was 'not a word of the price'. On the present length of the Sankey vessels only made two or three trips down to Liverpool and back per month, but the Liverpool Canal boats would be able to reach Ashton or Hindley in about twelve hours from Liverpool. The Liverpool Canal, too, would provide a better coal wharf at the port than that of the Sankey proprietors, for their place of delivery was 'so excessively dirty, there's no seeing the quality or measure before they are delivered, and no stocks ever kept on hand'. Against the claims of the Sankey proprietors that the crossing of their waterway by the proposed canal would obstruct its navigation, it was pointed out that the Irwell Navigation had been crossed by the Barton Aqueduct without any interference being suffered. In fact the Sankey proprietors would have little to complain of; the Liverpool Canal carefully avoided poaching on their present coal preserves, while against their claim that they had had their extension in mind since 1768 it could be argued that they had done nothing about it, while the Liverpool Canal, whose practicability they had denied, was now before the public.[44]

On 8 November another writer supported the arguments of 'Candidus' at some length. He declared himself to be a Leeds canal proprietor, but confessed that a great error had been made in planning the wide northerly sweep through Newborough and Halsall. The Liverpool Canal, on the contrary, would run through many mining areas which 'are certainly the most desirable and most advantageous object, for the town and trade of Liverpool, of any [canals] yet put into execution'. He agreed that the various canal projects should avoid needless competition, so as not to 'end in the destruction or loss of the different adventures'. But, 'as there cannot possibly be an overstock of the article of coals to such a trading port as Liverpool, private interest ought always to give way to public utility'. All the local navigation and canal projects had approached Parliament for powers on the basis of their value to the public, but coal was now 15 to 20 per cent dearer in Liverpool than when the Sankey undertakers applied to the legislature, while the owners were making an annual dividend of 20 per cent and over. He be-

lieved the new Sankey extension scheme to be a pretext introduced
'when they see the people of Liverpool will no longer groan under
their yoke'.[45]

The support which the Liverpool Canal had now gained in the
town can be seen from the mayor's calling a public meeting in the
Exchange to discuss 'an intended navigable canal . . . to or near
Wigan', when a full gathering approved it. A former mayor, John
Sparling, as one of the principal managers of the scheme, had opened
the Liverpool subscription, and books were also opened in Wigan,
Warrington and Chorley.[46] While the Liverpool Canal men were
striving to raise the £60,000 they estimated as required, the Sankey
proprietors, probably as a piece of camouflage, took in subscriptions
for their extension, insisting both that the project would be innocent
of private monopoly, and that the money was raised in the record
time of a quarter of an hour.[47]

It is at this point that canal politics become murky. On 21 December 1771 Hustler was directed by the Leeds & Liverpool Committee
to write to Jonathan Blundell and Mr. Earle of Liverpool to thank
them for their services as intermediaries in buying from Mr. Alexander Leigh of Wigan his majority share in the Douglas Navigation.
At the same time the Committee ordered Longbottom and others to
examine the collieries around Wigan, to pay Leigh his first one-
quarter instalment of the Douglas purchase money, and then to go
on to Liverpool, 'to consult with proper persons there about supplying the town with water from the Leeds & Liverpool Canal and
also about taking such steps as shall appear most advisable for op-
posing and rendering ineffectual the scheme for an Act for making
a . . . canal from Wigan to Liverpool'.[48] Early next month the emis-
saries reported favourably on their mission. The banks of the Douglas were well lined with coal measures. One of the party, Mr. Hardcastle, had had the opportunity of meeting the Corporation and inhabitants of Wigan, and, in return for their support, proposed that
the Company would engage to take no more than one shilling per
ton for merchandise carried from Wigan to the junction with the
Leeds canal. Hardcastle had then proceeded to Liverpool, where he,
Earle, and Blundell, for the Leeds–Liverpool proprietors, had signed
a pact with Dr. Bostock and Scrope Colquitt on behalf of the Sankey
proprietors, agreeing that the proprietors of the Leeds & Liverpool
Canal should join them and bear one-third of the expenses of oppos-
ing the Liverpool-Wigan Canal, 'the landowners bearing one-third,
and the proprietors of the Sankey Navigation the remaining third
part'.[49]

John Holt was thus entirely justified in stating that the purchase of the Douglas Navigation by the Leeds Canal was made 'as one means of preventing' the Liverpool Canal's being sanctioned and reaching the colliery districts.[50] The blow was indeed a damaging one, and the Liverpool Canal supporters immediately wrote to the press in an endeavour to prove that their scheme was still valid. Its course 'thro' a chain of coal mines 30 miles or more long' could not be improved upon; many of the Sankey and Leeds & Liverpool subscribers believed that the Liverpool Canal scheme was the most promising and had given it their subscriptions; £48,000 of the £60,000 needed was now guaranteed. If the Sankey and Leeds canals could, as they claimed, provide Liverpool with coal as cheaply as the new venture, 'let the poor, the mechanic, the trader, the merchant rejoice at the hope of so valuable an acquisition'—all the coal brought could be consumed. There was thus no need for 'jarring interests' or 'undue measures by any of the adventurers'.[51]

By the middle of December surveying for the Liverpool Canal was complete, the parliamentary plan was in preparation, and negotiations with the relevant landowners were about to open. But there were 'frequent and reiterated attempts' to obstruct this 'glorious undertaking'.[52] Many came from the Sankey proprietors. Not only had they 'cooked up a subscription among such of their choice friends as they think worthy of their society' for their extension scheme, but they had attempted, with fairer words, to get the Liverpool Canal supporters to run their canal into the Sankey Navigation, thus using the existing canal for part of their course, though this would have meant an immense array of locks.[53] This advance refused, they spread rumours among the people of the town that the Liverpool Canal, by running behind and above the built-up area, would cause flooding, while the landowners were told that their lands would be cut up unnecessarily.[54]

Forces were now gathered for the parliamentary struggle. The Liverpool Canal reached its £60,000 subscription target, but continued to entice the subscriptions of landowners[55] in order to counteract the adverse canvassing of that body by their rivals. There was some last-minute discussion of their past dissensions between those Leeds & Liverpool proprietors who had crossed permanently into the Liverpool Canal camp and others who had returned after the Douglas purchase, while the failure of the Yorkshire party under Hustler to provide the best line through Lancashire was once again criticised.[56]

In January 1772 the Liverpool Canal projectors petitioned Parliament for leave to bring in a Bill to make a canal from Liverpool to Wigan—the Runcorn Bridge plan seems to have been abandoned, as does the idea of continuing on from Wigan towards Chorley. In the next few weeks, however, they had to face counter-petitions from the Sankey proprietors, the Lancashire landowners and the Leeds & Liverpool proprietors.[57] The former claimed that their own canal supplied Liverpool efficiently, and that between the Leeds and Bridgewater canals and their own there was all the transport the district required. They also objected to the aqueduct which would be necessary to carry the Liverpool Canal over their own. The landowners, headed by Lord Derby, declared that additional transport was not needed, as the turnpike brought plenty of coal from Prescot and Whiston—an argument which was at least twenty years superseded. Finally, the Leeds & Liverpool proprietors contented themselves with emphasising the adequacy of the canals then building, and the merits of their own junction with the Douglas Navigation.

By the chance preservation of a series of letters between those Liverpool Canal promoters who acted as lobbyists in London and the main committee back in Liverpool, we are able to see the causes of their parliamentary defeat in some detail. The deputation managed to get the support of Mr. Gascoigne[58] and of Lord Sefton,[59] but as late as 25 January the plans prepared by Yeoman and Everard[60] had not yet reached London. They were also in need of someone to give expert evidence on the coal trade, and desired that Mr. Richard Melling of Wigan, a noted coal viewer, should be sent up. There was little generosity between the different industrial regions at that time, and it was quickly discovered that 'the very apprehension of Liverpool becoming a coal-port, will certainly bring upon us the opposition of Cumberland and Northumberland'.[61] As a counter to this the lobbyists tried to discover how many corn ships from the south of England to Liverpool returned in ballast for lack of a back-cargo, so as to obtain southern support for the canal both on the grounds of breaking the existing monopoly of Cumberland and the north-east and of assisting southern shippers.[62] Next the rather amusing claim of the Sankey owners in their petition concerning 'the great use of their navigation in raising seamen for His Majesty's Navy (a very popular idea) . . . must either be circumstantially confuted or it will carry great weight against us'.[63] Rebuttal could only be made by showing that Sankey flats carrying coal for the coal-masters were but a small part of the traffic, much being undertaken by the salt-boilers' own flats based on the Weaver navigation.

When eventually a meeting was held with Lord Sefton, Sir William Meredith, and other M.P.s at the Salopian coffee-house, the parliamentary prospects were found to be far from bright.

Lists were produced of the landowners through whose lands the canal was to run, but it was found that two-thirds of their number opposed the scheme, though they were estimated to hold less than half the acreage to be traversed. When it was considered that the House had 'a natural jealousy to all navigations', the likelihood of a Parliament of landowners passing the Bill was small. Even its warmest supporters could not be too open in their advocacy in such circumstances: 'Lord Sefton said that as many considerable Landowners were in opposition, although he himself did consent and in his private capacity did promote the scheme, that he could not in his public one solicit the votes of others in Parliament to support it.' Since the ensuing session was expected to be short, the members who were friendly to the plan suggested that the promoters should conciliate some of the landowners and apply again later. But here the Liverpool Canal promoters were in a cleft stick, for they knew that the Leeds canal would soon be complete from Liverpool to the Douglas, and that the Leeds & Liverpool and Sankey proprietors would then collaborate in furnishing Liverpool with a cheap and plentiful supply of coal for just as long as was required to convince Parliament of the inutility of an additional canal. They therefore decided that it had better be now or never; whatever its chances, they would submit their petition to the examination of a Commons Committee, and they would endeavour to 'make friends by our merits that we could not make by our connections'.[64]

On 27 February the scheme was before Committee for three hours, and the surveyor, Mr. Everard, gave his evidence very satisfactorily, Mr. Gascoigne giving him all the help he could. Between them they were able to show that 'it is not that unnecessary, chimerical scheme that our opponents have represented', but their friends in the House were still of opinion that they should, after exhibiting the merits of their plan, temporarily withdraw it and conciliate the landowners. This was done at the next session of the Committee, when Gascoigne and Meredith executed a graceful withdrawal on behalf of the promoters until such time as the scheme could be satisfactorily explained to the landowners. The deputation had to return to Liverpool empty-handed, 'hoping that what we have done in this business (notwithstanding our failing in success) will have the approbation of all the parties concerned'.[65]

To all practical purposes the plan for the Liverpool Canal died at this moment. It was advanced again, momentarily, and merely as a threat, in 1794. The Leeds & Liverpool proprietors had then a Bill in preparation which would allow them to vary the route to what was to be the final line and to raise additional funds. For this they wanted the support of the Liverpool Common Council, but their representatives who appeared before the Corporation's Canal Committee in the early weeks of 1794 got a rough reception. 'The Committee conceived it to be of great importance to the interest of the Town of Liverpool that an investigation should be made into the cause of the late extraordinary advance in the price of coals coming down the Leeds Canal by which the Inhabitants are so much aggrieved, and the important export trade almost put a stop to', and demanded a full explanation before they would back the petition. Two days later they relented and the Corporation affixed its seal, but insisted that the special tonnage dues which were enforcable on the Douglas Navigation should be removed, and the toll reduced to the penny per ton per mile which applied to coal on the remainder of the Leeds-Liverpool system:

'And further, that should the proprietors . . . abandon their application to Parliament for the Deviation in case of such interference on the part of this Corporation (as was intimated by the Gentlemen Proprietors who attended this Committee on the 8th instant) that it be commended to the Council to consider of the propriety of calling a General Meeting of the Inhabitants to take into consideration the expediency of making a new canal from this town to Wigan by a nearer line, which has been suggested to the Committee as a measure likely to secure an abundant, regular and cheap supply of the article of Coals to the public at large.' Ironically one of the delegates of the Leeds–Liverpool proprietors to the stormy meeting on 8 February had been Edward Chaffers, a strong supporter in former days of that Liverpool Canal of which the ghost was now alarmingly resurrected. Its appearance was not in vain; the Douglas tolls were revised as the Council had demanded.[66] Perhaps the very ghost of a ghost may be discerned in a plan of 1825 by Francis Giles, civil engineer, of London. He would not only have made an aqueduct and roadway across Runcorn Gap, but have linked the Bridgewater, Sankey, and Mersey–Irwell systems.[67] Thereafter canals were no longer an issue—in Lancashire the Railway Age had entered upon its vigorous life.

While the Liverpool Canal never came to anything, its story is worth telling because it teaches us much about the Liverpool attitude to canal construction at the most important period. While they were willing to assist the most ambitious cross-country canal projects, the Corporation and citizens of Liverpool placed the first emphasis on the efficiency of canals as coal carriers, and they were correct in regarding them as of more importance as short-distance rather than long-distance hauliers. The failure of the Leeds & Liverpool as a short-range coal supplier to Liverpool nearly caused the wreck of that scheme, and it was only after it had been threatened by a dangerous rival, and had made belated arrangements to connect with the Wigan coalfield, that it made good its privilege of being the only canal across Lancashire to Liverpool. The figures of coal carried from Wigan to Liverpool[68] in the first decades of the existence of this section of the canal are sufficient commentary on the value of the opening-up of that coalfield. On the other hand the Liverpool Canal must remain an intriguing might-have-been: while its chances of success were diminished by the many alterations the plan underwent, by the failure to engage a canal surveyor or engineer of national repute,[69] and by the forces of vested interest and reaction which marshalled themselves against it, it seems to have been an idea of real merit, likely to open up the South Lancashire hinterland of Liverpool more effectively than the Leeds & Liverpool Canal in its unrevised form would have done.[70] It failed, but its very proposal and discussion led to the satisfaction of its main object—the improvement of Liverpool's coal supply. The preoccupation of Liverpool's citizens with this coal question makes us realise how serious Merseyside's persistent fuel crisis seemed to contemporaries, and it partly explains why waterways so advantageous to the port as the Trent & Mersey and the Bridgewater canals had proportionately so little space devoted to them in the controversies of the time. Of course the Bridgewater scheme was in a sense above criticism—there was a recognition that the designs of the Canal Duke were inspired by something higher than profit, while in a concern owned by a single aristocratic proprietor there was no possibility of shareholders' quarrels occurring, or being aired in print.

The Liverpool canal controversies of 1769–72 are only an episode, but an episode to be set against the long perspective of Merseyside's transport history. In few regions of Britain can the story of transport over the past 250 years be more fascinating. There is the first dock in the outports in 1710; the Sankey Canal, the first of the Industrial Revolution; the speed with which Liverpool was connected to the canal system; the Rainhill trials and the Liverpool & Manchester Railway; the influence of Liverpool capital in the creation of a national railway system; the great dock schemes of the nineteenth century; the Manchester Ship Canal controversies; the Mersey Tunnel; the present port reorganisation scheme. Even so, this leaves out of the question sea transport, ships, shipowners and sailors. To the historian of Merseyside transport must always have a fundamental importance.

(1) Holt-Gregson Papers, 5/93, p. 95. Liverpool Record Office.

(2) The Sankey Canal was complete over its main course in 1757. The Liverpool–Wigan section of the Leeds & Liverpool was opened in October 1774, though that canal as a whole was not finished until 1816. The Bridgewater and Trent & Mersey schemes were under construction during the period of the Liverpool controversies, the former being completed in 1776 and the latter in 1777. The Duke of Bridgewater, however, was able to sell coal in Liverpool as early as 1774.

(3) T. C. Barker and J. R. Harris, *A Merseyside Town in the Industrial Revolution.* (1959), chapters II to V: T. C. Barker, The 'Sankey Navigation', *Trans. Historic Soc. of Lancs. & Cheshire*, Vol. 100 (1948), p. 121 *seq*: T. C. Barker, 'The Beginnings of the Canal Age in the British Isles' in L. S. Presnell, ed., *Studies in the Industrial Revolution* (1960) p. 1 *seq*.

(4) Barker and Harris, *op. cit.*, pp. 15–23.

(5) Holt-Gregson Papers, 10/177.

(6) Liverpool's coal-consuming industries at this period included breweries, potteries, sugar refineries, glasshouses, a salt refinery, and a copper smelting concern.

(7) *Williamson's Lpl. Advtr.*, 12 Feb. 1762.

(8) *Ibid.*

(9) *Ibid.*, 8 May 1761, 9 Dec. 1774; *Gore's Lpl. Genl. Advtr.*, 1 Nov. 1771.

(10) *Williamson's Lpl. Advtr.*, 8 Jan., 12 Feb. 1762.

(11) *Ibid.*, 14 Jan. 1774, quoted Barker and Harris, *op. cit.* p. 47. This bears out Smiles's observations on the Duke's consideration for his poorer Manchester customers: *Lives of the Engineers: James Brindley and the Early Engineers* (1874), p. 229.

(12) Barker and Harris, *op. cit.*, chapter III, *passim*.

(13) Canal boats, in the case of the Sankey almost invariably equipped with sails.

(14) Barker and Harris, *op. cit.*, pp. 41–42, 45.

(15) *Ibid.*, pp. 28–29.

(16) J. A. Picton, *Liverpool Municipal Archives and Records 1700–1835* (1907), p. 243.

(17) *Ibid.* J. Phillips, *A General History of Inland Navigation* (4th ed., 1803), p. 115, states that Liverpool Corporation supported a Trent & Mersey survey by Taylor and Eyes as early as 1755. For John Eyes see R. Stewart Brown, 'Maps and Plans of Liverpool and District by the Eyes family of Surveyors' who also mentions this survey: *Trans. Hist. Soc. of Lancs. & Cheshire*, Vol. LXII (1911), p. 143 *seq*.

(18) *Williamson's Lpl. Advtr.*, 28 Feb. 1766. John Rylands Library, Wedgwood corr., Wedgwood to Bentley, 5 Dec. 1765; 'Do you mean that His Grace's Canal [Bridgewater] should not proceed as now laid down in the plan . . . but should not [*sic*] cross the Mersey perhaps a little above Warrington and be carried on to Liverpool and so not fall into the Mersey at all? Where do you mean the Aqueduct to be?' This aqueduct continued to be advocated until it was made part of the early plans of the abortive Liverpool Canal in 1770. A Liverpool group headed by John Tarleton were its first supporters, Tarleton subsequently being one of the chief promoters of the Canal. Brindley who had originally backed the scheme continued his support for some years. 'I find he hath now [Nov. 1768] the same opinion of the Runcorn Aqueduct which he often expressed to me and others two or three years ago—That there is no doubt of the practicability of its being made nor of its answering to the undertakers'. The great engineer's support began to wane with disputes about the desirability of widening the Trent & Mersey and Bridgewater Canals beyond the originally proposed dimensions, which would have led to the use of wider vessels than the proposed aqueduct could take. Wedgwood Corr; Wedgwood to Tarleton 12 Nov. 1768; Wedgwood to Bentley 16 Jan. and 18 June 1769; Stronge to Wedgwood 22 July 1769; *Liverpool General Advertiser* 21 Oct. 1768. Picton, *op. cit.*, p. 244.

(19) H. F. Killick, 'Notes on the Early History of the Leeds and Liverpool Canal' in *Bradford Antiquary*, n.s., Vol. II (1897), pp. 175–79; J. Priestley, *Historical Account of the Navigable Rivers, Canals and Railways* (1831), pp. 385–86; Williamson's *Lpl. Advtr.*, 9 Oct. 1767.

(20) A canal between these places was constructed much later as the Rochdale Canal.

(21) *Williamson's Lpl. Advtr.*, 19 Feb. 1768.

(22) Killick, *op. cit.*, pp. 185–87; J. A. Picton, *Liverpool Municipal Archives and Records* (1907), p. 244; *Williamson's Lpl. Advtr.*, 10 Feb. 1769.

(23) *Williamson's Lpl. Advtr.*, 20 Jan. 1769.

(24) Killick, *op. cit.*, p. 190 *seq.*; *Williamson's Lpl. Advtr.* 10 Feb. 1769.

(25) *Williamson's Lpl. Advtr.*, 20 Jan. 1769.

(26) Killick, *op. cit.*, p. 191.

(27) *Ibid.*, p. 192.

(28) *Lpl. Genl. Advtr.*, 1 Dec. 1769. Burdett was an artist, engraver, and the inventor of an aquatint process (over which he quarrelled with Wedgwood), as well as a surveyor.

(29) Killick, *op. cit.*, p. 196.

(30) *Lpl. Genl. Advtr.*, 5 Jan. 1770.

(31) Killick, *op. cit.*, p. 198; *Lpl. Genl. Advtr.*, 5 Jan. 1770.

(32) 10 Geo. III, Cap. 114.

(33) *Lpl. Genl. Advtr.*, 9 Nov. 1770.

(34) *Ibid.*, 28 Sept. 1770.

(35) *Ibid.*, 5 Oct. 1770.

(36) *Ibid.*, 12 Oct. 1770.

(37) *Ibid.*, 26 Oct. 1770.

(38) *Ibid.*, 16 Aug. 1770.

(39) *Ibid.*, 6 Sept. 1771.

(40) Whitworth, on Brindley's behalf, surveyed part of the Lancaster Canal in 1772, but no Act was obtained till 1792. For its course when completed see Priestley, *op. cit.*, pp. 372–77.

(41) *Lpl. Genl. Advtr.*, 13 Sept. 1771.

(42) *Ibid.*, 11 Oct. 1771.

(43) *Ibid.*, 18 Oct. 1771.

(44) *Ibid.*, 1 Nov. 1771. Extracts are given in Barker and Harris, *op. cit.*, pp. 39–40.

(45) *Lpl. Genl. Advtr.*, 8 Nov. 1771.

(46) *Ibid.*

(47) *Ibid.*, 8 and 15 Nov. 1771.

(48) Killick, *op. cit.*, p. 219 *seq.*

(49) Killick, *op. cit.*, p. 221 *seq.* Actually 'Dr Boscough' is given in error for Dr John Bostock, who married a sister of Nicholas Ashton, principal proprietor of the Sankey Navigation, in 1771. 'Calcott' was written for 'Colquitt'.

(50) Holt-Gregson Papers, 10/215.

(51) *Lpl. Genl. Advtr.*, 6 Dec. 1771. The same letter gives the Committee of the Liverpool Canal as John Tarleton, John Sparling, and James Gildart Esqrs., and Messrs. Thomas Wickliffe, Edward Chaffers, Roger Fisher, and J. Hollingshead. Tarleton, Sparling, and Gildart were aldermen, all three were merchants, and Tarleton and Gildart both took part in the African trade. Tarleton was also a sugar baker, and owned estates in the West Indies. Gildart had an interest in the coal and salt trade. Chaffers was the son of the pioneer of the Liverpool porcelain manufacture. Fisher was in business as a shipwright, and published several

attacks on the management of the Leeds–Liverpool Canal. Hollingshead styled himself 'gentleman'.

(52) *Lpl. Genl. Advtr.*, 13 Dec. 1771.

(53) Liverpool Record Office, Binns Collection 31/212. Public letter of 19 Nov. 1771.

(54) *Lpl. Genl. Advtr.*, 21 Feb. 1772.

(55) *Ibid.*, 20 Dec. 1771.

(56) *Ibid.*, 27 Jan., 7 Feb. 1772.

(57) *Commons Journals*, XXXIII, 22 Jan., 10 Feb. 1772.

(58) Sir William Meredith, Bart., and Richard Pennant were M.P.s for Liverpool at this time; Bamber Gascoigne, sen., was M.P. for Weobley; his son, Bamber Gascoigne, jun., became M.P. for Liverpool in 1780.

(59) An important landowner in Liverpool and district.

(60) Thomas Yeoman was surveyor to the Stroudwater Navigation, 1774–79. See C. Hadfield, *Canals of Southern England* (1955), p. 61. William Everard (1723–92) had some reputation as an architect, designing among other buildings the uncompleted Liverpool Observatory. He was also founder of the Liverpool Library and writing-master to the Corporation. See P. Fleetwood-Hesketh, *Murray's Lancashire Architectural Guide* (1955), p. 79.

(61) Wigan Public Library, Liverpool and Wigan Canal Letter Book; Deputation to Staniforth, 6 Feb. 1772.

(62) *Ibid.*, Wycliffe to Dobson, 9 Feb. 1772.

(63) *Ibid.*, Deputation to Committee, 11 Feb. 1772.

(64) *Ibid.*, Deputation to Committee, undated letter (mid-Feb.) and 20 Feb. 1772.

(65) *Ibid.*, Deputation to Committee, 27 Feb., 2 Mar. 1772.

(66) Lancashire Record Office, Moore Canal MSS., fol. 354. Notes of a meeting of the Corporation Canal Committee held in Exchange, 8 Feb. 1794.

(67) *Ibid.*, fol. 592.

(68) Holt-Gregson Papers, 10/215, give the following tonnages (22 cwt. to the ton):

1781	31,401	1784	70,555	1787	98,246	1790	137,790
1782	39,326	1785	85,138	1788	109,209	1791	145,616
1783	57,376	1786	91,249	1789	124,874		

By 1791, except for some deliveries to breweries, the Leeds Canal had largely replaced the Sankey as the supplier of Liverpool's fuel, though there was a temporary falling-off in 1793–94 (see above). This followed a price-war between the two canals after 1774, and a three-cornered tussle with the Bridgewater after 1776. See also *ibid.*, 19/39.

(69) It may be worth noting that at least one of the supporters of the Liverpool–Wigan Canal had a dread of over-powerful individuals among the canal proprietors having too great an influence. He asked that 'not less than half a dozen men, endued with common sense', should be asked to view the intended canal before application were made to 'Mr. Smeaton, or any other Engineer'.

(70) That is, before the Douglas purchase. Later developments such as the further improvement of the Douglas, the arrangement to share part of the course of the Lancaster Canal, the Wigan–Worsley extension to join the Bridgewater system, lie outside the period under discussion.

(71) Wedgwood Corr., Wedgwood to Tarleton, 12 Nov. 1768; Wedgwood to Bentley, 16 Jan. 1769 and 18 June 1769; Stronge to Wedgwood, 22 July 1769; *Lpl. Genl. Advtr.*, 21 Oct. 1768.

(72) Smiles, *op. cit.*, p. 215; Picton, *op. cit.*, p. 244; J. Phillips, *General History of Inland Navigation* (4th Ed., 1803), p. 110.

CHAPTER FIVE

The Liverpool Campaign Against the Order in Council and the War of 1812

B. H. TOLLEY

'THE MISCALCULATION of merchants and politicians was . . . strikingly illustrated with regard to the trade with America. While that country was a colony of England the trade carried on from hence with our transatlantic possessions was considerable and it was imagined that the loss of America would prove its death blow: so far however was this from being the case that in the year 1783, the very first year after the continent of North America was severed from the mother country, the commerce of Liverpool experienced a small augmentation: in the year 1785 it was nearly doubled; and the commercial transactions between the United States of America and Liverpool at the present day exceed in amount the trade carried on by this port with all the world at the period of the declaration of American independence.'

In this way Edward Baines described the American trade of Liverpool in his commercial directory for the year 1824.[1] His description of the rapidity with which the Liverpool merchants resumed their contacts with the newly established United States and began to develop a commerce which was soon far greater than in colonial days, was typical of contemporary local pride in the achievement. It ignored, however, the serious interruption of this trade which occurred during the Napoleonic Wars when, determined to challenge the French hold over Europe and unable to do this in any way other than by exercising her maritime superiority, the British Government pursued a policy promulgated by Orders in Council which infringed the rights of neutrals and ultimately provoked America into a declaration of war.

The Berlin–Milan Decrees which inaugurated the French blockade of Britain and which were enforced throughout that part of Europe which lay under Napoleon's control, had a serious effect upon the British economy in 1808, but it was not until two years later that they combined with other circumstances to produce a major economic crisis. The French annexation of Holland, Westphalia and further sections of the North German coast which followed Napoleon's successful Austrian campaign, made it increasingly difficult to re-export the colonial merchandise accumulating in British ports. This had come not only from the West Indies but also from Latin America, derived as payment in kind for goods sent out during the speculative boom of 1808. The strict control applied by France at Hamburg caused a major contraction in exports to North Germany, whilst the situation was further exacerbated by the Fontainebleau Decrees which confiscated British property found in France or allied territories. Gloom and despondency overtook the commercial world during 1810, the prices of colonial produce and some manufactures fell sharply and the number of bankruptcies increased.[2]

In these circumstances the Anglo-American trade came to be of the greatest importance. Outside Europe, the U.S.A. was the second largest market for British exports, the largest in the case of the export of British manufactures, and she was also a source of essential raw materials. Trade between Great Britain and America had grown rapidly since her independence despite the unstable political relations which existed between the two countries, and in 1806 the official value of British exports to the U.S.A. had reached a peak of £8,613, 124.[3] This figure had fallen in the years which followed due to a succession of restrictions placed upon commerce by the American Government. They included non-importation controls, a total embargo on the movement of American vessels applied in 1808, and a Non-Intercourse Law prohibiting direct trade with Britain in 1809. Although designed to protect American shipping against depredation by France as well as Britain, these measures were principally an expression of American hostility towards the British Orders in Council of November 1807 and April 1809 which attempted to regulate the movement of neutral traffic on the high seas. This traffic was highly profitable to the United States during the European war when the merchant fleets of the belligerent States were committed and neutral American shipping was in great demand. However, neither Britain nor France had been coerced into changing their positions regarding neutrals and the pressure of both the New England shipping interest and the anti-war party in America had been sufficient to initiate a new U.S. policy in May 1810. The Macon Act of that month removed all restrictions on American commerce with the European powers with the proviso that complete prohibition of trade would be imposed against the recalcitrant party if one of the powers should repeal its ordinances against neutral shipping. Three months was allowed for the other power to take the same step.[4]

Britain gained most from the Macon Act because the effect of the

H

legislation was to open trade between the United Kingdom and the U.S.A. at a time when the continental situation and the over-speculation in South America were producing commercial depression. Consequently in 1810 the U.S.A. became the most valuable market for British exports, affording some relief to the depressed manufacturers. The official value of goods imported from the U.S.A. was also considerable at £2,614,405.[5] Ostensibly, America had become the commercial ally of Britain in the fight against France.

FIGURE 1

THE OFFICIAL VALUE OF BRITISH EXPORTS (1809–10) IN £ MILLIONS[6]

	Portugal & Spain	Sweden	Mediter-ranean	Germany	Brit. N. America	Brit. W. Indies	Foreign West Indies	U.S.A.
1809	3·8	3·5	5·8	6	1·7	6	6·4	5·2
1810	3·4	4·9	4	2·2	1·8	4·8	6	7·8

By the end of the year, however, the situation had changed again as a result of a diplomatic manoeuvre on the part of France. On 5 August the American representative in Paris, General Armstrong, was informed by the French Government that the Berlin–Milan Decrees in so far as they affected American shipping would be revoked, and called upon the U.S.A. to put into operation the sanctions envisaged in the Macon Act. On 2 November Madison gave Great Britain three months to renounce the Orders in Council, having accepted in good faith the French declaration of intent, and when the British Government did not comply non-intercourse was resumed against the United Kingdom in the spring of 1811. A Non-Importation Act was passed by Congress on the 2 February prohibiting the entry of British goods and ships to American ports. Unlike earlier legislation there were no exceptions to the list of prohibited articles and the Act was rigidly enforced.[7] As the year progressed, the effectiveness of the measure in reducing even more the outlets for British exports became increasingly apparent, and there was a general worsening of the economic situation in Britain.

Out of these circumstances there grew a widespread agitation against the Orders in Council which was inspired by the hope that some revival of the American trade would be a universal remedy for the ills which beset the economy. In Liverpool, however, at the centre of the American trade, the merchants were more acutely aware of the likely consequences of refusing to modify British policy. They appreciated that the Non-Importation Act was symptomatic of deteriorating political relations between Britain and the U.S.A., which if maintained would lead to war. Since their business interests were directly involved and the livelihood of the port was in jeopardy they brought to this new campaign against the Orders in Council a greater sense of urgency than it might otherwise have possessed.

I

Liverpool was the leading British port in the American trade. There were excellent dock and warehouse facilities and a network of roads and canals brought to the Mersey the coal, textiles, and miscellaneous manufactures of Lancashire, the salt of Cheshire, the woollen cloth of the West Riding, the iron of South Yorkshire, the pottery of Staffordshire and the hardware of Birmingham. In each case Liverpool became the outlet for industries producing a wide variety of articles suitable for the expanding United States market and, in reflecting the opinions of a large number of manufacturers in different parts of the country who, as Baring said, 'are never able to act in a body with a weight corresponding to their importance',[8] the merchants in the port expressed the views of a comprehensive section of the industrial and commercial world.

Because of the complex nature of the American trade and its many ramifications there had grown up within the port by 1800 a mercantile community whose principal interests were in this one field of activity. Knowledge of market conditions on both sides of the Atlantic, personal contacts in American ports and inland producing areas, the established facilities for handling certain specific goods, and experience of shipping operations involving of necessity the use of alien vessels, produced a specialist Liverpool–American merchant.[9] He was usually the intermediary between the manufacturer and the American customer, receiving goods as they came into the port for the spring and autumn sailings, warehousing them and loading them on to vessels bound for the U.S.A. For services rendered he charged a commission. Rarely did he export on his own account. As importer he would be acting on behalf of his American correspondent and might concentrate upon one or two chief articles such as cotton or grain. Again a commission would be charged when sales were made. Credit was often extended to the American correspondent and payment was usually by means of a bill of exchange made payable on one of the London American houses such as the Barings, or MacKenzie, Glennie and Co. Most of the important Liverpool merchants performed the function of agent for U.S. vessels using the port and for this, too, they charged their commission. The American Chamber of Commerce, founded in 1801, helped to co-ordinate the activities of its members, giving advice on the rates of freight to be charged, and on availability of docking space and other routine matters which arose out of the trade. It was also a means of organising opinion, and through the agency of the press its influence extended over a wide area outside the port. Members of the Chamber frequently sought the advice and guidance of James Maury, American Consul in Liverpool between 1790 and 1829, who transacted his own business on the Liverpool market as well as fulfilling his consular role. His knowledge of American political conditions and other information which he gained as a result of his diplomatic activities made him a valuable asset to the Chamber.

William Rathbone estimated in 1808 that the American trade accounted for five-sixteenths of Liverpool's commerce; after the abolition of the slave trade it had become the largest single enterprise undertaken by merchants in the port. In contrast to this the West Indies trade had experienced a relative decline, being seriously depressed by the recurring crises in the re-export trade to Europe. Like the shipowners the West India merchants had been angered and dismayed by the success of the Americans as neutral carriers. They strongly resented the conveying of foreign colonial goods into continental ports which excluded British ships, and they supported the Orders in Council because they attacked a trade which violated the Rule of 1756 and was so unfavourable to their interests.[11] In doing so they took a stand which placed them in direct opposition to merchants in the American trade, the latter being afraid that U.S. retaliation would jeopardize their trading prospects. Petitions had been presented to Parliament in 1808 on behalf of both parties setting forth their respective views. At the time it seemed to the American merchants that the continued operation of the U.S. Embargo, passed in anticipation rather than in consequence of the Orders, would have disastrous effects upon the Anglo-American trade, and Henry Brougham, who had acted as counsel for their representatives when they appeared before the Parliamentary Enquiry of 1808, made this the basis of his attack upon government policy.[12] It was unsuccessful. Few of Brougham's witnesses were leading businessmen known outside their own circle of associates, and most could be accused of self-interest. They represented only a small part of the commercial world and many of them were torn by conflicting loyalties. Some had their own business interests at heart and to this extent felt that the Orders in Council and the American

Embargo would seriously disrupt their affairs. Others, however, believed that the Orders, making full use of British sea power, were the only effective means of retaliation left to the Government in the war against France.

The Embargo proved serious but not disastrous for the Liverpool merchants, and after its removal their trade flourished, especially during the ten months' operation of the Macon Act. They felt sufficiently secure in November 1810 to reject an appeal by the Liverpool West India Committee for co-operation in a request to the Government for an issue of Exchequer bills to relieve the pecuniary embarrassments caused by the stagnation of trade. 'The members of the American Chamber of Commerce in consequence of the imports from the U.S.A. generally being calculated and intended for consumption in this country, and even now saleable, do not feel that they have similar grounds for such an application to the Government on their behalf, and that in the present state of prices, such application is not necessary.'[13] An appeal by the Chamber of Commerce in Glasgow to the Liverpool merchants in January 1811 received much the same response 'on account of the present state of the market for American goods in Liverpool'.[14]

Despite this stand, however, anxiety grew amongst the American merchants of Liverpool during the autumn of 1810 that the U.S. would put into effect the Macon Act if the British Government did not repeal the Orders in Council. So far there had been no indication that the Government would concede that France had revoked the Berlin-Milan Decrees and in these circumstances manufacturers had delayed the execution of orders for the American market until they were sure that shipment could be arranged.[15] Madison's November proclamation was known in Liverpool on 19 December and the worst fears seemed realised. The Liverpool *Courier*, expressing Tory opinion, was adamant in its condemnation of the Non-Importation Act:

'What America really wants is . . . to hit our maritime success. No time perhaps appears more favourable to America than the present to effect this purpose by shutting her ports in conjunction with those of the European continent against us and thus to compel us to give up the basis of our maritime power as the price of the re-admission of our trade.'[16]

There were a large number of American vessels in Liverpool at various stages of loading those goods which the manufacturers had already sent forward. These put to sea as soon as possible hoping that some provision would be made for their entry to American ports with the British merchandise on board. Most merchants were optimistic that these goods would eventually reach their destination.[17] At a special meeting of the American Chamber on 20 February 1811 those present drafted a letter to their Liverpool M.P.s, Generals Gascoyne and Tarleton, expressing their concern at the situation and asking for some guidance from the Government as to its intentions to remove the Orders in Council.[18] Receiving little in the way of assurance that things would improve, merchants were then left to weigh the risks and decide for themselves whether or not to ship the goods that remained on their hands. Congress, under pressure from the American importers, agreed to the entry of British cargoes which had left the United Kingdom before the 2 February 1811 and the last vessel from Liverpool to be accepted under this provision reached New York at the end of April. Ships continued to leave Liverpool for the U.S.A. throughout the spring months but those that departed with British cargoes ran the risk of confiscation and most seemed to have sailed in ballast only.[19]

The Liverpool merchants received orders from their correspondents during the summer with instructions that goods should be held by the exporters until there was a change in British policy. Then, as soon as ships could be procured, the merchandise was to be despatched. This was an important incentive to British manufacturers since it contributed to some industrial activity and helped maintain employment, but in the general atmosphere of uncertainty it was limited in its effects. There was no autumn shipment from Liverpool. The fact that ships had to return in ballast tended to discourage American captains coming into British ports when they could seek more profitable voyages elsewhere. On 26 September Maury commented: '. . . the state of our trade continues most discouraging and the arrival of our vessels greatly diminished. At this time there are no more than 17 vessels in this port. At the same date last year there were near 100.'[20] Few American vessels were advertised in the local press during the autumn months when normally agents would be seeking to make up cargoes if for some reason the holds were not already full. Those American ships which were advertised by the Rathbones, Cropper-Benson, Barclay-Salkeld, Alexander McGregor and John Richardson, carried passengers only. Many gave as their destination Amelia or a British North American port, and the advertisement of Hobson and Bolton in the *Mercury* was typical:

> '*American ship for Philadelphia*. If her cargo can there be legally admitted. Otherwise she will proceed to Amelia Island or some other port in North America to be determined by a majority of

the owners and consignees of the ship and cargo according to value.'[21]

Between 1 July and 31 December 1811 only 90 American vessels cleared from Liverpool compared with 349 during the same period in 1810.[22] Amelia Island, a flat desolate part of Spanish Florida, had become an entrepôt centre for goods entering and leaving the U.S.A. in 1808 when the Embargo operated. It was hoped that vessels would now be able to discharge at Amelia cargoes destined for American customers. However, the experience of Liverpool merchants in this respect was not encouraging either in 1811 or in the spring of 1812 when similar efforts were made. Hobson and Bolton received the following letter from their agent in New York concerning the plight of an American vessel on which they had some goods:

'Messrs. Hobson and Bolton of Liverpool.   New York.
                                                      1 February 1812.
'Dear Sirs,
        The Captain is placed in the most disagreeable and embarrassing situation imaginable at Amelia Island: the Governor there refusing him permission to remain unless he enters the cargo, the duties on which are about $33\frac{1}{3}$ per cent. Again I am requested by —— and others to do an illegal act and order the —— to the Delaware which I, of course, decline, unless I am completely indemnified from all possible loss, which perhaps is impossible. I shall proceed under the best legal advice I can get. I am mortified to the soul that the ship ever took on the cargo: and if you could have foreseen all the trouble I think for three times the freight you would not have given it to me. I wish the thing was at an end and the consignees in lawful possession of the goods in Philadelphia.

                              Your very obedient servant'[23]

John Richardson also made the attempt to get the goods ordered by a Philadelphia customer to their destination via Amelia but was unsuccessful. His ship, the *Amazon*, with a cargo worth £60,000 had been turned away.[24]

The editor of *Niles' Weekley Register* described the Non-Importation Act as one '. . . for the better encouragement of roguery and other purposes' for British goods were 'being feloniously introduced into the U.S.A. to a prodiguous amount' via Canada, and smuggling was an activity carried on along the New England coast with Boston as the key centre.[25] Liverpool merchants did try to land their cargoes at British North American ports with the intention of sending them on from there into the U.S.A., but few succeeded. John Richardson had two valuable consignments held up in New Brunswick whilst Martin, Hope and Thornely, hoping that goods sent to Canada would be allowed to cross the U.S. border immediately the Non-Importation Act was repealed, found that this was not a profitable venture. Dry goods were selling at '20 per cent and upwards' less than their cost in England.[26] By the end of 1811 the official value of British exports to the U.S.A. had fallen to £1,432,000.[27] There seemed no prospect of an improvement in the early weeks of 1812 and a spring shipment was out of the question.

As far as the import trade was concerned enormous stocks of American produce had been accumulating in Liverpool during 1810 as a result of the free intercourse of that year. Figures are given in *Table 1* showing the volume of imports of eight American commodities normally handled by the Liverpool merchants, and it can be seen from these that although there was a substantial fall in the level of imports during 1811 the proportion coming from the U.S.A. remained static or, in some cases, revealed a slight increase.[28] In fact the quantity of American produce held by the importers and the lack of demand for most of the articles involved had the effect of both depressing prices and discouraging an increase in supplies from alternative sources even where these existed. On 30 January Maury transmitted a price list of American produce on the Liverpool market to Washington with the comment:

'. . . most of which are depressed by the supplies being so much beyond the wants of the country for its own consumption, added to the discouraging prospect for export hence to the continent and not a little by the continuance of failures which for many months have gone on to an extent unknown.'[29]

The general industrial situation especially in the Lancashire textile areas reduced the demand for cotton and therefore the price of this article (see *Tables III, IV and V* at the end of the Chapter). The low selling price of yarn throughout the year caused reluctance on the part of the spinners to buy more cotton than they could immediately use, whilst dealers, too, were loath to speculate on a commodity which seemed totally depressed. In February W. & E. Corrie, general brokers, noted: 'Scarcely any demand for cotton. Public sales advertised for yesterday brought down several Manchester dealers who, however, buy sparingly owing to the depressed market for twist and manufactured goods.'[30]

A little speculation in April raised the price of Sea Island cotton momentarily but by the end of May the market was once more dull.[31] During June and July there was little change at a time when in the Manchester area alone one-third of the spinners were unemployed and there were over 2,000 working only a few days each week.[32] Occasional rumours of pending negotiations and the opening of trade subjected the market to change in the autumn months but generally there was no improvement. A few manufacturers closed their mills believing that it would be some time before they could hope to sell the yarn they had in stock.[33] A revival in December came with the news that Foster, the British representative in Washington, had failed to come to any agreement with the American Government on the issues dividing the two countries, but by January 1812 the excitement had subsided. W. & E. Corrie summed up the situation:

'We compute the present stock of cotton in Liverpool to be 135,000 bags, which is less than the quantity on hand at the close of 1810 by about 15,000 bags: so that the trade has taken out of the market the whole of the importation of the last year. . . . We are not of the opinion, however, that the whole of this quantity has been required for actual consumption, but that many of the spinners and dealers have been induced by the very low prices to supply themselves with larger stocks than they immediately wanted.'[34]

This pattern of oversupply, little demand and low prices characterised the market for American pot and pearl ash, tar, and turpentine, although all these articles were increasing in price towards the end of the year as stocks were slowly being eliminated and the prospects of a rupture with the U.S.A. seemed near. Tobacco remained low in price throughout 1811 (*Table XI*). Like cotton there was a large stock on hand at the beginning of the year and the inability to re-export tobacco to the continent held down prices.[35] On 15 July Maury, who usually imported tobacco on behalf of his Virginian friends, commented: '. . . The wretched state is such that our produce still continues depreciating and there being little or no export for cotton or tobacco the stocks of the two articles are immense and go far beyond the wants of this country. . . .'[36]

The relatively low prices of American grain—wheat, wheat-flour, and rice—on the Exchange early in 1811 were due to the good harvests and the large volume of foreign imports that had reached Britain during 1810. These prices were maintained until midsummer by which time most of the annual grain shipments from the U.S.A. were complete (*Tables IX and X*). Then, the prospect of a deficient harvest and the action of Napoleon in prohibiting French exports of wheat under licence to the United Kingdom forced a rise in price. The demands of the British army in the Peninsula for grain had a bearing on the situation and the only modification to the increase in prices arose out of short-lived rumours in December that the Government would prohibit distillation from grain.[37]

In these circumstances, conditions became increasingly difficult for the Liverpool American merchants during 1811. As exporters they held British merchandise but were unable to ship because of the Non-Importation Act. Despite their efforts to evade U.S. regulations by sending goods to Canada or Spanish Florida they achieved little and had to bear the costs of delays and frustrations since in most cases they could not expect payment until the goods actually reached the American customer. The situation was worse where they themselves had granted credit facilities to the correspondent. As importers seeking their commission from the sale of American produce they were in a difficult position because of the lack of demand for many articles associated with the industrial depression and the stopping of the re-export trade to Europe. This prevented them disposing of the large stocks they held and gave them little opportunity to sell those articles for which there was a demand at profitable prices.

It became increasingly difficult to negotiate American bills of exchange in Liverpool after February 1811, when the effectiveness of the Non-Importation Act made it impossible to accept the bills against consignments of British merchandise being sent to the U.S.A. There were more bills on the market than there was demand for, and the discount rate depreciated to $22\frac{1}{2}$ per cent at the end of the year. Some American bills on England were sold at a credit of six months, but as far as can be ascertained there was little direct payment in specie by the Liverpool merchant to his American correspondent.[38] The proceeds of American sales on the continent were in normal times transmitted to London for investment in British manufactures which were then exported to the U.S.A. This process normally involved the Liverpool merchants to the extent that remittances from the continent were occasionally sent direct to them for purchasing the required goods, but this practice ended in 1811, largely as a result of more stringent French controls over the large European exchanges such as Hamburg or Amsterdam.[39]

Remittances were being received in Liverpool during 1811 from the sale of American wheat and flour to Wellington's forces in Spain and Portugal. Cargoes of grain were paid for in British Government bills which were then transferred to some respectable London commercial house or directly to a Liverpool merchant to be placed to the credit of the American shipper.[40] The most important houses of the American Chamber handled the proceeds from these grain shipments. They could endeavour to transmit the funds thus accumulated by drawing bills even at the high discount rate, by purchasing American Government stock, Louisiana 6 per cents or the notes of the First Bank on the London market or, alternatively, await the opportunity to send British manufactures when the Non-Importation Act was removed.[41]

Because of the deterioration in the trading situation many of the smaller houses engaged in the American trade were unable to maintain solvency and swelled the long list of bankruptcies recorded in the port. Many more were financially embarrassed and hung on as best they could hoping for a change in the political relations between Britain and the U.S.A. which would restore commerce.[42] In a better position were those merchants who specialised in the importation of American timber, especially if they had secured contracts with the Admiralty for the supply of essential material for the naval shipyards. In Liverpool Thomas Mair, Morral and Borland, and Leigh-Sherlocks possessed such contracts, but the most prominent house involved was that of Logan Lennox and Co. who also imported a wide variety of American produce including cotton. Their affairs in the U.S.A. were managed by Peter Stubs, son of the Warrington industrialist.[43] Throughout the year they were responsible for deliveries of pitch pine from the U.S.A. to dockyards at Deptford, Woolwich, Chatham, Sheerness, Portsmouth and Plymouth, most of which was carried in American or foreign-built shipping since British craft were forbidden entry to American ports. In their zeal to carry as much timber as possible before the U.S. decided to stop this lucrative trade the vessels used under Board of Trade licences were often overloaded and between 10 July 1809 and 17 June 1811 some thirteen ships were reported missing on contract to Logan-Lennox.[44]

Even the most substantial houses found it difficult to foresee an improvement in the situation until the British Government removed the Orders in Council. From 1807 onwards their transactions had been conducted under threats and counter-threats of restrictions imposed by both sides in the clash of interests between the United Kingdom and America. Now it seemed that an uncompromising political position had been reached and only some concession on the part of the British Government could avert a war. It was therefore with great vigour that they joined the campaign against the Orders in Council.

II

It was alarming that past events seemed to have made the British Government insensitive to the dangers of an open breach with the U.S.A. It was exasperating that the attacks of the Whig Opposition against Perceval's administration were ineffective, particularly on the misuse of the licensing system to manipulate neutral trade. The issuing of licences for trade between Great Britain and the continent had developed rapidly following the Order in Council of April 1809, and whilst in theory there was no discrimination against American shipping, in practice the Board of Trade had tended to favour vessels which did not fly the American flag. Forged licences and false documents to overcome this difficulty could be purchased in Liverpool at the right price but the iniquities of the whole system had become the principal obstacle in the way of an understanding with the U.S.A. once the French announced that the Berlin–Milan Decrees had been revoked.[45]

Petitions against the Orders and the stoppage of the American trade were sent to Parliament from some of the manufacturing centres during May and June 1811 and had produced little response, but since then the depression had worsened.[46] It was urgently necessary therefore to present a new case to the Government with as much provincial support as possible. At the end of September, after printing a series of letters bemoaning the stagnation of trade, the *Mercury* gave support to the idea of a petition to the Prince Regent against the Orders in Council. Repeal of the Orders, it maintained, would do far more to restore Anglo-American amity than indeterminate negotiations.[47] Similar views were expressed during the following weeks by correspondents adopting the pseudonymns 'Mercator', 'Viator' and 'Civis'. On 18 October after viciously attacking James Stephen —'who had the temerity in a moment of premature triumph to boast in the House of Commons that the Orders in Council were the production of his brain, . . . many a poor starving family may lay their distress at the door of that gentleman'—it called for Liverpool to lead the way in a new attack upon the Government's American policy.[48] The appeal for support, as in 1808, was broadened to include all sections of the community including those who had originally supported the Orders. The shipowners were told that they would derive great advantages from a free intercourse with the U.S.A. particularly when their ships carried bulky cargoes such as coal, since the export duties then favoured British rather than American vessels. If the Orders were removed British shipping might then participate in the profitable grain trade from America to the Peninsula. Similarly the salt proprietors were led to believe that there would be an immediate improvement in their position if the removal of the British regulation opened American ports once more, whilst everyone from the dock trustees to Liverpool tradesmen would benefit from the renewed presence of American ships in the Mersey.[49]

On 30 November a special meeting of the American Chamber was convened to discuss the situation and it was decided to give publicity to the cause by holding a large meeting of interested parties at the Golden Lion, Dale Street.[50] Thomas Bolton inserted an advertisement to this effect in Billinge's *Commercial Advertiser* on 9 December, and at the same time a letter bearing the names of several important American merchants was sent to J. Bourne, the Mayor, requesting permission to hold the Dale Street meeting. James Cropper and Thomas Martin, whose names headed the list of merchants requesting the meeting, drew attention to the fact that they had presented the Liverpool petition against the Orders in Council to Parliament in 1808 accompanied by the late William Rathbone. Bourne, however, like Holinshead on the previous occasion, had the support of the Tory corporation with its West India merchant affiliation and permission to hold the meeting was withheld. In a letter to Bolton and William Rathbone V he suggested that the request was unreasonable, since it would inevitably lead on to counter meetings and further petitions, and there was a strong possibility that a breach of the peace would occur.

'The mayor put his veto on a measure of vital importance to this very town and to the nation at large. For the mayor to talk of charity as an adequate resource is like laying a handful of dirt to stop a torrent rushing from the hills and threatening to overwhelm the plains', commented the *Mercury* on 27 December. In a letter to the Liverpool freemen M.N. ('In my signature I trust that you will recognize an old friend') went further: '. . . it seems to me most mysterious that while the West India merchants can so easily obtain the sanctions of our municipal magistrates for any application which may further their views, a trade of such great extent, and affording employment to so many more hands, is at our Town Hall ever disregarded and discountenanced.'[51]

The resolutions of the American Chamber and the outline of the petition to the Prince Regent were left with W. Robinson in Castle Street for further signatures to be appended. It appeared that the campaign might be frustrated by die-hard Toryism and the pressure of vested interests blind to the real needs of the moment. Shortly after these events, however, Brougham resumed his correspondence with the American party in Liverpool.[52] He had remained in touch with the Rathbone family, Cropper, and Thornely largely through his correspondence with Roscoe. The latter had, for example, collected information from the Liverpool American merchants for use in an abortive opposition campaign against the Orders in 1809, but the Whigs had never seriously challenged the Government and it was not until the end of 1811 that they felt that political advantage could be gained out of a new campaign.[53] Brougham, therefore, as their most effective spokesman, placed great importance on the link that he had established with the American interest in Liverpool, and the merchants, in their turn, considered Brougham as the one politician who might yet bring down Perceval's administration and the wretched system which it continued to uphold.[54]

In January and February 1812 fears of an American war grew with every report from the U.S.A. of Presidential speeches and bellicose sentiments expressed by politicians and journalists. The intensity of the depression made the prospect of a revival of American trade to alleviate the situation more alluring and led to a renewed agitation against the Orders in Council in the Midlands, the industrial regions of Lancashire and Cheshire, south Yorkshire and the West Riding textile areas. With feelings running high in Liverpool Brougham was prompted to channel spontaneous movements into a concerted parliamentary attack. In the Commons, on 3 March, he moved for a Committee to examine once more the effects of the Orders in Council. This was defeated by a majority of 72 but the Government's position was obviously not as strong as on former occasions.[55] Even Gascoyne voted for the motion, and writing to Thornely afterwards Brougham was not downhearted: 'Our division is a good one and by following it up with petitions an American war may be prevented. If petitions come to Parliament this may be done and the Ministers may be driven from the Orders in Council. Those measures are materially damaged but the country must follow up the blow if it would see them given up. . . .'[56]

The appeal for petitions from the manufacturing areas and other sections of the commercial world was widely taken up.[57] In Liverpool, however, there was some doubt as to the wisdom of openly linking Brougham with the new movement. On 11 March Roscoe wrote to Brougham: 'It might in some degree prevent the good effects of your exertions to be told in the House that the petitions to which you refer were the consequence of your own representations. When the people are distressed they will be ready to speak of their own accord. In fact we are so sensible of your importance to the success of this great cause, that we are unwilling you should stand committed in a newspaper without it were absolutely necessary.'[58]

In the same letter Roscoe indicated that there were encouraging signs that the Corporation would at least agree to a meeting to draw up a petition against the East India Co. monopoly, and that if this could be achieved it should serve as a stimulus to the campaign against the Orders. When this meeting was held in the Town Hall Roscoe used the occasion to speak of the dangers of a rupture with America which would be precipitated if the Government maintained its restrictions upon neutral trade: 'We must above all avoid a war with America, that consumation of calamity to this country. By keeping open our trade with America we may perhaps have some chance of supporting our expenses until the benefits resulting from a free trade to the East can be fully realized.'[59]

Commenting upon Roscoe's speech the *Mercury* noted that the moment he got up to address the meeting 'a sacred ministerial awe was felt throughout the hall, a reverential shudder was perceptible on the bench, and the Worshipful Mayor, most devoutly alarmed mildly admonished the speaker not to trespass upon so fearful a matter'.[60] Undaunted by the request Roscoe proceeded to imply that in his opposition to the East India Co. he spoke for those who were not seeking instantaneous advantage. The principles involved were of much deeper significance:

'. . . our present want of confidence did not originate in our want of East India commerce. Liverpool flourished without participating in the trade to the East and Liverpool has ceased for the present to flourish because the War and the Orders in Council have compelled her to cease from being the great intermediate depot of traffic between America and British manufactories and between the West India planter and the marts of the continent.'[61]

The West India interest and shipowners of Liverpool were just as concerned to open Eastern trade as were the American merchants and on the committee formed to pursue this end, in conjunction with representatives from other towns, Moses Benson and John Gladstone, West India merchants and shipowners, took their place with J. Richardson, Joseph Leigh, Charles Lawrence, William Rathbone and Adam Lodge of the American party. It is hardly likely, however, that they agreed with Roscoe's denunciation of Government policy or placed so much emphasis upon the benefits of American commerce.

When the petition against the monopoly of the East India Co. was presented to Parliament on 23 March it was the occasion for a clash in the Commons between General Tarleton of Liverpool and Thomas Creevey. Tarleton who had reluctantly supported the Liverpool petition against the Orders in 1808 was now accused of misrepresenting the true state of commerce in the port and the causes of the depression in order to further his own position in the eyes of the corporation. Creevey, Liverpool born, claimed that the conditions in Liverpool were far worse than had been described and that they were due almost entirely to the stoppage of the American trade. With Alexander Baring, he was prepared to say that the corporation was deliberately confusing the issue for the sake of its own position:

'. . . for it was well known that in all the petty corporate towns of the kingdom, the mayor and corporation were always eager and mostly interested in supporting the measures of the minister of the day, and were ready to proclaim them as the best possible for the interests of the country. This was misrepresentation of the facts. The vitally important American trade had been destroyed.'[62]

Throughout March and April petitions were sent to Parliament from all parts of the country calling for the revocation of the Orders in Council,[63] and revealing both the widespread nature of the depression and—unlike 1808—the universal opinion amongst the manufacturing classes that the U.S. trade had become essential to their prosperity. Thomas Attwood's organisation of the petition from Birmingham (presented on 17 April) was given much publicity in the Liverpool press and copies of the speeches delivered in the Midlands by Attwood and others were printed and sold on the Exchange.[64] The difficulty of organising a formal meeting in Liverpool, despite Roscoe's expectations, was too great and the time too pressing to delay making further applications to the municipal authorities. The original petition to the Prince Regent was therefore modified and an appeal launched for more signatures.[65] On 27 April this was presented to the Commons by Gascoyne and to the Lords by the Earl of Derby.[66] It was supported by 6,662 signatures and set out in general terms the distress to be found in the port as a result of the Non-Importation Act and the failure to repeal the Orders in Council. These were assumed to be the chief points at issue between Britain and the U.S.A. Objections were made to the system of granting licences 'by which a power of dispensing with the laws is vested in the minister for the time being and has been exercised, as the petitioners humbly apprehend, to a most dangerous and alarming extent'.[67] The repeal of the Orders would bring immediate relief to the nation in general and to Liverpool in particular.

Brougham followed this petition with a second document prepared by the American party criticising remarks allegedly made by George Rose at the Board of Trade when meeting a Birmingham deputation. Rose had apparently expressed the view that the commercial contest between Britain and France could be likened to two men each having their heads in a bucket of water seeing which could stand drowning the longest. Though emphatically denied by Rose this had caused great offence and alarm in Liverpool because it implied that the policy of the Government was to remain unchanged. In view of the large number of petitions to Parliament the Liverpool merchants were hoping for at least a modification of the existing system:[68] '. . . however it might be a matter of merriment to others, it was a subject of a most melancholy nature to them because it shut a door by which even hope was excluded, and they were unwillingly compelled to believe not only that ministers would not remove the cause of their complaint but that they would not even listen to the propositions of enquiry.'

Like the first petition this document was ordered to lie upon the table after the Chancellor had accused the petitioner of 'exciting outrageous spirits throughout the country including the Luddites'. On the following day, however, the Government which had for so long resisted suggestions that a new parliamentary enquiry should be held into the effects of the Orders suddenly gave way and declined to oppose a new call for a Committee. It could no longer withstand the pressure to examine the depressed state of trade, but it doubted whether such an enquiry as the Whigs now proposed would reveal the solution to a problem for which, it argued, the Orders were not responsible. James Stephen reminded the Commons that nothing had been achieved by the 1808 Committee and he conceded an enquiry now simply to quieten the public mind.[69]

One hundred and fifty witnesses appeared before the parliamentary enquiry, representing a wide range of manufacturing and commercial interests. Brougham was supported by Whig pamphleteers and the radical press of those parts of the country where the depression was most acutely felt. The underlying theme of much of this publicity was not so much the desire for a genuine rapprochement with the U.S.A. but more the plea for an export outlet. Support for the Government came from the shipowners, West India traders, and merchants whose principal dealings were with the continent, the Mediterranean region, Latin America and Canada. In every case, fears of American competition were uppermost in the minds of the petitioners. It is significant that with the exception of a small contingent from Glasgow the Liverpool West India merchants were

I

the most consistent supporters of Government policy from the provinces. They were represented by John Gladstone, J. B. Aspinall, J. Yates and Joseph Poole. The Liverpool American interest was represented by William Rathbone, John Richardson, Thomas Thornely and W. R. Brown. James Cropper, who went with the party to London, was too ill to attend the enquiry.[70]

The assassination of Perceval on 11 May might have had disastrous consequences for the American interest since the assassin, Bellingham, was a Liverpool man, and there was the danger that this desperate act would be assumed to have political motivation. Brougham saw the likely implications and did his utmost to dissociate Bellingham from the Liverpool cause. The *Mercury* too drove home the same point: '. . . the petitioners have long perceived that their cause must be ultimately successful whether Mr. Perceval be minister or not'.[71] The murder did create a ministerial crisis which weakened the Government's stand, although the parliamentary committee laboriously proceeded with its business. There was little intimation that the Orders would be repealed despite confirmation that the Berlin–Milan Decrees had been rescinded and that the U.S. Government had placed the armed forces in a state of readiness for war.[72]

On 16 June Brougham at last introduced a formal motion that the Orders in Council should be repealed, and following a short debate Castlereagh announced the Government's intentions to suspend the regulations if America would consent to remove the Non-Importation Act.[73] Under further pressure Castlereagh made it known, seven days later, that the Orders had been withdrawn. This was a triumph for the new manufacturing and mercantile classes over Government policy and traditional vested interests. It was also a great personal success for Brougham who had become the national hero and the apparent saviour of commerce. Popular subscriptions throughout the country raised money for lavish presentations of silver plate which caused some embarrassment but were nevertheless accepted.[74] With great relief the commercial world looked forward to the immediate opening of the American market and the end of the depression. Even when news reached Britain that the U.S.A. had declared war on 18 June there was still optimism that Washington would negotiate a peace settlement as soon as the Americans received confirmation that the Orders in Council had ceased to operate.

In Liverpool tremendous jubilation greeted Castlereagh's announcement of the change in government policy. Roscoe wrote to Creevey suggesting that the town had risen from the dead.[75] The

American Chamber summoned a special meeting on 25 June and resolved that: 'It is the unanimous opinion of this meeting that American vessels may proceed with perfect safety with cargoes to America without any restrictions.'[76]

Those vessels which were available were quickly loaded with merchandise that had been stored for many months and put to sea. There had been no spring shipment and those American ships which had wintered in the Mersey hoping for the removal of the Non-Importation Act which would allow them to return home with a British cargo had, by the end of February, left in ballast, their masters and agents deciding that there was not likely to be a change in American policy.[77] The American Government's imposition of a sixty-day embargo in April as a prelude to war however, had been an incentive, as in 1807, for American ships to put to sea again to avoid being held in port. These vessels had reached Liverpool in May, sixty-five arriving between 9 May and 6 June,[78] some of them having departed in such haste that there were irregularities in their papers and cargo manifests.[79] As a precaution against hostile action being taken prematurely by either side, the Privy Council issued licences for the protection of the American ships on the return voyage but this issue of papers was to cease on 15 August, by which time it was assumed that the repeal of the Orders would be known in Washington.[80] The vessels which left Liverpool in the first weeks of July were in most cases protected by such licences, application for which had been made by the Liverpool American merchants acting as agents. Thus Cropper-Benson applied for licences for twenty-two American ships sailing for U.S. ports between 1 July and 15 August.[81]

The American declaration of war prompted the British Government to place an embargo on all British and American ships still in United Kingdom ports unless they could provide the required sailing papers. The customs officers in Liverpool did their work diligently, sealing hatches and putting additional tide waiters on the fifty American ships in port, but an examination of their papers revealed that all possessed the necessary documents and they were allowed to depart.[82] Undaunted by fears of a long war merchants continued to despatch goods to their American correspondents and there were few like Abraham Garnett who, having loaded a cargo of salt, earthenware, sacking and porter on the brig *Harriet* for Virginia, asked the customs officers for permission to take the goods off the ship and then reclaimed the export duties paid.[83] On 12 August, unable to complete the loading of vessels before the date fixed by the Board of Trade as the last sailing day on which licences would be operative, a group of Liverpool merchants asked for an extension of time for loading and clearing the port and this was granted until 1 September. There were, even then, complaints that the number of ships available was insufficient to take all the merchandise ready for despatch and the Privy Council indicated that it would consider applications for licences made after this date. However, by September it had become clear that tempers were hardening on both sides of the Atlantic and that the war would be protracted.

The official value of British exports to the U.S.A. in 1812 was £4,136,000. Most of the goods were in fact, shipped between July and September and for this very short period the Liverpool American trade was revitalised. Although the U.S. Government confiscated many of the cargoes on arrival in American ports most goods reached their destination eventually, especially if the American customer could prove that they had been ordered before the onset of war. Losses in this respect were not serious as far as the Liverpool merchants were concerned.[84]

What of the import trade during 1812? The official value of imports from the U.S.A. to Great Britain was £1,294,000.[85] This was a considerable reduction but must be set against the difficulties experienced in the early part of the year when the inability to return with cargoes to the U.S.A. made an eastward Atlantic crossing relatively unprofitable, and the war conditions which appertained after July. In fact most of the American goods imported at Liverpool arrived following the April embargo and the exodus of American shipping from home waters. After the arrival of three American ships in the week ending 11 July no other vessel was recorded as arriving direct from the U.S.A. until a prize was brought into Liverpool in December.[86] Government policy further discouraged the importation of American produce once the war had started, the exception being naval stores, especially timber and cotton. The Privy Council and Board of Trade were loath to grant licences on the application by the Liverpool merchants for importation even in British or non-American ships.[87]

The U.S.A. provided 46 per cent of the cotton imported at Liverpool during 1812 compared with 56 per cent in 1811 (*Table II*) but there was little difference in the total quantity of cotton landed. The reduction in American supplies was made up in volume (though not in quality) by an increase in cotton imported from Brazil.[88] There was actually an increase in the quantity of American rice and flour imported but the volume of wheat which arrived was greatly reduced. The annual grain shipments were usually complete by May and the embargo came too late to stimulate the trade from American ports. However, harvests in America, moderate in 1811, were bountiful in 1812 and like much of the grain shipped to Wellington's forces in Spain large quantities reached Britain via Halifax and other ports of British North America. This accounts for the significant increase in the volume of wheat landed at Liverpool from Canada during 1812.[89]

Smaller quantities of American tar and turpentine arrived than in the previous year but the U.S. proportion of the total importation of these articles remained much the same. Pot and pearl ashes showed much the same pattern. With tobacco, however, there were already large stocks of the leaf in the King's Warehouse and since it was difficult to get rid of these the amount of tobacco sent from the U.S.A. was deliberately kept to the minimum.[90]

Prices fluctuated with political events. The tension felt had a marked effect upon the demand for American goods during January and February when speculative buying forced them in many cases higher than they had been at any point during 1811. For most commodities the market was dull once more by the early weeks of March. In the case of cotton large stocks were held by the importers and the poor demand for yarn discouraged the spinners attending the market. The prices of all cottons were reduced in consequence. The exception to this picture was American grain, the prices of wheat, flour and rice climbing higher as the spring progressed and prospects for the British harvest seemed poor.

In April the declaration of the Prince Regent that Britain would not repeal the Orders unless France gave full notification of the removal of the Berlin-Milan Decrees aroused fears of an open breach once more and caused prices to rise. They would have increased more than they did in May had it not been for the assassination of Perceval which prompted rumours of a change in the British position. The arrival of embargo breakers had a moderating influence too, whilst popular disturbances in the cotton manufacturing districts reduced demand for the raw material.[91] There was then little change until mid-June when the repeal of the Orders caused a momentary reduction in the price of all American produce but by the second week in July rumours of war were circulating on the Exchange and speculative buying began in earnest.[92] In August news of peace between Russia and Sweden heralded the first real break in the French hold over Europe and the manufacturers were more optimistic. This had a particular effect upon the demand for cotton and spinners joined the dealers in Liverpool, large purchases being made.

The importers stood firm in these circumstances though the temptation to sell must have been great in view of the expectation that an Anglo-American peace would be concluded as soon as news of the removal of the British regulations was made clear to the president. The gamble paid off. In September, October and November prices climbed higher than at any time, though there was little American grain to be had and no regular prices were quoted for wheat, flour, and rice after 26 September.[93] By November the price of Sea Island and Upland cottons had risen so high that Brazilian cotton was being sold extensively to spinners and dealers because of its comparative cheapness. Favourable accounts from northeast Europe raised the demand for yarn and by the end of the year those importers who still held cotton in their warehouses looked forward to even better returns from sales made in the new year.

III

The absorbing task of renewing commercial intercourse with the United States delayed the full realisation of the fact that, despite the triumphant campaign against the Orders in Council, war had been declared. In spite of Brougham's uncertainty of the wisdom of large-scale celebrations, including a formal banquet held on his behalf, the Liverpool American interest pressed on, convinced that a peace would quickly be concluded.[94] It was not until September that there was a more sober realisation that the war would be prolonged and that the revival of American trade would soon be over. By the autumn the British Government had refused to accept a military armistice offered by the U.S.A. and had abandoned hope of a speedy reconciliation. There was a distinct hardening of attitude towards America and a resurrection of hostile sentiments reminiscent of the War of Independence, whilst in Government circles responsibility for the war was held to lie with the immoderate demands and grand pretensions of Washington. The Tories accused the U.S.A. of seeking not only to dominate world commerce, but also to seize the West Indies and Canada and destroy British power.[95]

Lord Liverpool's administration was strengthened by victory in the autumn elections of 1812, and Brougham's defeat at Liverpool was, in effect, a crushing defeat for the American interest which supported him. It is not known when Brougham was first approached by the Liverpool Whigs to stand as their candidate but negotiations for the election had begun as early as March. He had the support of Roscoe, Stephen, Colonel Williams and Thornely and he was well known for his opposition to the slave trade as well as for the part that he had played as counsel at the enquiry into the Orders in Council during 1808. On 30 June, following the repeal of the Orders, Brougham was proposed by Roscoe at a meeting held at the Golden Lion and on 4 July, he agreed to stand. Egerton Smith and the *Mercury* gave him unqualified support and the editorial columns of the paper were used to deliver a series of attacks upon the Tory Government and upon Brougham's chief opponent, Canning. Brougham and Creevey were defeated by Canning and General Gascoyne at the election and in so far as Canning was the candidate promoted wholeheartedly by the West India and shipping interest in the port, the result of the contest must be seen as an expression of support for the Government and the war, and for a candidate who believed that Britain was now fighting against 'the most desolating tyranny that ever afflicted the race of man'.[96]

The views of John Gladstone, chief promoter of Canning's candidature were typical of the unconciliatory attitude towards America of the sectional interests he represented.[92] At the dinner to celebrate Canning's victory he asked:

'Are we to be told, gentlemen, that the speculative theories of the leaders of those who have opposed us are better entitled to confidence and belief than the results of our long and practical experience as merchants, ship-owners and tradesmen; are we to be told that we must yield up our maritime right, our established commercial interests and consequence to America and our other enemies; that we ought to surrender the carrying trade into their hands in the hope of obtaining a truce, which in the visions of the night might present to us the illusions of universal peace and universal commerce, for it is only in such visions that these prospects have been realized.'[98]

Secure in his seat once more, Gascoyne was also able to deliver invectives against the U.S.A. which pleased his audience.[98]

Thus in the opening months of the war the Liverpool American merchants were in a minority. Their sentiments were shared only by those manufacturers for whom the U.S.A. was the chief market, and to this extent the situation was very similar to what it had been in 1808. The Orders in Council had then seemed justified as the most effective form of retaliation against the French claims to European domination. Now it was felt that the defeat of America was the only way to show that Britain would not accept United States claims to be the arbiter of international maritime rights. In both cases the consequences for Anglo-American trade were considered of secondary importance. Those merchants and manufacturers who had joined the campaign against the Orders in 1811 and 1812 simply because they felt that the commercial depression would be eased by the opening of the American market now turned to the continent which, following the French defeats in Russia and Spain, seemed to offer once more unlimited possibilities for British trade. By January 1813 Henry Brougham, while not actually despairing of peace, considered the emptiness of the victory against the Orders. In writing to Roscoe concerning the publication of some of his speeches he noted: 'The consequences of the repeal of the Orders might as well be pointed out . . . even if no more happens [the repeal afforded] a temporary relief to the manufacturers and indeed has restored part of their locked up capital and enabled them to help their men through this scarcity.'[100]

It is extremely difficult to assess the effects of the American war upon the exporting activities of the Liverpool merchants. There are no local sources of information to indicate the extent to which goods were despatched to American customers either directly or indirectly during the war period. To make matters worse the fire at the London Customs House destroyed the returns from the several outports so that there are no national figures for British exports to the U.S.A. in 1813. No official value was given to the trickle of goods which reached American ports from Britain in 1814. Confident that the repeal of the Orders in Council would restore amicable Anglo-American relations, goods were received for despatch long after the first news reached Liverpool that the United States had declared war. Before the end of the year, however, since there was no guarantee that merchandise would reach its destination, merchants were delaying shipment even when vessels and licences for them could be obtained.

The last American vessels with cargo space for the U.S.A. were advertised in January and February 1813 by John Richardson and Hobson and Bolton.[101] Cropper-Benson were the agents for the *Ann Alexander*, an American ship which in May was ready to sail with freight or on charter to an unblockaded American port if goods were forthcoming. Evidently they were not, for the *Ann Alexander* sailed to Boston in the autumn with passengers only, protected by a British licence. The risks involved were too great.[102] From this point until the end of the war the only vessels which left Liverpool to sail directly to U.S. ports were cartels carrying passengers and mail. These were usually under the care of Cropper-Benson, W. and R. Rathbone and John Richardson. There were still a number of American vessels at Gothenburg and in Spanish and Portuguese waters in the summer of 1813. In the latter case they were the last of the many involved in grain shipments to Wellington's forces in the Peninsula. Some attempt was made to use these for conveying goods to the U.S.A. since there was a chance that the American customs officers would accept their cargoes. Thus Hughes and Duncan and Hobson and Bolton applied for Board of Trade licences in June and July to send goods in American vessels via Cadiz and Lisbon but the applications were refused.[103]

Steps taken by the Admiralty to further the war at sea increased the dangers for American shipping and reduced even more the opportunities to export goods. In October 1812 letters of marque were issued authorising attacks upon American vessels not protected by licences.[104] After the humiliating surrender of His Majesty's ships *Guerrière*, *Macedonia* and *Java*, Admiral Warren was ordered to blockade the Chesapeake and Delaware coastlines in March 1813, and eventually the whole of the American coast south of Rhode Island. In the following spring, Admiral Cochrane extended the blockade to the New England States and it was rigidly enforced. The index of U.S. shipping activity consequently fell from 77 in 1812 to 32 in 1813, and finally to 9 in 1814.[105] Similarly, the tonnage of vessels arriving in American ports from foreign countries from 667,000 tons in 1812 to 59,000 tons in 1814.[106]

Anxious to limit the extent of losses for the mercantile marine, the U.S. Government imposed an embargo on the movement of American ships in December 1813. However, following protests by the New England shipowners this was removed after operating for only five months. At the same time, due to an acute shortage of British goods, the Administration removed the Non-Importation Law. After April 1814 the Liverpool exporters could thus send merchandise to the U.S.A. provided that it was carried in American or neutral vessels and was American property. Cochrane's blockade nullified the concession since very few ships could actually get through to American ports. Neutral shipping, especially Swedish and Russian, had slipped through the naval screen during 1813, being unmolested if they did not carry contraband. David Carruthers had used a Russian vessel to carry British goods to the U.S.A. via Lisbon in May that year.[107] In 1814, however, these vessels were stopped by the blockading forces and their cargoes confiscated unless satisfactory papers were produced. Applications to the Board of Trade for such licences after the removal of the Non-Importation Law were usually vetoed. On 30 May 1814, for example, B. and J. Grey had their application for a licence to allow a Swedish vessel to carry a cargo of British manufactures to Boston rejected.[108]

Alternative means of sending goods to American customers

were explored. It was impossible to use Amelia until 1814 since it was occupied by enemy forces at the beginning of the war, but a small volume of merchandise was smuggled into the U.S.A. via the West Indies which were provisioned by American vessels until 1813. The most important avenue for the entry of goods used by the Liverpool merchants was Nova Scotia, where Halifax developed an extensive trade with Maine and other parts of New England.[109] The official value of British exports to Nova Scotia rose from £243,856 in 1812 to £949,586 in 1814. Of the Liverpool American merchants who switched some of their business to British North America the most prominent were Cropper-Benson, W. and H. Matthie, William Dixon, J. Chapman, Coates and Hay, B. and J. Grey, and the Rathbones. For the remainder the war meant a period of suspended operations similar to that which preceded the repeal of the Orders. Those who had managed to clear most of their stocks in the months immediately following repeal were in a better position to withstand the new difficulties imposed by the war, but there were some whose capital resources had been overstretched by events and who had no alternative but to declare bankruptcy at an early stage. These included a number of houses which had been active members of the American Chamber such as Mason-Hodgson, Sloan and Mc- Millan, Thomas Mair and Co. and Conway Davidson. Similarly, among the fatalities of 1813 two more influential houses appeared, their partnerships broken. They were Morral and Borland and McIver, McViccar, and McCorquodale. Borland, writing to Josiah Wedgwood on 21 April 1813, pointed out that even after eight successful years of business it was now necessary to wind up the affairs of the house. In February 1813 Martin, Hope and Thornely dissolved their partnership, whilst Samuel Holland and Michael Humble, in business as American merchants for many years in Liverpool, terminated their association in 1814.[110]

It is possible to give more precise information concerning the wartime importation of American produce at Liverpool because there are a number of sources from which the volume of imports can be ascertained. The weekly handbills of W. and E. Corrie, general brokers, have survived for this period complete with annual statements of goods imported at Liverpool and stock held. They throw considerable light, too, on the state of the market for American produce. Similarly the shipping lists of the Liverpool *Mercury* for the war years give further data on the distribution of goods to the various importers when vessels arrived and discharged their cargoes. From these sources the figures given in *Tables III* to *XI* have been compiled.

Until 1814 the Government tolerated an extensive import trade from the U.S.A. The need for essential provisions for the British army in Canada as well as in Spain, and for supplies to the West Indies led to an encouragement being given to New Englanders to violate the restrictions imposed by their own government especially since it was known that the war was unpopular in the north-eastern States. Priority was given to naval stores including timber, and Logan-Lennox were again active in this respect until their bankruptcy in May 1813. Cotton and flax seed for the Irish linen industry were also allowed to enter the United Kingdom. This state of affairs, however, was not accepted passively by those sections of the commercial world who had welcomed the war as a means of destroying American trade. In May 1813 the London West India merchants presented a petition to Parliament deploring the issuing of licences which '. . . by allowing the importation of American produce, while it made no stipulation for the export of any British produce or manufacture, was peculiarly calculated to encourage the produce of the enemy, while it comparatively depressed our own'.[111] In response to this sort of pressure the Government attempted to restrict the importation of American rice and tobacco, but the licenced import trade using neutral as well as American shipping continued in other commodities, regulated by various Orders in Council.[112] After repeated parliamentary attacks the Government stopped the trade between the West Indies and the U.S. mainland and required American vessels to unload at Halifax cargoes destined for Europe which had been passing through the islands. In view of the number of ships sailing between Nova Scotia and the Mersey during the war it is hardly surprising that there was an increase in the importation of American produce from British North America.

The American embargo and Cochrane's blockade of the U.S. coast from New Brunswick to Florida had a serious effect upon the import trade during 1814, but the evacuation of Amelia by U.S. forces opened this island once more as an entrepôt for American goods en route for Britain.[113] A small number of craft had reached Liverpool from Amelia during 1813 but now there was a substantial increase in the volume of this traffic, fourteen vessels arriving during April and May, sixteen in July and August, and seventeen more before the end of November.[114] American cotton, pot and pearl ashes, some rice and tobacco were the most common cargoes carried on these vessels, which flew a wide variety of neutral flags. At the beginning of the year the Board of Trade was reluctant to grant licences for imports from Amelia and applications by Hughes and Duncan in February and by B. and J. Grey in March were all rejected. However, after midsummer there was no great difficulty in acquiring the necessary papers.[115]

Although there were thus opportunities to avoid the restrictions imposed by war, the volume of American produce imported at Liverpool was greatly reduced in 1813 and 1814. The effects of this reduction were not uniform over the whole range of goods normally handled by the Liverpool American merchants. They varied from article to article depending upon demand, extent of stock still held and the possibilities of alternative supplies. In the case of wheat and flour, for example, the absence of American imports coincided with an abundant British harvest in 1813, prices falling considerably in consequence. The harvest of 1814 was not so good but there was a large surplus from the previous year which kept prices down, and the possibility of importing grain from Europe after the defeat of Napoleon helped to depress the corn market even further. There was in fact a marked falling off in the number of applications to the Board of Trade to import American grain in the autumn of 1813.[116] The reduction in the quantity of American rice imported was offset to some extent by an increase in imports from Brazil. Some American rice did reach Liverpool via Lisbon.[117] Prices for this article were kept high by speculative dealings following Government attempts to limit the importation of rice except for re-exportation. During 1814 the prices quoted tended to fall due to the arrivals from Amelia.

A similar pattern can be seen in the case of pot and pearl ashes. The total volume of ashes imported from all sources at Liverpool in 1813 was half the quantity which had arrived during the previous year, and despite the supplies which came from Canada there was a deficiency of stock which caused prices of both pot and pearl ashes to rise at the end of the year. To some extent there was an improvement in the supply situation during the summer months of 1814 due to arrivals from Amelia, but by the autumn the increase in price had resumed once more. It was supported by speculative buying in view of the tardiness with which the negotiations at Ghent began, and also because the prospects of a re-export trade to Europe were once more unfolding.

There were no imports of American tar at Liverpool in 1813 and 1814 but imports from other sources during the first full year of the war were in excess of the American total for 1812, and although there was a decrease in the total amount imported in 1814 this was still substantial. Consequently the price of American tar never reached the same heights that were recorded at the time of the 1808 Embargo, when best American tar sold at 63s. per barrel. Increases in the price of American tar occurred as a result of speculative buying in the winter of 1812–13 when the full implications of the war were realised, and in the last two months of 1813 when news from Europe encouraged optimism that the re-export trade would soon reopen. At that time too there were rumours of the new American embargo. Fluctuations in the price of American turpentine were very much the same. A small quantity reached Liverpool from the U.S.A. in 1813, some of this via Lisbon, but in the last year of the war no turpentine was landed. Since most of the stock normally imported was sent coastwise to Hull or London markets the increasing availability there of supplies from non-American sources prevented prices rising excessively at Liverpool. As in the case of tar the price of American turpentine never reached the maximums recorded during 1808–09. The highest prices were due to speculative buying during the winter of 1812–13 and in the spring of 1814.

The quantity of U.S. tobacco imported directly was much reduced during the war. In 1813 a small amount arrived via Canada and Portugal and some was brought into Liverpool by coastal vessels from Ireland. Prices rose throughout the year but there was no spirited demand, since stocks accumulated in previous years had proved difficult to dispose of until there were more definite openings on the continental market. Maximum prices were achieved in the early spring of 1814 but declined with the arrival of vessels from Amelia during the summer months. There was some speculative buying towards the end of the year which fell off again once the Treaty of Ghent had been ratified.

Since most of the Liverpool merchants were importers of cotton the effects of the war upon this article was of major concern to them. As holders of cotton they were placed in the position of having to decide when best to sell in order to obtain the highest prices for their American correspondents. For this reason the naval and military events of the war and the attempts to reach a peace settlement were watched just as closely as the situation in the manufacturing districts and the probable demand for yarn which came with the re-opening of European trade.

In January 1813 stocks of cotton in Liverpool were smaller than they had been for some time due to the relatively small volume of imports of 1812 and the increasing demands of the manufacturers towards the end of that year. It was felt that the American war would last longer than had originally been anticipated and the importers were not anxious to sell. Prices of Sea Island and upland cotton rose in the spring, although the latter was more directly competitive with cottons from other sources, especially Brazil and the West Indies (see *Tables II* and *IV*). These conditions endured throughout February and into March, speculative buying being stimulated by news that Madison had been re-elected President. During March there were a number of memorials presented to the Board of Trade to prohibit the importation of American cotton in neutral vessels and the market was unsettled until the Government made its intentions clear. At the beginning of April it was known in Liverpool that a heavy duty was proposed on cotton imported from the U.S.A. in neutral bottoms and that the blockade of the southern cotton ports was ordered. Some 8,500 bales changed hands almost immediately on the Liverpool Exchange, bought by dealers rather than by the trade.[118] There was, in fact, parliamentary opposition to the exaction of a heavier cotton duty and this did not become operative despite petitions from the Liverpool West India interest, the Liverpool Shipowners' Association and the Brazil merchants in the port, presented on 13 April 1813.[119]

Prices fell during the early summer due to reports that Russia had offered to mediate between Britain and the U.S.A. and also to disappointing sales of cotton twist and yarn.[120] The arrival of two neutral vessels carrying cotton helped to depress prices in June. They flew Spanish colours and had left Charleston before the blockade had been imposed. Then in the autumn the tightening of the naval blockade of the American ports and the armistice talks in Europe renewed the demand for cotton and prices rose once more. The American merchants held out as long as they could before disposing of what stocks they still held but the demand was so great at the end of the year that they sold at the relatively high prices which could be obtained. Over 50,000 bales of cotton were sold during December 1813, mostly to speculators. 'The speculators have now become the chief holders, the importers being very bare of stock.'[121]

Some 14,076 bales of cotton arrived in Liverpool from the U.S.A. in 1813 compared with 78,188 in 1812. This represented only 10·25 per cent of the total cotton imported during the year. In the absence of American cottons Brazil made up 50 per cent of the total. William Corrie estimated this to have been 141,356 bales which was less than had been imported in any year since 1803 with the exception of 1808.[122] On 1 January 1814 approximately 55,000 bales of cotton from all sources remained in the warehouses compared with 100,000 bales in January 1813. It appeared that there would be a real shortage during the second year of the war. Prices were therefore maintained at a high level until the late spring. Then in April there were more rumours of peace moves and the first vessels began to arrive from Amelia. The removal of the embargo and the Non-Importation Law depressed prices in May although there was a temporary revival when Cochrane's blockade was made effective and news reached Liverpool of the fitting out of a large British military expedition for service in the American war.[123] Alarmed by falling prices the importers withdrew the new stocks of cotton until the state of the market became clear. The continued arrival of U.S. cotton from Amelia and the small demand from manufacturers caused the price of both Sea Island and upland varieties to fall to their lowest point in July.

This trend was reversed during the autumn months with the growing apprehension that Britain would not accept the arbitration of the Tsar and that the wranglings at Ghent were achieving nothing. Speculative buying forced prices high once more. In November, Sea Island reached 60 pence per lb., its highest price during the war. That the record prices of 1808–09 were not achieved was due principally to three factors. In the first instance supplies via Amelia were considerable, shippers being attracted by the promise of substantial profits from this clandestine trade. Some 38,353 bales reached Liverpool by this means during 1814. In the second instance, supplies of cotton from areas outside the United States were very large. In 1813, some 69,320 bales of cotton arrived in Liverpool from Brazil accounting for 50 per cent of the total imported, and in 1814, 95,235 bales of Brazilian cotton reached Liverpool which was more than 53 per cent of the total imported from all sources.[124] Thirdly, the expected demand did not materialise. As early as June reports were reaching the Lancashire area that orders for British cotton textiles at the Leipzig and Frankfürt fairs had been limited and that European trade in general was likely to remain depressed. In these circumstances although some speculative buying helped to increase the price of the raw material the uncertainties of the times restricted the willingness of the importers to risk all by refusing to sell at the prices then obtainable. On 31 December the Exchange was informed by express that an Anglo-American peace had been signed, and at that point only 30,000 bales of cotton remained on hand. It was not until March 1815 that the cessation of hostilities began to have an effect upon prices and then those merchants who had cotton to sell were anxious to dispose of this as soon as possible[125] (See *Table III*).

The course of the war perpetuated the divisions between the Liverpool American merchants and the West India and shipping interests. Every opportunity was taken by the former to attack and discredit the Tory administration, held responsible for the war and for the repeated failures to find a pacific solution to the problem of Anglo-American relations. Because they had so much at stake the views of the Liverpool American party were perhaps the most extreme throughout the country in their sweeping condemnation of Government policy.[126] The West India merchants on the other hand strongly defended British policy towards the U.S.A. To Gladstone and his associates America and France were in league and no efforts should be spared to crush the pretensions of both.[127] Their only criticism was the timidity with which the Government, having once accepted the American challenge, approached the task of destroying the enemy, especially his navy. They were particularly depressed by the success of American privateers which caused havoc with the sailings of the West India fleet, made convoys essential, and increased the already high mercantile insurance rates. Despite rewards of silver plate to the captains of naval vessels which helped clear Liverpool Bay and its approaches of Yankee privateers the menace continued throughout the war period, reaching its height in the summer of 1814 when the activities of the two American ships *Whig* and *Peacock* caused even the very loyal Tory corporation to voice its discontent and publicly criticise the Admiralty.[128]

Brougham continued to be extolled as the popular hero of all those connected with the American trade. During 1813 there were several more presentations to him for the part that he had played in the campaign against the Orders in Council. In his turn Brougham did not forget his friends in Liverpool and information about pending Anglo-American negotiations which he gleaned from his contacts in London, and which might be of commercial value, were passed on via Roscoe to those merchants who had been his allies in the campaign and had supported him in his unsuccessful attempt to become Liverpool's representative in Parliament.[129]

The war did not prove catastrophic for the American merchants in Liverpool and to this extent may be regarded as something of an anticlimax to the months of apprehension which had preceded it. Hostilities had important effects upon the livelihood of the port but to a lesser degree than anticipated. There was, for example, a reduction in the amount of dock duties collected by the trustees in 1812, but this was a continuation of a trend which was already apparent due to the operation of the Non-Importation Law.

The earnings of shipwrights, carpenters, chandlers and other tradesmen were affected by the absence of American shipping, but the situation improved during 1813 with the arrival of vessels from Brazil and the revival of the West India trade which followed the reopening of continental ports to colonial produce. Neutrals were

FIG. 2

THE AMOUNT OF DOCK DUTIES COLLECTED AT LIVERPOOL
(1810–16)

	Number of Ships	Tonnage	Duties
			£
1810	6,729	734,391	65,782
1811	5,616	611,190	54,752
1812	4,599	446,788	44,403
1813	5,341	547,426	50,177
1814	5,706	548,957	59,741
1815	6,440	709,849	76,915
1816	6,888	774,243	92,646[130]

attracted to the little American commerce which remained open whilst there was an increase in the number of voyages to and from British North America. In the second year of the war vessels arrived from Amelia and these added to the traffic using the port. Then, at the end of March 1815, the *Milo* arrived from Boston and was the first of a large number of ships which undertook the Atlantic crossing as soon as the Treaty of Ghent was ratified. From this point they helped to inflate the post-war dock revenues and to bring great activity once more to the Mersey.

There were casualties during the war amongst the American merchants of Liverpool, but the war itself was not wholly responsible for these. It was simply the final factor in overstraining the resources of merchants who had been operating under severe conditions since the enforcement of the Non-Importation Law of February 1811. The six months of trade with the United States which followed the repeal of the Orders in Council enabled them to get rid of some of the stock of merchandise they held, but the returns from this trade in the form of commissions were insufficient to enable them to meet all their commitments, especially if they had extended credit to their American customers. Funds normally transferred from European sales of American produce were not forthcoming during 1811 and 1812 and due to the general economic depression it was impossible for the merchants to offset their losses by selling American produce at high prices on the home market.

The most difficult time for the exporter was the period from December 1812 to December 1813. In December 1812 it was realised that despite the removal of the Orders America intended to pursue the war. There followed months of depression and pessimism as successive attempts to find alternative ways of placing goods on the

United States market failed. After December 1813, however, the situation began to improve. There were rumours of Russian mediation in the Anglo-American war and when the American commissioners took their place at Ghent in the early summer of 1814 there seemed to be good prospects for the resumption of intercourse. Furthermore in April 1814 the United States repealed the Non-Importation law so that when the opportunity to ship arose, British goods were legally free to enter American ports. American agents were placing orders for British merchandise long before the Treaty of Ghent had been signed and this was an important factor not only in raising the morale of the merchants concerned but also in encouraging the preparatory work necessary for the despatch of goods as soon as a treaty was ratified.

The war of 1812 seriously interrupted the flow of American produce to Britain but those who suffered most in these circumstances were the speculators rather than the importing merchants. This was especially the case with those who sought to profit from an expected shortage of cotton. In addition to the usual dealers and buyers from the trade the Liverpool cotton market attracted a wide variety of speculators during the war. 'There was nothing equal to cotton to speculate upon and therefore not only regular merchants but brokers, grocers, corn merchants, timber merchants, tobacconists, and coopers . . . joined in.' Inevitably, since so many people were involved, there were bound to be casualties. The price of American cotton, and indeed of American goods in general, never attained the expected heights.

TABLE I

SHOWING THE VOLUME OF AMERICAN PRODUCE IMPORTED AT LIVERPOOL (1810–14)

	Cotton (Bales)	Wheat (Bushels)	Flour (Barrels)	Rice (Tierce)	Tobacco (Hogshead)	Tar (Barrels)	Turpentine (Barrels)	Ashes (Pot & Pearl)
1810	174,270	200,528	98,389	37,695	10,925	51,158	48,783	22,546
1811	97,597	60,200	6,274	3,107	5,851	29,009	40,725	6,767
1812	78,188	130	11,589	3,700	3,174	19,442	19,276	3,314
1813	14,076	135	0	1,357	0	0	1,806	633
1814	38,553	0	3	1,360	172	0	0	1,859
	(Amelia)			(Amelia)	(Amelia)			

Source: Information contained in the weekly handbills of W. & E. Corrie.

TABLE II

COTTON IMPORTED AT LIVERPOOL (1811–14), SHOWING PROPORTIONS FROM ALL SOURCES

	1811	**1812**	**1813**	**1814**
U.S.A.	56·4	45·9	10·25	21·4 (Amelia)
Canada	0·1	0·16	2·67	0·24
Brazil	26·4	35·8	50·16	52·48
Portugal	0·4	0·85	12·9	5·02
Jamaica	0·47	1·14	2·85	4·46
Other W. Indies	3·17	2·97	4·27	4·4
Demerara, Berbice, etc.	12·03	11·3	11·1	9·3
Smyrna, Malta	0·2	0·34	0·10	—
Ireland	0·75	0·92	4·5	2·2
Other parts	0·04	0·58	0·64	0·39
Totals (Bales)	172,792	171,774	141,282	182,720

TABLE III

AVERAGE MONTHLY PRICE OF AMERICAN SEA ISLAND COTTON AT LIVERPOOL (1811–15) (pence per pound)

	1811		**1812**		**1813**		**1814**		**1815**	
Jan.	23½	25½	25	27½	30	35	42	48	45	49½
Feb.	21½	22½	25½	26	35	37	42	47	42½	45
March	21½	22	22	23	35	39	46	49	40	43
April	22	23	21	22	34	36	46	47	34	36½
May	20	23	22	24	34	36	44	48	32½	34¾
June	19	21	23	24	32	36	36	44	30½	32½
July	18½	20½	21¾	24	32	34	36	39½	32½	35
Aug.	18½	21	22½	25½	33	36	39½	45		
Sept.	18½	21¾	23½	25	35	37	42	51		
Oct.	17½	19½	27	30	33	37	42	44		
Nov.	18¾	22	28	29	36	40	48	60		
Dec.	25	26½	33	36	39	45	42	48		

AMERICAN UPLAND COTTON

	1811		**1812**		**1813**		**1814**		**1815**	
Jan.	12	13½	14	16½	23½	25	29½	31	21½	23
Feb.	11¼	13	14½	15½	22½	24½	30	31	18½	19½
March	12½	13¼	13¾	15¾	22	24	33	34	20	21¼
April	11½	13	12½	14¾	22½	24	27½	31	20	21½
May	11¼	13	13½	15	22	23¼	27½	30	20½	22
June	10¼	12½	14	15	20½	22½	24	26	17¼	19½
July	10½	12¼	13¼	15	21	22	24½	25	16½	18½
Aug.	11	12¾	14	15½	22	23	25½	27		
Sept.	11¼	12½	14½	16	21¾	22½	29¼	33		
Oct.	11	12½	15½	18½	22½	24¼	26½	28		
Nov.	12½	13¼	17¼	18¼	22¼	26	28½	30		
Dec.	13¼	15	21	21½	27	30	21½	26		

TABLE IV
AVERAGE MONTHLY PRICES OF COTTON AT LIVERPOOL (1811–15)
Maximum prices per pound given (pence)

1811	**Bourbon**	**Common West India**	**Bahia**	**Berbice**	**Surat**
Jan.	33½	17	21	21	10¾
Feb.	31½	16¾	20	20½	10½
March	30	16½	20	20	10½
April	30	16½	20	20	10½
May	30	16½	20	19	10½
June	30	15¼	18½	18	10½
July	30	14½	16	17½	10½
Aug.	30	14½	16	16½	10½
Sept.	30	13½	15½	16	10½
Oct.	30	13½	15	16	10
Nov.	30	14¼	16¾	17½	10
Dec.	30	16	20	20	11½

1812	**Bourbon**	**Common West India**	**Bahia**	**Berbice**	**Surat**
Jan.	30	16	19½	19½	11½
Feb.	42	16¼	19½	20	11½
March	39¾	16	18¾	19¾	11
April	39	16	17½	19	11
May	39	16	18	19½	11
June	39	15½	18	18¾	11
July	39	14¾	17	17½	11
Aug.	39	16	18	18	11
Sept.	39	16	18	19	11
Oct.	39	17¼	18½	20½	12½
Nov.	39	18½	19½	21½	13½
Dec.	38¼	23	24	25	14¾

1813	**Bourbon**	**Common West India**	**Bahia**	**Berbice**	**Surat**
Jan.	37¼	23¼	26	28½	16
Feb.	39¾	24	25¾	29½	18
March	40	23	24½	25¾	17½
April	39	24	25	27½	18
May	39	23	24½	26	16¾
June	39	22	23	24	16
July	37	22	23½	24½	16
Aug.	37	22½	24½	25	17
Sept.	37	23	25	25¼	17½
Oct.	37	24	26¼	27	18
Nov.	37	24¼	27	27½	18½
Dec.	40¼	27¾	30¾	31¾	20

TABLE IV—*continued*

1814	Bourbon	Common West India	Bahia	Berbice	Surat
Jan.	45	$30\frac{1}{2}$	$35\frac{1}{2}$	$35\frac{1}{4}$	$23\frac{1}{2}$
Feb.	45	$31\frac{1}{2}$	$35\frac{1}{2}$	$35\frac{3}{4}$	$24\frac{1}{2}$
March	45	$32\frac{1}{4}$	35	35	24
April	42	$31\frac{1}{2}$	$32\frac{1}{2}$	33	25
May	42	$27\frac{3}{4}$	$29\frac{1}{2}$	$31\frac{1}{4}$	23
June	$37\frac{3}{4}$	25	$27\frac{3}{4}$	29	20
July	36	$25\frac{1}{2}$	$27\frac{1}{2}$	$28\frac{1}{2}$	$19\frac{1}{2}$
Aug.	36	$26\frac{1}{2}$	29	30	$21\frac{1}{2}$
Sept.	$39\frac{3}{4}$	$30\frac{1}{2}$	34	$34\frac{1}{2}$	25
Oct.	42	30	$32\frac{3}{4}$	$33\frac{3}{4}$	25
Nov.	$43\frac{3}{4}$	31	34	34	24
Dec.	$45\frac{1}{2}$	$28\frac{3}{4}$	$31\frac{1}{2}$	32	$23\frac{1}{2}$

1815	Bourbon	Common West India	Bahia	Berbice	Surat
Jan.	46	26	28	$27\frac{3}{4}$	20
Feb.	46	23	25	$25\frac{1}{4}$	$15\frac{3}{4}$
March	46	$22\frac{1}{2}$	25	25	15
April	$32\frac{1}{2}$	$21\frac{1}{2}$	24	25	15
May	32	$21\frac{3}{4}$	25	$25\frac{1}{2}$	15
June	$30\frac{1}{2}$	21	25	25	15

Source: Monthly average prices calculated from weekly prices given in the hand-bills of W. & E. Corrie.

TABLE V

AVERAGE PRICE OF AMERICAN POT ASH, PER CWT. (1811–15)

	1811		1812		1813		1814		1815	
Jan.	44/3	45/6	40/8	48/4	63/-	66/3	72/6	76/6	71/3	77/6
Feb.	42/-	44/-	44/-	46/-	63/-	67/-	74/-	78/-	65/-	71/9
March	40/-	44/-	44/-	46/-	63/-	67/-	74/9	79/6	70/-	78/6
April	41/-	44/-	44/-	46/-	60/-	63/-	73/3	77/9	68/9	71/9
May	40/6	43/6	44/6	47/3	60/-	63/-	67/3	71/-	66/-	70/6
June	40/-	43/-	44/6	48/-	60/-	63/-	59/-	62/9	66/-	73/-
July	40/-	42/-	42/9	47/9	60/-	63/-	57/-	61/9	66/3	72/6
Aug.	37/8	40/-	49/9	52/9	62/9	66/3	62/9	67/9		
Sept.	38/-	40/-	49/-	52/6	65/-	70/-	75/3	78/6		
Oct.	37/-	39/-	51/-	54/6	65/-	70/-	80/-	84/3		
Nov.	38/9	41/3	54/9	58/9	65/-	70/-	90/3	93/9		
Dec.	40/-	43/-	61/-	63/-	67/6	71/6	95/-	101/9		

TABLE VI

AVERAGE PRICE OF AMERICAN PEARL ASH, PER CWT. (1811–15)

	1811		1812		1813		1814		1815	
Jan.	44/9	45/9	45/-	46/-	66/-	68/-	71/3	74/6	86/9	91/3
Feb.	44/-	45/-	47/-	48/-	66/-	68/-	73/-	75/-	98/3	103/9
March	42/-	45/-	47/-	48/-	63/-	65/6	73/9	75/9	80/-	91/3
April	41/6	43/6	46/-	47/-	60/-	62/-	70/6	71/9	80/-	90/-
May	43/-	45/-	46/6	48/3	60/-	62/-	68/3	71/4	78/9	82/6
June	44/-	45/3	47/-	49/-	60/-	62/-	63/-	65/-	75/-	79/6
July	43/9	44/9	45/9	48/-	61/-	62/6	63/-	65/-	79/3	81/6
Aug.	40/-	42/-	50/-	53/-	62/3	63/9	64/6	66/3		
Sept.	40/-	42/-	49/-	52/6	63/-	66/-	80/3	85/-		
Oct.	39/-	41/-	51/9	55/3	63/-	66/-	85/-	90/-		
Nov.	44/3	46/3	54/-	57/-	63/-	66/-	88/4	96/3		
Dec.	45/-	47/-	62/-	64/9	64/6	69/-	101/8	111/8		

TABLE VII

AVERAGE PRICE OF AMERICAN TAR, PER BARREL (1811–15)

	1811		1812		1813		1814		1815	
Jan.	27/-	29/3	28/-	32/-	38/-	40/-	34/6	37/3	30/-	
Feb.	25/9	27/9	29/9	33/9	38/-	40/-	34/-	36/-	28/-	
March	26/-	30/-	29/-	33/-	38/-	40/-	34/-	38/-	28/-	
April	27/-	31/-	28/4	32/-	35/4	38/8	34/-	38/-	28/9	31/-
May	29/4	23/4	28/-	31/-	36/-	38/-	31/-	34/8	30/-	33/-
June	28/8	31/-	27/-	29/6	36/-	38/-	27/3	28/3	36/-	41/6
July	26/6	28/6	26/3	28/-	36/-	38/6	31/-	33/6	26/9	30/3
Aug.	27/6	30/-	30/-	32/6	36/-	40/-	34/3	36/6		
Sept.	27/6	30/-	30/-	32/-	36/-	40/-	36/3	42/-		
Oct.	28/-	32/-	34/6	36/9	None quoted		37/6	44/-		
Nov.	28/-	32/-	38/-	40/-	40/-	42/-	38/-	44/-		
Dec.	28/-	32/-	38/-	40/-	40/-	42/-	38/-	44/-		

TABLE VIII

THE AVERAGE PRICE OF AMERICAN TURPENTINE AT LIVERPOOL (1811–15)
(maximum and minimum prices per cwt.)

	1811		1812		1813		1814		1815	
Jan.	15/-	17/-	15/-	19/-	40/-	45/-	38/9	42/-	17/9	19/3
Feb.	14/-	17/3	15/3	19/3	38/9	42/9	34/-	42/-	13/3	15/6
March	14/-	18/-	14/-	18/-	33/6	39/6	37/-	42/3	14/-	17/-
April	14/-	18/-	14/-	18/-	31/4	36/-	32/9	37/-	18/-	21/6
May	15/-	18/8	15/4	19/-	29/-	34/-	28/-	32/-	20/-	24/-
June	14/8	17/6	16/-	19/-	28/9	32/6	23/-	25/-	20/-	24/-
July	15/9	17/9	14/3	16/6	28/3	31/10	23/9	26/9	18/3	21/6
Aug.	15/3	17/9	19/6	23/3	33/-	36/9	25/-	30/-		
Sept.	14/-	17/-	20/-	24/-	35/6	39/-	35/-	36/6		
Oct.	14/-	17/9	24/3	28/6	38/-	40/-	35/9	36/6		
Nov.	15/6	18/9	35/-	39/-	38/-	40/-	36/3	39/6		
Dec.	15/-	20/-	37/6	41/9	38/-	40/-	35/-	40/-		

The monthly prices (Tables V to VIII) are based upon average weekly prices given in the handbills of W. & E. Corrie.

TABLE IX

WHEAT PER 70 LB. MONTHLY PRICES AT LIVERPOOL

	1811		1812		1813
Jan.	13/3	14/-	14/6	15/-	
Feb.	13/6	14/-	14/6	15/3	
March	13/-	13/6	16/10	13/7	18/- ⎱ Am.
April	12/9	13/3	18/-	19/6	18/- ⎰ Prize
May	12/9	13/3	18/6	20/8	
June	12/9	13/-	19/-	21/6	No Wheat
July	12/6	13/-	20/-	21/9	Prices
Aug.	13/-	13/6	21/-	22/10	quoted
Sept.	13/6	14/-	None		1814
Oct.	13/6	14/-	,,		1815
Nov.	14/1	14/10	,,		
Dec.	14/6	15/-	,,		

TABLE IX—*continued*

WHEAT-FLOUR PER BARREL 196 LB.

Jan.	58/-	61/-	None		
Feb.	58/-	61/-	65/-		
March	58/-	61/-	70/3	75/9	80–81/- ⎫ Am.
April	58/-	61/-	75/-	78/-	80–81/- ⎭ Prize
May	68/-	61/-	78/6	81/6	
June	58/3	61/3	82/-	85/-	None
July	56/-	58/-	82/-	84/6	quoted
Aug.	None		82/-	84/6	1814
Sept.	,,		None		1815
Oct.	,,		,,		
Nov.	,,		,,		
Dec.	,,		,,		

TABLE X

AVERAGE PRICE PER MONTH OF AMERICAN RICE AT LIVERPOOL (1811–15)
(price per cwt.)

	1811		1812		1813		1814		1815	
Jan.	20/3	23/6	32/-	35/-	–	–	65/-	68/-	44/6	
Feb.	21/-	23/-	32/-	35/-	63/-	70/-	65/-	68/-	41/9	
March	20/4	23/8	34/-	37/9	56/9	62/3	65/-	68/-	34/6	
April	21/-	24/-	37/6	41/9	54/-	58/-	65/-		35/-	36/9
May	21/4	24/4	49/-	51/8	56/6	59/-	50/-	55/-	39/-	43/-
June	22/-	25/-	49/-	51/6	56/6	57/9	49/-	53/6	46/6	50/9
July	22/-	25/-	46/-	49/6	53/9	54/6	48/-	52/-	48/-	52/-
Aug.	21/-	24/-	53/9		54/3	55/9	None quoted			
Sept.	21/6	24/6	62/-		57/-	58/-	,,			
Oct.	24/6	28/-	None quoted		60/-	62/-	,,			
Nov.	30/6	34/-	,,		63/-	65/-	,,			
Dec.	32/-	35/-	,,		63/-	65/-	,,			

TABLE XI

AVERAGE PRICES OF AMERICAN TOBACCO AT LIVERPOOL (1811–15) (pence per pound)

	1811		1812		1813		1814		1815	
	Stemmed	Maryland	Stemmed	Maryland	Stemmed	Maryland	Stemmed	Maryland	Stemmed	Maryland
Jan.	5 –8	4 –10	6 –9	3 –11	10–14	6 –13	13–20	8 –16		
Feb.	–	–	–	–	–	–	No further Prices quoted			
March	–	–	–	–	9 –14	5½–10				
April	–	–	–	–	–	–				
May	5½–8	4 –9	–	–	–	–				
June	–	–	–	–	–	–				
July	–	–	–	–	10–15	6 –10				
Aug.	–	–	6½–10	4 –11	11 –16	5 –10				
Sept.	5½–7	4 –9	–	–	12 –17	6 –18				
Oct.	–	–	–	–	–	–				
Nov.	5½–8½	–	8 –12	4 –10½	–	–				
Dec.	5½–9	3½–12	9 –13	5 –12	12 –18	8 –14				

(1) E. Baines, *History, Directory and Gazeteer of the County Palatine of Lancaster, with a variety of Commercial and Statistical Information* (1824), Vol. I, p. 189.

(2) F. Crouzet, *L'Economie Britannique et le Blocus Continental* (Paris 1958), Vol. II, pp. 563–640.

(3) *H. of C. Journals*, Vol. LXVI (1812), pp. 760–61, 763–65.

(4) Bradford Perkins, *Prologue to War; England and the United States, 1805–1812* (1961), pp. 238–42.

(5) A. D. Gayer, W. W. Rostow and A. Schwartz, *The Growth and Fluctuations of the British Economy, 1790–1850* (1953), Vol. I, p. 89.

(6) *H. of C. Journals*, Vol. LXVI (1812), p. 761.

(7) H. Heaton, 'Non-Importation, 1806–1812', *Journal of Economic History*, Vol. I (1941), p. 194.

(8) A. Baring, *An Enquiry into the causes and consequences of the Orders in Council; and an Examination of the conduct of Great Britain towards the Neutral Commerce of America* (1808), pp. 4–5.

(9) B. H. Tolley, *The American Trade of Liverpool and the War of 1812* (M. A. Thesis, Liverpool, 1967). Chapter II deals more fully with this subject.

(10) Parliamentary Papers, 1808, Vol. X, p. 76. *Minutes of Evidence taken before the Committee of the Whole House to whom it was referred, to consider of the Petition of several merchants of Liverpool, and also the Petition of several merchants, manufacturers and others, of the City of London, interested in the trade with the United States of America* . . . See also: Parliamentary Papers, 1812, Vol. XI, p. 497. *Minutes of Evidence taken before the Committee of the Whole House, to whom it was referred, to consider of the several Petitions which have been presented to the House in this Session of Parliament, relating to the Orders in Council.* Some three-fifths of the total British trade with the United States passed through Liverpool.

(11) *The Cambridge History of the British Empire* (1929), Vol. I, p. 551. Neutral vessels should not engage in a trade opened up to them in time of war but closed to them in time of peace.

(12) B. H. Tolley, *op. cit.*, Chapter III. The Liverpool protest against the introduction of the Orders in Council and the effects of the Embargo are examined here.

(13) *The American Chamber of Commerce*, Liverpool, Minute Book I. 14 November 1810.

(14) *Ibid.*, 9 January 1811.

(15) The possibility that France might remove the Berlin–Milan Decrees was suggested in the Liverpool *Courier*, 22 August 1810, but this was overshadowed by the news of the revolution in the Spanish Colonies.

(16) Liverpool *Courier*, 19 December 1810.

(17) H. Heaton, 'Non-Importation, 1806–1812', *op. cit.*, p. 195.

(18) *American Chamber of Commerce*, Liverpool. Minute Book I, 20 February 1811.

(19) Parliamentary Papers, 1812, Vol. III, p. 345. Evidence of Thomas Thornely. Between 1 January and 30 June 1811, 196 American vessels sailed from Liverpool. This was far more than had departed during the same period of 1810, but then the Non-Intercourse Law had operated.

(20) *Liverpool Consular Reports.* James Maury to the Secretary of State, Washington, 26 September 1811.

(21) Liverpool *Mercury*, 6 September 1811.

(22) Parliamentary Papers, 1812, Vol. III, *op. cit.*, p. 345.

(23) *Ibid.*

(24) Parliamentary Papers, 1812, Vol. III, *op. cit.*, p. 426.

(25) *Niles Weekly Register*, Boston, Vol. I, p. 133, 26 October 1811. Hezekia Niles

was well known for his pronounced anti-British views. The Library, University of Keele.

(26) Parliamentary Papers, House of Lords, 1812, Vol. XI, p. 266. *Select Committee on the Orders in Council.* Evidence of John Richardson. Parliamentary Papers, 1812, Vol. III, *op. cit.*, p. 346. See also the *MacConnel amd Kennedy Papers*, The University of Manchester. Letter to G. Marsden from MacConnel and Kennedy requesting information about vessels sailing to the St. Lawrence so that shipment of goods could be arranged. Letter dated 22 November 1811.

(27) *H. of C. Journals*, Vol. LXVI (1812), *op. cit.*, p. 761.

(28) In the case of tar, imports in 1811 came from many small sources to make up any deficiency on the Liverpool market. British North America on the other hand supplied 48 per cent of the pot and pearl ashes in 1811 compared with 32 per cent in 1810 and this accounted entirely for the increase in this commodity from an area outside the U.S.A.

(29) *Liverpool Consular Reports*. James Maury to the Secretary of State, Washington, 30 January 1811.

(3) *W. and E. Corrie Handbills*, 2 February 1811.

(31) *Ibid.*, 27 April: 4, 11 and 25 May 1811.

(32) Parliamentary Papers 1810–1811, Vol. II, pp. 390–91. *Minutes of Evidence taken before a Select Committee of the whole House, to whom was referred the Petitions of several weavers* . . . See also *Monthly Magazine*, Vol. XXXI, p. 600.

(33) *W. and E. Corrie Handbills*, 14 September and 26 October 1811. See also G. W. Daniels, 'The Cotton Trade during the Revolutionary and Napoleonic Wars', *Transactions of the Manchester Statistical Society* (1915–16), p. 80.

(34) *W. and E. Corrie Handbills*, 4 January 1812.

(35) *Liverpool Consular Reports*. James Maury to the Secretary of State, Washington, 30 January 1812. See also the letter from Mercator in the Liverpool *Mercury*, 4 October 1811.

(36) *Liverpool Consular Reports*. James Maury to the Secretary of State, Washington, 15 July 1811.

(37) *Liverpool Consular Reports*, James Maury to the Secretary of State, Washington, 24 December 1811.

(38) Parliamentary Papers, House of Lords, 1812, Vol. XI, *op. cit.*, p. 324.

(39) Liverpool *Mercury*, 4 October 1811. Letter from 'Mercator'.

(40) W. F. Galpin, 'The American grain trade to the Spanish Peninsula, 1810–1814', *The American Historical Review*, Vol. XXVIII (1922), p. 26.

(41) Parliamentary Papers, 1812, Vol. III, *op. cit.*, p. 350; see also H. Heaton, 'Non-Importation', *op. cit.*, pp. 195–96.

(42) Thomas Robinson and Nathaniel Lawrence had survived the rigours of the Embargo and Non-Intercourse Law but were declared bankrupt six months after the operation of the Non-Importation Law. Liverpool *Mercury*, 5 July 1811. Similarly Abraham Binns and his family fell upon hard times due to the conditions now experienced in the American trade. *Occasional notices and remarks of the late Margaret Binns of Liverpool, Her Diary, 1763–1812*, Liverpool Records Office. See particularly the entries of 8 and 11 February 1811.

(43) B. H. Tolley, Thesis *op. cit.* Chapter II deals with some of the activities of individual merchant firms engaged in the American trade of Liverpool.

(44) P.R.O. Adm. 106/1561. In Letters, 17 June 1811, Logan Lennox to the Admiralty.

(45) Forged licences and ships' papers could be obtained without difficulty in Liverpool, Parliamentary Papers, 1812, Vol. III, *op. cit.*, p. 351; Liverpool *Mercury*, 13 March 1811. There was also the feeling that the operation of the licensing system had transferred some of the West India business to London. Liverpool

Mercury, 20 December 1811. In his evidence before the Committee of Enquiry of 1812, Thomas Thornely produced a letter circularised by a Liverpool firm which boasted of its ability to produce exact replicas of the licences required by American vessels. See also *Cobbett's Parliamentary Debates*, Vol. XXI, p. 1113.

(46) *Cobbett's Parliamentary Debates*, Vol. XIX, pp. 1017–18, Petitions from Paisley and Lanark, 8 May 1811; Vol. XX, p. 339, Petitions from Bolton and Manchester.

(47) Liverpool *Mercury*, 20 September 1811.

(48) *Ibid.*, 18 October 1811.

(49) *Ibid.*, 8 November 1811. There was a substantial fall in the quantity of white salt exported to the U.S.A. from Liverpool. In 1810, 1,870,368 bushels had been despatched but this fell to 394,541 bushels in 1811. This last figure has considerably less than the low volume exported during the operation of the Embargo of 1808, viz. 1,014,086 bushels. *H. of C. Journals*, Vol. LXVII (1812), p. 760.

(50) *The American Chamber of Commerce*, Liverpool, Minute Book I, 30 November 1811.

(51) Liverpool *Mercury*, 20 December 1811.

(52) H. Brougham, *The Life and Times of Henry, Lord Brougham* (1811), Vol. II, p. 9.

(53) Roscoe Papers, p. 456, Liverpool Records Office. Undated manuscript, William Roscoe to H. Brougham. See also *Cobbett's Parliamentary Debates*, Vol. XII, pp. 771–803, 1159–210.

(54) Bradford Perkins, *Prologue to War, op. cit.*, p. 323.

(55) *Cobbett's Parliamentary Debates*, Vol. XXI, pp. 1092 *et seq.*, 1164.

(56) H. Brougham, *The Life and Times, op. cit.*, p. 12. Letter to Thornley, 4 March 1812.

(57) Brougham's letters were duplicated and sent to the provincial centres. See *Parliamentary Papers*, 1812, Vol. III, *op. cit.*, p. 153. The evidence of Ebenezer Rhodes, cutlery manufacturer of Sheffield, gives details of a letter sent by Brougham to Attwood in Birmingham which had also been used in Sheffield at a meeting there to gain support for the campaign against the Orders.

(58) Roscoe Papers, *op. cit.*, p. 484, 11 March 1812. William Roscoe to Henry Brougham.

(59) Liverpool *Mercury*, 20 March 1812.

(60) *Ibid.*, 27 March 1812.

(61) *Ibid.*, 27 March 1812.

(62) *Cobbett's Parliamentary Debates*, Vol. XXII, p. 114.

(63) *H. of C. Journals*, Vol. LXVII, pp. 216, 266, 285, 317, 321, 348, 374–75, 381, 385, 390, 412.

(64) Liverpool *Mercury*, 17 April 1812.

(65) Liverpool *Mercury*, 24 April 1812.

(66) *Ibid.*, 1 and 8 May 1812. See also *Cobbett's Parliamentary Debates*, Vol. XXII pp. 1041, 1058.

(67) *Cobbett's Parliamentary Debates*, Vol. XXII, *op. cit.*, p. 1058. The Liverpool Petition was presented by General Gascoyne.

(68) *Ibid.*, p. 1063. The second petition from Liverpool was presented by H. Brougham. See also B. M. Add.MS.42773, Letter 302, 12 May 1812. Correspondence of George Rose.

(69) *Cobbett's Parliamentary Debates*, Vol. XXII, *op. cit.*, p. 1109.

(70) The Liverpool West India Petition was presented on 13 May 1812, *H. of C. Journals*, Vol. LXVII, p. 375. William Rathbone V excused James Cropper on the grounds of ill-health. Parliamentary Papers, 1812, Vol. III, *op. cit.*, p. 434.

(71) Liverpool *Mercury*, 15 May 1812. See also H. Brougham, *The Life and Times, op. cit.*, Vol. II, p. 16.

(72) Ratification by France occurred on 20 May 1812.

(73) *Hansard*, Vol. XXIII, pp. 486–548.

(74) H. Brougham, *The Life and Times, op. cit.*, Vol. II, pp. 31–33.

(75) C. W. New, *The Life of Henry Brougham to 1830* (1961), p. 69.

(76) *The American Chamber of Commerce*, Liverpool, Minute Book I, 25 June 1812. See also J. C. Brown, *A Hundred Years of Merchant Banking* (1909), p. 32. Alexander Brown in Baltimore was just as surprised as his son, William Alexander, in Liverpool that the American government had declared war. Letter dated 22 June 1812.

(77) *Liverpool Consular Reports*, 26 February 1812. James Maury to the Secretary of State, Washington.

(78) *W. and E. Corrie Handbills*, May and June 1812.

(79) R. C. Jarvis, *Customs Letter Books on the Port of Liverpool* (1711–1813), (Chetham Society, 1954), Letter 430. J. C. Brown *op. cit.*, pp. 27–29, Letters to G. Brown, then in Liverpool, 2 and 7 April 1812.

(80) P.R.O. Privy Council Unbound Papers, 27 June 1812. Form of American Licences. See also F. Couzet, *op. cit.*, Vol. II, pp. 705–06.

(81) P.R.O. BT.6/207. Registers of Applications for Licences made to the Board of Trade, June to August 1812.

(82) R. C. Jarvis, *op. cit.*, p. 433, 2 August 1812; 434, 4 August 1812. *Liverpool Consular Reports*, 20 August 1812, James Maury to the Secretary of State, Washington.

(83) R. C. Jarvis, *op. cit.*, p. 437, 21 August 1812.

(84) H. Heaton, 'Non-Importation', *op. cit.*, pp. 197–98. See also C. N. Parkinson, ed., *The Trade Winds. A Study of British Overseas Trade during the French Wars 1793–1815* (1948), p. 224; R. G. Albion and J. B. Pope, *Sea Lanes in Wartime. The American Experience, 1775–1942* (1942), p. 114. *Niles' Weekly Register, op. cit.*, Vol. III, p. 227.

(85) F. Crouzet, *L'Economie Britannique, op. cit.*, Vol. II, p. 707.

(86) *W. and E. Corrie Handbills*, 12 December 1812.

(87) P.R.O. BT.6/208. Registers of Applications for Licences made to the Board of Trade, September to December 1812.

(88) Parliamentary Papers, 1812, Vol. III, *op. cit.*, p. 484.

(89) W. R. Copp, 'Nova Scotian Trade during the War of 1812', *Canadian Historical Review*, Vol. XVIII (1937), p. 151.

(90) Parliamentary Papers, 1812, Vol. III, *op. cit.*, p. 345. There were 17,000 hogsheads of tobacco in the King's Warehouse.

(91) *W. and E. Corrie Handbills*, May 1812.

(92) *Ibid.*, 25 July 1812.

(93) *Ibid.*, August to September 1812.

(94) *Roscoe Papers, op. cit.*, p. 487, 24 June 1812. Henry Brougham to William Roscoe. Liverpool *Mercury*, 4 September 1821.

(95) *Hansard*, Vol. XXIV, p. 14, 363–77, 3 February 1813. Declaration of the Prince Regent, *The Times*, 15 December 1812.

(96) *Hansard*, Vol. XXIV, p. 641. Canning had supported Brougham in the demand for an enquiry into the effects of the Orders in Council. Now he saw that his best interests would be served by taking a hostile attitude towards the U.S.A.

(97) Brougham explained Gladstone's hostility towards him by referring to the Committee proceedings of the spring when Gladstone had been ruthlessly cross-examined in the witness-box. There was still a lingering resentment against Brougham for his opposition to the slave trade. Liverpool Record Office, Manuscript of B. W. Jones, p. 226.

(98) Liverpool *Mercury*, 30 October 1812.

(99) *Ibid.*, 4 December 1812.

(100) *Roscoe Papers, op. cit.*, p. 501, January 1813. Henry Brougham to William Roscoe.

(101) Liverpool *Mercury*, 29 January, 19 February 1813.

(102) *Ibid.*, 7 May, 4 June, 23 July, and 12 November 1813.

(103) There were over forty American vessels still at Gothenburg in November 1812 and it was hoped that some of these would put in to Liverpool on their way home. Liverpool *Mercury*, 13 November 1812. See also P.R.O. BT.6/210, Registers of Applications for Licences to the Board of Trade, June 1813 to January 1814.

(104) Liverpool *Mercury*, 16 October 1812.

(105) D. C. North, *The Economic Growth of the United States 1790–1860* (1961), p. 231.

(106) R. B. Albion and J. B. Pope, *op. cit.*, p. 116 *et seq.*

(107) P.R.O. BT.6/209/51868, 18 May 1813. Registers of Applications for Licences to the Board of Trade.

(108) P.R.O. BT.6/211/56151, 30 May 1814. Registers of Applications for Licences to the Board of Trade.

(109) J. W. Pratt, *The Expansionists of 1812* (1957), p. 101; see also Bradford Perkins, *Castlereagh and Adams. England and the United States, 1812–1823* (1964), p. 35; and W. R. Copp, *op. cit.*, pp. 141–49.

(110) B. H. Tolley, *op. cit.*, Chapter V. examines the effects of the war upon individual merchant houses in Liverpool. *Wedgwood Papers* Box No. 135/27037, 21 April 1813.

(111) Liverpool *Mercury*, 28 May 1813.

(112) P.R.O. Adm.1/5219, James Buller to Croker, 2 February 1814. Copies of the Orders in Council to this date are attached.

(113) J. W. Pratt, *op. cit.*, p. 234. See also *Niles Weekly Register, op. cit.*, Vol. IV, p. 158, 30 March 1814. Ezekiah Niles warned that Amelia would become once more 'a mighty scene of smuggling and treasonable intercourse'.

(114) Liverpool *Mercury*, Apr. to Nov. 1814.

(115) P.R.O. BT.6/211. Registers of Applications for Licences to the Board of Trade, Feb. to July 1814.

(116) W. F. Galpin, *The Grain Supply of England during the Napoleonic Period*, New York (1925); Chapter VIII deals with the general question of American grain supplies to Britain.

(117) *W. and E. Corrie Handbills*, 13 Mar. 1813.

(118) *Ibid.*, 3 Apr. 1813.

(119) *H. of C. Journals* (1813), Vol. LXVIII, p. 407, 13 Apr. 1813.

(120) *W. and E. Corrie Handbills*, 15 and 22 May 1813.

(121) *Ibid.*, 27 Nov. 4, 11, 18 and 24 Dec. 1813.

(122) *Ibid.*, 1 Jan. 1814.

(123) *Ibid.*, 28 May 1814.

(124) *Ibid.*, 7 January 1815.

(125) *MacConnell and Kennedy Papers, op. cit.*, Purchase Book. Hughes and Duncan sold Sea Island Cotton regularly to MacConnell and Kennedy between Jan. and Mar. 1815, in increasing amounts each time. No business had been transacted previously.

(126) Bradford Perkins, *Castlereagh and Adams, op. cit.*, pp. 10–16; Liverpool *Mercury*, 10 Dec. 1813, reporting the Concentric Society Dinner.

(127) Liverpool *Mercury*, 13 May 1814. The occasion was a public meeting to prepare a message of congratulation to the Prince Regent on the occasion of victory in Europe.

(128) Liverpool *Mercury*, 5 and 26 Aug., 2 Sept. 1814.

(129) *Roscoe Papers op. cit.*, p. 504, 16 Sept. 1813. Henry Brougham to William S. Roscoe; 528, undated, H. Brougham to William Roscoe.

(130) E. Baines, *op. cit.*, p. 188.

(131) Liverpool *Mercury*, 31 March 1815.

(132) H. Heaton, 'Yorkshire Cloth Traders in the United States (1776–1840), (*Thoresby Society Transactions (1941–1942)*, p. 265. Liverpool *Mercury*, 16 December 1814.

(133) T. Slack, *Remarks on Cotton and Retrospective Occurrences for more than thirty-six years last past*, (Liverpool, 1815), p. 17.

CHAPTER SIX

Liverpool Shipping in the Early Nineteenth Century

F. NEAL

I

IN VIEW of the importance of Liverpool as a port during the nineteenth century it is surprising that an adequate economic history of the city has not yet been written. Historians have concerned themselves either with general surveys of the town's development, touching lightly upon matters concerned with trade and shipping, or with histories of specific shipping companies or business organisations. There has been no major work concerned with analysing the mechanics of the port's general growth and, surprisingly at a time when the statistical and analytical approach to economic history is rapidly gaining ground, there are very few detailed studies of key developments in the expansion of this world-class seaport.[1] A major omission is a detailed study of the growth of shipping belonging to the port in the conventional period of the Industrial Revolution, 1780 to 1830.

What do we gain by establishing the growth of a port's shipping in tonnage terms? It is hoped to show that in the particular circumstances of the early nineteenth century it gives a good indication of the prosperity of the port and the immediate hinterland. Before elaborating on this statement it may be useful to examine more closely what is meant by the phrase 'the tonnage of shipping belonging to a port'. Here it means the registered tonnage of British ships at particular ports as prescribed by various Acts of Parliament in the seventeenth, eighteenth and nineteenth centuries. The Acts were the manifestation of the mercantilist view that all trade to the United Kingdom should be carried in British ships except in the case of goods carried by vessels of the country from which the goods originated. The motives behind mercantilist philosophy were varied but some themes stand out. Such legislation would harm the carrying trade of Britain's main maritime rivals, particularly the Dutch; it would help the trade balance by reducing freights paid to foreign shipowners, and it would also help to build up a large merchant marine which would provide Britain with seamen in times of war. Given the fact that certain trades were restricted to British ships by law, it was a logical consequence that there had to be some method of certifying that a ship was in fact British, so that its right to be used in certain trades could be established if the master were confronted by suspicious naval or customs officers. It was this necessity to have some means of identification which gave rise to the registration of ships at British ports. The Act which gave rise to the most comprehensive registration requirements was that of 1786, known as Lord Liverpool's Act.[2] It was passed as a direct consequence of the successful revolt of the American colonists resulting in an independent nation which was, by definition, excluded from using its ships in certain trades with Britain. These American ships had previously been classified as British plantation vessels, many had English shareholders and their owners had strong business connexions in Britain. If the Law regarding the exclusion of foreign ships from certain trades with Britain was not to be flouted then a tighter system of registration had to be imposed: Lord Liverpool's Act provided the remedy.

This laid down that all British merchant ships of over 15 tons had to be registered at a British port. In practice the owners normally chose the port in which they resided and from which the vessel operated. The sole owner, or a managing owner on behalf of a group of shareholders, had to produce evidence from the builder of the physical dimensions of the vessel. Before registration was effected a customs officer, or surveyor, had to go on board and measure the vessel, recording her physical features. This ensured that the vessel was the one described on the certificate. These measurements of length, breadth, number of masts, and depth of hold were entered in the Register Books at the particular port and a copy of these dimensions was made on a certificate of Registration issued to the master so that should his ship's right to be carrying certain cargoes ever be questioned, he could produce the Certificate of Registration. The Register Books contained additional information such as the name of the vessel, owners, their occupation, place of residence, name of master, dates of change of masters. Any change in the physical characteristics of the ship or in its ownership had to be recorded in the Register Books kept at each port and such endorsements were to be entered on the Certificate of Registration, as soon as was practicable. Thus, when speaking of the tonnage of shipping belonging to a port we mean the tonnage of shipping registered at that port. A vessel's Certificate of Registration at a particular port would be cancelled if the vessel were sunk, sold to foreigners, broken up or registered at another port, thus reducing the tonnage of shipping belonging to the particular register. At the port of Liverpool the Register Books exist from 1786 onwards and contain a mass of information regarding the shipping of the port.

What is the economic significance of a statistic such as the tonnage of shipping on a port's register? Movements in such a magnitude at the period we are concerned with would indicate changes in the prosperity of the port and surrounding area, for in 1815 almost all the vessels registered at Liverpool would be operating from Liverpool, their home port. This contrasts with the situation today, when vessels registered at Liverpool may operate continuously between Southampton and New York or London and Mombasa. Changes in the tonnage of ships registered at Liverpool at the present time do not necessarily reflect changes in the volume of trade passing through the port or the amount of auxiliary work provided in the Liverpool area.

In 1815 the situation was quite different. Given the communications existing at the time, it would not be easy for Liverpool owners to register a vessel at Liverpool and allow it to trade regularly from London or Newcastle to say, the Gulf ports or South America. To supervise from Liverpool the paying off of a crew in London and the preparation for a voyage from that port, involving buying of victuals, repairs, marine insurance and so on, would have been highly inconvenient. The master would have had to undertake most of these duties and the Liverpool owners could have exercised only the most tenuous control, a situation fraught with danger.[3] Also, given the fact that most Liverpool vessels were owned by merchants who used them to carry their own goods, the likelihood of chartering vessels to ply between other ports was reduced. Thus, changes in tonnage of vessels registered at the port normally reflected changes in the trade and prosperity of the Liverpool merchant community.

It is true that the registered tonnage of shipping does not in itself indicate the volume of goods passing in and out of a port—ships may be laid up because of a lack of business—but it is a reasonable premise that if the stock of shipping in a port is increasing over a period of time, this reflects a growth volume of overseas trade. Merchants did not invest money in ships to have them laid up. An increased tonnage of vessels operating from the port meant not only more trade in terms of goods carried into or out of the port, but also more work for ship repairers, shipbuilders, marine insurers, seamen, dockers, ships chandlers and others connected with ships and dock work. For this reason alone the tonnage of shipping belonging to the port is of interest. Additionally, changes in this magnitude would also reflect changes in the level of economic activity in Liverpool's industrial hinterland, for instance in Lancashire and the Black Country. By 1815 the port was linked by canal with the most rapidly developing centres of manufacturing industry, the products of which left the country via Liverpool. In the case of the cotton industry, all the raw cotton needed to feed the voracious appetite of Lancashire's rapidly mechanising industry came in through Liverpool, and her merchant shipowners handled the bulk of the trade.

It ought to be pointed out that the tonnage of vessels registered at a port is quite a different matter from the tonnage of vessels entering and leaving a port. This latter figure would include not only Liverpool-registered vessels entering and leaving, but also vessels registered at other British and Colonial ports, as well as foreign-owned ships. Thus any increased trade passing through might have been carried by ships other than Liverpool-owned vessels. If this had been true to any great extent we could not deduce, for instance, that a decline in the tonnage of ships belonging to the port reflected a decline in the prosperity of the port and its hinterland. In fact, the bulk of the trade passing through Liverpool in the period 1815 to 1835 was handled by locally owned ships. Despite the fact that other vessels shared in Liverpool's trade, the deduction that there is a clear correlation between changes in the port's registered tonnage and the level of prosperity in the port and its hinterland therefore remains valid.

The scope of this essay is limited. It examines quantitatively the shipping belonging to the port of Liverpool during a crucial period in Lancashire's industrial development, namely the twenty-one years from 1815 to 1835. The questions posed and answered are these: What happened to the tonnage of shipping belonging to the port over this period? Who owned the ships? Where did the Liverpool owners obtain their vessels? What type of business unit predominated among the shipowners? The choice of 1815 as the beginning of the period under review is based on the feeling that this year can reasonably be described as something of a watershed in the port's history. The eighteenth century had witnessed developments in the world economy that had favoured Liverpool, changes which the merchant community had been quick to exploit. The causes of Liverpool's growth at this time can be summed up in the words slaves, rum, tobacco, sugar, salt and cotton, and, with respect to Ireland, provisions. An upsurge of humanitarian feeling resulted in the abolition of the slave trade in 1807 and for a while it might have seemed to the Liverpool mercantile community that it had suffered an irreparable loss. However, this was the gestation period that ultimately gave birth to new and important trades, which did not merely replace the triangular and other declining trades but completely overshadowed them in terms of tonnage of shipping involved. The trade with South America was beginning to grow; the North American trade was of increasing significance as commercial relations had been rapidly restored after the War of 1812; the West African trade in palm oil flourished under the leadership of such people as John and Thomas Tobin and Henry Laffer; the abolition of the East India Company's monopoly of the trade to India in 1814 created an opportunity that Liverpool merchants, with their insatiable appetites for profits, were quick to exploit; as a result of an increasing rate of technological innovation the growing cotton industry devoured an increasing quantity of raw cotton, mainly from the Gulf ports of the U.S.A., and from South America. The Napoleonic wars ended in 1815 and there commenced a period which despite fluctuations was to witness the port's rapid growth and which also saw the steam engine applied to locomotion on land and propulsion on sea, developments that were further to stimulate Merseyside's importance as a centre of trade and shipping.

II

Not surprisingly, the officials responsible for collecting statistics in the first decades of the nineteenth century did not have the needs of future economic historians in mind when they were collating the masses of information that came into their hands. Such a basic statistic as the total tonnage of shipping on a port's register in any one year does not appear to have been compiled by H.M. Customs for the decades immediately following Lord Liverpool's Act. Parliamentary papers have also proved to be lacking in information regarding tonnages over the years 1815 to 1819, though there are figures for the period 1820 to 1832. Lastly, various works on Liverpool published during the first half of the nineteenth century quote tonnages for the odd year but there is no way of checking whether or not they are accurate, and rarely is the source of the information given. However, the Liverpool Statutory Registers of Merchant Ships enable the tonnage added to the Liverpool stock of shipping in any year to be calculated, and this is the source of the statistics that follow. The method adopted is quite simple. The Registers contain details of all the ships registered at the port in any one year and the tonnage of all such registrations can be called the gross tonnage registered. Because many vessels registered in any one year were already on the Liverpool Register and were merely re-registered following a change of ownership or a change in the physical characteristics of the vessel, it is necessary to deduct their tonnage from the gross tonnage, leaving a figure that can be called the net tonnage registered. This magnitude is, overwhelmingly, the tonnage of ships newly acquired by Liverpool owners and registered by them at their home port, thus adding to the stock of shipping registered at Liverpool. Against this must be set the losses of ships from the Register. These mainly occurred because Liverpool owners sold their vessels to owners outside of Liverpool who then registered the vessels elsewhere, or because ships were lost at sea or broken up and thus lost to the port. When the tonnage registered elsewhere or lost at sea in any one year is set against the net tonnage registered in that year, the balance is the amount by which the volume of shipping registered at the port increased. This can be called the net accretion. The following table shows how the figure for the net accretions to the stock of shipping has been arrived at for each of the years 1815 to 1820 and 1829 to 1835:

TABLE I

NET ACCRETIONS TO THE STOCK OF SHIPPING REGISTERED AT THE PORT OF LIVERPOOL

Year	No. of ships	Gross tonnage	Tonnage already registered	Net tons registered	Tonnage lost	Net accretions (tons)
1815	156	30,683	12,735	17,948	8,710	+9,238
1816	163	31,120	11,164	19,956	7,601	+12,355
1817	140	29,860	14,851	15,009	11,768	+3,241
1818	157	31,382	14,666	16,716	8,331	+8,385
1819	127	23,290	13,396	9,894	9,435	+469
1820	130	26,988	16,079	10,909	11,740	−831
1829	163	32,897	13,956	18,941	13,633	+5,308
1830	159	34,516	16,883	17,633	15,222	+2,411
1831	154	27,895	13,455	14,440	18,276	−3,836
1832	182	39,363	18,399	20,964	15,340	+5,624
1833	204	45,904	18,847	27,057	17,910	+9,147
1834	218	49,520	20,399	29,121	16,823	+12,298
1835	229	55,722	16,232	39,490	19,821	+19,669

Thus in 1815 156 vessels were registered, representing 30,683 tons. Some of these 156 ships were already on the Liverpool Register and were being re-registered. The tonnage of such vessels came to 12,735 tons which, when deducted from the gross tonnage, leaves a figure of 17,948 tons added to the Register. In the same year ships totalling 8,170 tons were lost to the port, either because they were sold and registered elsewhere or because they were lost at sea. After deducting such losses from the tonnage newly registered the net accretion is

9,238 tons. The figures for the subsequent years are derived in the same manner.

The net accretions over the six years 1815 to 1820 display two significant features. Firstly, in each of the years except 1820, tonnage is added to the Liverpool Register. Secondly, the rate at which tonnage is added slows down. The period has been described by Clapham as 'economically, probably the most wretched, difficult and dangerous in modern English economic history'. If one looks at the tonnage of shipping registered in the United Kingdom as a whole the picture is one of general depression in overseas trade and shipping. The total tonnage on the United Kingdom Register in 1815 was 2,479,000; in 1820 it was down to 2,413,000, a decline of 2 per cent. As will be shown later, the additions to the Liverpool Register over the same period represented an increase of 16 per cent; the only effect of the general depression on Liverpool's shipping was to slow down the rate at which it was increasing. Growing activity at the port is indicated by other factors. In 1815, 6,440 vessels, totalling 709,849 tons, paid dock dues of £76,915. In 1820 the vessels numbered 7,276, totalling 885,033 tons, paying £94,412 in dues.[4] Thus accompanying a 16 per cent increase in the volume of Liverpool-owned shipping was a 24 per cent jump in the volume of traffic using the port. In 1820 the tonnage of foreign vessels entered inwards at Liverpool was 72 per cent greater than in 1815, whilst the corresponding figure for British vessels was 13 per cent. The proportion of the extra British tonnage that was Liverpool owned is not known, but almost certainly it was the greater part. All of this suggests that whilst British overseas trade and shipping in general was depressed, Liverpool prospered and was subject to special and peculiar influences.

It is beyond the scope of this paper to try to analyse the wider aspects of Liverpool's trade but general points are worth noting. Firstly, over the years 1816 to 1820 the volume of imports into the United Kingdom increased overall and the imports of raw cotton increased particularly rapidly, especially in the years 1817 and 1818. Liverpool was the main port of entry for this commodity, and though American vessels would carry much of this, Liverpool ships had a big share in the trade. The East Indian Company's monopoly of trade with India ended in 1814 and Liverpool merchants were quick to exploit this new opening, particularly welcome after the ending of the slave trade. The first Liverpool ship to return from Calcutta was John Gladstone's *Kingsmill* which arrived back in Liverpool in 1815 with what was reputed to be a cargo of record value.[5] Between 1815 and 1820 there was a rapid increase in the number of vessels trading between Liverpool and the ports of Calcutta and Bombay. Similarly, there was an increase in the North American trade. There had been the fear that the war of 1812 might have damaged our trading interests in America and that the French might have stepped in. However, when the French war ended in 1815 there was a rush to export to the United States and, though the trade suffered something of a decline by 1820, the initial post-war upsurge would have helped to sustain the extra tonnage registered over this period. Lastly, the trade to South America was also increasing under the drive of such men as Charles Tayleur, who was so well established in Buenos Aires by 1823 that he sent his son over there as agent for his firm. Imports of wet and dry hides and cotton formed the basis of this trade.

It would be pretentious to claim that there was a precise causal relationship between the annual volume of shipping registered at the port and fluctuations in the general level of economic activity, particularly as it appears that Liverpool's trade was partially insulated from the effects of the general economic malaise that characterised the period 1815–20. Yet the basic thesis is attractive. Modern economic theory assumes that changes in the expectations of profits accruing to increments of investment in plant and equipment will influence directly the amount of investment taking place in the near future. Thus if overseas trade was depressed, one would expect that there would be some falling off in the purchase of ships on the part of merchants involved in such trade. Conversely, an upsurge in overseas trade ought to have led to an increase in the purchase of ships. Losses of shipping as a result of shipwreck were purely fortuitous and depended on the accident of storms and bad seamanship and had nothing to do with economic decisions concerning profit or loss. Thus, such losses ought to be ignored when assessing the tonnage added to the Liverpool Register from purely commercial motives. If the tonnage of vessels taken off the Liverpool Register because of registrations elsewhere is deducted from the net tonnage registered in any one year, the balance left represents the addition to Liverpool's shipping as a result of purely economic factors and this is the tonnage that might be expected to fluctuate with changes in the overall level of economic activity. The following table shows the balance between the tonnage for net registrations and the tonnage of ships registered elsewhere.

The year 1815 has been identified as a peak in the recovery from the depression of 1810–11, whilst 1816 was a year of decline.[6] The tonnage added to the Register in 1816 (ignoring losses at sea) was 16,120 tons, an increase over the 14,561 tons in 1815. This could be

TABLE II

The Balance between net Registrations and
the Tonnage Removed from the Liverpool
Register to Other Ports

Year	Net registrations (tons)	Registrations elsewhere (tons)	Balance (tons)
1815	17,948	3,387	14,561
1816	19,956	3,836	16,120
1817	15,009	4,489	10,520
1818	16,716	3,699	13,017
1819	9,894	3,216	6,678
1820	10,909	3,602	7,307

explained by the argument that the decline in general economic activity did not become apparent to merchants until 1816 was nearly over. A similar time-lag in the awareness of contemporary business opinion regarding fluctuations in business activity may have been responsible for the fact that in 1817, a year of recovery, the tonnage added to the Register declined from 16,120 tons to 10,520 tons. The recovery continued in 1818 and the tonnage registered increased from 10,520 tons to 13,017 tons. In 1819 there was a dramatic falling off in the tonnage added, to 6,678 tons; 1819 was a year of depression and the decline in purchases of ships was immediate. This quick reaction to depressed conditions could possibly be explained by the timing of the trade cycle. If the depression was under way at the end of 1818, it might have been obvious to shipowners early on in 1819. In 1820 there was a slight increase in the amount registered, to 7,307 tons. In fact the recovery continued until about 1824. Thus there appears to be a considerable degree of correlation between purchases of vessels and fluctuations in the general level of economic activity. However, more analysis is needed to establish a functional relationship between the variables.

So far the discussion has been about the net accretions to the Liverpool Register but obviously the significance of these figures is only really appreciated when placed against the total stock of shipping belonging to the port. For example, in Table I it can be seen that 9,236 tons were added to the Register. Was this a lot or a little? It has not been possible to find any figures, official or otherwise, that give the total tonnage of shipping belonging to Liverpool in each of the years 1815 to 1820. However, a Parliamentary Paper gives the total amount of shipping belonging to Liverpool over the years 1820 to 1832 and this has been used as the basis of the calculations of the figures shown below.[7] If the tonnage given for the year 1820 is used as a starting point the figures for the net accretions over the years 1815 to 1820 can be deducted in order to find the annual stock for each year. For example, there was a loss of 831 tons from the Liverpool Register in 1820 so that if this is added to the official figure of 173,782 tons for 1820, it gives a figure of 174,613 for 1819. Similarly, 469 tons were added in 1819 and if this is deducted from the 1819 total of 174,613 tons we get 174,144 tons for 1818. The following table shows the annual stock of shipping calculated in this manner.

TABLE III

THE TOTAL AMOUNT OF SHIPPING BELONGING TO THE
PORT OF LIVERPOOL 1815 TO 1820

Year	Total (tons)	Net accretions (tons)	increase (+) or decrease (−)
1815	150,163		
1816	162,518	12,355+	8%+
1817	165,759	3,241+	2%+
1818	174,144	8,385+	5%+
1819	174,613	469+	−
1820	173,782	831−	−

Over the whole period, the stock of shipping increased by 16 per cent, compared with a decline in the national tonnage of 3 per cent, so the only effect of the general depression seems to have been a slowing down of the rate of increase. These figures probably overstate somewhat the volume of shipping at Liverpool, for many vessels were left on the Register books long after they had ceased to exist. In 1827, however, many defunct vessels were written off, so that after this date shipping statistics of this sort are likely to be more accurate.

The picture revealed by the statistics for the period 1829–35 has similar characteristics, namely that the port's tonnage increased over the period and there was some correlation between the fluctuations in the level of economic activity and the purchases of ships. In each of the seven years (except 1831) tonnage belonging to the port increased and by 1835 the total tonnage was 28 per cent greater than in 1829, compared with a national increase of 7 per cent. Given the developments in the port's hinterland, this is what one would have expected. By 1835 its communications had been greatly improved by the opening of the Liverpool–Manchester railway. The development of the power loom broke the technological bottleneck in the cotton industry, greatly increasing output and so causing a rapid increase in the consumption of raw cotton, the importing of which was a staple Liverpool trade. The period from 1827 to 1832 has been described as a period of falling prices and profits, increasingly severe competition and falling industrial output. By 1829, foreign trade was picking up and by 1833 industrial output began to increase rapidly. In 1833–34 and 1835 imports and exports expanded at an ever-increasing rate, reaching a peak in 1836. In 1829, 223 million lb. of raw cotton was imported; in 1835 the figure was 364 million lb., most of which came through Liverpool. The trades to India, South America, the Gulf Ports and Ireland were all booming. After 1833 Liverpool merchants entered the expanding trades to South America in greater numbers. These developments are mirrored in the increased actitivy at the port. In 1835, 787,009 tons of shipping entered inwards, 47 per cent higher than in 1829. If this figure is broken down into British and foreign vessels, 517,172 tons of British shipping entered inwards, 60 per cent more than in 1829, and most of this extra British tonnage would be Liverpool owned.[8]

The national stock of shipping over these years increased by only 7 per cent compared with an increase of 28 per cent at Liverpool. The table shows the stock of shipping in each of the years under review.

TABLE IV[9]

THE STOCK OF SHIPPING REGISTERED AT THE
PORT OF LIVERPOOL 1829–35

Year	Total tonnage registered	Net accretions (tons)
1829	161,780	
1830	164,191	+2,411
1831	160,355	−3,836
1832	165,979	+5,624
1833	175,126	+9,147
1834	187,424	+12,298
1835	207,093	+19,669

The increase in the stock of shipping registered at the port is a reliable indicator of the secular trend of shipping activity. A more sensitive barometer of change in trading activity is the figure showing the net tonnage registered at the port in each year. In 1829, for example, 18,941 tons of shipping were added to the Liverpool Register as a result of shipowners buying ships which were not already registered at the port. In the same year, 8,461 tons of shipping were taken off the register as a result of their registration being transferred to another port, leaving 10,840 tons as the balance of tonnage registered in that year. Such a balance of registered tonnage reflects the sale and acquisition of vessels from purely commercial considerations and so is a rough indicator of the fluctuations in trade passing through the port. It does not reflect net accretions to the Register because losses from shipwreck have not been deducted. However, such losses were purely fortuitous and so do not reflect trading conditions. It must be added, however, that losses at sea would affect future purchases of ships but it is not possible to allow for this rather unpredictable element in ship buying.

TABLE V

SHOWING THE BALANCE BETWEEN THE NET
REGISTRATIONS AT LIVERPOOL AND REGISTRATIONS
AT OTHER PORTS

Year	Net registrations (tons)	Registrations elsewhere (tons)	Balance (tons)
1829	18,941	8,461	10,480
1830	17,627	7,443	10,184
1831	14,440	9,552	4,888
1832	20,964	9,495	11,469
1833	27,057	6,129	20,928
1834	29,121	8,930	20,191
1835	39,490	12,392	27,098

The years 1829–31 were years of relative stagnation in the nation's trade in general, and in fact additions of shipping to the Liverpool Register declined over the three years, but if losses at sea had not been so great, the port's stock of shipping would have slightly increased. In 1831 there was a significant increase, from 4,888 tons to 11,469 tons, whilst in 1833 the growth was even greater; it was almost equalled in 1834 and exceeded in 1835. These years were years of boom conditions in overseas trade and Liverpool had more than her share of this prosperity, particularly in the trade to the U.S.A. and, less spectacularly, in trade to Asia, Africa and the Mediterranean.

III

It is a well-established fact that the commonest forms of business unit in manufacturing industry during the Industrial Revolution were the one-man business and the partnership. A similar situation existed in shipping at Liverpool during the first half of the nineteenth century. The atomistic nature of the industry is revealed if one examines the structure of shareholdings from the point of view of the number of owners per vessel. The striking feature is the fact that in each of the years, on the average, nearly 80 per cent of all vessels registered had three or fewer owners. Given the circumstances of the time this is understandable. The overwhelming majority of vessels were owned by merchants, either individuals or partners in a trading concern. They normally used the vessels to carry outwards both their own goods and those of other persons, and to carry inwards goods on their own account and some freight for other merchants. The extent to which a particular merchant shipowner depended on carrying other traders' goods varied, but it was unusual at this time to find any shipowner functioning purely as a shipowner in the sense that he, or a group of persons, invested money in a vessel which then carried only the goods of other traders.

It is not obvious that the conditions under which vessels operated at the time would have made shipowning, as such, profitable.[10] The profits of commerce normally came from the sale of goods and raw material rather than freights. For example, sailing ships could not operate on fixed time schedules, if weather conditions were adverse then a vessel might be on the berth for weeks. Also, given the primitive business communications, a vessel might wait months for a full cargo for the outward journey. Though the fact that the owners were willing to let their vessels wait long periods whilst advertising their loading suggests that freight was not an unimportant item to many owners, it was seldom the main reason for owning a ship. The amount of capital needed to purchase the average-sized merchant vessel of about 220 tons was well within the means of most trading partnerships, particularly as few of them owned many vessels. It was the steam engine and iron hull that put the cost of a ship outside the means of the small partnership and led increasingly into the realm of joint stock company ownership. There were examples of vessels owned by large numbers of people, without a joint-stock, but these were not common, particularly after 1820. When they did occur, the owners were persons who had invested small amounts of money; such people as seamen, ships' chandlers, shipbuilders, or ships' masters receiving payment in the form of shares. Occasionally they were gentlemen or other uncommercial persons, buying or inheriting a small share in a vessel owned by a relative, friend or local personality. They were rarely people with risk capital to invest who deliberately chose shipping as the best

TABLE VI

THE NUMBER OF OWNERS PER VESSEL ON THE DAY OF REGISTRATION

No. of owners per ship	Number of vessels registered in each of the following years												
	1815	1816	1817	1818	1819	1820	1829	1830	1831	1832	1833	1834	1835
1	46	60	50	52	45	35	68	70	69	74	67	93	83
2	42	50	43	45	35	32	54	33	34	29	55	56	56
3	30	19	22	32	23	22	16	23	13	31	30	32	33
4	11	10	11	10	13	19	12	12	12	20	17	15	22
5	13	5	5	7	2	8	4	5	7	5	6	6	9
6	5	6	4	3	4	6	2	3	3	4	4	4	6
7	2	2	2	1	2	3	1	3	9	6	4	2	5
8	4	2	1	2	—	1	2	2	1	3	2	3	4
9	1	2	—	1	—	2	—	3	2	1	4	2	2
10	1	—	—	2	—	1	—	1	—	1	—	2	1
over 10	1	7	2	2	3	2	4	2	4	8	15	3	8
Total	156	163	140	157	127	130	163	157	154	182	204	218	229

investment outlet open to them. As already stated, most of the profits came from trading rather than freights as such.

In addition, ship owning was subject to many other risks apart from the shifting of economic forces. Wars resulted in loss of shipping; in peace time the incidence of shipwreck was quite high as a result of both adverse weather conditions and bad seamanship. For example, in 1819 twenty-five Liverpool-owned vessels were lost at sea or broken up because they were unseaworthy. In addition there were hazards, statistically less significant, such as pirates and dishonest masters. For example, in November 1820 the *Nymph* of Liverpool was captured by pirates at St. Domingo; in 1818 the *Alicia Hill* of Liverpool was also captured by pirates, whilst the *Lord Cochrane* was stolen by her master, Andrew Wallace, who was believed to be using her for trade along the South American coast. For the cautious investor there were better outlets for capital than shipowning; the separation of capital from management had to wait the coming of the steam engine. Over the period 1820 to 1835 several joint stock companies were formed in Liverpool to promote the use of steamships on certain runs, particularly to Ireland and in the coasting trades, but these were relatively uncommon in the shipping industry in general.

If the ownership of the vessels is analysed on the basis of the occupation of shareholders as given in the shipping register, the predominance of merchant shipowners is at once apparent. Of course the term 'merchant' as recorded in the Register may have been very loosely applied. Information contained in the Liverpool Directories, together with that in the standard works on the city, reinforces the view that for the majority of shipowners buying and selling of goods was their main occupation and shipowning was an ancillary function.[11]

The grouping of occupations under the headings given on the table is straightforward. In the first group (commerce and industry) are people described in the Registers as merchants, bankers, brewers, cotton manufacturers, etc. In the second group (maritime) are placed all persons such as master mariners, seamen, ships' chandlers, ship builders and others whose trade is connected with the sea and ships. Lastly, the professional and direct services group contains such people as doctors, lawyers, accountants, widows and spinsters.[12] It can be seen that the first grouping 'commerce and industry' is by far the most important group of occupations. In 1815, 83 per cent of all shareholders of vessels registered in that year had occupations of a commercial or industrial nature. In fact, on the average 84 per cent of such shareholders were described as merchants. This merely

TABLE VII

OCCUPATIONS OF OWNERS OF SHIPS REGISTERED AT LIVERPOOL

Year of registration	The percentage of shareholders in the occupations shown		
	Commerce & Industry ‰	Maritime ‰	Professional, direct services and private persons ‰
1815	83	12	5
1816	67	23	10
1817	76	16	9
1818	74	19	7
1819	77	16	7
1820	69	22	9
1829	66	24	10
1830	65	27	8
1831	65	25	10
1832	67	18	15
1833	63	23	14
1834	66	24	10
1835	63	23	14

emphasises the view that the bulk of the capital put into the port's shipping at this time came from mercantile profits rather than industry.

Though the importance of the merchant shipowner had declined slightly by 1835 this did not mean that capital was coming into the shipping industry from new outside sources. It reflected the increased number of shareholders among shipbuilders, master mariners, mariners, ships' chandlers, sail makers, etc. It was a common practice for the builder of a ship to receive part of his payment in the form of shares in the ship and in the same way ships' chandlers, sail makers and others concerned with the fitting out of a vessel would often receive payment in kind. Though over the years 1829–35 there was some increase in the proportion of shareholders classified under the heading 'professional and direct services' their significance as a source of capital remained small. The spinsters, doctors, lawyers, and clergymen who bought shares in vessels were not entrepreneurs risking their capital in an effort to maximise the return on their investment. Examination of the Certificates of Registration suggests that they were people who bought the odd share together with friends, in something of the nature of a light-hearted flutter or because they knew the main shareholder of the vessel and the purchase of a share was something of a sign of local patriotism.

TABLE VIII

AREAS OF RESIDENCE OF OWNERS OF SHIPS REGISTERED AT LIVERPOOL

Area	1815	1816	1817	1818	1819	1820	1829	1830	1831	1832	1833	1834	1835
	‰	‰	‰	‰	‰	‰	‰	‰	‰	‰	‰	‰	‰
Merseyside	84	77	82	75	74	79	86	82	79	85	76	82	76
Northern Counties[13] and Scotland	11	13	8	11	8	8	6	7	11	7	10	7	14
N. Wales and Cheshire	2	4	3	3	7	4	1	3	4	1	1	3	3
Ireland	–	1	2	4	4	1	1	–	2	1	2	2	1
Colonies	1	3	2	2	4	1	1	4	–	2	2	2	1
Others	2	2	3	5	3	7	5	4	4	4	9	4	6

M

Yet again, many of these people simply inherited the shares they owned. Government stock or the mortgage market would probably have provided a better outlet for the capital of the person seeking a steady income.

This concentration of ownership in the hands of the mercantile community is further emphasised if shareholdings are analysed on the basis of place of residence. The majority of the owners classified as living in Merseyside lived in Liverpool itself, whilst the remainder lived in Runcorn, Frodsham, Tranmere and other places near to the town of Liverpool. The importance of Liverpool as a place of residence for the shipowners is not surprising in view of the fact that they were mainly merchants. One noticeable feature is the fact that a large proportion of the shipowners coming from outside Liverpool resided in other seaports. In some cases this may have been the result of the coasting trade, in that a Hull shareholder in a vessel may have had business interests in Liverpool, particularly when the other shareholders in the vessel were Liverpool merchants. Several Liverpool business houses had members of their firms living abroad as agents and these persons made up the greater part of the owners of vessels living in the colonies. The proportion of the shareholders of Liverpool vessels drawn from Merseyside remained relatively stable over the whole period. In 1815 it was 77 per cent and in 1835 it was 76 per cent. It was the coming of steam and the joint stock company that was to break this pattern of ownership.

From what sources did Liverpool owners obtain their vessels? A ship registered at Liverpool which was not already on the Register would fall into one of three categories. Firstly, it might be a vessel that was newly built and was being registered for the first time. A merchant may have commissioned a shipbuilder to build the vessel or he may have bought it off the stocks, that is, a shipbuilder may have first built the vessel and then looked for a buyer. Secondly, a vessel may have been bought from an owner in another port. It was usual for the Liverpool owner to cancel the registration at the other port by registering the vessel at the Liverpool customs house. Thirdly, a vessel may have been previously employed on canals and rivers, for which purposes registration was unnecessary. If such a vessel was to be used in the coasting or foreign trades, it would have had to be registered. Thus in these ways vessels were added to the Liverpool Register in contrast to the re-registration of vessels already registered at the port; the tonnage added in these ways is referred to in Table I as net registrations. Looking first at the years 1815–20 the tonnage of the net registrations can be broken down in the following way:

TABLE IX

A BREAKDOWN OF NET TONNAGE ADDED TO THE LIVERPOOL REGISTER ACCORDING
TO ORIGIN

Year	New vessels	Vessels brought from other ports	Vessels previously in inland trade	Total of net registrations
	tons	tons	tons	tons
1815	7,781	10,042	125	17,948
1816	6,119	13,574	263	19,956
1817	3,940	10,764	305	15,009
1818	4,965	11,605	146	16,716
1819	4,131	5,547	216	9,894
1820	5,900	4,819	190	10,909

In each year except 1820 the tonnage of vessels brought from other ports exceeds the volume of newly built tonnage added to the Register. In 1817 and 1818 the proportion of newly registered tonnage represented by vessels from other ports is 63 and 70 per cent respectively. The significance of the relative proportions represented by the tonnage of newly built vessels and second-hand vessels is difficult to assess without having access to contemporary views on the economics of shipping at the time.

Nevertheless, it is possible to hazard a few guesses. The years from 1815 to 1820 were years of depression and the stock of shipping belonging to the nation was declining. The stagnation in shipping did not prevent Liverpool's shipping from increasing overall during the period and it may have been the case that the laying-up of vessels in other ports caused the prices of ships to fall, and Liverpool owners, enjoying relative prosperity, took the opportunity to buy on advantageous terms. This view would be tenable only if it could be shown that Liverpool owners were net purchasers of vessels from particular areas. It must be remembered that whilst they were buying ships in other ports and registering them at Liverpool, Liverpool ships were sold to merchants in other ports who then cancelled the Liverpool registration by registering them elsewhere. If it could be shown that, on balance, Liverpool was drawing vessels from particular areas this would support the view that these areas held particular attractions at this time for purchasers of ships. The following table shows the extent to which the Liverpool Register was a net gainer or loser to ports in other areas. The figures have been arrived at by calculating the tonnage of Liverpool vessels registered at other ports and deducting this from the tonnage of vessels brought to Liverpool from these same places. In the years

TABLE X

LIVERPOOL'S GAINS (+) AND LOSSES (−) IN RELATION TO PORTS IN OTHER AREAS

	1815	1816	1817	1818	1819	1820
West Indies	−429	−239	−1,142	−329	−228	+54
Scotland	−403	+1,192	+457	+460	−491	+178
North-west Ports	+1,061	+576	+180	+771	+544	−205
East Coast Ports	+925	+2,068	+2,975	−119	+571	+914
Ireland	−1,125	−713	−356	+212	+33	−450
London	+894	−192	−270	+1,195	−186	−104
Btitish N. America	+2,436	+2,490	+2,134	+5,115	+1,175	+646
Others	+383	+1,535	+1,019	+601	+544	+112

1815–17, East Coast ports such as Newcastle, Whitby, Hull and Scarborough were places from which Liverpool owners obtained a relatively large number of vessels. These ports were well known as shipbuilding centres and so it is not surprising that Liverpool owners made purchases on the East Coast. Prices of ships in these ports may have been falling, or size, too, may have been a factor in such purchases. The average size of vessels built at Liverpool in these years was below two hundred tons, but the average size of the vessels purchased in the East Coast ports was 232 tons. Most Liverpool builders were operating under cramped conditions and this may have been the limiting factor regarding the size of vessels that they built. Given the fact that larger vessels would be needed in the developing trades to Africa and India, the East Coast may have had larger vessels to offer at attractive prices. Certainly the area had a high reputation for shipbuilding.[14] The importance of British North America as a source of vessels stands out. In three of the six years, over 2,000 tons of shipping were brought to Liverpool, and in 1818 the figure was 5,115 tons. Price would most certainly have been the attraction of this source of ships, although size may have been an additional factor, the average size of such vessels being 238 tons. In 1825 a 300 ton vessel built in Canada cost from ninety dollars to one hundred dollars per ton, whilst in England the cost was from one hundred to one hundred and ten dollars.[15] The abundance of soft woods in Canada was a major factor in explaining this price differential. With regard to tonnage of newly built vessels it is not surprising that Liverpool itself was the main source.

New ships were bought in a large number of ports other than Liverpool itself, and the fact that in each year (except 1820) Liverpool-built vessels represented less than 50 per cent of the total

TABLE XI

THE SOURCES OF NEWLY BUILT VESSELS REGISTERED IN LIVERPOOL IN THE YEARS
1815–20

Place	1815	1816	1817	1818	1819	1820
	tons	tons	tons	tons	tons	tons
Liverpool	3,286	2,565	1,898	2,462	1,898	4,458
Chester	370	1,004	389	457	1,080	598
Workington	1,092	284	531	244	–	–
New Brunswick	1,231	361	153	–	–	–
Greenock	403	–	–	506	–	413
Monkswearmouth	150	134	182	–	–	–
Northwich	78	–	11	77	77	89
Runcorn	64	–	–	–	–	–
Frodsham Bridge	85	233	90	–	–	–
North Shields	101	–	–	360	–	–
Maryport	114	–	–	–	–	–
Others	807	1,538	686	859	1,076	342
Total	7,781	6,119	3,940	4,965	4,131	5,900

of newly built vessels added to the Register only emphasises the varied sources of new ships. The fact remains unchanged that Liverpool was the most important source of such vessels. This is not surprising. A developing port would have plenty of repair work to sustain shipwrights and for local merchants there would be the advantage of being able to supervise the building of the vessels. Relatively little is known of Merseyside shipbuilding at this period and it is not possible to say whether the local builders were fully extended in an effort to meet a growing demand for ships. If they were, then poor delivery dates and prices may have been a major factor in promoting purchases of ships elsewhere. The local industry did decline sufficiently for an enquiry to be set up in 1850 to investigate the causes of this stagnation, but in the period up to 1835 the local yards seem to have been as busy as they ever were. This will be examined later. For the moment the noteworthy feature of the above table is that British North America was not an important source of new, previously unregistered, ships. This may be partly explained by the number of vessels that were brought to the port from that area after first being registered in Canada and Nova Scotia. Many of these were registered and then brought over to Liverpool in the first year of their life, so that even though their tonnage was shown under the heading of vessels previously registered elsewhere they were, for all practical purposes, new ships.

The years 1829 to 1835 display similar trends to the 1815–20 period. The table below shows the breakdown of all newly registered vessels in each of the seven years.

TABLE XII

SOURCES OF NEWLY REGISTERED VESSELS

Year	Newly-built	Vessels brought from other ports	Vessels previously in inland trade	Total of net registration
	tons	tons	tons	tons
1829	6,204	12,340	397	18,941
1830	5,343	12,023	267	17,633
1831	6,998	6,885	557	14,440
1832	7,936	12,660	368	20,964
1833	10,946	15,905	206	27,057
1834	12,747	15,467	907	29,121
1835	17,244	21,136	1,110	39,490

In every year except 1831 the tonnage of vessels brought from other ports represented the greater proportion of the tonnage newly registered. In view of the sales of Liverpool ships to owners in other ports the question must be repeated, were the Liverpool owners, on balance, net purchasers of vessels from any particular area?

TABLE XIII

LIVERPOOL'S GAINS (+) AND LOSSES (−) IN RELATION TO OTHER PORTS

	1829	1830	1831	1832	1833	1834	1835
West Indies	+20	–	–	–	+76	+49	−230
Scotland	−1,303	+389	−4	−742	+396	−1,059	−826
North-west Ports	−213	+882	+1,064	−59	+1,281	+677	−491
East Coast Ports	+435	+814	+348	+496	+3,002	+3,260	+1,665
Ireland	−623	−420	−2,953	+216	−1,463	−767	−2,173
London	+79	+803	−480	+504	+749	−375	+211
Brit. N. America	+7,363	+3,648	+1,036	+2,992	+5,272	+5,599	+11,028
Others	+695	+992	−709	+1,405	+1,087	+72	−1,586

Once again, the predominance of British North America as a source of 'second hand' ships is noticeable; in 1835 11,028 tons, representing over thirty vessels, were brought to Liverpool. Once again, the lower price prevalent in Canada would be a major influence here. In 1833 and 1834 a relatively large tonnage came from the East Coast ports and one can only guess that price and size of ships were two possible reasons for the attraction of these ports, Newcastle and Sunderland being particularly important. In most years Liverpool was a net loser of tonnage to Ireland. This was a period when Irish trade was expanding and as Liverpool had strong connexions with Ireland it is not surprising that in some years Irish owners were purchasers of vessels registered in Liverpool. Taking the period as a whole no other significant areas can be discerned, the item 'Others' covering some thirty-seven different ports.

At the present time the centre of shipbuilding on Merseyside is Birkenhead; the last ship launched on the Liverpool side of the river came from the yard of Thomas Royden and Sons in 1899. Long before this time, however, shipbuilding on the Liverpool shore was dying. Relatively little is known of the shipbuilders of Liverpool but the Register Books can give some help in assessing their importance and in identifying the individuals involved. Before the coming of iron frames and steam engines, the building of the typical merchantman was a relatively small-scale operation and early prints of the Liverpool shore contain pictures of wooden ships on stocks situated in odd places near the docks and sea front. The Registration Acts up to 1824 did not lay down any procedure for the recording of the name of the builder of any new vessel that was registered, only the place and date of the building. After 1824 the name of the builder was also recorded, so that for new vessels registered in the years 1815 to 1820 we have a record of the place of building and the date, whilst for the years 1829 to 1835 we also have the name of the builder.

The scale of the shipbuilding operations can be appreciated by breaking down the number of vessels built at Liverpool into vessels of various sizes, remembering that these figures refer only to Liverpool-built vessels registered at Liverpool. It is probable that some vessels were built and sold to owners residing in other ports who registered the ships for the first time in their home ports.

In the years 1815–19 the majority of the vessels built were below 200 tons, the average for the years 1815–20 being 173 tons; 1820 appears to have been something of an unusual year in that seven vessels of over 300 tons were built, one being over 500 tons. In the years 1829 to 1835 there was an increase in the average size of vessels built locally, to 233 tons. Relatively large vessels were built in both periods; for example, in 1820 a ship of 556 tons was built whilst in each of the years 1834 and 1835 tonnages of 618 tons and 608 tons were recorded. However, the general design of the vessels may have been dictated by habit rather than a desire to produce vessels

TABLE XIV

A Breakdown of the Number of Vessels Built and Registered at Liverpool, According to Size

Year	Below 100 tons	100 up to 200	200 up to 300	300 up to 400	400 up to 500	500 up to 600	600 up to 700	Total No.	Total tons	Average tons
1815	4	8	4	1	1	–	–	18	3,286	183
1816	7	5	4	2	–	–	–	18	2,565	142
1817	6	8	–	2	–	–	–	16	1,898	119
1818	9	3	4	–	2	–	–	18	2,462	134
1819	3	4	3	–	1	–	–	11	1,898	172
1820	1	5	2	5	1	1	–	15	4,458	297
1829	3	–	4	6	–	2	–	15	4,336	289
1830	7	2	3	3	1	–	–	16	2,907	182
1831	5	4	2	3	–	–	–	14	2,541	182
1832	2	4	4	2	–	–	–	12	2,446	204
1833	1	4	5	2	–	–	–	12	2,494	208
1834	4	1	7	2	1	–	1	16	3,736	234
1835	3	3	6	6	3	–	1	22	6,178	281

capable of achieving certain performances. Shipbuilding at this time was a conservative industry, characterised by small yards and craftsmen rather than innovators. Not only were the vessels relatively small but their design was very conventional. The tonnage laws influenced the shape of the vessels, if not the weight. The result of the Tonnage Act was that the registered tonnage was based on a measurement of length and breadth only, and on the basis of this measurement the owners had to pay port duties; by deepening the hold the carrying capacity of a vessel could be enlarged without increasing its taxable dimensions. This resulted in a 'general' type of vessel being produced, reflected in the dimensions of nearly all the vessels registered at Liverpool over the years 1815–35. In the main, the length of such vessels was less than 100 feet, the breadth about one-third of the length, and the hold was about half the breadth of the ship, thus producing the rather squat vessels that appear on prints of this period. The Americans were the innovators with regard to the clipper ships, and in the building of this type of ship the British builders long lagged behind. They came into their own when they turned to iron-framed sailing ships and steam ships.

With regard to the tonnage of new vessels built at the port, it can be seen that there was no notable decline over the whole period, the 6,178 tons registered in 1835 being the highest of all the years examined. In his *Liverpool Ships in the Eighteenth Century* R. Stewart-Brown gives a list of the number and tonnage of vessels built at the port. In 1787, 5,731 tons were built; this figure had not been exceeded by 1808, the last year he quotes. Over the years 1787 to 1800 the average annual output was 3,728 tons. Compared with this figure, the local yards appear to have been slightly less busy in the years 1815–35 with the notable exceptions of 1820, 1829 and 1835. Two points must be borne in mind. Firstly the volume of repair work after 1815 may have been greater, given the greater volume of shipping using the port compared with the years before. The local builders may thus have been even busier after 1815, despite the apparent decrease in their average output of new ships. Secondly, the figures of new vessels built and registered at Liverpool do not give any clue to the number of vessels built there and registered elsewhere. Almost certainly some Liverpool-built vessels must have been registered elsewhere, and the fact that in 1835 the local yards could increase their output from 3,736 tons to 6,178 tons suggests that some capacity in the local yards was either idle or switched from repair work to the building of new ships at a time when demand was high.

Fifteen years later, in 1850, a Committee of Enquiry was set up by the Corporation to investigate the causes of the decline in ship-building at Liverpool. The shipbuilders who gave evidence claimed that their costs were higher than elsewhere because combinations among the shipwrights had forced up wages. In addition they argued there was no motive for a builder to install equipment in his yard because of the Corporation's policy of short leases. Such installations were expensive and the builder would not get the full benefit of his investment if the lease of the yard was soon to be terminated. The Corporation's policy of dock building resulted in many of the yards being squeezed more and more into confined spaces so that timber was difficult to store and a great deal of time and money was lost in constantly sorting piles of timber for lengths needed for a particular job. Whatever the reasons for the running down of the industry, decline must have come rapidly after 1835, for up to that time the figures do not indicate a contracting industry, though they may imply one whose limit of expansion had been set.

Stewart-Brown gives a list of the Liverpool builders and the number of shipwrights and apprentices employed by them in 1805.

TABLE XV

LIVERPOOL SHIPBUILDERS AND THEIR EMPLOYEES, 1805

Owner of Yard	Shipwrights	Apprentices	Total
Humble and Hurry	80	14	94
Dwerryhouse	5	5	10
Leather and Co.	19	16	35
Baldwin and Co.	8	10	18
Smallshaw	13	14	27
P. Quirk	29	15	44
Grayson	19	5	24
Fisher and Co.	12	21	33
Rathbone and Co.	57	24	81
Mottershead and Hutchinson	16	12	28
Wm. Quirk	–	–	–
Wm. Wilson	3	–	3
Hamer and Richardson	12	–	12
Hind and Son	36	6	42
Wm. Hill	8	5	13
Richard Bushell	7	8	15

Source: R. Stewart-Brown *Liverpool Ships in the Eighteenth Century*, p. 34.

If the number of shipwrights and apprentices employed by each builder is taken as a rough indication of the relative importance of each, then Humble and Hurry were the biggest builders in 1805, followed by Rathbone and Company, P. Quirk and Hind and Son, in that order. The picture revealed by the Register over the years 1829 to 1835 is shown in the following table. A rough guide to each builder's importance is the tonnage built by the firm over the seven years and registered at Liverpool.

It can be seen that many of the twenty-four builders listed in the table were very small contributers to the local output of new ships. For example, of the twenty-four builders named, ten have only one vessel listed against them over the seven years whilst another four have only two vessels. Of the seven leading firms in existence in 1805 only one appears to be a going concern in 1829, that of Humble and Hurry, who seem to have taken on Milcrest as an additional partner; two more firms also reorganised their partnerships and continued in a different form, Mottershead and Hutchinson becoming Mottershead while Heyes and Fisher and Company became John and Roger Fisher. Four other firms were no longer in existence, i.e. Rathbone and Company, Hind and Son, P. Quirk and Leather and Company. The firm of Grayson, listed in 1805, was not responsible for any registrations in the years 1829 to 1835, but in 1830 and 1835 one Mathew Clover built vessels and he may have been the person who was in the partnership that formed the present day firm of Grayson, Rollo and Clover. The Grayson family thus appears once again, its connexion with shipbuilding not having been severed by the death of the earlier Grayson as a result of a duel fought in 1806.

In 1835 the leading builders appear to have been Thomas Royden, Clarke and Nickson, Mottershead and Heyes, Humble, Hurry and Milcrest, John Wilson and Bland and Chaloner. In the 1850 enquiry into the bad state of the local shipbuilding industry some of the builders listed in the above table gave evidence, including Robert Clarke (of Clarke and Nickson), Thomas Royden, Mr. Humble (of Humble, Hurry and Milcrest), John Dawson, Mathew Clover and Joseph Steel. Michael Humble stated that the municipal dock building policy was a major factor in his firm's decision to give up shipbuilding, this policy resulted in short leases of land to builders and the consequent insecurity of tenure that this brought about. Robert Clarke (formerly of Clarke and Nickson) stated that he had been moved from his premises three times and that the removals cost him £3,000. Given the growth of traffic at the port, the dock building policy was the more rational use of resources. The technical developments in shipping in the late nineteenth century meant that more room was needed for building operations and this was to be had on the other side of the river. At any rate specialist shipbuilding areas were springing up on the Clyde,

TABLE XVI

THE TONNAGE OF NEW VESSELS BUILT REGISTERED AT LIVERPOOL DISTINGUISHING BY YEAR AND BUILDER

Builder	1829	1830	1831	1832	1833	1834	1835	Total
Clarke and Nickson	365	300	694	–	462	–	416	2,237
Thomas Royden	765	292	461	183	523	909	575	3,708
John Steel	–	–	378	–	489	216	747	1,830
Mottershead and Heyes	377	449	53	436	193	628	79	2,215
James Gordon	–	–	–	–	–	271	608	879
Humble, Hurry & Milcrest	389	–	340	–	469	498	983	2,679
Cabel and Jas. Smith	552	–	–	–	–	–	–	552
John Dawson	36	–	145	234	–	228	245	888
Bland and Chaloner	902	334	–	–	–	–	–	1,236
John Wilson	510	175	302	418	–	630	449	2,484
J. and R. Fisher	374	433	–	–	330	–	–	1,137
John and Wm. Taggert	66	–	–	–	–	–	–	66
Jas. Smith	–	304	–	460	–	–	–	764
Jas Moffat	–	–	–	–	28	–	–	28
Mathew Glover	–	271	–	–	–	–	363	634
Pearson and Melling	–	29	–	–	–	58	–	87
Wm. Jones	–	65	–	–	–	–	–	65
Joseph Steel and Co.	–	–	–	188	–	–	–	188
Peter Craigie	–	11	–	–	–	–	–	11
Bannister	–	26	–	–	–	–	–	26
P. Chaloner	–	191	168	196	–	298	602	1,455
T. J. & W. Russel	–	27	–	–	–	–	256	283
Wm. Dickinson	–	–	–	–	–	–	855	855
Ormondy Steel Co.	–	–	–	331	–	–	–	331
	4,336	2,907	2,541	2,446	2,494	3,736	6,178	

at Tyneside and at Birkenhead, and the local industry became relatively less important as steam and iron came in. It was preferable that docks and warehouses should be on the Liverpool side of the river to facilitate the movement of goods in and out of Liverpool's industrial hinterland. The firm of Sir Thomas Royden struggled on at the Liverpool side of the river until 1899 when the last ship to be launched in Liverpool went down the slipway. By this time the prosperity of the port was firmly based in shipowning and trade. Shipbuilding was a matter of history.

V

The early development of steam navigation in Britain has been often described. Progress at first was slow, and though Symington and Miller had met with considerable practical success as far back as 1788 it was not until 1812 that Bell, though not able to prosper himself, achieved enough to convince others that steamers could be a commercial proposition. For some time the Clyde had a predominance in steamboat building and operation.

On Merseyside similar experiments had little immediate result and it was only after 1820 that a local engineer, William Laird, emerged to attract attention to his merits as a marine engineer.[16] By 1815 local shipowners had shown little, if any, interest in steam boats. The development elsewhere had been entirely of vessels engaged on river or canal work and the engines were too primitive to think in terms of applying steam engines to vessels engaged on the deep sea routes. What potentially useful function could the early steam vessels perform for the Port of Liverpool? There were two spheres in which they could be of immediate use, as ferries across the Mersey and in the towing of sailing vessels that were becalmed or held up by adverse winds. In the *Liverpool Mercury* of 1812 a report appeared concerning the building of a vessel on Clydeside, the *Comet*, that was driven by a 12 h.p. steam engine. She was intended to ply on the Clyde between Glasgow, Port Glasgow, Greenock, and Gourock. The same newspaper carried a report on 11 June 1813 in which the success of another of Henry Bell's vessels, the *Clyde*, was reported as being so great that the four stage coaches running between Glasgow and Greenock had been put out of business. Thus, through the medium of the press, the capabilities of steam boats became known to Merseyside shipowners.

It is possible that the first steamboats were seen on the Mersey in 1814 and that they were used on the short runs to Runcorn, Warrington, and the opposite bank of the river. The Register books record the registration of a steam driven vessel for the first time in 1817 but there is plentiful evidence that this, the *Prince Regent*, was not the first to be used. In the autumn of 1815, Mr. Egerton Smith, the proprietor of the *Liverpool Mercury*, wrote a series of letters in his own newspaper, strongly urging local shipowners to use steam vessels for towing sailing ships out to sea when a north west wind was blowing. In some instances adverse winds kept vessels in dock for several weeks, bringing a large element of uncertainty regarding times of departure and arrival of goods in foreign trade. In a letter of September 1815 he stated that the *Runcorn Packet* had been becalmed and the Runcorn steamboat towed her for ten miles. Mr. Smith's advice did not fall on stony ground for in 1816 another newspaper report stated that the *Harlequin* was towed out to sea by 'one of the steam ferryboats'.

It seems that by the beginning of 1816 there was a ferryboat service from Liverpool to the opposite bank of the river. Whether or not this was the Runcorn steamboat is not clear, but in 1816 the Ellesmere and Chester Canal Company initiated a steamboat service to run from Ellesmere Port, the end of the canal connexion with Chester, to Liverpool. In June the first vessel undertook an experimental trip from Liverpool to Ellesmere and was a resounding success. Thus, by 1817 there was at least one steamboat running from Runcorn to Liverpool and two Mersey ferryboats, one of which belonged to the Ellesmere & Chester Canal Company. It may be that the omission of the vessels from the Register books is because they were considered too novel to be registered as vessels that would undertake deep sea voyages and they were treated as boats engaged solely on canals and rivers. In March 1817 the Tranmere Ferry Steam Packet proprietors announced that a new vessel, the *Etna*, would commence a ferry service from Liverpool to Tranmere on 10 April 1817. The *Etna* does not appear to have been registered and her unusual design may have had something to do with this, as she was really two vessels joined together by beams.

In 1817 two steam vessels were registered. The first was the *Prince Regent* of fifty-eight tons, owned by a group of owners from Runcorn, who included a school master, an innkeeper, a cabinet maker, a waiter, a butcher and a seaman. The second vessel was the *Duke of Wellington*, of fifty-nine tons, also owned by a group of shareholders from Widnes and Runcorn. This is probably the vessel referred to in a report in the *Liverpool Courier* of 3 July 1819.

'The Perfection to which the navigation of steamboats has been carried, and the celerity with which they sail, will be evidenced by a history of the voyage of one of the Runcorn steam packets on Sunday last. The *Duke of Wellington* steamer left Runcorn at four o'clock in the morning and arrived at this port at seven. She sailed hence with passengers about eleven and landed them at Runcorn. She departed from Runcorn for Warrington, where she arrived at two o'clock. She left it again at half past two for Runcorn, where she landed her passengers and, having taken in a fresh cargo, sailed for Liverpool and arrived here at half past seven in the evening. The whole distance she sailed in the course of the day was upwards of eighty miles, a distance, we imagine, which no vessel ever performed in the same time on this river.'

Thus steamboats were to be seen on the Mersey by 1820, and though the total tonnage of such vessels was an insignificant proportion of the total tonnage of shipping at the port their importance is not to be judged in this light. They provided a degree of reliability in communication by water which had previously been missing and started the first tightening up of business communications which ultimately manifested itself in the fixed times of sailings and arrivals of the Conference liners. Immediately, this very reliability showed itself in an increase in the population living on the bank of the river opposite to Liverpool. After 1820 the steam-driven vessel began to give Liverpool more regular communications with areas farther afield than Birkenhead and Runcorn. This process had begun in 1819 when the *Robert Bruce* began regular sailings to Glasgow, a voyage of thirty hours. This was a Glasgow-owned vessel; as yet the Liverpool merchants showed little or no interest in steam which had little to offer them on the long ocean runs, although the arrival in 1819 of the *Savanah* from New York caused a stir because of the fact that she had been assisted by a steam engine on part of the trip. The main developments between 1820 and 1835 were in the coasting trades and the Irish trade. On 17 May 1821 the *Cambria* was launched. She was owned by John Jackson, Samuel Parkes and James Owen, all of Liverpool and none of them shipowners or merchants of any substance. The *Cambria* was used to open a regular service from Liverpool to Bagilt in North Wales. In 1822 Jackson and Owen joined forces with a large number of shipbuilders, including some of the more important merchants, to finance the building of the *Albion*, a steam driven vessel of 102 tons which was used on the Liverpool–Menai Straits run. The register implies that these shareholders were not members of a joint company but ordinary shareholders in a vessel that was operated by managing owners elected on their behalf, possibly Jackson and Parkes. Though the *Albion* and *Cambria* both carried passengers to and from North Wales, grain was a staple of this trade route. By 1823 there was a Liverpool–Whitehaven–Dumfries service, but it was in the Irish trade that the innovation of steam shipping was most dramatic.

The cross-channel battle between the first steamship companies opened in 1823 when Charles Wye Williams, a gentleman of Liverpool, acting on behalf of a large number of Irish investors, asked Thomas Wilson, a Liverpool shipbuilder, to build him a steamship for service on the Liverpool–Dublin run. In 1822 the *City of Dublin*, of 207 tons, was launched at Wilson's yard. She was the first vessel of the City of Dublin Steam Packet Company. In 1824 the Dublin Liverpool Steam Navigation Company came into being, the proprietors including William Dixon and William Potter, well known Liverpool merchants, and Joseph and Jonathan Pim, Quakers of Dublin. This company launched the *Liffey*, the *Mersey* and the *Commerce*. The City of Dublin Steam Packet Company added the *Hibernia* and *Shamrock* to their fleet and a fierce struggle developed between the two companies. In February 1826 the Dublin Liverpool Steam Navigation Company sold out to the triumphant City of Dublin Company, competition having been so fierce that the former company could not continue at the level to which rates had dropped. Between 1825 and 1835 steamship companies operating in the Irish and coastal trades multiplied. In 1824 owners joined forces with a group of Irishmen to promote the Liverpool Belfast Steam Navigation Company. In the following year the Mona & Liverpool Steam Packet Company registered the *Mona* at Liverpool, whilst the *Lee* of 201 tons was registered in the name of the Cork & Liverpool Steam Navigation Company. Then followed the registration of vessels by the Liverpool & Newry Steam Navigation Company (1826), the St. George Steam Packet Company (1826), the Liverpool & Dundalk Steam Navigation Company (1826) the Liverpool & Londonderry Steam Navigation Company (1827) and the Liverpool Steam Navigation Company (1828). Between 1828 and 1835 a further twenty-four steamships were registered at Liverpool by owners other than the companies listed above, many of them small vessels for the coasting trade.

Most of the companies mentioned were small by present-day standards, owning at the most three or four steamers, often only one. The men behind these companies can be identified from an examination of the Shipping Registers, people such as Joseph Robinson Pim, a Quaker of Dublin, Charles Wye Williams, of Liverpool and Dublin,

Sir John Tobin of Liverpool, William Heap Hutchinson of Liverpool, William Fawcett, civil engineer of Liverpool. Unfortunately, with the exception of William Fawcett, little is known of these men or their motives when investing in a new form of transport.[17] The Irish trade was an important one both from the point of view of provisions and passengers to and from England. The steam vessels brought a reliability in travel to Ireland that must have had beneficial effects on the Irish economy. Were these early entrepreneurs very shrewd men who saw early on the possibilities of steam vessels when others neglected them, or were they men who invested in what was, from the outset, an obviously profitable investment? The spate of company formations suggests that the application of steam propulsion in this trade did present obvious attractions, yet the very presence of so many companies brought profits down and priced some firms out of business. This does not invalidate the view that the Irish trade presented obvious attractions to investors in steamships, it merely reflects the fact that competitive forces take time to establish a level of normal profits.

What can be said in conclusion? The picture revealed by the statistics of the shipping registered at the port of Liverpool substantiates the more general claim made about the structure of British industry at the time, namely that business units were mainly in the form of the sole trader and partnership. The joint stock company form of organisation had made relatively little progress in the shipping industry by 1835. This is understandable given the scale of operations. The fact that the overwhelming majority of ships were owned by merchants meant that shipowning as a business in itself was not likely to flourish, the exception being the steamship lines, which were most common in the Irish trade. The cost of a small wooden sailing ship would be well within the means of a single merchant or partnership of merchants. At this time the purely technological developments that necessitated large amounts of money beyond the means of the partnership were almost entirely in the realm of canal and railway building. The source of long-term capital for the shipping industry was almost entirely local, mainly from trading profits, whilst short-term capital came from the usual sources such as the Bill of Exchange. The progress in the development of marine engines and iron-framed vessels ultimately meant that more capital was needed for the purchase of a ship and this in turn meant the raising of capital by the joint stock company method. In the sixties the large shipowning company became more common, a process that was helped by changes in the law regarding limited liability and the greater liquidity of investments in shares provided by the parallel growth of the Stock Exchange. These developments ultimately brought about the separation of risk-taking and management, functions that the early Liverpool shipowners combined. Even so, quite late on in the nineteenth century, many Liverpool shipping companies still operated as partnerships.[18]

Many other questions regarding the port's shipping in the period 1815–35 are left unanswered. How competitive were freight rates in a market characterised by many sellers? When did the industry begin the development into the more oligopolistic structure characteristic of the early twentieth century? When did shipowning as a function become widely separated from trading?[19] To what extent did the merchant shipowners have ideas that influenced the designing of ships? It is beyond the scope of this paper to attempt any answers but the laying bare of the structure of the industry from the point of view of the tonnages involved, the sources of shipping and the patterns of ownership is a useful prerequisite to the investigation of these other questions.

(1) A recent study goes some way towards filling the gap; this is Stuart Mountfield's book *Western Gateway—a History of the Mersey Docks and Harbour Board* (1965).

(2) 26 Geo. III Cap. 80. Mr. R. C. Jarvis has written extensively on port records and it was his article 'Liverpool Statutory Register of Merchant Ships' that first drew my attention to these documents. See *Transactions of the Historic Society of Lancashire and Cheshire*, Vol. 105 (1953). Regrettably, the work by Mr. R. Craig and Mr. Jarvis, *Liverpool Registry of Merchant Ships*, published by the Chetham Society, which discusses the situation in 1786 and a representative period thereafter, only appeared after this paper went to press.

(3) For detailed description of the limited control of owners over ships' masters see R. Davis, *The Rise of the English Shipping Industry* (1962), Chapter V.

(4) T. Baines, *A History of the Commerce and Town of Liverpool* (1852), p. 590.

(5) T. Baines, *op. cit.*, p. 569.

(6) Rostow, Gayer and Schartz, *Growth and Fluctuations in the British Economy, 1790 to 1830* (1953), Vol. I, p. 110.

(7) 'An Account of the number and tonnage of ships belonging to the Principal Ports of the North of England', Parliamentary Papers, 1833, Vol. 1., p. 722.

(8) Most of the British tonnage entered inwards was registered at Liverpool rather than at other British ports. See *Liverpool Customs Bills of Entry* for records of ships entering inwards. Extant copies for some of the years 1829–35 are in H.M. Customs Library, King's Beam House, London.

(9) The basis of the calculations giving rise to the figures in Table IV is the same as that adopted in the earlier period. The official figures state that the tonnage on the Register at Liverpool in 1832 was 165,979; the figure for total tonnage in each year is again arrived at by adding or subtracting the relevant number of annual totals of net accretions to the Liverpool Register.

(10) For a detailed examination of profits in the shipping industry during the seventeenth and eighteenth centuries see R. Davies, *op. cit.*, Chapter XVII.

(11) One of the earliest documented Liverpool instances of a purely shipowning partnership is that of Thomas Harrison and Richard Williamson, who in 1836

were shareholders in the *Tom Tough*, a vessel used for carrying wine from France. See F. E. Hyde, *Shipping Enterprise and Management 1830–1939; Harrisons of Liverpool* (1966), Chapter I.

(12) For a detailed analysis of the occupations and residences of shipowners see F. Neal, *Investment in Liverpool shipping 1815 to 1835* (M. A. Thesis, Liverpool 1962).

(13) The classification 'Northern Counties' includes Cumberland, Northumberland, Yorkshire, Durham, and Lancashire other than Merseyside.

(14) See R. Davis, *op. cit.*, p. 374.

(15) G. S. Graham, 'The Ascendancy of the Sailing Ship 1850 to 1885', *Econ. Hist. Review*, Vol. 9, p. 80.

(16) For an account of the use of a steam boat on the Sankey canal in 1797 see J. R. Harris, 'The Early Steam Engine on Merseyside', *Trans. Historic Soc. of Lancashire and Cheshire* (1954), p. 115.

(17) For a history of the company of Fawcett, Preston and Co. see H. White, *Fossets* (privately published, 1958).

(18) For instance, it was as late as 1884 that Thomas and James Harrison, with their partners, transferred their shipping interests to a limited company, the Charente Steam Ship Company.

(19) For the relationship between shipowning and merchanting in the cotton and timber trades, see D. M. Williams's essay below, and his recent article 'The Liverpool Timber Trade', *Business History VIII*, (1966), pp. 103–17.

CHAPTER SEVEN

Liverpool Merchants and the Cotton Trade 1820–1850

D. M. WILLIAMS

I

OUR KNOWLEDGE of merchanting and commerce in Liverpool in the first half of the nineteenth century is surprisingly slight. Even in the case of the cotton trade, rightly by virtue of its size and importance the best documented of the port's trades, there are remarkable gaps in our understanding. The eighteenth-century origins of the trade, its dramatic expansion after 1780, the evolution of the cotton market, the emergence of the specialist broker as the lynch pin on which sales depended, and the beginnings of future trading, have all been subjects of scholarly study,[1] yet many features of the trade and its organisation still await research. One such feature is the structure and character of that section of the merchant body which imported cotton into Liverpool. Very little is known about the Liverpool cotton merchant; true the names of Cropper, Brown, Baring and Collman are familiar enough and there is Dr. Marriner's excellent study of the Rathbones and their trading operations,[2] but of the cotton merchants as a group, or as individual entrepreneurs, our information is really superficial. We do not know who the cotton merchants were or how many importers were active in the trade. Similarly, the importer's scale of operation and the reaction of the merchant body to the tremendous growth of the trade are issues of doubt. The purpose of this short paper is to remedy these deficiencies in our knowledge through a study of Liverpool's cotton merchants in the first half of the nineteenth century with particular reference to the period after 1820. The choice of the year 1820 as an opening date was influenced by two factors, namely, the regaining of stability in the trade following the dislocations of the war and of the immediate post-war period and the availability of source material. It is proposed to consider first the degree of concentration prevailing in the cotton trade between 1820 and 1839 and then to examine more generally the changing role and function of the individual merchant over the slightly longer period from 1820 to 1850.

182

II

The period 1820 to 1850 was one of immense expansion in the cotton trade. Within thirty years imports of cotton into Liverpool increased threefold, from under half a million bales in 1820 to well over a million and a half bales in 1850. This huge increase in imports is revealed in Table I, which shows the total receipts of cotton at Liverpool subdivided into the various sources of supply and the total imports of the country as a whole.[3] Comparing the Liverpool and the national totals, the dominance of the port in this particular trade is striking. In every year over 80 per cent of the country's supplies of this vital raw material came through Liverpool and in some

TABLE I

RECEIPTS OF COTTON AT LIVERPOOL AND TOTAL BRITISH IMPORTS OF COTTON
1820–50 (in bales)

Date	U.S.A.	E.I.	Liverpool Egypt	Brazil	Other	Total	G. Britain Total
1820	272,574	7,668	—	161,628	16,823	458,693	571,651
21	240,257	3,273	—	70,060	54,673	367,673	491,658
22	274,832	1,613	—	67,106	95,380	439,031	533,444
23	390,914	13,684	—	84,598	58,797	557,993	688,797
24	265,413	13,863	28,170	94,460	55,722	457,628	540,092
25	419,490	15,060	71,486	140,057	82,820	728,913	820,883
26	371,143	11,573	36,767	35,765	35,366	490,614	581,950
27	579,134	12,902	12,524	93,373	30,590	728,523	894,063
28	403,255	15,076	19,636	121,586	49,367	608,920	749,552
29	422,109	17,453	22,259	128,707	39,645	630,173	746,707
1830	570,808	12,276	11,023	161,225	38,538	793,870	871,487
31	560,181	33,601	25,019	138,312	32,511	789,624	903,367
32	581,695	39,778	32,196	104,760	18,489	777,278	902,322
33	612,031	52,694	2,450	123,688	43,329	834,192	930,216
34	664,023	47,216	1,886	94,598	29,203	836,926	951,034
35	700,359	54,560	26,255	106,071	50,785	938,030	1,081,253
36	708,994	103,248	21,397	143,761	46,233	1,023,633	1,201,374
37	769,408	69,684	25,817	97,701	48,321	1,010,931	1,175,975
38	1,066,790	60,592	22,820	94,743	74,287	1,312,212	1,428,600
39	787,900	82,800	17,029	66,749	57,300	1,011,778	1,116,200
1840	1,155,270	92,643	34,594	64,035	53,984	1,400,528	1,599,500
41	843,755	153,396	35,332	101,192	28,919	1,162,584	1,344,000
42	931,612	165,026	17,340	80,662	22,620	1,217,260	1,392,800
43	1,291,807	108,729	45,649	97,004	19,679	1,562,868	1,744,100
44	1,028,811	145,165	37,551	116,333	28,018	1,355,878	1,681,600
45	1,370,455	86,888	64,127	107,051	11,549	1,640,070	1,855,700
46	933,833	49,521	60,767	77,998	10,578	1,132,694	1,243,700
47	809,809	114,730	21,712	113,747	8,099	1,068,147	1,232,700
48	1,284,689	133,168	27,840	99,467	9,948	1,555,112	1,740,000
49	1,342,771	106,127	70,117	168,046	7,070	1,694,181	1,905,400
1850	1,084,644	198,138	83,052	152,498	3,820	1,522,152	1,749,300

years such as 1837 the proportion reached 90 per cent. Both sets of figures reveal an upward trend, national imports rising some 300 per cent in the thirty years and Liverpool's imports by over 400 per cent. Only in 1839 and 1846–47 is there any major departure from this movement and this was entirely due to poor crops in the U.S.A., the smaller quantities imported in 1826, 1828 and 1841 being the result of exceedingly large imports in the preceding years which allowed unusually large stocks to be accumulated.[4] Liverpool's supplies of cotton were drawn from the U.S.A., Brazil, Egypt and the East Indies. Supplies from other sources, mainly the West Indies, the Mediterranean and later Australia fell considerably over the period and were negligible by 1850. United States' cotton dominated Liverpool's imports of cotton, averaging 75 per cent of the total, and rose from around a quarter of a million bales to well over a million bales in the thirty-year period. Imports from Brazil enjoyed no such increase, fluctuating in absolute terms, generally between 90,000 and 160,000 bales, but declining continuously in relative terms from over 30 per cent of total imports in 1820 to around 10 per cent in 1850. The East Indies on the other hand rose from insignificance to a figure of nearly 200,000 bales (13 per cent) in 1850. Even more spectacular was the growth of supplies from Egypt. Imports from this source, unknown in Liverpool before 1823, represented 6 per cent of total imports in 1850. Overall the trend was one of great expansion. Braithwaite Poole, one of the more accurate commentators on Liverpool's commerce, calculated that of the port's total trade valued at £50m. in 1850, cotton accounted for some £20m.[5]

In seeking to enquire who handled these immense amounts of cotton and how the merchant body responded and reacted to the very rapid increase in imports, the greatest problem facing the historian is that of source material. What is required is not a collection of business-house records but a comprehensive source which provides full and detailed information on the import trade of the port and on the activities of all merchants engaged in import operations. These requirements are admirably fulfilled by the Customs Bills of Entry, a source which has been surprisingly neglected by both economic and business historians. The Customs Bills of Entry were a daily publication published by the Customs' authorities for the convenience of the merchant community. Over the period 1820 to 1850 there were some slight changes in the form of presentation but the content of each daily Bill remained the same. Each Bill contained a list of all vessels arriving in Liverpool and particulars of the port of registration, the tonnage, crew, master, dock, ship's agent in Liverpool, and last port of clearance, together with a full account of all merchandise carried and to whom it was consigned. Apart from these 'Ships' Reports' as they were termed, summaries of imports and exports, and of articles entering and released from the bonded warehouses, appeared in every issue, as did information regarding ships entered outwards, ships cleared outwards and ships loading. It is, however, only the ships' reports which are of value in a study of merchanting for it is they which contain data on imports relating to the individual merchant.

The search for empirical evidence on concentration in the cotton trade and the changing function of the cotton merchant took the form of a detailed examination of the ships' reports for four years taken at ten-yearly intervals in the period 1820–50. The absence of the Bills of Entry for the year 1840 necessitated the use of those for 1839.[6] For each of the years 1820, 1830, 1839 and 1850 a list was compiled of all merchants who during the year either imported cotton or acted as a ship's agent to a vessel carrying cotton as part of its cargo. The date of every appearance of these merchants in the Bills of Entry was noted, special notation being used if the reference was to cotton being imported or to a vessel carrying nothing but cotton. From the resulting lists, four in all, it was possible to see from the hundreds of merchants engaged in the trade, who were the most important. It was not at this stage possible to establish those who were importing the largest amounts of cotton (although it may often be a reasonable inference that a merchant who imported cotton on fifty occasions during a year, imported more in absolute terms than one who imported cotton on ten occasions), but an examination of the lists did reveal those importers who were of little significance in the trade. Merchants who imported cotton on fewer than five occasions during a year could be safely disregarded, for even if on each occasion the amount imported had been the entire cargo of a vessel, their annual total would have been under 1 per cent of the quantity imported for the port as a whole.

For all merchants who imported cotton on more than five occasions in a year (and in any marginal case where there was an element of doubt) a chart was constructed of all the references to each individual in the Bills of Entry. Each chart noted the date of the reference, the commodity or commodities imported and the quantity, the port of origin, and the name, tonnage and port of registration of the vessel. The compilation of these charts, some two hundred in all, many of which contained over one hundred references, was a lengthy procedure, but once completed a very clear picture of each merchant's activities could be seen. His scale of operation, the commodities he dealt in, the markets he traded with, and his performance of the function of ship's agent were but a few of the facts which were visible. More important still, the quantities of each commodity that the merchant imported could be totalled up and set against the port's total import of that commodity. It thus became possible to discover to what extent the cotton trade was concentrated into the hands of a group or groups of importers. This object was attained by examining the combined imports of the largest importers in each year. For each of the years studied the thirty largest importers of cotton were selected and subdivided into sub-groups of ten, the order of size being the guiding factor. The imports of each group were then added together and compared with the total imports of cotton in that year. As the degree of concentration is best expressed as a proportion of total imports, both absolute and percentage measures were used at this stage of the analysis.[7]

One further point remains to be mentioned before presenting the results of the analysis. In theory the comprehensive survey described above would account for all imports of cotton, i.e. every bale of cotton imported would be allocated to an individual merchant, but in practice such a complete breakdown was not possible. The ship's reports appearing in the Bills of Entry were made up from ship's manifests which embodied a list of the vessel's cargo and information regarding its markings and consignees. In certain cases, however, the name of the consignee did not appear; instead the phrase, 'to order', or just 'order'. Sometimes this was because the consignee did not wish it to be known that he was importing, but more often it was because the goods were not consigned to any one in particular. The significance of this practice of consigning goods to order is that it prevents the complete division of total imports into the imports of individual merchants, for it is impossible to discover who actually purchased and thus imported goods consigned in this manner. The proportion of cotton imports consigned to 'order' remained under 20 per cent of total imports in the first three years examined and hence is not sufficient to invalidate the survey or significantly distort the basic trends which occurred within the group of merchants importing cotton, but in the decade after 1839 the practice of consigning bales to 'order' increased rapidly. By 1850 around 60 per cent of total imports of cotton were consigned in this manner.[8] With over half of total cotton imports being untraceable any attempt to trace the degree of concentration prevailing in 1850 would be futile, hence the analysis of concentration was confined to the years 1820, 1830 and 1839. It was, however, possible for the year 1850 to draw up a list of the leading thirty importers which could be used for the examination of changing merchant functions where the quantification of imports was not required.

III

The dominant position occupied by the cotton trade in the

commerce of the port, and the importance of the Liverpool cotton trade to the nation's industrial economy, have quite naturally led, in the past, to the view that the majority of Liverpool's merchants devoted their commercial energies to the importation of cotton. This view is correct only in so far that the number of merchants who imported some cotton during the course of any one year ran into hundreds. Table II illustrates this.

TABLE II

TOTAL NUMBER OF IMPORTERS OF COTTON SUBDIVIDED BY FREQUENCY OF IMPORT
IN THE YEARS 1820, 1830 AND 1839

	Total number of merchants importing cotton on some occasion	On one occasion	On two occasions	On three to five occasions	On six and more occasions
1820	607	318	77	92	120
1830	318	153	40	47	78
1839	341	155	58	41	87

It is, plain, nevertheless, that the total figure of cotton importers gives an entirely erroneous impression, for in each year around half of them imported cotton on one occasion only, and between 70 and 80 per cent of the total number of merchants fell into the category of importing on five occasions or under. Clearly the majority of these merchants were individually of little account in the trade although taken collectively they were of some importance. The information which can be drawn from Table II is limited, as the accounting unit is 'occasions on which cotton was imported', and quite obviously the amount imported on any one occasion could vary from one to a thousand bales, but the table does throw some light on the nature of the trade.

Of most interest is the high number of (if the term may be used) 'occasional importers of cotton', and a striking feature is the fall in the total number of merchants engaged in the trade from 607 in 1820 to 318 in 1830 and 341 in 1839. This was due to several factors. Firstly there was a larger number of small operators in business in 1820; secondly, the dominance of the U.S.A. as a supplier of cotton was by no means as great in 1820 as in 1830 and in subsequent years, and thirdly, perhaps of lesser importance, there was a change in the attitude held by Liverpool's mercantile classes towards the trade. In 1820 the growth of the cotton trade was still viewed with wonder and amazement, and even at this late date a desire to share in its prosperity prevailed in all sections of the merchant body, and amongst men not fully engaged in merchanting. An enthusiasm similar to that which the slave trade had inspired fifty years earlier, when 'he who could not send a bale sent a bandbox',[9] existed until the need for specialised knowledge made apparent the futility of haphazard and amateur participation in the trade.

The degree of hypothesis which analysis based on Table II must inherently contain, prevents any definite conclusions being formulated. Concrete evidence on concentration requires the consideration of merchants in the light of actual quantities of cotton imported. Table IIIA shows the amount imported by the thirty leading importers of cotton subdivided into three groups, I, II, and III in order of size, together with the total receipts of cotton at Liverpool and the amount consigned to order. Table IIIB gives exactly the same information expressed in percentage terms.

TABLE IIIA

IMPORTS OF THE THIRTY LEADING COTTON MERCHANTS AT LIVERPOOL IN THE YEARS 1820, 1830, and 1839 (in bales)

	1820	1830	1839
Total receipts at Liverpool	458,693	793,870	1,011,778
Amount imported by Group I	109,272	259,156	368,595
Amount imported by Group II	48,020	105,107	153,351
Amount imported by Group III	24,794	58,385	64,228
Total imports of the thirty leading importers (Groups I, II and III)	182,086	422,648	586,174
Consigned to 'order'	89,935	117,403	161,911

TABLE IIIB

IMPORTS OF THE THIRTY LEADING COTTON MERCHANTS AT LIVERPOOL IN THE YEARS 1820, 1830 AND 1839 EXPRESSED AS A PERCENTAGE OF TOTAL IMPORTS

	1820	1830	1839
Total receipts at Liverpool	100	100	100
Amount imported by Group I	23·82	32·64	36·44
Amount imported by Group II	10·47	13·23	15·16
Amount imported by Group III	5·40	7·35	6·35
Total imports of the thirty leading importers. (Groups I, II and III)	39·69	53·22	57·95
Consigned to 'order'	19·60	14·78	16·00

The tables show that in 1820 the thirty leading importers handled 39·69 per cent of total imports. An examination of the appendix, which shows the imports of each individual merchant, reveals, not surprisingly, that most of the leading importers were dealing in United States' cotton. Nine members of Group I, eight of Group II and six of Group III fell into this category, the exceptions in each case importing their cotton from South America, mainly Brazil. By 1830 the imports of the thirty leading merchants had risen to form 53·22 per cent of total imports. Group I's imports rose to 260,000 bales (32·64 per cent) a rise which exceeded that of Groups II and III. Once again only one merchant in Group I was not engaged in the United States trade, and the presence of but one Brazilian merchant in each of Groups II and III, reflected the relative decline in importance of this market as a supplier of cotton; for while imports from the U.S.A. had trebled over the decade 1820–30, the Brazilian figure had just remained constant. The year 1839 saw the upward trend of the previous decade continuing, although at a slower pace, the share of the thirty leading importers in total imports rising to 57·95 per cent. Group I's imports rose to 36·44 per cent of total imports, and Group II's to 15·16 per cent but Group III's share fell from 7·35 per cent to 6·35 per cent. In absolute terms, however, the imports of all three groups showed an increase on the 1830 figure. A survey of the markets traded with again shows the changing sources of cotton supplies, United States' merchants completely monopolising Group I while the Brazilian trade could only muster one merchant in Group II and one in Group III. Significantly one East Indian importer appeared in the ranks of Group II.

IV

If the entire period covered by the tables is examined, certain trends are plainly visible. Most outstanding is the fact that in the twenty years from 1820 to 1839, a period of very rapid expansion, the cotton trade became more and more concentrated into the hands of a small group of merchants. The amount handled by the thirty leading importers rose greatly in both absolute and percentage terms. Whereas they had controlled under 40 per cent of the trade in 1820, in 1839 their share was nearer 60 per cent, a remarkably high proportion when one remembers that at this date 16 per cent of total imports were untraceable through being consigned to 'order'. Hence, in 1839 almost three-quarters of traceable cotton imports were handled by this small group of thirty importers. The increasing dominance of the cotton trade by a small number of importers is all the more apparent if the figures of total receipts are compared with the total imports of the leading importers. Between 1820 and 1830 total imports of cotton increased by some 345,000 bales, and between 1830 and 1839 by 218,000 bales. Imports of the thirty leading importers over the corresponding periods rose by 240,000 bales and 164,000 bales. In other words over 70 per cent of the increments were being handled by the leading merchants. Table II showed that the number of merchants actually importing cotton was subject to a great decline between 1820 and 1830, and that the 1839 figure was only slightly higher than that of 1830. Thus up to 1839 the increase in imports was not met by a greater number of importers but by an expansion in the leading merchants' scale of operation. This expansion was not uniform but was geared towards the larger importers as evidenced by the increasing proportion of total imports handled by the leading thirty merchants. Even within this group of leading merchants the gap between the large merchant and the small merchant widened. This can be seen most fully by looking at the scale of operations of individual merchants as given in the appendix to this article but it is illustrated in Table IV which compares the imports of the three largest and three smallest importers in Groups I, II and III in the years 1820, 1830 and 1839. This small sample reveals the extent to which the large importer of cotton left behind his smaller counterpart between 1820 and 1839.

TABLE IV

COMPARISON OF THE IMPORTS OF THE THREE LARGEST AND THREE SMALLEST IMPORTERS IN GROUPS I, II AND III IN THE YEARS 1820, 1830 AND 1839 (in bales)

	Three Largest Importers		Three Smallest Importers	
1820	Richards A. S.	17,632	da Costa A. J.	2,258
	Brown W. & J. & Co.	12,696	Ewart, Myers & Co.	2,209
	Alston, Eason & Co.	12,219	Haworth & Co.	2,175
1830	Bolton & Ogden	40,185	Burn J.	5,179
	Brown, W. & J. & Co.	39,448	Barclay & Co.	5,081
	Alston, Finlay & Co.	26,297	Cardwell Bros.	5,043
1839	Molyneux & Witherby	53,122	Dawson, R. L.	4,657
	Brown W. & J. Co.	48,238	Gilliatt W. H. & Co.	4,569
	Humphreys & Biddle	46,018	Rushton J.	4,322

The analysis of the process of concentration in the cotton trade between 1820 and 1839 shows that while the number of merchants in any one year ran into hundreds, a large portion of the trade was handled by a small group of some thirty operators who gained increasing control as they absorbed a larger part of increased imports. Within this group, all merchants increased their scale of operation and the gap between the big importer and the small importer considerably widened. This was very marked; in 1839 the twenty leading importers accounted for over 52 per cent of total imports, while the next leading ten importers accounted for only 6 per cent of the total. Clearly, after 1820 the cotton trade became the preserve of large operators dealing in United States' cotton.

IV

The merchant houses which made up the group of leading importers in each year were of varied form and origin. The greater part were Liverpool-based family firms or simple partnerships often long established in the port and engaged in the cotton trade before, sometimes long before, 1820. Firms such as Rathbones, Bolton and Ogden, Cropper & Co., Isaac Lowe & Co., and Ewart, Myers & Co. fell into this category. Not all importers, however, were Liverpool houses. W. & J. Brown & Co. and Brown, Shipley & Co. were branch houses of the American firm of W. & J. Brown of Baltimore.[10] Baring Bros. was a branch of the London parent firm. A. Dennistoun & Co. had their headquarters in Glasgow, as did Rankin, Gilmour & Co., Pollock, Gilmour & Co. being the parent firm.[11] Gibbs, Bright & Co. was an associate house of Anthony Gibbs & Co. of London, and the firm of Humphreys & Biddle who were active in the late 1830s were the Liverpool agents of the American speculator Nicholas Biddle. Regrettably, the absence of merchant house records and the present level of research into Liverpool's commerce make it impossible to form any real conclusions on the composition of the port's merchant body, but it may reasonably be suggested that as the cotton trade, and particularly the United States' section of the trade, expanded and became more sophisticated in its organisation and finance, the structure of the merchant body engaged in the trade became more complex as important operators both in the United States and in London and Glasgow set up branch, associate or agency houses in Liverpool.

The absence of merchant house records also prevents any positive pronouncements being made on the nature of the import business undertaken by the leading importers in the cotton trade. Imports were made on a commisssion basis or on own account, but it is not wholly clear which form of business predominated or whether importers engaged in one or both forms of business. N. S. Buck in his pioneer work on the organisation of Anglo-American commerce in the first half of the nineteenth century concluded that most cotton was imported on commission by merchants acting on behalf of others but that there was a general tendency for the merchant who acted on his own account to become more important.[12] Witnesses before the Select Committee on Commerce, Manufacturers and Shipping in 1833 giving evidence on the Liverpool cotton trade stated that cotton was chiefly imported on commission but that importing on own account was increasing.[13] This was certainly the predominant form of business by the mid-century, when the coming of the steam packet and the increased speed with which market information was communicated caused a decline in consignment business generally. The conservative, cautious Rathbones found it increasingly difficult to obtain sufficient commission business from the late 1840s, for most Liverpool houses were by that date importing solely on own account. In the twenties and thirties, however, it would appear that most merchants conducted a mixed business, partly receiving consignments on a commission basis and partly on own account, the proportion of each type of business depending on the state of the market, contacts overseas, and the individual merchant's spirit of risk, commission business being safer but less profitable than business on own account.

V

Whatever the form of merchant house operating and whether the import business prosecuted was on own account or on a commission basis, a common feature of all cotton importers in the years after 1820 was that their scale of operation increased. An important feature which must be considered is how this increased scale of operation affected the operator's other commercial activities; in particular, did the importer as he handled greater and greater amounts of cotton come to devote more and more of his attention to this one operation? In other words, did the large-scale importer of cotton become more specialised both in the sense of importing only cotton or importing only from certain areas, and in the sense that he came to deal specifically in import business and to cease to perform other mercantile functions such as those of exporter, broker, shipowner and ship's agent?

It is by no means an easy matter to discover whether import merchants specialised in terms of commodities dealt in or markets traded with. The use of commercial directories in this respect has long since been regarded as totally unsuitable and registers of trade associations though perhaps less unreliable are open to widespread misinterpretation as it was common practice for a merchant to belong to a variety of associations.[14] Again, there is the problem of definition; while a specialist is clearly a merchant who confines his dealings to one particular commodity or one particular market, what criteria does one use to assess specialisation?

When only a single firm is being examined and the actual records of the firm in question are available, it is possible to consider a variety of criteria before formulating the final evaluation of the degree of specialisation attained. The quantities of commodities imported from various sources, the value of the several branches of the merchant's business, the amount of time and energy devoted to each, and the regularity of trade can all be taken into account. No such comprehensive examination can be made when the merchant body as a whole, or a large number of merchants is being considered. The absence of sufficiently detailed information about each merchant's activities, and the need to establish a set of common criteria necessitates judging import specialisation solely by the quantities of goods imported and the countries traded with. Even the use of this seemingly simple yardstick does, however, present some problems. Extreme cases are straightforward enough, the merchant who imported 20,000 bales of cotton and nothing else was clearly a specialist, and at the other end of the scale the merchant who in the course of a year imported 10,000 bales of cotton, 5,000 tons of timber, 7,000 barrels of flour and quantities of cheese, turpentine, tar, maize, wheat and sugar was equally clearly not a specialist. It is in instances where the merchant's imports do not allow a clear-cut decision to be made that difficulty arises. No common scale can be adopted to help in the balancing of the merchant's imports of one commodity against those of another, for the numerous problems involved in expressing imports in value terms, and the sheer magnitude of the task, render such compilation impracticable. In any event such an exercise would give results which were severely distorted towards more valuable commodities. Again, there is the question of whether specialisation should be assessed by balancing the merchant's imports of one commodity against his imports of any other single commodity, or against his imports of all other commodities taken together. Even if the latter definition is accepted as being the more satisfactory of the two, the weakness of comparing quantities of one commodity against those of others still remains. The presence of this inherent difficulty results in decisions on marginal cases being in the last resort arbitrary judgments.

The examination of the degree to which the thirty leading importers of cotton specialised in importing that commodity took the form of classifying importers into one of four categories according

to the degree of specialisation attained, perfect specialists, near perfect specialists, marginal specialists and non-specialists. The degrees
of specialisation represented by these four classifications are as follows: perfect specialists are merchants who import one commodity
to the exclusion of all others, near-perfect specialists are merchants
who import more than one commodity but whose imports of cotton
completely outshadow all others, marginal specialists are merchants
whose imports of cotton are greater than those of any other commodity but not to the extent that these other commodities are rendered
negligible, and finally, non-specialists are merchants importing a
variety of commodities, no one of which is distinguishable as being
more important than any other. Examples of merchants falling into
each category and the classification of each of the leading importers
are contained in the appendix. An overall view of the degree of specialisation attained by the thirty leading importers of cotton in the
years 1820, 1830 and 1839 is depicted in Table V. If the number of
specialists (i.e. perfect specialists, near-perfect specialists and marginal specialists) is compared with the number of non-specialists in
each year, two features emerge from the table. Firstly, the majority
of merchants were specialising in the importing of cotton, and
secondly, there was little increase or decrease in the number of
specialists between 1820 and 1839. The ratio of specialists to non-
specialists in the years 1820, 1830 and 1839 was 24 to 6, 24 to 6 and
25 to 5 respectively, and within the 'specialist group' the distribution
between perfect, near-perfect and marginal specialists shows no
major change. It would appear then that the period 1820 to 1839, a
period when the scale of operation of leading importers of cotton was
increasingly rapidly, saw no movement towards specialisation in
importing but rather merely the maintenance of the very high
degree of specialisation which already existed in 1820.

TABLE V

DEGREE OF SPECIALISATION ATTAINED BY THE THIRTY LEADING
IMPORTERS OF COTTON OF LIVERPOOL IN THE YEARS 1820, 1830
1839

	Perfect specialists	Near-perfect specialists	Marginal specialists	Non-specialists
1820	2	13	9	6
1830	6	12	6	6
1839	6	13	6	5

As yet, no consideration has been given to specialisation by country or area traded with, as opposed to specialisation by commodity.

However, an analysis of import specialisation by commodity is to a great extent an analysis by country traded with also, for the geographical sources of supply of a commodity are generally strictly limited. The specialist cotton importer must obtain his supplies from the U.S.A., Brazil, the East Indies or Egypt. If he obtains the great bulk of his supplies from one country only he must obviously be a specialist importer both in terms of commodity dealt in, *and* in terms of area traded with. Table VI shows that with insignificant exceptions importers gained their supplies almost entirely from one country only.

The conclusion that the great majority of the leading importers of cotton were specialising in their importing business in importing cotton from one source only (nearly always, as might be expected, the U.S.A.) does, however, require some qualifications. Firstly, it is worth remembering that a small number of importing houses were actually branches of merchant houses centred outside Liverpool, set up specifically to handle imports of cotton. This was true of the

TABLE VI

DEGREE TO WHICH THE THIRTY LEADING IMPORTERS OF COTTON OBTAINED THEIR SUPPLIES OF THE COMMODITY FROM ONE COUNTRY ONLY

	1820	1830	1839
Merchants importing cotton from one country only	25	29	26
Merchants importing over 90% of cotton imports from one country only	5	1	3
Merchants importing under 90% of cotton imports from one country only	—	—	1

near-perfect specialist firm of Humphreys & Biddle which was operating in 1839, and an even better example from the same year is the perfect specialist firm of Purton, Parker & Co. which was set up to take over the business of the Liverpool branch of T. Wilson & Co., which handled cotton imports for the parent firm in London.[15] Secondly, as a study of the appendix will reveal, there was a distinct tendency for the very largest importers of cotton to be non-specialists, so that the ratio of the imports of non-specialists to those of specialist importers is not the same as the ratio of the number of non-specialists to the number of specialists. Thus the proportion of total imports of cotton handled by specialists is less than might be imagined at first sight. Thirdly, it is very important to remember that the conclusion that the majority of the leading cotton importers specialised in the importing of cotton from one area, refers to the leading cotton importers in *any one* year. The pattern of business of the individual firm was frequently changing as market conditions fluctuated and new opportunities presented themselves. Firms might at any time move from one degree of specialisation in cotton to another and occasionally switch from specialisation to non-specialisation. Such movement was constantly occurring, but in each of the representative years chosen in the period 1820 to 1839 the majority of the leading thirty importers of cotton, around 80 per cent in fact, were specialising in importing cotton from one area.

VI

In specialising in importing one commodity from one area the merchant engaging in the cotton trade in the years after 1820 had moved a far cry from the typical merchant of the eighteenth century who tended to be a general merchant with widely spread interests. The interests of the eighteenth-century merchant were diffuse not only in the sense that he traded in many commodities and with many countries, but often also in the sense that he performed a variety of mercantile functions additional to that of importing. While even in the eighteenth century men specialising in providing well-defined services emerged in the fields of banking, insurance, shipowning and general brokerage, many merchants in the late eighteenth century remained men of many parts, importing and exporting, selling and purchasing supplies of goods, owning shares in vessels, acting as ship's agent to vessels docking in his local ports and sometimes dabbling in banking business or the underwriting of vessels and their cargoes. This is in no way to suggest that all merchants performed each of these functions, but simply that the average merchant of the eighteenth century did engage in a wide range of activities. Gradually, however, as the scale of trade increased, as commercial organisation became more intricate and as the need for specialised knowledge became more apparent, the merchant of necessity had to surrender many of the functions which had traditionally been part and parcel of his everyday business to specialist operators, and, in doing, became more of a specialist himself, restricting his dealing to a narrower range of activities. The remaining section of this paper attempts to assess how far the leading importers in the cotton trade had moved in this direction by 1820 and whether the trend towards

specialisation of function continued as the importer's scale of operation expanded over the period 1820 to 1850.

In Liverpool certain functions had by 1820 been generally given
up by virtually all merchants and become solely the province of
specialist operators. The activity normally described as Country
Banking was one such function and a similar development was
apparent in the insurance field. Other functions had been surrendered wholly or partially in some trades but not all. In many import
trades general brokers were taking over the business of selling produce in the Liverpool market, but this trend was most noticeable
and most complete in the cotton trade, where merchants were
almost completely dependent for the disposal of their imports on the
specialist cotton broker, who had provided, from the turn of the
century, the vital link between the Liverpool importer and Manchester manufacturing interests.[16]

In the case of other functions the break was less pronounced and
is less easy to determine. For example, conclusions on the degree to
which importing and exporting were combined by one merchant are
impossible without a close survey of the business records of individual houses. It is to be regretted that there is no general source of
information on exports such as the Bills of Entry provide for imports.
I have not, however, come across any evidence to suggest that importing and exporting were becoming separate functions and I
know of no example of a firm operating only in the import trade or
only in the export trade. On the other hand, examples of merchants
engaging in both functions are legion and it is well worth repeating
the words of a Mr. A. H. Wylie (himself both an importer of cotton
and an exporter of manufactured goods to the U.S.A.), who stated
in evidence before the Select Committee on Commercial Distress
of 1847–48 that, 'the importers of raw materials are generally exporters of manufactured goods'.[17]

One group of operators engaged in the importing of cotton who
most certainly dealt in imports and exports were the merchant
banking houses who figured so prominently amongst the leading
cotton importers throughout the period 1820 to 1850. A. Dennistoun & Co., W. & J. Brown & Co., Baring Bros. & Co., Wildes,
Pickersgill & Co., Reid, Irving & Co., McAlmont Bros, and
Brown Shipley & Co., were all important merchant bankers in the
Anglo-American trade.[18] As such they handled imports and exports
on commission and on own account and performed a host of international banking services, acting as agents, guaranteeing credit,
and financing trade all over the world as well as on the Atlantic
route.

VII

Amongst the other functions undertaken by the merchant banking firms were those of ship's agent and shipowner. These are two functions which can be examined thoroughly and statistically because of the availability of fully comprehensive source material. Information on the performance of the function of ship's agent is to be gained readily from the Bills of Entry, while the Statutory Register of Merchant Shipping so fully utilised by Mr. Neal in an earlier essay provides a clear indication of shipowning interests. The function of the ship's agent, that of looking after a vessel and its interests while the vessel was in port,[19] was a customary function of the eighteenth-century merchant, but by 1820 specialist ships' agents were operating in certain trades, notably the Mediterranean, Baltic, Coastal and South American trades. In other trades the function was still performed by a large number of merchants. Table VII shows that this was certainly true of the majority of importers in the cotton trade.

TABLE VII

PERFORMANCE OF THE FUNCTION OF SHIP'S AGENT AMONGST THE
THIRTY LEADING COTTON IMPORTERS IN THE YEARS 1820, 1830
1839 AND 1850

	Number of Merchants acting as ship's agent on some occasion	Number of merchants not acting as ship's agent
1820	24	6
1830	26	4
1839	28	2
1850	26	4

The table reveals a remarkable level of consistency; in each year more than three-quarters of the leading thirty importers acted as ship's agent on some occasion, and the proportion rose slightly between 1820 and 1839 as importers dealing in S. American cotton declined in importance in the leading group and were replaced by merchants trading with the U.S.A. Knowing that the merchant had surrendered many other functions and that specialists in the business of acting as a ship's agent had appeared in other trades, it may appear surprising that almost all the leading importers of cotton should continue to perform the function. One feature, however, which is revealed by a detailed study of the Bills of Entry, is that whenever importers in the United States' cotton trade acted as ship's agent they invariably had a heavy interest in the cargo of the vessel in question. This would suggest that the performance of the function was very closely allied to that of importing and that the leading cotton merchants looked on it as part of their operations as importers. It remains, nevertheless, somewhat strange that the practice should have been retained and performed so generally in the United States' trade where specialisation of function so often first appeared.

One occasion when an importer always acted as ship's agent was on the arrival in Liverpool of a vessel in which he had a personal interest as a shipowner. Shipowning was for the greater part of the eighteenth century a secondary function of the merchant. Most shipowners were merchants, and conversely most merchants were shipowners.[20] At the beginning of the nineteenth century, a slight difference between trading and shipping interests was beginning to appear,[21] and as the century progressed the specialist shipowner became increasingly more important.[22] There was not, however, and indeed never has been, a complete separation of the two functions of shipowning and importing, and in trades involving bulky low-value commodities the functions were very closely linked; the most outstanding example of this was to be found in the British North American timber trade. In the cotton trade, as Table VIII shows, the majority of the leading importers did not engage in ship owning.

TABLE VIII

NUMBER OF SHIPOWNERS AMONGST THE THIRTY LEADING IMPORTERS OF COTTON IN THE YEARS 1820, 1830, 1839 AND 1850

	Merchants with shipowning interests	Merchants without shipowning interests
1820	9	21
1830	8	22
1839	7	23
1850	15	15

The table shows that in 1820, 1830 and 1839 some two-thirds of the leading importers of cotton were without shipowning interests, and the departure from this trend in 1850 is due not to an increased desire on the part of importers of cotton to own vessels but to the fact that six of the leading importers of cotton in this year also possessed interests in the colonial timber trade where shipowning was the rule.[23] The extent of shipowning interests amongst those importers of cotton who performed the function varied enormously, but whatever the size of the holding, the merchant did not use his ships exclusively for the furtherance of his trading activities. If the information gained from the Registers of Shipping and the Ship's Reports of the Bills of Entry is brought together, it emerges that cotton importer/shipowners were neither shipping all their imports in their own vessels, nor using the vessels solely to carry their own imports. Thus whereas the function of ship's agent was clearly regarded by all cotton importers as ancilliary to importing, in cases where the cotton importer possessed shipowning interests he regarded these in a different light. It seems that shipowning was held to be a business interest in itself, apart from importing, on which returns were to be made from freight charges rather than in the free carriage of imports.

VIII

Viewing the entire range of functions which were customarily performed by the merchant of the eighteenth century it would appear that the typical importer of cotton of the first half of the nineteenth century, that is one of the leading thirty importers, was much more of a specialist. True, all merchants continued to engage in both importing and exporting and nearly all acted as ship's agent at some time in a year. Again, some as international merchant bankers conducted far-ranging financial business, but the functions of country banker, underwriter, and broker had been wholly taken over by specialist operators and the majority of importers no longer possessed shipowning interests. The majority of leading importers of cotton in the first half of the nineteenth century were relative specialists in terms of function. This stage had been reached by 1820 and the following decades saw no increase in the degree of functional specialisation. This was partly because it was already very high in 1820, and also, because specialisation had gone sufficiently far to render the merchant body capable of coping with the increasing scale and pace of the trade. Not until the laying of the Atlantic cable and the appearance of an immensely complex and sophisticated futures market was there any pressure towards a higher degree of functional specialisation amongst importers operating in the cotton trade.[24]

The conclusions reached from the foregoing examination of the Liverpool cotton trade in the first half of the nineteenth century are simple and straightforward. Between 1820 and 1850 the cotton trade was increasingly concentrated into the hands of a small group of operators who generally undertook only a narrow range of functions and who tended to specialise in their import business in the one commodity, cotton. While attention throughout this paper has focused on one trade, and the conclusions must strictly be seen as referring only to the cotton trade, the statistical exercises undertaken and their findings do, I think, have a wider relevance. One of the greatest weaknesses of our entrepreneurial and commercial history to date had been a lack of information on merchants as a class, and there has been a dangerous tendency to try to overcome this deficiency through sweeping generalisations based on only a few case studies often of an incomplete nature. Any value which this study possesses lies not so much in its findings which tend merely to substantiate prevailing views about specialisation, but in the fact that changes in the import merchant's function and scale of operation are examined through a study of empirical evidence which relates to a large section of the merchant body. In providing statistically based evidence of concentration and specialisation in the cotton trade, the surveys of the Bills of Entry add greater plausibility to views about specialisation in other trades in the first half of the nineteenth century. At the same time they bring to light a valuable source of information which, it is hoped, may be used by other students to enlarge our understanding of merchanting and commercial practice in this period of dynamic trade expansion.

APPENDIX

LIVERPOOL'S THIRTY LEADING IMPORTERS OF COTTON IN THE YEARS 1820, 1830, 1839, and 1850

Note on presentation

For the years 1820, 1830 and 1839 each importer's activities are presented in the following sequence: name, quantity of cotton imported and the area of origin [United States of America (U.S.A.), East Indies (E.I.), or South America (S.A.)]. In cases where not all imports of cotton came from one source, the area quoted refers to the area from which over 90 per cent of cotton imports were obtained. In the one instance where less than 90 per cent of an importer's supplies came from one area, both the areas in question are given. There then follows the percentage of total imports represented by the individual operator's imports. On the right-hand side of the page appears the degree of specialisation which the merchant is adjudged to have attained (Perfect Specialisation (P.S.), Near-perfect Specialisation (N.P.S.), Marginal Specialisation (M.S.), or

Non-specialisation (N.S.))* and the other commodities (if any) handled by the importer together with their port or country of origin. Unless otherwise stated, where no quantity is given, imports are on a very small scale. *An asterisk denotes a merchant with shipowning interests and a dagger denotes an importer who performed the function of ship's agent on some occasion during the year.*

For the year 1850, the year in which it was not possible to determine the full cotton imports of individual operators, a list is given of the leading importers (of that cotton which was actually consigned to specific Liverpool merchants) indicating as above their performance of the functions of shipowner and ship's agent.

LIVERPOOL COTTON IMPORTERS 1820

Group I	Bales	Per cent	
†Richards, A. S.	17,632 (U.S.A.)	3·82	(M.S.) Turps, 4,474 brls—*U.S.A.* Tobacco, Tar, Rice, Flour, Apples —*U.S.A.*
†Brown, W. & J., & Co.	12,696 (U.S.A.)	2·77	(N.S.) Flour, 20,560 brls—*U.S.A.* Tobacco, 475 hds—*Virginia* Rice, Turps, Staves—*U.S.A.* Ashes—*N. York, Belfast* Molasses—*Demerara*
†Alston, Eason & Co.	12,219 (U.S.A.)	2·66	(N.P.S.) Rice, Mahoghany, Indigo —*U.S.A.* Coffee, Sugar, Ginger—*India*
*†Rathbone & Co.	11,139 (U.S.A.)	2·43	(N.S.) Turps, 4,554 brls—*N. York* Tar, 679 brls—*N. York* Ashes, 766 brls.—*N. York* Tobacco, 429 hd.—*U.S.A.* Flour, 2,179 brls—*U.S.A, &* 1,781 brls—*Ireland* Hides, 2,632—*M. Video* Wheat, 6,680 qrs—*Ireland, Baltic, Canada* Apples, Bark, Flaxseed, Staves— *U.S.A.* Oats, Mats, Port, Barley—*Ireland* Mahoghany, 238 lgs—*Belize* Sugar—*Demerara*
†McGregor, A., & Co.	10,587 (U.S.A.)	2·31	(M.S.) Flour, 8,557 brls.—*N. York* Staves—*N. York* Tobacco—*N. Orleans*
†Lowe, I., & Co.	10,387 (U.S.A.)	2·27	(N.P.S.) Tobacco—*N. Orleans*
Dyson Bros.	9,291 (S.A.)	2·03	(N.P.S.) Orchella Weed, 787 bgs— *Lisbon*

* A full explanation of this classification is contained in the text of the essay.

	Bales	Per cent	
Group I (*cont.*)			
*†Cropper & Co.	9,030 (U.S.A.)	1·98	(N.S.) Flour, 14,625 brls—*U.S.A.* Flour, 211 tons—*Ireland* Tar, 1,839 brls—*N. York* Tobacco—*U.S.A.* Turps, 1,573 brls—*U.S.A.* Oats, 7,313 qrs—*Ireland* Wheat, 6,824 qrs—*Ireland* Ginger, 3,233 bgs—*Calcutta*
†Marshall, J.	8,203 (U.S.A.)	1·79	(N.P.S.) Flour, Rice—*U.S.A.*
*†Lodges & Tooth	8,088 (U.S.A.)	1·76	(M.S.) Ashes, 6,879 brls—*U.S.A. Canada* Tar, Turps, Apples—*U.S.A.* Rice, 350 tcs—*Charleston*
Group II			
*†Duff, Finlay & Co.	5,929 (U.S.A.)	1.29	(M.S.) Sugar, 8,187 bgs—*Manilla* Sugar, 595 bxs—*Cuba* Flour—*U.S.A.* Hides, 10,763—*Argentina, W. Indies* Timber, 305 tons—*N. Brunswick* Gum, Valonea—*Smyrna*
†King & Gracie	5,576 (U.S.A.)	1·22	(M.S.) Flour, 500 brls—*N. York* Rice, 1,000 tcs—*Savannah* Turps, 408 brls—*U.S.A.* Staves—*U.S.A.*
Otis, T.	5,138 (U.S.A.)	1·12	(N.P.S.) Ashes, 591 brls—*Canada*
†Crowder, Clough & Co.	5,081 (U.S.A.)	1·11	(M.S.) Flour, 700 brls—*U.S.A., Canada* Wheat, 3,214 bsls—*Quebec* Ashes—*Quebec* Tobacco—*Charleston* Rubber—*Brazil*
†McAdam & Co.	5,068 (U.S.A.)	1·11	(N.P.S) Turps, 500 brls—*Boston* Ashes—*N. York, Quebec* Rice—*U.S.A.*
*†Campbell, C. & J.	5,002 (U.S.A.)	1·10	(M.S.) Hides, 5,871—*N. York* Tobacco, 225 hds—*N. Orleans* Rice, Sago, Indigo, Saltpetre, Ginger—*Calcutta*
†Bolton & Ogden	4,622 (U.S.A.)	1·01	(N.S.) Flour, 7,468 brls—*U.S.A.* Turps, 410 brls—*N. Orleans* Tar, Apples, Bones, Rice—*U.S.A.* Sugar, Rum—*Demerara*
*†Heyworth, O.	4,518 (S.A.)	0·98	(N.P.S.) Hides, 7,292—*Brazil* Sugar—*Bahia* Flour—*Quebec*
†Dixon & Dickson	3,558 (U.S.A.)	0·78	(N.P.S.) Fruit—*Malaga* Tobacco, Rice, Turps, Resin— *U.S.A.*

Group II (cont.)	Bales	Per cent	
*†Earle, T. & W., & Co.	3,428 (S.A.)	0·76	(M.S.) Flaxseed, 800 tcs—*N. York*
			Turps, 1,648 brls—*U.S.A.*
			Flour—*N. York*
			Tobacco—*N. Orleans*
			Sugar, Fustic, Molasses—*Trinidad*
			Sugar—*Berbice*

Group III

†Wainwright & Co.	2,959 (U.S.A.)	0·65	(M.S.) Turps, 600 brls—*N. York*
			Rice, 321 csks—*Savannah*
			Flour—*N. York*
†Barber, W. & Co.	2,717 (U.S.A.)	0·58	(N.P.S.) Rice—*U.S.A.*
			Flour, 500 brls—*U.S.A.*
Pedra, A. M., & Co.	2,713 (S.A.)	0·58	(P.S.)
Milne, J. & A.	2,662 (U.S.A)	0·57	(N.P.S.) Tobacco—*N. Orleans*
*†Watson J.	2,415 (U.S.A.)	0·54	(N.P.S.) Rice, 495 tcs—*Charleston*
†Maury & Latham	2,369 (U.S.A.)	0·52	(N.S.) Tobacco, 947 hds—*Virginia*
			Flour, 1,274 brls—*U.S.A.*
			Rice, Staves, Apples—*U.S.A.*
Roach, G., & Co.	2,317 (S.A.)	0·52	(N.P.S.) Orchella Weed—*Lisbon*
†Da Costa, A. J.	2,258 (S.A.)	0·49	(N.P.S.) Coffee, 400 bgs—*Para*
			Cocoa—*Para*
*†Ewart, Myers & Co.	2,209 (U.S.A.)	0·48	(N.S.) Tobacco, 434 hds—*U.S.A.*
			Flour, 500 brls—*Richmond*
			Beans, 840 qrs—*Baltic*
			Iron, Hemp—*St. Petersburg*
			Sugar—*W. Indies*
			Cutch, Saltpetre, Coffee—*Java*
Haworth & Co.	2,175 (S.A.)	0·47	(P.S.)

LIVERPOOL COTTON IMPORTERS 1830

Group I	Bales	Per cent	
†Bolton & Ogden	40,185 (U.S.A.)	5·06	(N.S.) Tar, 2072 brls—*N. York*
			Turps, 4,014 brls—*U.S.A.*
			Flour, 82,914 brls—*U.S.A.*
			Flaxseed, 1,150 tcs—*N. York*
†Brown, W. & J., & Co.	39,448 (U.S.A.)	4·96	(N.S.) Flour, 17,714 brls—*U.S.A.*
			Bark, 1,279 hds—*Philadelphia*
			Turps, 5,962 brls—*N. York*
			Tobacco, 226 hds—*Virginia*
			Apples, 334 brls—*N. York*
			Hides, 1,479—*N. York*
			Linen—*Ireland, Scotland*

Group I (*cont.*)	Bales	Per cent	
†Alston, Finlay & Co.	26,752 (U.S.A.)	3·37	(M.S.) Turps, 1,600 brls—*N. York* Tar, 2,340 brls—*N. York* Flour, 4,000 brls—*N. Orleans* Tobacco—*N. Orleans*
†Wainwright & Co.	26,297 (U.S.A.)	3·33	(N.S.) Maize, 29,474 bsls—*N. York* Flaxseed, 338 tcs—*N. York* Turps, 3,860 brls—*N. York* Flour, Tar—*N. York*
†Cearns & Cary	24,391 (U.S.A.)	3·07	(N.S.) Turps, 8,758 brls—*N. York* Flour, 4,331 brls—*U.S.A.* Hides, 1,059—*U.S.A.* Ashes, Tar, Seed, Apples—*U.S.A.* Tin Plates, 2,080 bxs—*Bristol*
*Moon Bros.	24,044 (S.A.)	3·03	(N.P.S.) Butter, 1,205 frks—*Cork* Linen, Calicoes—*Ireland, Scotland*
*†Cropper, Benson & Co.	23,363 (U.S.A.)	2·94	(N.S.) Sugar, 7,202 bgs—*Calcutta* Wheat, 8,299 bsls—*Baltic, Ireland* Oats, 3,851 qrs—*Ireland* Flour, 11,590 csks—*U.S.A.* Tar, Turps—*N. York* Large variety of E.I. goods— *Calcutta*
*†Taylor, A., & Co.	19,861 (U.S.A.)	2·50	(N.P.S.) Flour, 6,300 brls—*N. York* Cedar Wood, Canes, Reeds— *N. Orleans* Ashes—*Quebec* Molasses—*Demerara*
†Lowe, I., & Co.	18,285 (U.S.A.)	2·30	(N.P.S.) Rice, Nuts—*Africa*
*†Rathbone & Co.	16,530 (U.S.A.)	2·08	(N.S.) Wheat, 3,321 scks—*Dublin* Oranges & Lemons, 682 bxs— *Palermo* Flour, 6,062 brls—*U.S.A.* Wool—*Sydney* Logwood, Mahoghany—*W. Indies* Ashes—*Canada* Tobacco—*Virginia* Bran, Butter—*Ireland*

Group II

	Bales	Per cent	
*†Tayleur, C. Son & Co.	13,400 (U.S.A.)	1·69	(N.P.S.) Hides, 22,580—*S. America* Logwood—*W. Indies* Calicoes—*Ireland*
†Collman, Lambert & Co.	12,786 (U.S.A.)	1·59	(N.P.S.) Oranges & Lemons 288 chsts—*Lisbon*
†Maury & Latham	12,494 (U.S.A.)	1·57	(M.S.) Flour, 7,260 brls—*Virginia* Tobacco, 873 hds—*Virginia* Tar, Turps—*U.S.A.*
†Hagarty & Jerdein	12,187 (U.S.A.)	1·54	(M.S.) Tobacco, 492 hds—*Virginia* Flour, 3,282 brls—*U.S.A.*

Group II (cont.)	Bales	Per cent	
*†Buchannan, Laird & Co.	10,257 (U.S.A.)	1·29	(N.P.S.) Coffee, Logwood—*W. Indies*
			Indigo, Sugar—*Calcutta*
†Martineau, Smith & Co.	10,196 (U.S.A.)	1·28	(P.S.)
Inglis, W.	9,185 (S.A.)	1·16	(P.S.)
†Hobson, J.	8,614 (U.S.A.)	1·09	(P.S.)
†Gordon, A.	7,997 (U.S.A.)	1·01	(N.P.S.) Calicoes—*Ireland*
*Ewart, Myers & Co.	7,991 (U.S.A.)	1·01	(M.S.) Flour, 3,000 brls—*U.S.A.* Sugar 1,000 hds—*W. Indies*

Group III

	Bales	Per cent	
†Peck & Phelps	7,361 (U.S.A.)	0·93	(N.P.S.) Tinplates, 11,535 bxs—*S. Wales*
†Sands, Hodgson & Co.	7,270 (U.S.A.)	0·92	(M.S.) Flour, 5,018 brls—*U.S.A.* Tar, Turps—*U.S.A.*
†Thornley, T. J. & D.	6,130	0·77	(N.P.S.) Tar, Turps—*U.S.A.*
*†Heyworth & Co.	5,664 (S.A.)	0·71	(N.P.S.) Hides, 18,000—*S. America*
†Jackson, D.	5,656 (U.S.A.)	0·71	(P.S.)
†Leech & Harrison	5,576 (U.S.A.)	0·70	(N.P.S.) Rye—*London* Indigo—*Calcutta* Fruit, Wine—*Opporto*
†Molyneux, W. E., & Co.	5,425 (U.S.A.)	0·68	(P.S.)
Burn, J.	5,179 (S.A.)	0·65	(P.S.)
†Barclay, G.	5,081 (U.S.A.)	0·64	(N.P.S.) Tobacco—*N. Orleans*
†Cardwell Bros.	5,043 (U.S.A.)	0·64	(M.S.) Flour, 7,932 brls—*U.S.A.* Cochineal, Tar, Turps, Bark—*U.S.A.*

LIVERPOOL COTTON IMPORTERS 1839

Group I	Bales	Per cent	
†Molyneux & Witherby	53,122 (U.S.A.)	5·25	(N.P.S.) Tea, 665 chsts—*Bristol* Flaxseed, Turps—*N. York* Ashes—*Montreal*
†Brown, W. & J., & Co.	48,238 (U.S.A.)	4·77	(N.S.) Flour, 10652 brls—*Philadelphia* Tobacco, Apples, Tar—*U.S.A.* Turps, 4,296 brls—*U.S.A.* Iron, Tinplates—*Newport*

Group I (*cont.*)	Bales	Per cent	
†Humphreys & Biddle	46,018 (U.S.A.)	4·55	(N.P.S.) Turps, 4,193 brls—*Philadelphia* Flour—*U.S.A.* Iron—*Cardiff*
†Dennistoun, A.	42,234 (U.S.A.)	4·17	(N.P.S.) Logwood—*N. Orleans*
†Roskell, Ogden & Co.	35,578 (U.S.A.)	3·52	(N.P.S.) Turps—*N. York*
†Purton, Parker & Co.	33,341 (U.S.A.)	3·29	(P.S.)
†Baring Bros.	29,000 (U.S.A.)	2·89	(N.S.) Turps, 3,064 brls—*N. York* Flour, 10,922 brls—*U.S.A., Leghorn* Wheat, 2,025 qrs—*Leghorn* Timber, 950 tons—*Canada* Tea, 3,350 chsts—*Canton* Pork, 555 brls—*Belfast* Iron, 4,173 tons—*S. Wales* Logwood, Wax, Rubber—*W. Indies* Sugar—*Calcutta* Cochineal—*Vera Cruz*
†Holford, J.	29,000 (U.S.A.)	2·87	(N.P.S.) Flour, 2,008 brls—*Baltimore* Flaxseed—*N. York* Iron—*Glasgow* Rye, Tallow—*Baltic* Wool—*Trieste*
†Reid, Irving & Co.	26,426 (U.S.A.)	2·61	(N.P.S.) Beeswax—*U.S.A.*
†Brown, Shipley & Co.	25,638 (U.S.A.)	2·54	(M.S.) Turps, 3,002 brls—*U.S.A.* Flour, 7,790 brls—*U.S.A.* Tobacco—*U.S.A.* Iron—*S. Wales*

Group II

	Bales	Per cent	
†Todd, Jackson & Co.	24,306 (U.S.A.)	2·40	(N.P.S.) Iron, 582 tons— *S. Wales*
†Collman & Stolterfront	22,857 (U.S.A.)	2·28	(M.S.) Flour, 7,875 brls—*N. Orleans* Turps, 3,605 brls—*U.S.A.* Flaxseed—*N. York* Indigo—*Valpariso*
†Maury, J., & Sons	17,465 (U.S.A.)	1·73	(M.S.) Flour, 2,500 brls—*U.S.A.* Turps, 5,000 brls—*N. York* Tobacco, 806 hds—*U.S.A.* Flaxseed, 480 tcs—*U.S.A.*
†de Lizardi, F.	16,945 (U.S.A.)	1·67	(N.P.S.) Logwood—*U.S.A.* Iron—*Cardiff*

Group II (*cont.*)	Bales	Per cent	
†Wildes, Pickersgill & Co.	15,325 (U.S.A.)	1·51	(N.S.) Timber, 20,618 tons—*Canada* Turps, 7,303 brls—*N. York* Flour, 3,187 brls—*N. York* Tar, Tea—*N. York* Ashes—*Montreal*
*†Moon Bros.	14,012 (S.A.)	1·39	(N.P.S.) Rubber, Hides—*Maranham*
*†Rathbone & Co.	12,472 (U.S.A.)	1·23	(M.S.) Tobacco, 619 hds—*Virginia* Copper Ore, 749 tons—*N. York* Oranges & Lemons, 3,057 bxs—*Palermo* Hemp—*Riga* Ashes—*Montreal* Flour, Turps—*U.S.A.*
*†Tayleur, C., Son & Co.	11,850 (U.S.A.)	1·17	(M.S.) Logwood, 620 tons—*Laguna* Wool, 4,534 bls—*S. America* Skins—*Monte Video*
*†Barton, Irlam & Co.	9,117 (E.I.)	0·91	(M.S.) Sugar, 5,887 hds—*W. Indies* Sugar, 4,895 css—*Mauritius* Pepper, Ginger, Coffee, Molasses—*W. Indies* Ginger, Indigo, Pepper, Ivory—*Bombay*
†Fountain & Price	8,912 (U.S.A.)	0·88	(P.S.)

Group III

	Bales	Per cent	
*†McAlmont Bros.	3,507 (U.S.A.) 5,347 (S.A.)	0·88	(N.P.S.) Rum, Sugar, Logwood—*W. Indies* Cordage—*Baltic*
†Waddington, Holt & Co.	8,510 (U.S.A.)	0·84	(N.P.S.) Turps, 1,625 brls—*N. York* Tar—*U.S.A.* Fruit—*Malaga*
†Poutz, V.	8,406 (U.S.A.)	0·83	(P.S.)
*†Mure, H., & Co.	6,675 (U.S.A.)	0·66	(N.P.S.) Iron Ore, Apples—*N. York* Flour, 2,000 brls.—*N. York*
†Green, G., & Son	6,465 (U.S.A.)	0·64	(P.S.)
Pope A.	6,005 (U.S.A.)	0·59	(P.S.)
†Hagan, Magee & Co.	5,765 (U.S.A.)	0·57	(P.S.)

Group III (*cont.*)	Bales	Per cent	
†Dawson, R. L.	4,657 (U.S.A.)	0·46	(N.S.) Turps, 1,840 brls—*U.S.A.* Flour, 1,507 brls—*Baltimore* Timber, 589 tons—*Canada* Porter—*Dublin*
*†Gilliatt, W. H., & Co.	4,569 (U.S.A.)	0·45	(N.S.) Timber, 474 tons—*Canada* Tobacco, 1,555 hds—*Virginia* Tar, Turps—*U.S.A.*
Rushton, J.	4,322 (S.A.)	0.43	(N.P.S.) Rubber, Sarsparilla— *S. America*

LIVERPOOL COTTON IMPORTERS 1850

†Dennistoun, A.
†Jackson, W. & Sons
*†Moon, W.
*†Johnston, S.
*†Rankin, Gilmour & Co.
*†Zwilchenbart, R., & Blessig
†Brown, Shipley & Co.
*†Gibbs, Bright & Co.
†McHenry, J.
†Duckworth & Williams
Melly, Romilly & Co.
†Bird, Gillian & Co.
†Baring Bros.
Petrochino, E.
*†McAlmont Bros.

*†Fielden Bros.
†Crook, J. T.
*†Rathbone & Co.
*†Zwilchenbart, E.
Ryder & Tetley
*†Moon, E.
*†Hutchinson, R.
Rushton, J.
†Lowe, I. & Co.
†Collman & Stolterfont
*†Cater, J. W.
†Morewood Bros.
*†Holderness & Chilton
*†Toole, J.
*†Kleingender Bros.

(1) See for example: S. Dumbell, 'Early Liverpool Cotton Imports and the Organisation of the Cotton Market in the Eighteenth century', *Economic Journal*, Vol. XXXIII (1923), pp. 362–73; S. Dumbell, 'The Cotton Market in 1799', *Economic History*, Vol. I (1926–9), pp. 141–48; S. Dumbell 'The Origin of Cotton Futures', *Economic History*, Vol. I (1926–29), pp. 259–67; G. W. Daniels, 'The American Cotton Trade with Liverpool under the Embargo and Non-intercourse Acts', *American Historical Review*, Vol. XXI (1916), pp. 276–88; F. E. Hyde, B. B. Parkinson and S. Marriner, 'The Cotton Broker and the Rise of the Liverpool Cotton Market', *Economic History Review*, 2nd series, Vol. VIII (1955), pp. 75–83.

(2) S. Marriner, *Rathbones of Liverpool* (1961).

(3) The absence of the Liverpool Port Books for much of the eighteenth century and the first half of the nineteenth century necessitates statistics of the port's trade being assembled from secondary sources. The sources for Table I were as follows: national figures were obtained from T. Ellison, *The Cotton Trade of Great Britain* (1886), p. 85, and Liverpool figures from E. J. Donnell, *Chronological and Statistical History of Cotton* (1873), *passim*. In both cases the original sources were brokers' circulars, Ellison relying on the circulars of George Holt & Co. and Donnell those of Collman & Co. As Donnell's statistics date only from 1821, figures for 1820 were obtained from H. Smithers, *Liverpool* (1825). Smithers' reputation as a

statistician is to say the least, weak, but in his table of imports of cotton 1790–1823 he does obtain a high degree of accuracy. Checking his figures with others which exist for the period reveals only very slight discrepancies.

It is regrettable that the unit of measurement, bales, is not a strictly homogeneous unit, for bales from the southern states of the U.S.A. were larger and weighed more than those from Brazil. Moreover, over the period 1820–50 there was a steady tendency for the average weight of all kinds of bales imported to increase. As figures, however, in pounds weight are unobtainable and impossible to construct, Table I represents the nearest approximation we have to the trend of cotton imports over this period. On the question of the size and weight of bales, J. A. Mann, *The Cotton Trade of Great Britain* (1860), p. 51, provides valuable information.

(4) On market movements over the period 1820–50 see Donnell, *op. cit.*, and T. Ellison, 'History of Cotton Prices and Supply 1790–1862', *Exchange Magazine*, Vol. I (1862), pp. 306–15, Vol. II (1863), pp. 45–54.

(5) B. Poole, *The Commerce of Liverpool* (1854), pp. 196–97. The figure of £50m. excludes imports of bullion valued at £7m. in 1850.

(6) No complete set of Liverpool Bills of Entry is available and the earliest existing volume is for the year 1819. Odd volumes between this date and 1842 are in the Customs House Library, London. A complete sequence from 1842 on is available in the Liverpool Record Office. I should like to express my gratitude to Prof. F. E. Hyde for allowing me to use the volumes for 1820 and 1839 while they were in his possession, and to Mr. R. C. Jarvis, until recently Librarian, H.M. Customs & Excise, for permission to consult the 1830 volume.

(7) For a more detailed discussion of the method followed in examining concentration see D. M. Williams, 'The Function of the Merchant in Specific Liverpool Import Trades. 1820–50' (unpublished Liverpool M.A. thesis 1963), pp. 26–35.

(8) The reason why this tremendous rise in the quantity of cotton consigned to 'order' occurred is not clear. The most likely explanation is that it was linked with the arrival of the steam packet ship on the Atlantic route which meant that for the first time information could travel more swiftly than goods. This situation would permit the sale of 'cotton afloat' which may have been an earlier development than has hitherto been supposed.

(9) F. W. Wallace, *History of Liverpool* (1795), p. 273.

(10) A. Ellis, *Heir of Adventure: The Brown Shipley Story, 1810–1960* (1960), p. 10.

(11) J. Rankin, *A History of our Firm* (1921), p. 49 *et seq.*

(12) N. S. Buck, *The Development of the Organisation of the Anglo-American Trade 1800–1850* (1925), pp. 37–45.

(13) *Report from the Select Committee on Manufacturers, Commerce and Shipping*, 1833 (690) vi, Qs. 1510, 4086–122.

(14) For example, John Gladstone was a member of the West Indian, E. Indian, Baltic, Portugal and Brazil Associations in Liverpool at the beginning of the nineteenth century.

(15) A. Ellis, *op. cit.*, p. 57.

(16) F. E. Hyde, B. B. Parkinson and Sheila Marriner, *op. cit.*, pp. 76–77.

(17) Quoted in N. S. Buck, *op. cit.*, p. 45.

(18) R. W. Hidy, 'The Organisation and Function of Anglo-American Merchant Bankers, 1815–60', *Journal of Economic History*, Vol. I (1941), supplement, pp. 53–66. For a comprehensive survey of the activities of one of these merchant banking firms see R. W. Hidy, *The House of Baring in American Trade and Finance: English Merchant Bankers at Work, 1763–1861* (1949).

(19) See R. H. Thornton, *British Shipping* (2nd ed. 1959) p. 139, for an excellent description of the function of ship's agent.

(20) R. Davis, *The Rise of the British Shipping Industry* (1962), p. 81.

(21) C. R. Fayle, 'Shipping and Marine Insurance', in *Trade Winds*, ed. C. N. Parkinson (1948), p. 25.

(22) N. S. B. Gras, *Business and Capitalism* (1947), p. 174.

(23) D. M. Williams, 'Merchanting in the First Half of the Nineteenth Century: The Liverpool Timber Trade', *Business History*, Vol. VIII (1966), pp. 111–14.

(24) Sir J. H. Clapham, *An Economic History of Modern Britain* (1932), Vol. II, pp. 315–16.

CHAPTER EIGHT

The African Steam Ship Company[1]

P. N. DAVIES

BY THE end of the nineteenth century the British possessions in West Africa consisted of the Gold Coast, the Gambia, Sierra Leone and the area which in 1914 was to become Nigeria. All of these territories lay on the coast between latitudes 4 and 14 degrees north, and they had many geographical similarities; for instance, all four were divided into two distinct zones. These were the jungle near the seaboard and the savannah in the interior. The peoples of such separate regions had naturally developed differently. Thus the jungle peoples were backward, relying on what could be gathered from the forests for their livelihood, while those of the interior lived in large communities with an advanced economy based on the cultivation of crops and the keeping of livestock.

Both zones suffered from a lack of adequate communications. Only the Gambia and Niger Rivers and coastal creeks provided a reasonable means of transport before railways were introduced in the 1890s. Even draught animals could not be used in many places because of the presence of the tsetse fly, and these areas were completely dependent upon native porters. In these circumstances the trade of the jungle regions was restricted to areas near the sea or a navigable river, while the savannah districts were almost completely isolated from the western seaboard. The peoples of the interior, in fact, found it easier to establish trade links with the Mediterranean and Red Seas than with the Atlantic Ocean, although the caravans which regularly crossed the Sahara Desert were very limited in the amount of goods they could carry.

The first Europeans to do business with West Africa were the Portuguese, and their first ship sighted the Coast in 1445. Many nations disputed the Portuguese claim to an exclusive trade and by the seventeenth century the West Coast played an important role in the economy of Britain and her colonies because it was the source of the slave labour needed for the American and West Indian plantations. Although large numbers of slaves were required it was not found necessary to establish formal colonies in West Africa to ensure an adequate supply. The native rulers were well used to the idea of slavery and were not only prepared to trade with the European merchants, but insisted that all commerce with the interior must pass through their hands. From an early date most of the British trade was organised by chartered companies. The most important of these was the Royal African Company which was formed in 1672, but which lost its monopoly in 1697.[2] The competition between Liverpool, Bristol and London which then followed led to a demand for some regulation of the trade, and in 1750 the 'Company of Merchants Trading to Africa' was set up by Act of Parliament. This meant in practice that all British subjects having business in West Africa were able to join the Company without difficulty. The only obligation was that members were to contribute a small annual sum to help pay for the upkeep of the forts established on the Coast.

In 1807 the slave trade became illegal for British citizens. Although this had been anticipated it was still a severe blow, particularly for Liverpool men who had come to predominate in the trade. However, the trade was prohibited just when an alternative to the export of men was presenting itself. This was the growth of the palm oil industry, and the quantity imported into Liverpool rose from 55 tons in 1785 to 1,000 tons in 1810 and to 30,000 tons in 1851. In spite of the development of this trade the oil was much less valuable than the slaves had been, and the ensuing difficulties led to a reorganisation of British commerce with West Africa. In 1821 the Company of Merchants Trading to Africa ended its activities and after that date the trade was completely free of all restrictions. Even so legitimate trade grew only slowly, for the reluctance of the British Government to undertake direct responsibilities in West Africa and the terribly high rates of mortality from tropical diseases were strong limiting factors. In addition, trade could not be significantly increased until the merchants or their agents penetrated to the interior, and this could not be achieved until the outlet of the Niger was discovered.

In fact, it was not until 1830 that it was realised that the 'Oil Rivers' were branches of the Niger. This discovery was made by the Lander brothers who made their way overland to the upper reaches of the river and then followed its course by canoe to the delta on the coast. Macgregor Laird, a member of the Birkenhead shipbuilding family, then joined with Richard Lander to form a company which was designed to complete the exploration of the river and to establish trade links with the interior. An expedition was organised in 1832, Laird providing two small steamships, the *Quorra* and the *Alburkah*, and a brig, the *Columbine*. The steamers ascended the Niger and were careful not to antagonise the King of Brass who claimed exclusive trading rights in the coastal strip through which they passed. They therefore moved through the oil-producing areas without stopping and eventually reached Fundah in the far north of the territory. Here they attempted to trade, but business was poor because of civil war and anarchy, and the expedition was not a financial success. Most significantly, of the forty-eight Europeans who took part in the venture, thirty-nine died of disease.

Laird then turned his attention to other matters, and in 1837 he became the Secretary of the British and North American Steam Navigation Company. Against his advice a second expedition was sent up the Niger in 1841. This had the full support of the British Government, but the dreadful death-rate—forty-eight out of 145 Europeans died—seemed to end all hope that a large and legitimate commerce could be developed with the interior. In 1844 Macgregor Laird rejoined the family shipbuilding firm in Birkenhead, but his interest and enthusiasm continued to be inspired by a belief in the future of West Africa. In 1849 he gave up his work and moved to London, and from then until his death in 1861 he was continuously associated with the West African trade. This decision to move was undoubtedly influenced by the knowledge that business with the coastal areas was increasing each year, and by 1850 this amounted to a considerable volume of trade.[3] In Laird's opinion this meant that great scope must exist for a regular steamship service, and his conviction was turned into action in 1851. He approached the Government and after long negotiations was successful in obtaining a ten-year mail contract, together with a substantial subsidy.[4] Armed with this contract, Laird sought and received the support of a body of influential men who were prepared to join with him in organising the new concern, and thus the African Steam Ship Company came into existence.

Sir John Campbell became the chairman of the new firm, and also on the board was James Hartley, a director of the Peninsular and Oriental Steamship Company. It was arranged that Macgregor Laird would be the managing director and a prospectus was issued. This stated that the Company had been formed to carry out a contract for the monthly conveyance of mail to West Africa, and that suitable vessels had been ordered for this purpose:

'Five iron screw steam ships for this service are in the course of construction by Mr. John Laird of Birkenhead, with engines by Messrs. George Forrester and Company, and Fawcett Preston and Company of Liverpool: the first of these vessels is to be launched on the 3rd July, and will be ready to commence the Mail Service, in accordance with the terms of the Contract on the 1st of September. Two of them have capacity for 700, two of them for 1,000 and one for 250 tons of cargo, with excellent accommodation for first and second class passengers.'[5]

Shares in the new company were quickly taken up, and the Report of the Directors at the 'First Ordinary Meeting of the Proprietors' on 11 June 1853, showed that 11,008 shares of £20 each had been issued. The capital account was then as follows:[6]

Deposit on 11,008 shares at £5	£55,040	0	0
First Call of £5 on 11,008 shares	£55,040	0	0
Amount paid in anticipation of calls	£19,712	10	0
	£129,792	10	0

The directors also reported progress in the construction of the ships and in the completion of their early voyages. The first trip was undertaken by the *Forerunner* of 400 tons. In accordance with the terms of the mail contract she was ready to sail at the beginning of September 1852 but at the request of the Board of Admiralty her departure was put back to the 24th of that month. The *Forerunner* was subsequently delayed again after being dismasted in the Bay of Biscay during a violent gale, but repairs were completed satisfactorily at Gibraltar and she then concluded her journey without further incident. Delays in the construction of the other vessels resulted in a loss for the company, because the compensation received from the builders did not altogether offset the cost of chartering alternative steamers. However, the delivery of the *Faith* in January 1853, and the *Hope* in April 1853, ended these initial difficulties.

The first half year's working, of only five voyages, resulted in a net profit of £1,929 8s. 3d., so a dividend of 2s 6d. per share, clear of income tax, was declared. Perhaps of even more importance was the fact that not a single man was lost by accident or from tropical disease. This may have been a reflection of the careful way in which the company was organised, as can be clearly seen from the ships' documentation. A typical sailing vessel of the time would carry only a log and a manifest, while her captain might or might not write a letter or a report for the owners at the end of each voyage. Yet even the earliest of the African Steam Ship Company's vessels carried a set of documents and returns that was almost equal to those carried by a modern cargo liner.[7]

Some details survive of the maiden voyage of the *Faith* which left London on 27 January 1853. She burned 352 tons of coal on the outward voyage and 533 tons on the homeward run, averaging about 9½ knots. Homeward cargo was loaded at Fernando Po, Cape

Coast Castle, Sierra Leone, Bathhurst, Teneriffe and Madeira. The main items of cargo were palm oil, gum, ginger, camwood, pepper, ivory, arrowroot, beeswax, cochineal and gold dust.

In the African Steam Ship Company's second year it was found that while receipts increased steadily, the increase was more than offset by the rise in wages, coal, oil, stores and provisions (amounting to nearly 35 per cent) engendered by the onset of the Crimean War. As a result the directors thought it prudent to dispose of their two larger ships, the *Charity* and the *Northern Light* (both of 1,062 tons, the latter still on the stocks) and these were sold at a profit to the Canadian Steam Navigation Company. The *Hope* and later the *Faith* (both of 922 tons) were then chartered to the Government's Commissariat Service, so the *Candace* and the *Ethiope* (of 675 tons) were built to take their place.

While these actions proved to be financially rewarding to the Company its West African service naturally suffered and was disrupted still further in 1854. This was because of the loss of the *Forerunner* after striking a sunken rock off Madeira. Many lives were lost and the subsequent investigation held under the Mercantile Marine Act returned a verdict of gross negligence. The company was thus forced to pay £5,000 into the Court of Chancery, 'to stop and bar the numerous actions commenced by different parties'.[8] The loss of this vessel could not be absorbed by the depleted fleet, so an immediate search was made for a replacement. The best available ship, the *Retriever*, of 440 tons, was therefore purchased.

The end of the Crimean War left the Company with only six ships—the *Faith* having been sold to Turkey. The *Candace*, *Ethiope*, and *Retriever* then ran the West African service with the aid of the newly built *Gambia* and *Niger* but the *Hope* was laid up when she was released from the Government's requisition as she was considered to be inefficient. In a further attempt to improve efficiency the *Candace* and *Ethiope* had their engines removed and replaced by new geared ones of 120 h.p. with improved boilers.

The year 1856 was also significant in other ways. In October 1855 Macgregor Laird resigned his position as managing director, although he remained on the board of the Company. This left a gap which was filled in theory by a committee of directors, but in practice the control of the line fell into the hands of its secretary. His period of authority, however, was only shortlived for the ending of the Crimean War and the poorness of the West African trade led the directors to consider winding up the entire business. At the recommendation of their Liverpool agents they agreed to give direct sailings from the Mersey a trial before reaching a final decision.

These voyages began in July 1856 and from that time the running of the Company was in the hands of Messrs. W. & H. Laird,[9] and the secretary in London reverted to a less important role. The new arrangement was an improvement and it was decided to continue the sailings from Liverpool, but in spite of this the level of trade was poor (only four out of the six vessels were continuously employed) and no dividend could be paid. However, the directors were convinced that the trade would improve, so they had the *Hope* fitted with a lifting screw to improve her sailing qualities and she was adapted to carry palm oil and other bulky cargoes.

The following half year, from July to December 1857, saw the Company in a better financial position and a dividend was paid in spite of the *Niger* being lost at Santa Cruz. No dividend was paid for the next period because of a further chapter of accidents. The *Gambia* broke her main shaft at Bathurst and was six weeks late in getting home, while the *Armenian* (acquired in 1857) lost over a fortnight by getting stranded in the River Cameroons and the *Candace* was lost after a collision. These difficulties were followed by the commercial crisis of 1857/8 which restricted trade to such an extent that freight receipts declined by £1,600 compared with the same period in 1857.

The second half of 1858 was much more favourable for the African Steam Ship Company. No losses were reported, and while revenue fell slightly, the fall in expenses was far greater and so there was a net gain. A new seven-year mail contract was entered into and this gave rise to certain economies, for Liverpool was recognised as the centre of the trade and was made the mail port. It was then no longer necessary to call at Plymouth and costs were accordingly reduced. The payment under the mail contract was increased to £30,000 per annum and as no losses were experienced in 1859, the Company made substantial progress, and the *Cleopatra* was purchased to replace the *Candace*. The *Cleopatra* was the first of the line's ships to be fitted with a super heater, and its success led to this equipment becoming standard throughout the fleet. It was soon found that the *Gambia* of 650 tons was too small to operate the new mail contract and she was sold. It is perhaps worth recording that all the Company's ships carried sails, but the extent to which these were used for propulsion—apart from steadying—is not clear.[10]

The death of Hamilton Laird in 1860 made little difference to the position of the Liverpool agents, although when a new partner was taken in their name was changed to Messrs. Laird and Fletcher. The death of Macgregor Laird in 1861 was followed by the retirement of William Laird in June 1863. A Mr. Parr was then taken into partnership by Fletcher and the Liverpool agents became known as Fletcher & Parr. The retirement of William Laird, had, however, a more significant meaning than the mere loss of his name would suggest. Instead of being the organisers of the Company the Liverpool agents became purely its representatives, and the control passed back to the London office. The board of directors were nominally in command there, but the real power was quickly assumed by the secretary, Mr. Duncan Campbell.[11]

The period from 1863 to 1868 was a time of increasing trade, and the ships provided by the African Steam Ship Company were insufficient to bring home all the cargo that was offered. The Liverpool agents made strong and repeated representations for additional ships, but until 1869 the fleet was not increased. This decision on the part of the directors was quite deliberate, for although the resources of the Company were comparatively small it would have been quite easy for it to have raised additional capital as it did at a later date. The directors' reluctance to accept further responsibilities derived from their views on the uncertainty of the trade. Their memory of past disappointments and their reliance on the certain but limited returns offered by the mail contract were in direct contrast to the views of their agents who were paid on a commission basis and naturally wished to see an expanding business.

The failure to expand, however defended, had the unwelcome result that it led to the intervention of another line in the West African trade. This was the British and African Steam Navigation Company and its entry was an especially bitter pill for Messrs. Fletcher and Parr because the promoters of the new line were their own ex-employees:-John Dempster and Alexander Elder. A policy of price cutting followed immediately and the secretary of the African Steam Ship Company wrote to their shippers:

'I am desired by the Directors of this Company to state that their attention has been drawn to an Advertisement and a List of Rates of Freight, issued by a new Company, called the "British and African Steam Navigation Company", which has been established to meet the alleged requirements of the Trade, between Glasgow, Liverpool and the West Coast of Africa.

'Under these circumstances, and in view of the interests of this Company, which was the first to establish Steam Communication with the West Coast of Africa, the Directors have resolved on making very considerable reductions in their Rates of Freight. These new Rates will be in your hands in the course of a few days, and will come into operation on the 24th Inst.

'The Directors have at all times endeavoured to meet the requirements of the Trade, and, looking to the superior class of Vessels belonging to this Company, and the manner in which the Service has hitherto been, and will in future be conducted, they hope to retain your support.'[12]

The second effect of this competition was to induce the African Steam Ship Company to increase its fleet,[13] and in spite of the reductions in freight and passenger rates which tended to diminish profits, the issue of all unallotted shares was carried into effect—the entire amount being quickly subscribed for by the Company's own shareholders.

In fact, the competition with the British and African Steam Navigation Company lasted only for a twelve-month period and then the two lines came together and agreed to share their sailings. The new agreement was at first in the nature of an uneasy truce and the Directors of the African Steam Ship Company felt it necessary to have more capital at their disposal. They accordingly called up an additional £2 per share, and having applied to the Government for the requisite authority, issued debentures to the value of £83,000 (a third of the subscribed capital of £250,000). The fleet was then gradually increased and improved, but the steady progress of the Company was to be impaired by two events in 1872.

The first of these concerned the secretary, Mr. Duncan Campbell for it was discovered that he had embezzled a sum which 'approached £20,000'.[14] The second event of 1872 that ended any complacency still existing in the minds of the directors of the African Steam Ship Company was the termination of the mail contract. This was not an unmitigated disaster, for the Company still received the actual sea postage for whatever it carried, and was relieved of the responsibility of running unprofitable services. What it did mean was that a new approach had to be made to the business, and proof that the directors recognised this fact can be seen by their change of policy. The older, uneconomic ships were sold immediately and were replaced with larger and more suitable vessels.[15]

A new agreement with the British and African was made in 1873. This provided that a steamer of each company should sail every alternate week and illustrated the increasing harmony between the lines. The basic reason for the success of these agreements was the fear of competition from outside firms; both concerns accepted the principle that co-operation with a friendly rival was preferable to unrestricted competition with innumerable interlopers. Under these circumstances the African Steam Ship Company paid a small but regular dividend, and came under heavy criticism from Messrs. Fletcher and Parr for not building up the fleet more quickly. The latter firm, dependent upon commission for their income, were naturally eager to expand trade while the London Office was mainly concerned with reducing risks and cutting costs. With two such divergent viewpoints it is not surprising that antagonism developed between Liverpool and London and this reached a head in 1875 when the agency agreement came up for renewal. The Liverpool representatives were then asked if they would be prepared to accept a reduced commission. Fletcher and Parr stated that they were prepared to discuss a reduction, but they 'hoped the proposed economy was not to be limited to the Liverpool Agency'. The chairman seems to have taken this as a personal slur on himself and his fellow directors, and the atmosphere worsened. In February 1875 the Liverpool agents were again asked if they were prepared to accept the reduced rates of commission. They replied that it was the 'indisposition of the directors to replace the *Soudan* wrecked at Madeira that was affecting the profits of the Company, and it would therefore be unfair to expect them to pay for the omissions of others'. They further offered to take over the sailings which this ship should have made if the Company continued to feel unable to replace her by purchase or charter. In this way they would be able to prevent the British and African, or any interlopers, from getting the benefit of the African Steam Ship Company's reduced sailings. A reply from the London Office came by return of post to say:

'. . . that the directors had unanimously decided to open an office of their own in Liverpool with a manager who would be under the more immediate control of the board'.[16]

This decision was eventually to result in a complete change in the structure of the West African carrying trade. The loss of the agency meant less work for Fletcher and Parr, and consequently less scope for one of their most able and ambitious employees, Alfred Lewis Jones. Jones had been born in Carmarthen in 1845, his father being a currier by trade. When Alfred was three years old his family moved to Merseyside. His own description of his childhood was that it was 'happy and uneventful', but at the age of fourteen Jones found that the prospects of employment for a youth without influence and only an elementary education were strictly limited. He decided that the sea offered him his best opportunity of a worthwhile career, and he began to make frequent visits to the city docks. Eventually he persuaded the master of a vessel of the African Steam Ship Company to give him a job as a cabin boy. Jones was only to make one voyage to West Africa, however, for he made a very favourable impression on his captain. When the vessel returned to the Mersey he was re-commended to Fletcher and Parr as a junior clerk and Mr. Parr took a strong liking to him. He gave Jones much encouragement and paid for him to attend evening classes at the Liverpool College in Shaw Street. Jones spent a lot of his spare time at Mr. Parr's home, and this was an invaluable help in strengthening his social back-ground at an impressionable age.

Alfred Jones stayed with Fletcher and Parr throughout the sixties and was in their employ when the British and African started its competition in 1869. In 1870 he helped to negotiate the truce be-tween the two lines, for by then he was in a senior position and earning £125 a year.[17] The loss of the agency of the African Steam Ship Company in 1875 then caused Jones to re-examine his position and prospects. He was aware of the success of Elder and Dempster's agency, and no doubt knew that his former office colleague, John Holt, had returned from West Africa after having laid the founda-tions of a profitable and lasting business. He felt he was in danger of being left behind by his more progressive colleagues, so he decided to open up in business on his own account.

At first Jones was concerned only with shipping and insurance broking, so the experience gained with Fletcher and Parr stood him in good stead and he prospered. His credit was good, and together with his profit and savings this enabled him to branch out in his second year. He chartered a number of small sailing vessels and used them to carry goods to and from West Africa. Finding these ventures profitable he purchased the ships and began to extend his activities still further. The success of these voyages was a key factor in Jones's progress, but he did not allow this to alter his opinion that the future of the carrying trade lay with the steamship. When, therefore, an advantageous moment arrived he disposed of his little fleet and made arrangements to charter a small steamer. This had immediate repercussions, for Elder, Dempster's, the Liverpool agents of the British and African, recognised that in Jones they had a dangerous rival, who though small was very efficient. With this in mind they decided to avert future difficulties by offering him a junior partnership. After much careful consideration Jones agreed to their suggestion and dissolved his own firm on 1 October 1879. Jones was to be a junior partner with Elder, Dempster's for five years. During this time he became very friendly with Alexander Sinclair who had been appointed manager of the Liverpool office of the African Steam Ship Company after the break with Fletcher and Parr. The British and African had its head office in Glasgow, while the African was controlled from London, so the close liaison between the two firms was greatly assisted by the proximity of Jones and Sinclair in Liverpool. In fact, most of the working arrangements and agreements were largely the result of their consultations, and together the two lines were successful in resisting the opposition of many companies and tramp steamers that were trying to enter the trade.[18]

In 1884 Alfred Jones became the senior partner of Elder, Dempster and Company. The way in which this was achieved is not too clear, but Alexander Elder (aged 50) and John Dempster (aged 47) certainly retired very much earlier than might have been expected.[19] Under Jones's leadership co-operation between the two lines became even closer and reached its logical conclusion in 1890. In that year the African Steam Ship Company closed its Liverpool office and appointed Elder, Dempster's as its managing agents. The former manager of their Liverpool office, Alexander Sinclair, then joined Elder, Dempster's as a partner, and this firm then represented both lines. In effect, this gave Jones almost complete control of the West African shipping trade, for his commanding position with the British firms enabled him to make advantageous arrangements with his sole remaining rival, the Woermann Line of Hamburg.

Under the agreement signed in 1890, Jones arranged to sell the vessels actually owned by Elder, Dempster's to the African Steam Ship Company. To do this meant that the capital structure of the latter had to be enlarged and it was increased from £200,000 to £424,000.[20] The advantages of possessing large reserves and a joint working agreement were clearly demonstrated during the next few years when both the Prince Line and the General Steam Navigation Company attempted to enter the trade.[21] When these opponents were defeated efforts were made to interest Sir Christopher Furness in the West African trade, and although Alfred Jones was able to divert this unwelcome prospect it made him appreciate more fully the vulnerability of his position. He therefore consulted the Woermann Line, and with their agreement decided to establish a conference system or shipping ring. This was inaugurated in 1895 and the efficient technique adopted to introduce the new system was well described by Mr. George Miller when giving evidence before the Royal Commission on Shipping Rings.[22] Miller stated that he received a copy of the rebate circular through the post. This was the first intimation he had had that a conference system was being established. The circular asked him (with all other West African merchants) to sign an agreement giving his whole carrying to the conference lines. He had less than a month in which to do this, and in the absence of a satisfactory alternative he decided to sign. He could have provided his own ships, but this would have been expensive and more trouble than he cared to take.

Miller was typical of the West African merchants. None wished to join the scheme, yet all did so, and once having shipped with the conference the deferred rebate ensured their continued support. In practice the conference operated as the original circular had laid down. All freights were increased by 10 per cent and this increase became known as primage.[23] Freight was only accepted from merchants who signed the declaration to the effect that all their shipments would be made via the Conference Lines for the succeeding six months. Once the six-month period had elapsed the rebate due could be claimed by the shipper for all outward cargo, and for palm oil and kernels on the homeward journey. This claim would not be paid until a further period of six month's exclusive shipment had taken place. Thus Elder, Dempster and Company always had in their possession a sum equal to 10 per cent of nine months' freight receipts. This gave them an interest-free loan which was a valuable addition to their working capital, and although it was continually being repaid it was simultaneously being replaced by fresh payments of primage.

To a merchant like John Holt this meant that the deferred rebate owing to him, approaching £10,000, was always being held by the shipping companies, so this was an irresistible incentive for him to continue to use their services. Smaller merchants had proportionately smaller sums held by the conference lines, but the general effect was the same. Under these circumstances it is not surprising that other companies were wary of entering the trade, and only one British firm commenced a rival service between the setting up of the Conference in 1895 and the death of Jones in December 1909. This was the Sun Line which was started by the Gold Coast Mining Companies in 1906. It owned no vessels of its own, but used chartered ships to carry coal and machinery out to West Africa. The line was naturally anxious to obtain return cargoes of produce, but the deferred rebate system proved to be too powerful to permit the merchants to take advantage of its service. Consequently the only return cargo was the gold produced by the mining companies and when this proved insufficient the line left the trade after running for two years at a loss.

The lack of competition by regular lines from 1895 to 1910 did not mean that Jones had no problems. Many tramp steamers attempted to break into the trade, but few could overcome the deferred rebate system. This was particularly true after Jones had purchased the boating companies which on the almost harbourless coast of

West Africa were responsible for most of the loading and unloading of cargo. But the details of at least one successful venture have survived. This concerned the steamer *Prestonian* which was managed by Henry Tyrer and Company Limited. This vessel of 1,152 gross tons was normally used to carry salt from Fleetwood to Denmark, returning with cargoes of Baltic wood pulp for Preston. In 1906 she made two trips to West Africa carrying salt, stockfish and general groceries outward, and returning with mahogany for the account of W. B. MacIver and Company. The shallow draught of the *Prestonian* enabled her to go up river, and she used her own gear to load the logs. This naturally took time, and after a lengthy delay Henry Tyrer telegraphed to her captain:

'YOU MUST MOVE HEAVEN AND EARTH TO SAIL SATURDAY.'

To which her master, Captain William Kerr, replied:

'HEAVEN AND EARTH IMMOVABLE AM RAISING HELL.'[24]

In spite of the success of these two voyages they were not repeated the following year, probably because of pressure brought to bear by Alfred Jones. The shipping companies did not particularly wish to ship the logs themselves as this type of cargo was difficult to handle and easy to obtain. On the other hand they felt it unwise to allow a precedent to be established. Jones had £3,000 invested in MacIver's, which might have given him some influence with them. He could also threaten to withhold the rebate held to MacIver's credit from the shipment of their other cargoes. In the event, a compromise was achieved. MacIver's agreed not to charter again, and they continued to receive their rebate in the normal way. The importance of these voyages lies in the fact that MacIver's were subsequently taken over by Lever Brothers, and the experience gained with the *Prestonian* was passed on and influenced Lever's decision to enter the West African shipping business.[25]

Although Alfred Jones was largely successful in keeping outside lines and tramps from gaining a foothold in the trade, these were not his only difficulties. He had to ensure that the merchants themselves did not become shipowners, and while the rebate system was a help it was not the complete answer. The Royal Niger Company was the largest concern on the Coast. It possessed enough capital and could provide sufficient cargo to justify the running of its own vessels. It did not do so, partly due to its preoccupation with internal expansion, but also because it had reached an agreement with Jones under which he retained his monopoly of sea transport but agreed not to use his ships on the Niger itself.[26] The Royal Niger

Company was also permitted to charter four ships a year to clear the seasonal glut of produce. Another important concern was the African Association. This was made up of many firms of West African merchants who traded collectively, and in some cases also singly, on various parts of the Coast. The group owned two steamers and four sailing ships, but these were sold to Elder, Dempster's in 1896 in return for what were believed to be special rates. John Holt was a prominent member of the African Association and also an important merchant on his own account. He was frequently tempted to start his own line, but it is significant that he did not begin serious activities in this direction until Jones was dead. Miller Brothers of Glasgow[27] also had big merchanting interests in West Africa and at times were dissatisfied with the Conference over freight rates. Jones, however, was always able to prevent a rupture with the merchants because he realised that so long as the rates were not extortionate they would gladly pay a little extra for the convenience of regular sailings.

Thus Alfred Jones had many serious problems to overcome, but the rewards of success were very great. From the thirty-five ships totalling 53,000 tons of 1884 (when he became senior partner) his fleets rose to 101 ships of 301,000 tons in 1909, and for the last fourteen years of his life he monopolised the shipping and financial activities of British West Africa. His commercial empire on the Coast included the surf boat companies and the branch boat lines. He owned barges, lighters, river craft, engineering shops and repair work facilities. He provided hotels, cold storage and victualling establishments. He founded the Bank of British West Africa and organised the Liverpool West Africa Syndicate which was designed to exploit the mineral resources of the area. In Liverpool he was his own master porter, insurance company and ships chandler, and had a large share in both the Liverpool Cartage Company and the African Oil Mills Company. He owned his own coal mine at Maesteg in Glamorgan, and this not only provided fuel for his ships, but supplied the Sierra Leone Coaling Company and the Grand Canary Coaling Company (both of which he controlled) as well as selling a huge quantity of coal to the colonial governments at high cost. Jones also made it his business to acquire the shares of the African Steam Ship Company and by 1909 he controlled 26,328 out of the total of 33,731 shares. In other words, his interest amounted to £526,560 out of the total issued capital of £674,000. In addition, Jones secured the major share holding in the British and African Steam Navigation Company (1900) Ltd., after it was reorganised in 1900.

To some extent Alfred Jones's success was only gained by allowing the Woermann Line to grow rapidly under the aegis of the Conference, this expansion being the price which Jones had to pay for its co-operation. But had he tried to exclude his German competitor it is unlikely that he would have succeeded. Woermann had the advantage of a steady trade with the German colonies on the Coast, and many of the trade goods used by the British merchants were obtained from German sources or via German ports. Apart from this, West African produce found a ready sale in Hamburg whence it was distributed to many parts of the continent. This was especially true of palm kernels, for three-quarters of the amount exported from British West Africa was crushed in Germany.[28] Thus even if Alfred Jones had been prepared to face a serious struggle with Woermann he would have found it exceedingly difficult to have won a final victory. The economic advantages of a German-based firm were such that if Woermann could have been defeated a new competitor would soon have arisen. On the other hand, Jones's policy of co-operation with his German rival gave stability to the British shipping companies as it put them on a permanently profitable basis. This enabled them to borrow large sums on favourable terms, and much of this money was ultimately invested in one or other of Jones's companies and hence in West Africa.

If these huge investments had not been made, development might not have been stifled but it would certainly have been retarded, and this could have had important political effects on the future of the British West African Colonies. Once the French and German governments had decided on a policy of expansion it required very vigorous action if Britain's possessions were not to become merely isolated settlements on the West African seaboard. If these colonies had not promised an adequate return in the future—and without the investment instigated by the shipping companies they probably would not have done—it is doubtful if such a great effort would have been made. This suggestion, however, may be criticised on two points. Firstly, although steam shipping services were provided in 1852 it was not until 1879 that Alfred Jones became associated with Elder, Dempster and Company. It was not until after this date that the shipping companies became prosperous enough to have significantly accelerated the growth of the economy, and this was only five years before the British Government had to make its crucial decision at Berlin. If, therefore, we take the view that the activities of the shipping companies were sufficient to influence the policy of the Government, we may have to add the rider that it was the way in which they were organising matters—their potential, in fact.

rather than what they had actually achieved—that was important. Secondly, it can be argued that in spite of its reluctance to accept new colonial responsibilities, the British Government could not have stood by and allowed other nations to have developed the West African hinterland. If this is true and the Government would have acted on political grounds without the need for economic justification, then the work of Alfred Jones and the shipping companies can only be regarded as a secondary factor in the expansion of British West Africa.

The death of Alfred Jones made little commercial difference to the situation. This was perhaps due to the excellence of the policies he had initiated, but it may also be attributed to the calibre of his immediate successors, namely Sir Owen Philipps, (later Lord Kylsant) and Lord Pirrie (the chairman of Harland and Wolff). From 1909 to the outbreak of the war in 1914 the trade continued in much the same way as it had in Jones's day and the African Steam Ship Company continued to make good progress. From 1895 to 1909 the Company had paid an average of 5 per cent tax free, but in the four years following Jones's death an average of $7\frac{1}{2}$ per cent was paid.[29] The authorised capital was increased to £2,000,000 in 1912 and the issued capital reached £1,000,000 during the next year. There were, however, two significant differences in the situation and the first of these concerned John Holt and Company. Holt's, founded in 1867, had always utilised the services provided by the regular steamship lines, albeit with many complaints, but in 1907 they had purchased the *Balmore* of 1,920 tons deadweight, at a total cost of £8,534. This vessel was intended to act as a tender for their fleet of river craft, but it did carry occasional cargoes to and from West Africa.[30] When Jones died in 1909 Holt's decided that it was an opportune moment for them to extend their shipping interests and they ordered two new ships of 2,350 tons deadweight, the *Jonathan Holt* and the *Thomas Holt*. They cost £23,250 each and were delivered in 1910.

Under the terms of the deferred rebate circular which governed the West African shipping trade, this action ought to have cost Holt's the rebate due to them for their previous nine months' working. By agreement with Philipps and Pirrie they did not, in fact, lose this money but in return had to promise to use their ships exclusively for their own trade. They were not to build any further vessels, but were to carry the balance of their goods by the regular lines. So long as these conditions were fulfilled it was agreed that Holt's would continue to receive rebates on all cargoes shipped with the Conference lines.

Q

It is clear that Philipps and Pirrie soon regretted their arrangement with John Holt and wished to bring it to an end. It is equally clear that Holts' rapidly discovered the profitability of owning their own vessels and wished to expand, rather than contract, their activities. At the same time Holts' appreciated that the existing situation gave them the best of both worlds. On the one hand they were always able to keep their ships full both outwards and homewards, whereas with a larger fleet their load factor might well have fallen significantly, with a consequent rise in expense. This was of particular importance in a trade where the homeward cargoes were twice as large as the outward ones. On the other hand the balance of their goods and produce was carried by the Conference at rates equal to those paid by their competitors. They thus enjoyed all the advantages of a regular service on about half their shipments, without penalty, and carried the remainder themselves at what was really a preferential rate.

The second change in the West African shipping trade which followed the death of Alfred Jones concerned Lever Brothers. In 1910 they purchased the old-established firm of W. B. MacIver and Company, and, as we have seen, this gave them a unique insight into West African shipping conditions, for MacIver's were the only firm with recent knowledge of successful chartering in this region. Lever's quickly extended their interests,[31] and soon realised that the traditional method of exchanging goods for crudely produced palm oil, based on the collection of wild fruit, was a most inefficient method of organisation. They, therefore, proposed to establish mills on the Coast so that modern machinery could be used to improve both the yield and the quality of the oil, and where conditions permitted it was intended to develop plantations so that the fruit could be improved and a steady supply ensured. When the mills were built, however, they ran into many difficulties and the carriage of the oil presented a major problem. The usual method of shipment was by cask, but the net effect of back loading was to double the freight. The alternative of breaking down the casks into shooks[32] was helpful in that it greatly reduced the freight charged on the return jour- but native coopers were inefficient and European ones were expensive, so little was gained. As a result of these problems, Lever's organisation—West African Oils Limited—lost over £50,000 in 1913. Lever's then came to the conclusion that the only way they could reduce this loss by a substantial amount was by the chartering of a tank steamship. Unfortunately, Elder, Dempster's refused to permit this, and with the aid of the deferred rebate system were able to prevent any action being taken.[33] Levers then decided that it was not a viable proposition to run the mills on the coast, and early in 1914 they were closed down.

Lever's failure to obtain any concessions from the shipping companies makes it appear that Philipps and Pirrie were completely successful in maintaining the structure erected by Alfred Jones. But this achievement was more apparent than real for the sailings of the John Holt vessels were developing frictions and jealousies which were not easily controlled. Even more important than this, however, was the growth of the interest of Lever Brothers. For the first time an organisation which could really rival the power and authority of the shipping companies was concerning itself with West Africa, and Lever was not the man to forget Elder, Dempster's refusal to allow him to charter a tanker.

These changes may be partly explained by the preoccupations of the dominant owners of Elder, Dempster's. Lord Pirrie was primarily concerned with shipbuilding activities, and his connexion with West Africa and its shipping companies was basically as a means of ensuring continuing orders for vessels. Sir Owen Philipps was interested in the shipping line itself, but it was of no greater interest to him than his other shipping companies, and he had no special concern for West Africa. Philipps' interests were large and growing rapidly. By 1915 he directed 295 steamers totalling 1,520,060 gross tons, and it was not possible for him to exercise personal control over every aspect of his organisation. This, of course, was in direct contrast to Alfred Jones whose whole world centred upon the West Coast of Africa. Jones made it his business to keep in close touch with everyone connected with West Africa. This applied particularly to the merchants and even the least important had ready access to him. He always kept his ear to the ground for possible difficulties and was thus able to deal with them before they reached significant proportions. The real secret of his success was not so much the establishment of the Conference, or even the deferred rebate system, as his intimate knowledge of the trade and its leaders. Philipps's and Pirrie's other responsibilities effectively precluded them from continuing this aspect of Jones's policy, and the daily running of Elder, Dempster's was left in other hands.

When war broke out in 1914 the Royal Navy quickly ended the activities of all the German ships engaged in the West African trade, and most were either sunk or took permanent refuge in neutral harbours. A few were captured, but these only counterbalanced the loss of three Elder, Dempster steamers which were detained at Hamburg. The loss of the German vessels was of the utmost importance to the trade for the remaining ships found it impossible to cope with the volume of cargoes available for shipment, even though these were below those of normal times. As the Woermann Line was unable to fulfil its obligations the Conference was ended, the rebate system was abolished and all merchants were free to charter without fear of financial loss. However, this newly found freedom came at a time when chartering was both difficult and expensive, and so in the early days of the war Elder, Dempster's continued to carry nearly all of the cargoes to and from West Africa.

It is now clear that this was the opportunity for which Lever Brothers were waiting. The ending of the Conference left the way clear for other lines to enter the trade, and in 1916 the Bromport Steamship Company was formed to serve the Lever interests in West Africa. This was accomplished by the purchase of eight ships from H. Watson and Company, and the new line was place under the management of Henry Tyrers' who had, as we have seen, been responsible for the chartering of the *Prestonian* to MacIver's in 1906. Another firm to enter the trade during the Great War was the Holland West Africa Line. Once hostilities had ceased this firm began a regular service, and in the shipping boom of 1919 and 1920 Elder, Dempster's could do little to discourage them.

The boom of the immediate post-war years was a major factor influencing the whole of the shipping situation in the inter-war period. In common with the other companies controlled by Lord Kylsant, the African Steam Ship Company invested large sums of money in the purchase of many ships to replace their war-time losses. As these vessels were procured at the height of the boom they cost up to four times as much as similar ships built a year or two later. The subsequent growth of a surplus of shipping capacity then led to a considerable fall in the level of freight rates, and made it almost impossible to obtain a satisfactory return on the investment. In the cirumstances it was inevitable that Kylsant[34] and Pirrie would look back to the period before 1914 as a kind of golden age, and this led to a desire to reintroduce the Conference.

Suitable plans were therefore made with the Holland West Africa Line, and with the Woermann Line which had recommenced its sailings in a small way in 1921. But before these could be put into operation it was obviously necessary to come to terms with Lever Brothers. Lever's acquisition of the Niger Company in 1920 had considerably increased its stake in West Africa, but the financial difficulties involved in the take-over had seriously affected the liquidity of the whole group. The four vessels of the Bromport Steamship Company that had survived the war continued to carry a part of Lever's goods and produce, but the high cost of ships and then the need for economy had prevented any expansion of the fleet. Under these conditions agreement was quickly reached. In return for an exclusive freight arrangement, Elder, Dempster's undertook to carry Lever's cargoes at a preferential rate. They also promised to dispose of the vessels of the Bromport Steamship Company, and in 1923 three of these were purchased by MacAndrews Limited, and the fourth was bought by James Moss and Company. The significance of this will be seen when it is realised that both MacAndrews and Moss were part of Lord Kylsant's Royal Mail group of which Elder, Dempster's and its associated lines were all members.

Following these events came the reintroduction of the Conference in 1924. This was ostensibly at the request of the smaller merchants who could not afford to charter and who saw in the regular lines an equalising factor of some importance. The new stability in the trade may have helped profitability for the African Steam Ship Company paid a 5 per cent dividend from 1923 to 1928, but the extent to which this may be attributed to genuine earnings, and the amount which was merely transferred from reserves is difficult to determine.[35]

The shipping slump of the twenties was not the only problem to worry the members of the newly formed West African Lines Conference. The threat of outside competition was always present, and efforts to prevent merchants from carrying their own cargo were constantly required. The challenge from external lines was dealt with by the use of a deferred rebate on outward cargo, but the satisfying of the merchants was a more complex problem. John Holts continued to own a small fleet which they used purely for their own trade. This was supplemented as required by the regular lines, and Holts received a rebate in the normal way on these shipments. After 1924 all the Lever cargoes were carried by the Conference at normal rates less a secret rebate, and with only one exception the other merchants also used the services of the established lines and paid the tariff rates. The exception concerned the African and Eastern Trade Corporation. This firm was an amalgamation of many smaller concerns which had previously been loosely connected in the African Association, and next to the Niger Company it enjoyed the largest share of the West African trade. The size of their business convinced its directors that they ought to receive preferential freight rates, and when these were not forthcoming they decided to run their own ships. This decision was taken in 1923 at the time that the Bromport Steamship Company was being acquired by MacAndrews and Moss, and as Henry Tyrers handled both the Bromport and the African and Eastern vessels, most of the former's redundant staff found employment with the latter concern. Thereafter, most of the

African and Eastern's cargoes were carried by its own ships or in chartered vessels, and no rebate was received if it became necessary to use the services provided by the Conference lines.[36]

With the acquisition of the Niger Company in 1920, Levers had become the most important merchants in West Africa. They were then heavily committed in both the Coast and the Congo as both were large sources of raw materials necessary for the manufacture of soap and margarine. Apart from an old ship called the *Ars* which the Niger Company purchased in 1928, the Conference carried all Lever's cargoes until 1929. The situation was then drastically changed because Levers purchased their main rival on the Coast, the African and Eastern Trade Corporation. Lever's West African interests were then amalgamated into a new concern—the United Africa Company Limited—and this entered into fresh negotiations with the Conference in order to obtain even keener rates for the shipment of the larger quantities of freight which they now controlled. These discussions failed and the United Africa Company decided to carry its own cargoes. It therefore expanded the small fleet it had inherited from the African and Eastern (plus the *Ars*) and began to charter on a large scale.

The effect of this disagreement was to cause the Conference lines to lose a disastrous amount of freight. The Official Receiver later suggested that this was of the order of 40 per cent of the previous quantities and it naturally caused the companies concerned to become unprofitable.[37] Thus the African Steam Ship Company paid only a $2\frac{1}{2}$ per cent dividend in 1929 and nothing thereafter. It is not suggested that the break with the U.A.C. was the sole reason for this collapse. The decline in the level of world trade in the twenties meant that the ships purchased during the post-war boom were hopelessly overvalued, and it was the failure of the Royal Mail group under Lord Kylsant to deal with this colossal depreciation that was the underlying cause of its weakness. Thus the break with the U.A.C. was only part of the reason for the failure of the African Steam Ship Company and the other British West African shipping firms,[38] and it is very likely that even if the breach had been healed they would have fallen with the rest of the Kylsant empire. Conversely it can be argued that if the West African interests of the group had remained viable they might possibly have provided the prop which Kylsant needed to support him until the general level of trade improved. The extent of the difficulties of the Royal Mail group, however, makes it extremely probable that nothing could have saved it from liquidation.

As we have seen, Kylsant's problems dated from the short-lived post-war boom. Once this was over he was left with an enormous fleet which at the prevailing rates of freight could not pay its way. In the circumstances there were two courses of action open to him. The most sensible would have involved a revaluing of the capital assets of the group and a reconstruction of its financial structure so that the preference shareholders and debenture stockholders placed a smaller burden on its resources. From Kylsant's point of view, however, action of this kind might have reflected on his ability to conduct the affairs of the combine and could easily have resulted in his being replaced as its leader. At the very least it would have prevented the expansion of his interests, and in spite of his difficulties he was still anxious to enlarge his empire. In fact he purchased the shares of the Oceanic Steam Navigation Company for £7,000,000 in 1926. This brought the White Star Line into the Royal Mail group, but it proved to be a disastrous investment.[39]

The other alternative open to Lord Kylsant, and the one which he chose—or into which he drifted—was a very dangerous policy, but it promised complete vindication of his actions if it succeeded. This plan was to maintain a façade of profitability over the entire group, paying dividends in the normal way but financing them from secret reserves until trade 'turned the corner'. In practice he was able to publish balance sheets and profit and loss accounts which did not show whether profit had been earned or not, and during a seven-year period he paid dividends to the value of £5,000,000 which had not been found from current earnings, but from non-recurring items of revenue and undisclosed transfers of hidden reserves.[40] Unhappily for Lord Kylsant the depression in world trade not only continued, but worsened, and in 1929 and 1930 the group could not repay certain loans which the Government had made to it under the Trade Facilities Act of 1921. Kylsant made an application for these to be extended, but before the Government would agree to this it asked that an impartial investigator should undertake an independent enquiry. The true facts then came to light, and Kylsant—together with Morland, the group's auditor—was charged with issuing misleading accounts. Kylsant alone was further charged with issuing a misleading prospectus. Both were acquitted on the first count, but Kylsant was found guilty on the prospectus charge and was sentenced to twelve months' imprisonment.

This was the final blow which caused the Royal Mail group to disintegrate, for the shock to public confidence was great. It proved impossible to borrow, and such reserves as remained were invested in other shipping companies and had little realisable value. Accordingly a 'Scheme of Arrangement' between the Royal Mail Steam

Packet Company and fourteen of its subsidiary and associated companies was sanctioned by Order of the High Court of Justice in June 1932. One aspect of this arrangement was the setting up of Elder Dempster Lines Limited, and this acquired most of the vessels and assets of Elder, Dempster and Company Limited, the African Steam Ship Company, the British and African Steam Navigation Company, the Elder Line and the Imperial Direct Line. *Fairplay*, the foremost shipping journal of the time, estimated the financial loss to the shareholders of the Royal Mail group as £37,565,071 out of a total capital of £38,815,071 but this was not the final account, for many creditors and debenture holders were never paid in full and the true deficiency approached £50 million.[41]

Throughout the difficulties of the Royal Mail group its West African services were continued under the supervision of the 'Voting Trustees'. As a result no new lines were able to enter the trade and, once the situation was resolved the new company benefited substantially by its fresh start and lack of liabilities. Some of the vessels of the African Steam Ship Company were transferred to Elder Dempster Lines Limited and continued to sail to West Africa, but the African Steam Ship Company itself was wound up on 13 July 1936. At this time it was stated that unsecured liabilities amounted to £722,897 and as assets were valued at only £6,900 the deficiency was £715,997. To this must be added the whole of the issued capital —£2,500,000—so the total deficiency amounted to £3,215,997.[42]

Thus the activities of the African Steam Ship Company came to an end. Though latterly its identity had been partially submerged in that of the Elder, Dempster section of the Royal Mail group, it had for over eighty years provided a regular and efficient service to British West Africa. It had grown as the territories it served expanded and might justifiably claim—with the help of its associated companies—to have instigated much of the economic development on the West Coast of Africa.

(1) The following abbreviations are used in reference to the source material:
   A.S.P.   African Steam Ship Company Papers in the author's possession.
   F.P.P.   Fletcher and Parr Papers in the author's possession. These include the records of their predecessors, W. & H. Laird and Laird & Fletcher.
   R.C.S.R. Royal Commission on Shipping Rings, H.M.S.O. Cmd. 4668–70, 1909.
   H.T.P.   Henry Tyrer and Company Papers in the author's possession.
(2) K. G. Davies, *The Royal African Company* (1957).

(3) By the parliamentary return of 1850 the total quantity of registered tonnage employed in the trade to and from the West Coast of Africa amounted to 40,410 tons outwards and 42,057 tons inwards, and the quantity of tonnage actually carried may be fairly reckoned at one-third more.

> A.S.P. Prospectus issued on the formation of the African Steam Ship Company. Appendix: Statement of the trade between England and the West Coast of Africa.

(4) The contract was in the name of Macgregor Laird, and the annual payment for the service was to commence at £23,250 and diminish at the rate of £500 yearly making an average payment during the ten years of £21,250 per annum. A.S.P. Prospectus.

(5) A.S.P. Prospectus.

(6) A.S.P. First Ordinary Meeting, 11 June 1853.

(7) F.P.P. The author has the following items in his possession:

Three Manifests of Cargo
Three Epitomes of Cargo
Three Passenger Lists
Three Specie Lists
Three Parcel Lists
Bills of Lading—cargo
Bills of Lading—specie
Report on Conduct of Servants
Surplus Stores List
Manifest Book
Report on Conduct of Officers
Admiralty Log
Ship's Log Book
Bills of Lading for Outward Cargo
Cargo Receipt Book
Parcel Receipt Book
Admiralty Returns, *viz:* Journal
Abstract of Journal
Average Speed
List of Mails
List of Vessels Spoken
List of Admiralty Packages
Cash Keeper's Department
Victualling Account of Passengers
Victualling Account of Captain, Officers and Crew
Portage Bill

Wine Account—Captain, Officers and Engineers
Abstract Wine Account
Abstract Intercolonial Freight out and home
Vouchers for Stores purchased on the Coast
Passenger Lists, with amounts extended
Cash Book
Wine Book
Towage Account
List of Stores supplied to other vessels
Government Passengers' Wine Accounts
Account of Wines, etc.
Visitors, Cooking, Medicine, Breakage
Agents' Accounts
Kroomen's Wages Accounts
Kroomen's Victualling Accounts
List of Draughts, and what taken for
Ship's Disbursement Account and Vouchers
Account Current
Government Requisitions and Dinner Certificates
To be handed in within 3 days of Arrival
Indent for next voyage
Inventory and Expenditure Book

(8) A.S.P. Directors' Report, June 1855.

(9) William and Hamilton Laird had been in business as coal merchants for many years, but when the African Steam Ship Company was formed in 1852 they readily agreed to their brother Macgregor's suggestion, and became its Liverpool agents. Their office was very small, but the staff included men who were destined to make important contributions to the development of West Africa. These included John Holt, later to become an eminent merchant, and Alexander Elder and John Dempster, who in future years were to join together to form the firm of shipping agents that became known as Elder, Dempster and Company.

(10) In 1856 Macgregor Laird presented a copy of M. F. Maury's *Physical*

Geography of the Sea to Captain McIntosh of the S.S. *Hope* (this is now in the author's possession). An accompanying letter states:

> '. . . I particularly desire your attention to it with reference to the trade between Liverpool and the Bights direct—using steam power only in calms, going into and out of Port and getting clear of the Guinea current on the homeward voyage.'

Maury's essential thesis was that a scientific knowledge of prevailing winds and currents would assist the master of a sailing vessel to cut down the times of his voyages. Macgregor Laird hoped that these studies would be valuable in finding routes where the use of sails could help to reduce fuel consumption, and that they would assist a steamer to reach her home port when her engines were out of action. Pictures of the early vessels of the African Steam Ship Company show clearly that their lines and rig made this a feasible proposition and in 1860 the *Cleopatra* which broke her propeller shaft at Freetown was brought home under canvas by her Captain. The introduction of super heaters and compound engines in the 'sixties and the development of more reliable machinery gradually lessened the importance of these factors.

(11) At this time an arrangement was made to revalue the Company's assets. This was in accordance with the terms of the agreement originally made with Macgregor Laird, and his executors received £1,000—this being a fifth of the revenue account.

(12) F.P.P. Letter from the African Steam Ship Company to its shippers, 9 January 1869.

(13) The *Benin* (1,500 tons) was built in 1869 while the *Soudan* (1,500 tons) and the *Eboe* (750 tons) were constructed in 1870. Other ships including the *Don* and the *Norway* were chartered so that the service could be rapidly increased (A.S.P.).

(14) 'It is, we believe, no exaggeration to say that for several years previous to this, and down to 1872, the influence of the late Secretary with the Board was very strong, and that the greatest confidence was reposed in him. This confidence was rudely shocked in the beginning of 1872 by the discovery of his very serious defalcations. We made an attempt in 1870 to expose some of his jobbery in ships' stores, which under his "management" it had become the practice to purchase in London and send down to Liverpool at prices very much in excess of those ruling at the latter port. The attempt, however, was "sat upon" by the Board, and was received with little less than positive insult by the Chairman, who declared his personal conviction that the Secretary was an "honest man and a gentleman". To this day, however, the wines and spirits continue to be sent from London under the very transparent fiction that they are cheaper and better than can be had in Liverpool.

'So far as we could discover, there was nothing particularly novel or clever in the Secretary's method of falsifying the accounts, but, beyond doubt, he managed to get through a very considerable sum of money during those years in which the directors deemed it advisable to centre the management more in the London Office. The bulk of the money it appeared was squandered, but a large sum was found to have been invested in jewels, doubtless for convenience in levanting, in case of need. We entertained no doubt ourselves that Mr. Secretary was full prepared to be "off" at the shortest possible notice, and we determined that he should not escape with the plunder if we could prevent him. With infinite pains we succeeded in recovering and turning into money some £6,000 worth of property which the Directors evinced no objection to receiving and turning to account, though they have never yet said to much as "Thank You", for the trouble we took in the matter.

'As to what may have been the actual sum total of these depreciations we cannot affect to be much wiser than the rest of our fellow shareholders, we only know that the investigation did not go back more than two years and that the deficiency in that period approached £20,000' (A.S.P. Pamphlet issued by Messrs. Fletcher and Parr).

(15) The *Mandingo* and the *Lagos*, both of 1,284 tons, were replaced by the *Ethiopia*, 1,750 tons. It was also found necessary to build two additional smaller ships. These were the *Monrovia* and the *Elmina*, built in 1873, and they were specially designed so as to be able to cross the bars of the rivers on the Coast.

(16) A.S.P. Pamphlet issued by Messrs. Fletcher & Parr, p. 9.

(17) F.P.P. Private ledgers.

(18) By 1884 the opposition of Messrs. Steermore, Watson and Company, the West African S.N. Company and the Anglo-African S.S. Company had been broken, but interlopers continuously attempted to break into the business and, from June 1884 to June 1885, fifteen outside vessels sailed from Hamburg and Liverpool to West Africa.

(19) P. N. Davies, *Sir Alfred Jones and the Development of West African Trade* (M.A. Thesis, Liverpool, 1963), pp. 56–61.

(20) 1889—12,500 shares of £20 each (£16 called) = £200,000.
    1891—26,500 shares of £20 each (£16 called) = £424,000.

(21) By 1896 the issued capital of the African Steam Ship Company amounted to £539,696, and its debenture issue had been raised from the £83,000 of 1890 to £212,786.

(22) R.C.S.R. Evidence of Mr. George Miller. Q. 4311–4.

(23) The introduction of this conference and deferred rebate system was by no means an innovation. Regulation of shipping began in the Calcutta trade in 1875, and by the 1890s was a common feature on many routes.

(24) H.T.P. Story told by Mr. Frederick Cutts, still (1968) Chairman of Henry Tyrer and Company at the age of 87. In 1906 he had already been with the firm for 9 years.

(25) This was particularly true because Mr. W. K. Findlay, the organiser of MacIvers, joined Levers when the company was acquired and was able to guide their development on the Coast. He subsequently became Chairman of the Niger Company, and died in December 1966 at the age of 99. He had given the author of this paper considerable help in his research.

(26) *Royal Niger Company Papers*, Vol. 7, p. 160. MSS. Afr. S. 95. Memorandum dated 21 August 1907 (at the Rhodes House Library, Oxford).

(27) Alexander and George Miller traded as Alexander Miller, Brother and Company until 1904, when 'Millers Limited' was set up to deal with the Gold Coast, and 'Miller Brothers (of Liverpool) Limited' was formed to deal with the Nigerian side of their trade.

(28) *Report of the Committee on Edible and Oil Producing Nuts and Seeds*. (H.M.S.O. 1916), CD.8248. Table 1, p. 5. This state of affairs was partly because of the early start enjoyed by the German firm of Gaisers and also the lack of demand in England for cattle cake made from the residue of the crushed kernel.

(29) To some extent this may have been caused by the cyclical upswing in trade which occurred in these years.

(30) P. N. Davies, *A Short History of the Ships of John Holt & Co. (Liverpool) Ltd., and the Guinea Gulf Line Ltd.* (published privately by the Company, Liverpool, 1965).

(31) Messrs. Peter Ratcliffe & Co. Ltd., and the Cavalla River Company were purchased in 1912.

(32) A shook is a cask that has been broken down into its component staves and packed into the smallest possible bundle.

(33) *Committee on Edible and Oil Producing Nuts and Seeds. Op. cit.*, Q. 2584.

(34) Sir Owen Cosby Philipps became Lord Kylsant in 1923.

(35) This was a major criticism of all the lines controlled by the Royal Mail group when Lord Kylsant was charged with fraud in 1931.

(36) The African and Eastern later made an arrangement with the Conference whereby they did receive the normal deferred rebate, but their shipments by the regular lines remained small.

(37) *West Africa* (19 September 1936), p. 1305.

(38) Elder Dempster & Co. Ltd., British & African Steam Navigation Company (1900) Ltd., Elder Line Ltd. and Imperial Direct Line Ltd.

(39) 'A shipping Company was at one time regarded as an "adventure" but when the White Star Line Ltd., was formed by Lord Kylsant it had all the elements of disaster, and the accounts of the Company for the past year, which are reproduced elsewhere in this issue, show the extent of the disaster. The Oceanic Company's shares had already been refused by the head of one well-known shipping Company in 1926, and yet, without apparently making any enquiries into the working results of the Company, Lord Kylsant acquired the shares for £7,000,000; formed the White Star Line in January 1927 to take them over, and today the capital of £9,000,000 is irretrievably lost' (*Fairplay*, 12 July 1934, p. 71).

(40) Collin Brooks, *The Royal Mail Case* (1933), p. xiii.

(41) *Fairplay* (14 December 1933), p. 474.

(42) *West Africa* (19 September 1936), p. 1305.

CHAPTER NINE

The General Strike on Merseyside, 1926

D. E. BAINES and R. BEAN[1]

I

THE NINE-DAY General Strike of 1926 was the most outstanding single event in the history of British industrial relations. Some observers see it as a watershed in trade union history,[2] separating a period of syndicalist belief in direct action and force as the ultimate weapons in industrial relations from one of disillusion with strike action and the replacement of open conflict by conciliation.[3] The strike arose when the Government's temporary subsidy to the coal industry came to an end. This subsidy had been given in order to maintain the existing level of wages and hours for the miners in a period of depressed trade, and to stave off the threat of a national coal stoppage. It was intended as a stop-gap pending the enquiries into the state of the industry by the Samuel Commission, set up in July 1925. When the Commission published its report, complete deadlock ensued. The coalowners, anxious to lower labour costs, pressed for reductions in wages even more rigorous than those suggested by the Commission itself. The miners were equally immovable and resisting with 'much spirit and little subtlety',[4] refused to accept any solution which entailed wage cuts or longer hours. Negotiations with the Government for a settlement of the miners' claims were therefore taken up by the Trades Union Congress, already pledged to full support of the miners, and now provided by the unions with authority to act on behalf of the whole movement.[5] It was empowered to call a national stoppage in support of the miners should a coal settlement not be reached. When negotiations were arbitrarily broken off by the Government, the T.U.C.'s General Council was left with no alternative but to declare a strike that it did not want and for which it had not prepared.

The ensuing strike was one of sympathetic action on an unprecedentedly large scale but was not all-embracing in any literal sense. It was in fact a partial strike by some sections of the labour force with others held in reserve for action at a later date. Yet the Government, playing upon public fears of great strikes for their latent possibilities of revolution,[6] successfully presented it as something more: as a direct constitutional challenge to the State itself. The strike ended in total capitulation by the General Council. The miners gained no assurances and were left to continue alone for another six months. The strike was thus in its inception and outcome a 'sorry business',[7] not in terms of the response of the rank and file, whose solidarity and local initiatives in conducting the strike are usually considered quite remarkable, but rather because of the conduct of its leadership. Their determination, it has been said, 'came nowhere near to matching that of the strikers',[8] and their watchword was caution; they feared the consequences of complete victory more than those of a negotiated defeat.[9] Therefore, despite the attempt of the T.U.C. to run the strike with a good deal of centralised control, it is to the *local* organisations set up by Trades Councils with responsibility for the conduct of the strike that we should turn in order to examine the impact of the strike and the problems it presented.

II

Liverpool and the rest of Merseyside[10] have a long history of organised labour, with trade societies beginning to appear in the eighteenth century in the older, luxury trades and especially in trades associated with shipping, such as the shipwrights and ship joiners. But these were generally shortlived[11] and it is not until nearer the middle of the nineteenth century that there is evidence of permanent organisation, consolidated for the Liverpool trade union movement as a whole by the setting up in 1848 of the Liverpool Trades' Guardian Association, the embryo Trades Council. However, in order to understand the particular nature of the labour movement in Liverpool it is necessary to note several distinctive, yet interrelated, features which have characterised its position in the city. The commercial expansion of the port by the mid-nineteenth century—tonnage entering and clearing from the port of Liverpool doubled at each fifteen-year interval between 1815 and 1860[12]— brought with it a great growth of population, much of it caused by Irish immigration. By 1841 about one-sixth of the total number of Irish migrants to England and Wales was to be found on Merseyside[13] and twenty years later a quarter of the total population of Liverpool consisted of Irish immigrants.

Two important results of this influx were a significant increase in the number of unskilled workers and the importation of bitter antagonism between Nationalists and Orangemen which transformed Liverpool into a storm centre of religious strife, enabling political parties to make capital out of religious differences which came to form the main line of cleavage between them.[14] The effect of this most important feature was to militate against attempts at trade union unity,[15] and on the political front the Protestantism always latent in the majority of Liverpool electors could be easily aroused. At one election in 1907 the socialist candidate, assailed with the customary charges, 'found himself regarded not only as one who denied the Bible, but as an advocate of free love and the State ownership of children'.[16] The near-dominance of politics by religious issues helped the Conservative Party to achieve remarkable control in the city council. An ascendency which they had enjoyed for the previous half century was broken in 1892,[17] only to be regained three years later and retained without interruption until 1955.

This prolonged period of Conservative rule seems to reflect the party's claim to represent the established and native-born section of the population. For these people, conscious of wave after wave of immigration, 'support was given to that party which seemed least to threaten the amazing growth and increasing prosperity of the city'.[18] The Conservatives' success derives equally, however, from their greater skill in political organisation and in particular the adaptation of their organisation to meet changed conditions. For instance, in order to appeal to the newly enfranchised working-class voters, the party in Liverpool accepted the principle of municipal housing and sponsored the inclusion of a fair-wage clause in Corporation contracts; in return it leaned very heavily upon the support of the Tory working man. In a city where religious loyalty counted for more than political loyalty this support was channelled through the Workingmen's Conservative Association, which in Liverpool was as much a religious organisation as it was a political one. It absolutely declined to admit Catholics and a perceptive local observer remarked that the W.C.A. and the Orange Institute were 'identical in political outlook as in personnel'.[19] The municipal election results of the 1890s and early 1900s also reflect, however, a lack of cohesion between the component parts of the labour movement in Liverpool, which often ran rival candidates in the same ward as well as dissipating its efforts by contesting too many seats at each election.

These influences, many of them peculiar to Liverpool, gave the city a reputation for religious strife, sectarian riot and Tory dominance in local politics, together with a notoriety for labour troubles often bordering on violence.

III

The first important strikes organised in Liverpool[20] took place in

1889 under the impetus of 'new unionism'. The seamen came out on a six-week unofficial strike for a wage increase and the shipowners retaliated by recruiting pauper-labour at the Brownlow Hill Work-house and the 'riff-raff of any county' for the purpose of breaking the strike.[21] Moreover, a closely allied section of workers, the Liverpool dockers, were encouraged by the successes gained by the dockers in London that year and endeavoured to weld themselves into a fighting unit.[22] After pressing the employers unsuccessfully for an increase in the daily rate of pay, this newly formed union came out on strike early in 1890. During the first week of the stoppage one of the biggest demonstrations ever seen in Liverpool took place with a march through the city of forty thousand strikers and supporters, yet 'the men behaved with great decorum all through'.[23] Despite the orderly behaviour, the city authorities called out troops as a precautionary measure for what they regarded as a potentially explosive situation. The strike was indeed a bitter one, not least because the employers imported more than six thousand blacklegs from other parts of the country. It succeeded in gaining only slight concessions for the men and was perhaps more notable for its strengthening of the union which by, 1894, with Sexton as its leader, had maintained membership at nine thousand.[24]

The period of relative prosperity at the turn of the century resulted in increased real wages, but this changed to a decline in the subsequent decade and unemployment rose.[25] Liverpool, with the rest of the country, shared the growing tide of working-class unrest and militancy which marked the years from 1909 to the beginning of the First World War. This discontent, although widespread, was particularly concentrated among the unskilled and lower-paid workers. It would, therefore, be felt with particular severity in Liverpool, a port with a distinctive industrial structure concentrating on services (especially transport) and thereby attracting a high proportion of unskilled labour, and being especially deficient in major manufacturing industries such as metals and engineering.[26] The Trades Council in 1909 lamented that 'Liverpool undoubtedly seems to be the last city in Great Britain to catch the hand of prosperity and the first to relinquish its grasp'.[27]

In 1911 Liverpool became the centre of one of the widest and most energetic strike movements ever initiated in this country which convulsed the city for at least seventy-two days. A series of overlapping stoppages began with the seamen and culminated in near civil war when Tom Mann, for many years a leader in movements of revolt and probably the most prominent trade unionist of his day, led a general transport strike of seventy thousand seamen, carters, tramwaymen and railwaymen. According to the Trades Council 'the docks were deserted, mills stopped and engineering works shut down, and Liverpool's industrial population stood to arms'.[28] The original intention of the strike committee—set up as a co-ordinating body responsible to the Trades Council—was to demonstrate the sectional gains that could be secured by combined action within an industry. In this case the particular section was the seamen. It would appear that the transport unions saw Liverpool as a centre with a decisive body of support for this strike and where pressure could be most effectively brought upon the shipping employers, particularly as several of the largest shipping lines were weakened by their non-affiliation to the Shipping Federation.[29] The successes obtained by the seamen, who secured union recognition and better wages and conditions, led other sections of transport workers to put forward their own demands. Indeed, the significantly new element in this struggle was the unity achieved not only between the different sections and their respective unions but also between unionists and non-unionists, with the result that the employers could no longer break the strike with blacklegs because the unemployed were now flooding into the unions. The dockers and carters, in particular, were working in unison, a 'remarkable fact' since the dockers were largely Roman Catholic and the carters largely Protestant.[30]

Much of the credit for this unity was due to Mann's insistence on excluding religious differences from the proceedings of the strike committee as well as the syndicalist element in the strike which gave the strikers 'a perspective, a consciousness of aims beyond mere rectification of current grievances'.[31] Certainly, the strike was important in welding together the labour movement in Liverpool and in instilling trade union discipline into thousands of inexperienced unionists whose enthusiasms required restraint. It was also perturbing to the civic authorities because the strikers controlled the means of distribution in the city and essential foodstuffs could not pass without either 'permits' issued by the strike committee, or a military escort. The events of 1926 were therefore foreshadowed. Again, although the strike had to that moment been relatively quiet and orderly, the city magistrates increased resentment among the strikers by calling on the Home Secretary for reinforcements. Fourteen thousand troops were sent together with police from Leeds, Birmingham and Bradford, and two warships were brought into the Mersey. The outcome was that violence appeared where none had been before.

A demonstration was held on the Plateau[32] of St. George's Hall on Sunday, 13 August, to celebrate the strike victories and to cement the newly won solidarity. Though authorised by the police, it pro-

R

duced one of the most unhappy incidents in Liverpool's history, an episode since commemorated locally as 'Bloody Sunday'. An observer later reported that the police had 'tendered their fraternal greetings with batons deftly used on the heads of innocent people'.[33] The huge procession comprised both Catholic and Orange marchers who had 'disregarded the dictum of some of their clericals on both sides who affirmed that the strike was an atheist stunt'.[34] Converging in orderly fashion on the Plateau it swelled a crowd estimated at some eighty thousand strong. A disturbance among spectators on the fringe of the crowd caused the police to intervene and, according to a Conservative local newspaper, 'in a second or two the scene beggared description. Hundreds of people were practically shot out of the mouth of Lord Nelson Street, flying for their lives before a furious baton charge of dozens of policemen. People were knocked over like ninepins. Many were felled to the ground with blood streaming down their heads.'[35] The meeting was abandoned but with tempers inflamed a general mêlée resulted between police, demonstrators and spectators. Hundreds required hospital treatment and the Plateau resembled a battlefield. It was an episode which 'bred bitterness, strengthened the doubtful and confirmed the militant'.[36] That night looting took place in the city and sectarian riots broke out when religious factions took the opportunity to pay off old scores. Later in the same week two men were shot dead by soldiers during a riot in Vauxhall Road.

The wave of militancy and unrest continued in the city over the next decade and many bitterly contested strikes took place with little abatement except during the war years. In 1912 a strike meeting of bobbin-workers at Garston was attacked by the police, and a hard fought strike at Bootle ended after eight weeks when the men were effectively starved into submission.[37] Nor were all the disputes on a small scale. In 1919 a strike of tramwaymen, always a low paid and downtrodden group of workers in Liverpool, stopped all trams for five days, and during the great rail strike of the same year a battleship was brought to the Mersey and the main railway stations were placed under 'military protection'. The difficulties of the authorities were increased still further when the police union went on strike in July 1919 in protest against the Police Bill, which had made trade unionism illegal in the force. In this dispute the most important strike centres outside London were Liverpool and Bootle, with respectively one-third and two-thirds of their forces out. Reinforcements drafted into the city after the 'orgy of looting and rioting' which resulted, consisted of 2,500 soldiers, four tanks, a battleship and two destroyers. A further feature adding to the significance of the strike on Merseyside was the very wide and powerful sympathy which the strikers inspired among local labour organisations. This went so far as to include the threat of direct action in the form of widespread local stoppages together with the possibility of a general strike in Liverpool to support the police.[38] The outcome, none the less, was the failure of the strike, mass dismissals from the force and a long period of unemployment for most of those who had taken part.

The collapse of the post-war boom and the onset of depressed trade conditions were reflected in an ebbing of strike activity and rising labour militancy was transferred temporarily to another sphere, the reaction against unemployment. Towards the end of 1921 marches of unemployed demonstrators took place daily through the streets of Liverpool, most of them conducted at a snail's-pace but with no violence. However, following one particularly large demonstration on 12 September a group of the unemployed who tried to occupy the Walker Art Gallery as a protest designed to gain publicity were attacked by the police. When the demonstrators appeared in court 'the heads of a number . . . were swathed in bandages'[39] and the Recorder[40] censured the police for their 'unnecessary violence' and remarked that he hoped the incident was not generally characteristic of the way in which the police behave on such occasions. It is, perhaps, indicative of the attitude of the authorities in the city that mainly as a result of these remarks and the fact that he 'refused to allow [his] judgment as to the sentence to be influenced by the prejudices of a political caucus' the Recorder claimed many years later that he had suffered a carefully calculated ceremonial and professional boycott at the hands of the Corporation in that,

'From the day I spoke those words I have never been briefed on behalf of the city, and I have never been invited as Recorder to any civic function or ceremony other than the Lord Mayor's Dinner to the Judges of Assize'.[41]

It is apparent therefore that by 1926 the experience of the first two decades of the twentieth century had brought about in Liverpool an upsurge in trade union activity, a development of the labour movement and an experience of major stoppages which was to be reflected in the solidarity of the General Strike itself. By then a good deal of sectionalism among unions in various trades had been overcome with the result that trade union forces in the city were more consolidated. This was partly due to the formation in 1921 of the Transport and General Workers' Union which replaced the numerous unions catering for dockers and road transport workers, previously co-ordinated only by the federal Transport Workers'

Federation. In the same year the local Labour Party and the Liverpool Trades Council formally amalgamated. By this time the opposition provided by the 1917 breakaway movement of dockers and seamen to form a rival Trades Council[42] was no longer active. Even more significant, however, was the solidarity acquired during the strikes and the growth of the idea of 'sympathetic action'. There had also been some waning of those religious differences which had always proved one of the main stumbling blocks for the labour movement in Liverpool.[43]

The first twenty-five years of the twentieth century were a stormy period which saw great industrial unrest, often of a spontaneous and unofficial nature, on the big occasions involving outside leadership to make it more articulate and effective. Tom Mann, for instance, spoke at mass meetings in 1890, led the 1911 strike and came to assist during the Police Strike. But following each period of strife there was a marked extension of unionism together with great gains in membership. This was reflected in the strength of the Trades Council whose total member representation increased in the two years 1889 to 1891 from 10,000 to 46,000. During the 1911 disputes union membership had again risen significantly, the main accessions being 8,000 to the dockers (with a further 16,000 by the end of the dispute), 4,500 to the sailors and firemen and 2,500 to the ships' stewards.[44]

The developing labour movement also proved a catalyst in that, paralleling gains secured by industrial militancy, Labour became a growing political force in the city. In the municipal elections of 1911 seven Labour candidates were returned compared with only two in 1905, thus inaugurating something of a break-through. Again, following the turbulence in 1919, there was a further advance when ten gains were made on the Council. Thus began the acceptance of Labour as a significant political force, replacing the Liberals as the chief opposition party. Not long afterwards parliamentary representation was secured, Labour winning its first seat at a by-election in Edge Hill in 1923. Yet throughout the period the affairs of the city were still dominated by an overwhelming anti-Labour majority. Furthermore, the civic authorities, assuming that disorder would inevitably accompany strikes of unskilled workers, provoked violence by summoning troops and outside police who would deal harshly with the disturbances. They granted extra pay to non-striking tramwaymen and to the police for their services in 1911. The authorities were supported even by the city's Medical Officer of Health who blamed the increase in infant mortality that same summer on interference by strikers with food and milk supplies and on the neg-

lect of children whilst 'the distracted women were lounging or fighting in the streets'.[45] Such was the labour situation in Liverpool before 1926, a year which from the national standpoint was to mark
the end of a chapter of bargaining strategy and trade union thought.
Many of these attitudes were, in fact, pre-war.[46]

IV

With such a troubled history behind them, the Merseyside unions
were prepared for a General Strike should one be forced upon them
and some of the unions seemed ready to welcome it as an opportunity to settle old scores.[47] Merseyside was in fact one of the few
areas in the country where the trade unions had made adequate
preparations for such an eventuality. Machinery for the co-ordina-
tion of the various unions functioned from the first day, while elsewhere it frequently had to be improvised. In July 1925 the Liverpool Trades Council, anticipating a prolonged struggle in the mining industry, called an 'industrial conference' attended by delegates
from eighty-four organisations[48] designed to bring about unified
action among the Merseyside trade unions. At this meeting a resolution was carried to set up local 'councils of action' throughout
the region with a central co-ordinating committee in Liverpool.
However, the executive of the Trades Council decided instead to
take up an invitation received that month from the T.U.C.'s
General Council to set up its own Provisional Council of Action,
and act in accordance with instructions received directly from the
T.U.C. Its first meeting was held in the following March when it
was decided to broaden representation by inviting delegates from
unions in other parts of Merseyside. There was a precedent for setting up a body in Liverpool prepared to accept national directives.
In 1920, at the time of the threatened war with Soviet Russia, a
Liverpool Council of Action had been formed including representatives of every trade union in the city, with power, in the event of war
being declared, to carry out any orders received from London.[49]
On Sunday, 2 May 1926, the Provisional Council of Action was
called together and constituted the Merseyside Council of Action
(M.C.A.) for an area comprising Liverpool, Bootle, Birkenhead
and Wallasey. It was a federal organisation including representatives
of all the major trade unions and each local (sub) council of action
together with the secretaries of the trades councils and Merseyside's
three Labour M.P.s,[50] who were co-opted members of the council.
It was in continuous session from the beginning of the strike until

its termination, printing bulletins, issuing permits and calling meetings. During the strike half a million bulletins were issued, seventy-two meetings were held and in many cases huge overflows had to be held in open spaces. Grouped around the Council of Action were the respective strike sub-committees, for the transport, building and distributive trades, which maintained contact with the council through liaison officers. Later, there was some criticism of the T.U.C.'s failure to grant full responsibility for the conduct of the strike to local councils. The Merseyside Council's report to the T.U.C. (7 July 1926) stressed that the main weakness of the Council was the channel of communication with the T.U.C., for directives came via the Strike Committees of the individual unions and not directly from the T.U.C. to the Council and then to the Committees. There was 'a lack of definite instructions and contact with the Trades Union Congress General Council. Any instructions . . . received were indirect.'

The initial T.U.C. directive which began the strike called out all transport workers, including those engaged in repairs and maintenance, and all workers in printing, the iron and steel, metal, heavy chemical and building industries. The 'usual' exceptions for health and food services were made and provision of these and other essential supplies were to be in the hands of the trades unions themselves. The extent of union support for the strike varied throughout the country but it was expected that given the strong union organisation on Merseyside the directive would be followed to the letter. This would bring out 100,000 in the area, including 70,000 in Liverpool itself.[51] In fact the response which was described as 'magnificent' by the secretary of the Trades Council[52] was undoubtedly well above average. Postgate[53] has classified those centres for which he had detailed reports according to their 'solidarity' and 'staying power'. He placed Liverpool and Birkenhead in 'Class I', that is where the response was 'unexpectedly and amazingly fine' (90–100 per cent), and Bootle in 'Class II', where the strike was 'wholly effective'. Given the occupational distribution of Merseyside it is not surprising that a high proportion (nearly one-third) of the employed population would come out. But it was not just the 'expected' unions that showed solid support. The railway clerks, for example, although they later wavered, had the highest response for this group in the country (95 per cent) and the distributive workers showed an 'unprecedented response'. The Unemployed Workers, whose intention was to prevent the replacement of strikers, had 5,000 members in Liverpool, and the Teachers' Labour League provided financial support for the strike as well as speakers.[54]

This brief account, however, conceals considerable modification of the T.U.C. directive on Merseyside. The response of some groups called out was not total, whereas some that were not specifically asked to do so ceased work. Many 'essential' services, moreover, were maintained by volunteers. Some, for instance, might remain at work for local internal reasons. Thus, although the Birkenhead and Wallasey tramways stopped completely, only a momentary and partial stoppage of trams was achieved in Liverpool despite the occupation's long history of disputes. The evidence is inconsistent— often because the Government-controlled *British Gazette*[55] and the local emergency authorities were at pains to give the appearance of 'normality' to the municipal services—but something like 30 per cent of the Liverpool trams appear to have been running by 4 May, rising to 80 per cent by 8 May.[56]

Presumably it was the differing local circumstances in Liverpool that tipped the scales in favour of the tramwaymen returning to work, or not coming out at all, since the advantages of a steady, pensionable job that would be lost if the Corporation's threats[57] were carried out, would be just as real in depressed Birkenhead as in depressed Liverpool.[58] It was, for example, commonly held in Labour circles that 'appointments on the Liverpool tramways go by favour and those people who know a Tory town councillor get the jobs'.[59] The Liverpool tramways position was further complicated by the existence of two rival unions, the Municipal Employees' Association (N.U.G.M.W.), with unskilled antecedents, and the newer Vehicle Workers' Union which had been backed by the carters and was known to be associated with the Working Men's Conservative Association. It was believed by the Trades Council to be the 'tool of the Conservative party'. Not unnaturally these unions had been in conflict before.[60] Similarly the workers at Lister Drive power station—the main Liverpool electricity supply—were all back at work by 6 May.[61] At the power station and on the tramways, then, such initial enthusiasm as existed soon waned.

The situation on the buses was even more complex since some firms were non-union. Indeed, the relative lack of trams gave many operators the windfall advantage of enabling them to continue their services into Liverpool city centre.[62] This was true even of private charabanc operators. Similarly, motor coach services operated from Liverpool to London and all the main centres in the north and west.[63]

Some services were treated as utilities by the Council of Action. The Mersey ferries, owned by Wallasey Corporation, never ceased operation although most of the hands were T. & G.W.U. members.

They were held to be 'essential to the movement of food'. Similarly the unions were prepared to carry necessities for hospitals and schools and aid the maintenance of sanitary services.[64] These essential services were to be regulated by union (transport) permits. In the case of the ferries, however, the unions had nothing to lose in regarding them as 'essential' since there is little doubt that they would have continued to operate even if there had been union opposition. They had done so for a month in a previous strike. The officers were non-union and not prepared to come out; stokers and deckhands could be obtained from the various naval vessels that the well-prepared Government had sent to the Mersey; also two months stock of coal was held, and failing this the ferries were easily convertible to oil-firing.[65]

Although most transport services ceased, the unions were not given the chance to prove their contention that they alone were able to guarantee the movement of essential supplies. The Government's emergency regulations had the express and sole purpose of maintaining such supplies, and the unions' hand was further weakened by additional organisations such as the Organisation for the Maintenance of Supplies (O.M.S.) whose motives appeared to be more partisan. The Council of Action was, in fact, in an impossible position. It had to allow food and essential supplies to be transported—for example grain from Merseyside's important milling industry—or the unions would lose support among the general public. Written requests by local merchants for permits to deliver commodities such as coal, however, were invariably refused by the Council. But the strike, as we have already seen, was not total. Blacklegs and volunteers, who were released from the necessity of carrying essentials, could therefore be used to maintain the output of non-essential industry. Also, the permit system was open to great abuse through mislabelling as 'food', metal, machinery or even blacklegs.[66] Moreover, from an early date the various Chambers of Commerce stated that they would not go to the trade unions for permits, thus forcing the unions into a potentially violent situation in which the courts, fortified by the Emergency Powers Act of 1920, would come down against the strikers, for example for interfering with motor transport.[67] A carter was indicted for attempting to impede the loading of foodstuffs at Hutchinson's Flour Mills. He claimed that he had merely inquired for the Carters' Union permit but the magistrate in sentencing him to two months hard labour observed that 'People can use the King's Highway without permits from unions'. This was the first prosecution in Liverpool under the Emergency Powers Act.[68]

The permit system was therefore impossible to maintain and it was largely abandoned on 8 May, ostensibly because of its 'abuse', the Council of Action blaming any public inconvenience entirely on 'blackleg labour utilized by the authorities'.[69] There was now little point in working in those industries where such difficulties were at their worst and union labour was withdrawn, firstly from the slaughterhouses and then from the milling firms. Efforts were made to mitigate the effects of their closing, however. All abattoir stock was slaughtered in advance and as late as 12 May union men at Vernon's Mill were loading flour. In the event, the milling industry was maintained by volunteers. The unions would obviously have preferred their own men to operate the mills because of their 'essential' nature, but the authorities and employers were in effect not going to allow the unions to reap the benefits of public responsibility.

Workers in some firms were not called out immediately but were held in reserve should the unions wish to intensify the strike. The T.U.C. had the so-called 'second line', including workers in shipbuilding, who were called out during the second week. Cammell Laird, the Birkenhead shipbuilders, were enabled to maintain full-scale production until 11 May, but were increasingly hampered by shortages of essential materials through the transport stoppage.[70] The building trades were also called out in the second week, except for those engaged on hospital construction and (a nice distinction) on houses built for letting. By 11 May 6,000 building trade workers were out

The rail stoppage in the area was almost total. The railwaymen and transport workers had constituted two-thirds of the Triple Alliance and they were the first to be called out,[71] and although in the early stages an occasional passenger train ran (for example, the odd local service, or a daily train to London or Manchester) there was effectively no freight traffic at all. The railwaymen on the whole remained firm and despite the efforts of volunteers no line had more than the merest skeleton service until the strike was officially over.[72]

The situation in shipping, however, was very different. Given the local and national backgrounds, it was to be expected that the dockers would cease work. Only those at Garston, who were working in a railway-owned dock and belonged to a different union, held back briefly. Nevertheless, large numbers of ships managed to clear the Merseyside ports during the period of the strike. It is true that those ships which had to meet delivery dates sailed only partially loaded,[73] but even so the number clearing the Mersey underlines the incomplete nature of the stoppage. Out of 92 ships of over 1,000 tons (g.r.t.) in the Merseyside ports on 4 May, 25 had left by 15 May and 50 more had arrived. (In a similar period preceding the strike 68 out of 103 had left and 57 arrived.)[74] The Seamen's Union was not directed to come out by its executive but a successful attempt was made to bring out the Liverpool Branch. By the constitution of the union this had to be on a ballot (in order to qualify for strike pay), but the ballot was restricted to the Merseyside Branch and the lengthy procedure of balloting those currently at sea was put aside. The president, Havelock Wilson, obtained a temporary injunction on behalf of the National Sailors' and Firemen's Union to prevent local officers calling the men out without sanction of the executive. The national union's case was upheld by Mr. Justice Astbury who incidentally observed that the General Strike was illegal as, except in the case of the miners, no trade dispute existed: 'The orders of the T.U.C. were therefore unlawful and the defendants were at law acting illegally in obeying them and could be restrained by their union in doing so.'[75] Charles McVey, the Liverpool Secretary who had defied the order, was immediately suspended. Later, eighteen Liverpool union officials were dismissed for their 'unconstitutional action'. The Liverpool branch remained out, however, but since the majority of seamen in the port were members of other branches most ships were assured of crews. Furthermore, 137 safety men on the dock gates were sent back on 7 May after initially coming out. Serious damage would have been caused if the gates had not been opened with the tides, which would have been to no one's advantage. This situation paralleled that of the safety men in the mines. Indeed, when the gate men at Barrow refused to open the dock gates seventeen volunteers from Liverpool were sent to do so.

The printing unions came out in Liverpool as elsewhere. As Pelling has shown,[76] this meant abandoning the information services to the Government-controlled *British Gazette* and to the wireless. On Merseyside the local newspapers managed to produce editions, although often in a severely attenuated state and virtually all violently anti-strike.[77] Nationally, of course, there were papers better disposed to the strikers, but there was no harm done by calling out the Merseyside press.

The chemical and metal-refining industries of Widnes and Runcorn continued to operate. Over a long period Widnes had experienced proportionally fewer disputes[78] than Liverpool, presumably because union demands could more easily be accommodated in her highly capitalised industries. Similarly, the giant Lever plant at Port Sunlight also ran throughout the strike.[79] The several iron works at Ellesmere Port did, however, come out. For those other

Merseyside plants continuing to operate during the strike the main problem was not labour but transport. Finally, the local police remained on duty, despite rumours to the contrary current in Lancashire and elsewhere. Rumours that they were on strike were denounced as a 'wicked falsehood' by the Liverpool Chief Constable and two men were arrested in London for distributing leaflets to that effect.[80] The non-violent nature of the strike will be discussed later, but it is partly explained by this failure of the local police to come out and the fact that police from other areas were not needed, nor were troops.

The inescapable conclusion is that even on Merseyside with its peculiar labour situation and its history of disputes, the strike was by no means 'General'. Furthermore, there are some indications that from the unions' point of view the difficulties of maintaining the strike increased. Those Liverpool tramwaymen, for instance, who had little sympathy with the T.U.C.'s position were soon back at work. In the case of the general workers, the District Secretary of the N.U.G.M.W. had apparently not anticipated a rail stoppage but promised, if necessary, to use his influence with the railway unions to transfer coal stocks needed for Pilkington's Glass Works at St. Helens. When the strike was declared, he criticised the town's Trades Council leaders for encouraging it.[81] There is also some limited evidence that those men who wanted or needed more money than strike pay provided or who disagreed with the local policy of their union enrolled as volunteers in their own industry, or occasionally in another. A number of Liverpool dockers were said to have enrolled at the Town Hall and some T. & G.W.U. members took the jobs of tugboatmen on strike.[82] Sometimes entire union branches wavered; for example, the railway clerks, initially so enthusiastic, had a meeting arranged in order to 'buck them up'. These doubts and defections, however, do not constitute a drift back to work that would threaten to break the strike. For Merseyside, at any rate, it is difficult to accept the view of the T.U.C. General Council that the movement back to work 'was sufficient to create serious perturbation',[83] by the time the strike was called off. It was the superior organisation of the authorities rather than the drift back to work which was the major factor.

V

The possibility of a general strike had been anticipated well in advance and its declaration on 3 May found the local authorities in a state of general organisation and preparedness.[84] This was in considerable contrast to previous disturbances. On the last day of the coal subsidy the Government declared a state of emergency by Royal Proclamation.[85] Coal exports and even bunkering were prohibited and a previously arranged system for the distribution of food and fuel was set into motion. That is, the nine-months truce had given the Government time to set up more than the mere framework of the emergency services. The whole country was to be administered by divisions and one of these (the North-west Division) had Liverpool as its centre. It stretched from Cumberland to Merioneth. Since Liverpool was at that time the second most important seaport in Britain and handled about one-fifth of total imports,[86] the city was vital as a distribution centre. The authority could institute coal rationing, assign volunteers, commandeer vehicles and require the local authorities to regulate gas and electricity consumption.[87] Over 1,200 special constables had been enrolled by 8 May.[88] Two battleships and three destroyers entered the Mersey, the former landing food supplies. A troopship arrived from Plymouth and two fully equipped battalions marched off under sealed orders.[89]

The response to the call for volunteers was considerable, 20,000, or over three times the national average, offering their services in Liverpool by 12 May.[90] To this number must be added any clerical workers who took unfamiliar jobs in their own firms without registering as volunteers. It seems difficult to believe, however, that the majority of the 20,000 'official' volunteers were white-collar workers already in employment, students, or strikers willing to work away from their own firms. The only concentration of white-collar workers for which evidence can be found was in the Liverpool Docks, where half of the 3,500 volunteers said to be working there on 11 May were shipping clerks, accommodated in warehouses to avoid trouble at the dock gates.[91] It would, therefore, appear probable that the majority of 'official' volunteers were previously unemployed. This assertion is supported by the numbers of unemployed who were found jobs after the strike because they had acted as volunteers. A bureau to assist those seeking work (ranging from ships' captains and skilled engineers to dock labourers) had found jobs for 5,650 of them by the end of June, but even this number was said to be a 'small fraction' of all the unemployed who volunteered.[92] Furthermore, as we discuss below, had not so many of the volunteers been previously unemployed fewer problems of reinstatement of strikers would have arisen. It is true that there did exist the National Unemployed Workers' Committee Movement whose declared intention was to try to ensure that 'no unemployed worker is allowed to blackleg upon those already on strike'.[93] But it never spoke for more than a fraction of the 33,000 unemployed on Merseyside,[94] most of whom were not members of trade unions, and it was further impeded by the action of the local Boards of Guardians.

The problems for the unemployed, and the N.U.W.C.M., were apparent. Dockers, for example, who had been unemployed for the four weeks prior to the strike were considered as strikers in Birkenhead, and were refused National Insurance benefit. This the authorities were able to do because once the strike was declared such unemployed could be held to have lost work through a trade dispute, which disqualified them from benefit under Section 8 of the 1920 Unemployment Act. Those refused benefit, or already out of it, could always apply for Poor Law relief. But local practice in granting relief varied and, indeed, there seems to have been little distinction between the treatment of unemployed and strikers, for both could be debarred for refusing to take another man's job. In Birkenhead and in St. Helens able-bodied strikers were debarred, although their families were eligible. In West Kirby, a much richer Poor Law area, one striker was given relief when he refused to work with blacklegs.[95] The huge West Derby Union comprised the fourteen Poor Law institutions of the Liverpool area and was supposed to be 'in the forefront of enlightened and progressive unions'.[96] However, the unemployed were instructed to go to the Town Hall 'as there is plenty of work there' and the Guardians sometimes refused to pay anything and at other times paid only a minimal amount to strikers whose unions could not afford strike pay. In any case their 'special' relief averaged only 2s 1½d. per striker in Liverpool for the whole period—hardly enough to justify the later assertion that the 'Poor Law stepped in the breech . . . and the West Derby Union undoubtedly saved Liverpool during that terrible time from riots'.[97] Even so, the Liverpool Guardians were more enlightened than many elsewhere, for in some places even strikers' dependants were barred.[98]

Thus the volunteers came forward for a variety of reasons. However, they swelled rather than stiffened the existing labour force as their efficiency was not high. Volunteer dock labour, by official calculations, had only one-fifteenth of the productivity of regular dockers (that is each volunteer shifted less than half a ton per 12-hour day, compared with 5 tons per 8-hour day for the regulars).[99] Their employers were, nevertheless, prepared to praise them. According to them, there was 'a good quality of volunteer labour at the docks' but 'deliveries are not being pressed for fear of violence from the crowds at the back of the pickets'.[100] Yet it is readily apparent that below-average productivity was normal while the volunteers in the docks were only one-third of the number of those on strike. There was no question under existing conditions of the city's normal daily requirements being met. Merseyside kept going by moving only the most essential commodities and by running down stocks.

A somewhat similar situation existed for the other emergency arrangements. From the outset, attempts were made to stop hoarding. The *Birkenhead News* reported that it had been informed 'on the very highest authority that supplies of essential foodstuffs in the borough were plentiful' and that there was fourteen days' supply of food in the borough at that moment.[101] This, like similar 'no panic' appeals from the other authorities, was insufficient to prevent steep rises in prices. At the Birkenhead retail market every single item had increased in price between 30 April and 4 May and some had gone up by more than 50 per cent (including mutton, beef, potatoes and apples).[102] Indeed, before the strike was declared there were already complaints that prices of coal and foodstuffs had risen.[103] There is some evidence that the wealthy householders of West Kirby were laying in provisions, although they, being customers of the large stores, were able to get deliveries by telephone and van in any case. The small shopkeepers were in this sense much more severely hit by the transport stoppage.[104] When examining retail prices it is to be remembered that most farmers supplying the shops and markets had their own transport, and that the Liverpool importers and wholesalers were reporting relatively steady prices as late as 12 May.[105] In the case of fuel, coal rationing was severe, despite the authorities' constant declarations that considerable stocks were held, not more than 1 cwt. per week being allowed for domestic use. This was further restricted on 28 April to 1 cwt. a fortnight for domestic consumption[106] and the practice of hawking it around the streets was banned in favour of allowing householders to pick up not more than 28 lb. per week. This precipitated a rush for coal on 29 April. It would appear therefore, assuming of course that the consumer had enough disposable income, that it was much more difficult to hoard coal than it was food. The public utilities, however, were rarely short of fuel as all had been holding considerable stocks for some time. Again, the activities of the emergency services were just enough.

It is apparent that it was not only the Government which was well prepared. The emergency authorities who claimed throughout the strike that their sole purpose was to maintain essential supplies had working alongside them organisations whose object was rather that of crushing the unions. This poses two problems. Firstly, in a general strike, for reasons discussed above, *any* attempt to maintain supplies is effectively strike-breaking unless it is performed by the unions themselves. Secondly, since the anti-union political organisations worked to maintain supplies, their activities are indistinguishable from those of the Government. For example, the Government's emergency haulage committee which had been inaugurated 'some months ago' had the Liverpool Chamber of Commerce as its headquarters. It claimed to have distributed 10,000 tons of foodstuffs during the strike.[107] The Organisation for the Maintenance of Supplies was, however, a private body set up in London in the summer of 1925. It was effectively a recruiting organisation to help maintain essential services whose members became indistinguishable from other volunteers. In any case it seems to have been relatively less important on Merseyside than in London.[108]

The preparations of industry itself were less systematic. One must, however, distinguish between stocking-up in anticipation of a coal shortage, which had occurred before, and the anticipation of the lesser danger of a short-lived general strike.[109] Moreover, at that time most industries were operating under conditions of excess capacity.[110] The public utilities, as we have noted, were well prepared, holding stocks of coal more appropriate to winter than early summer conditions.[111] The coal dealers had endeavoured to keep some surplus in hand instead of liquidating their stocks at Easter as usual but were afraid to hold very large amounts because they would lose heavily in the event of a slump following the dispute.[112] In the wholesale coal trade the situation was similar. Everyone had been anxious to ship out as much as possible immediately before the strike. In April the output of the Lancashire, Cheshire and North Wales fields had been the highest for twelve months and a rush of shipments for Ireland had left Liverpool in the week before the dispute. Quayside stocks at the beginning of May were not large, however, and those shippers holding coal preferred to await developments rather than sell, unless at very high prices.[113] There were considerable elements of speculation. For example, a firm of wharfingers[114] had purchased briquettes which they stored in Preston. Some of these had to be sold at a loss when the strike was over.

Grain stocks in Liverpool were in the main lower than in the previous week and also lower than the corresponding week in May 1925.[115] The trade was not prepared to buy Canadian and River Plate wheat even if 6d. or 9d. a quarter cheaper than the April prices, as purchasers would not risk spoilage should the wheat have to remain in the warehouses. The market eased only when it was clear that the unions were allowing wheat supplies to move and that the mills were beginning to operate with volunteer labour.[116]

The cotton trade also was depressed and had already agreed on a week's curtailment from 1 May. There had been a bumper crop in 1925 but the trade outlook was poor and prices probably reflected this far more than any temporary stoppage. The volume of business was somewhat restricted by the strike, but over the whole of 1926 such slackness would not be distinguishable statistically.[117]

The general lack of business concern was emphasised by the quietness of the Liverpool Stock Exchange. Some prices were marked down but in depressed conditions the members of the Exchange were not unduly troubled by a stoppage that must have appeared only temporary. Many had in fact been reducing their commitments since the beginning of the year, but with an eye more to the general economic indications than to the labour situation. The Exchange then, was untroubled and there was no panic selling. The committee did not even hold a special meeting nor were any special trading arrangements made.[118]

Had the strike been conducted in a less orderly manner, it is doubtful whether business would have shown such relative unconcern. Indeed, many had expected that the disorders of 1911 or 1919 would return to Merseyside. This never happened and, in general, Merseyside was quiet. Some observers confused this orderliness with the 'holiday spirit' which was supposed to exist in the West of England. Liverpool, however, was hardly 'a city of happy idlers'[119] who spent their time in 'banter and laughter',[120] as the opponents of the strike claimed. There were, in fact, serious incidents at the dock gates, and ugly scenes at the tram and bus depots on the Cheshire side of the Mersey, but these were isolated.[121] It was sufficient to deal with the malefactors in the normal way. For instance, there were not more than seven arrests under the Emergency Powers Act,[122] although it is true that some quite harsh sentences of up to three months hard labour were imposed. Petty crime also, was less than usual. Despite abnormally large numbers of unattended vehicles in the city there were fewer crimes against property than in any similar period that year. In addition, convictions for drunkenness were also down, but that probably owed more to the interruption of beer deliveries than any other cause.[123]

The conduct of the police was in the main exemplary. There were a few complaints from Birkenhead where 'truncheons were drawn and used freely on the more combative'[124] and the trades council claimed there was 'considerable interference'[125] with pickets; but the general opinion, both during and after the strike, was that the police had behaved with remarkable restraint. Moreover, the fact that the unions were never able to paralyse traffic in the city was felt to have done much to preserve more normal conditions and hold tempers in check. The continued operation of the trams in Liverpool was held to be particularly important in this connexion. Also, the weight of official opposition made it necessary on grounds of prudence for the unions to conduct themselves 'like gentlemen'.[126] Because of this the leaders refused to hold processions or countenance any form of violence. The preservation of peace and order on Merseyside was, therefore, the common aim of both the unions and the authorities.[127]

VI

The attitudes of the various parties in the dispute were, in the main predictable. There is evidence that the declaration of the strike was received with a good deal of enthusiasm among workers and some of their unions on Merseyside.[128] In any event it represented something of a culmination of a period of rising local militancy. Early in 1924 a national railway strike had resulted in a general train stoppage which spread even to the Mersey Railway drivers. Soon after, a dockers' strike for a wage increase brought about a complete stoppage on the docks, with 30,000 men out. This was followed in June by a three-month strike of Liverpool bricklayers and masons who had refused to accept a national agreement and were demanding a settlement on their own terms. In the autumn of 1925 the seamen were out on unofficial strike. It is significant that the Liverpool labour movement had been in favour of direct action in support of the miners for a number of years prior to 1926. After 'Black Friday', 1921, a telegram was despatched to the Miners' Federation urging them to resist the lock-out and a fund was started for those who were out. This was followed by a resolution from the Liverpool Trades Council and Labour Party to the T.U.C. proposing 'that a special Trades Union Conference be called to consider the advisability of declaring a general strike of all workers unless the miners' lock out is called off by the Government and the coalowners, and the men guaranteed a decent standard of life'.[129]

On the eve of the General Strike it would appear that the local labour leaders had come to see the dispute in a wider context, having implications far beyond the immediate situation in the mining industry. An official of the Bootle branch of the T. & G.W.U. declared 'if the miners are defeated in this instance defeat will certainly accrue to us in the near future'.[130] At the annual May Day demonstration in Liverpool every mention of the miners or of the impending strike was greeted with cheers by the large crowd,[131] and Luke Hogan, soon to be the Labour leader in the city council, spoke the language of class conflict: 'The day has come when the working classes of the country have thrown down the gauntlet to capitalism, the haves and the have nots are arrayed against each other.'[132] Another city councillor went even further and called upon the crowd 'in the name of international socialism to say now that you are going to destroy the system of capitalism'.[133] However, the speakers appealed to the men to remain quiet and create no disturbance. If the ultimate purpose of the strike could be the transformation of society, revolutionary action was not considered even by the militants as an appropriate means of bringing it about at that time.

Certainly, the bulletins published by the Council of Action during the strike were very moderate in tone and played down the more far-reaching implications of the dispute. They followed the T.U.C. very closely in insisting that the strike was a 'purely economic, industrial struggle' and that disorder must be avoided. The Council required: 'Complete discipline, absolute loyalty—and No Disorder. Carry out instructions and the victory will be won.'[134] Centralised control of the strike was particularly important in Liverpool because during the 1919 police strike the serious looting and hooliganism which occurred had discredited the strikers with the public. As a result in 1926 no meetings other than those summoned by the Council were to be regarded as official, and meetings called in Liverpool by the National Unemployed Workers' Movement, for instance, were banned by the Council.[135] This organisation was refused representation on the Council of Action because it was claimed that the Council was composed entirely of trade union representatives. Other smaller, militant bodies, such as the Marine Workers' Union were also refused inclusion on the grounds that the Council was already too big and unwieldy. One of these, the Shipbuilding, Shiprepairing and Engineering Industrial Union, wrote a very bitter reply to the Council's 'narrowminded parochialism' in refusing them a representative, stating that 'your subterfuge . . . is entirely too thin and so contemptible, as to be unworthy of place in this the greatest movement the Trade Unionists have ever attempted. . . . Even your professed thanks for our so called loyalty is a gratuitous insult.'[136] It has already been shown, however, that the moderates won the day.

On the other side it appeared to the municipal authorities and local employers that the constitutional issues of the strike overshadowed the more limited industrial ones. At the monthly meeting of the City Council following the strike's declaration (5 May) the

National Anthem had been sung 'with great enthusiasm'.[137] When the Lord Mayor appealed for volunteers he was 'determined to secure generous justice for the miners' but 'a General Strike is an attack upon the liberties and freedom of each one of us. . . . We cannot consent to be governed by this Trades Union Congress. That usurpation must be laid aside. The lawful Government of our land must be maintained.'[138] It was to this appeal that many volunteers came forward.

This attitude was mirrored in the local press which was almost universally hostile to the strikers, in contrast to its position in some previous disputes. The major Liverpool papers managed to produce shortened 'bulletins' and the like, supplemented by the local official broadsheet. The *Official News Bulletin*, however, took much of its material straight from the *British Gazette*. The two Birkenhead papers were less affected since they only appeared twice weekly, and could produce a reasonably sized newspaper in that time. Virtually all these papers attacked the unions on a broad front. Even where a newspaper had previously showed some sympathy with the miners[139] it would not accept the means chosen to further their cause. The threat of a General Strike was 'a pistol placed ruthlessly at the head of the Government and people'[140] and 'threatened the very foundations of the state'.[141] Interruption of food supplies was directly contrary to the implied undertaking given at the beginning of the strike.[142] Not unnaturally the strongest attack came from the trade press. 'Democracy or anarchy' was the issue, according to one such journal, which hinted at Soviet aid to the strikers.[143] Virtually the only local paper to take a less hard line was the *Birkenhead Advertiser*. Its leader on 1 May was obviously attempting to offend no one. May would be 'a month of hope'.[144] Later issues tended to stress how the strikers were 'taking it' or asserted that 'the characteristic phlegm of the British nation prevails'.[145] The Catholic press was eloquent when describing the miners' situation. However, it felt that the breakdown of communications made it impossible to apportion blame, and it was the duty of all to support the legally constituted authority.[146] Not one Merseyside publication was prepared to take the unions' side. The means taken to further the miners' cause cut too deeply into the fabric of society.

VII

The General Strike was called off by the T.U.C. at midday on 12 May although for some days they had been convinced that it could not succeed. The local union branches, however, were to wait for instructions from their own executives. On Merseyside, where both the numbers involved and the solidarity had been above the national average, the strikers and sometimes their local officials were more reluctant to concede defeat. The following day the Labour members of the Birkenhead Council, for example, would still not believe that the strike had ended,[147] and at a full meeting of the Liverpool Trades Council on 27 May a resolution condemning the T.U.C.'s action was lost by only five votes. Once they believed it,[148] the rank and file took the news calmly, although few on Merseyside could have seen the outcome as anything but a defeat for the unions, despite the speeches of their leaders to the contrary.[149] For some local Labour leaders the problem was that during the strike itself their position had so hardened that it was doubly difficult to accept the final defeat. On the Birkenhead Council, for example, the Labour members had refused to serve on the Emergency Committee and threatened that if any emergency buses ran 'people would get out of control and all the municipal services would cease except by voluntary labour'.[150] When the Mayor retorted that the buses were a public service, and as such deserved to be supported, the councillor in question exclaimed 'This is war and I will not allow it'.

The main reason why the resumption of work was so slow on Merseyside was the problem of reinstatement. Prime Minister Baldwin had specifically asked that firms treat the men 'magnanimously' but that was exceedingly difficult to do in those industries which had taken on volunteers, particularly if those volunteers had previously been out of work. How could the 'deserving unemployed' be rewarded if all the strikers were reinstated? Moreover, in the existing economic circumstances no firm was willing to expand its labour force. The stoppage was thus prolonged as the men fought to get back to work on the old terms. The M.C.A. had recommended that nobody return to work until the reinstatement problem had been agreed with the respective employers[151] but in the end the unions were glad to accept what was offered. Surrender, however, often came only after a fight. On Merseyside feeling was intense,[152] and railway workers, ship-repairers, dustmen, tramwaymen, dockers (in Garston), slaughterhouse and milling employees prolonged the strike either because they themselves, or some group with whom they were in sympathy, were unwilling to accept the terms offered. It was in fact difficult, particularly in Birkenhead, to tell whether the strike was over or not for some days after it had been called off.[153]

The railway unions tried to hold out against the proposed national settlement which, for example, insisted that the General

Strike was a 'wrongful act'[154] and only half the passenger trains were running four days after the strike was officially over. The Mersey Railway even had to revert to its emergency service. The men at Clover Claytons, the Birkenhead ship-repairers, downed tools only three hours after they had all been re-engaged when they learnt that the railwaymen were not back.[155] The Garston dockers who were railway employees held out for a further six days, unlike the main body of dockers who were all back within forty-eight hours.[156]

The problems caused by the unions' unwillingness to accept some of the national settlements were made worse by the vindictiveness of local employers. Many firms, oppressed by general trade conditions and the continuing coal dispute, saw the end of the General Strike as an opportunity to purge their labour force. The issue was complicated by the existence of volunteers and it was around them that the subsequent disputes revolved. It was many months before all the tugboatmen and floating crane operators were taken back by the Mersey Docks and Harbour Board. Merseyside was the only area of the country where such a group was victimised[157] and the T. & G.W.U. set up a committee to examine each case of victimisation.[158]

The possible 'solutions' open to a local company can be demonstrated from the experience of the three local tramway undertakings, all of them municipally owned and controlled by Conservative Councils. The summer season lay ahead of them and therefore they had some leeway in engaging extra staff. In Wallasey, the Corporation used the strike as a means of 'weeding out the malcontents'.[159] Eight months later, sixty Wallasey tramwaymen were still not reinstated.[160] In Birkenhead the company had taken on volunteers plus some forty permanent employees and had managed to run buses but not trams. All the strikers were given notice. But after various deputations from the men and from several local unions and a two-day continuance of the strike by the local dockers, the Council agreed to reinstate all 380 strikers as jobs became available. By 27 May there were only thirty-one still out of work, but feelings had run high and police protection was necessary on the first day of the trams' operation.[161] The Labour members of the local council were furious, and as late as 23 June refused to travel to an official function in a bus driven by an ex-volunteer.[162] Liverpool, however, was in a different position. The Corporation had been in favour of disciplining the strikers and could probably have done without the fifth of their labour force who had stayed out the whole nine days, but Salvidge persuaded them to relent in view of the Prime Minister's lead[163] and they were all reinstated. The problem in Liverpool was quite different, however, since enough men had turned in during the strike to run a service and no jobs had been given to volunteers. In Birkenhead and Wallasey the existence of volunteers not only made it impossible to reinstate everyone but had also created an attitude where it was more likely that the authorities would take a hard line.

The most protracted post-strike dispute was in milling. In general, labour relations in the industry had been good,[164] but on Merseyside the rate of reinstatement was lower than in any industry in the area and much lower than in the milling industry elsewhere. The mills had begun to operate with volunteers only on 11 May and carried on entirely with voluntary labour until 20 May—that is, a week after the 'end' of the strike. Moreover, the master millers, sensing they were in a strong position, were determined to 'take on what they like when and as required'.[165] The union (the T. & G.W.U.) was equally adamant and demanded that all men taken on during the strike should be dismissed before their members returned but, since the mills could have continued to operate with volunteer labour for a considerable time, it was forced to accept a day-to-day agreement on terms that were a complete victory for the employers. Reinstatement was painfully slow and Ernest Bevin later claimed that the Mersey-side millers had not 'played straight [believing] that they have the ball at their feet' and had broken the national settlement.[166] In November 'some hundreds' of strikers were still not reinstated and the Minister of Labour was asked in the House whether he was aware of this situation 'in defiance of an agreement between the milling unions and the employers; and a promise on behalf of the latter that all employees would be reinstated in accordance with the Prime Minister's suggestion . . .' [167] On Merseyside there was a general reluctance to resume work, but nowhere was the unions' defeat shown more than in those industries where the men could not regain their jobs at all.

With the strikers punished in a number of industries and the 'duty to the unemployed' done, it remained only to reward those who had worked through the strike. Lewis's, the big department store, had some 6,000 employees, mainly in local clothing factories. During the strike, by which it was unaffected, the firm agreed not to reduce wages for three years—in 1926 a remarkable undertaking.[168] Cunards later offered all their staff who had volunteered to work on the docks a return trip to Canada.[169] In Birkenhead a fund was started for the police.[170] The Liverpool City Council encountered considerable opposition when it was proposed to pay non-striking tramwaymen an additional week's pay (at a cost of £10,000). The

Labour members not surprisingly opposed the grant as 'a dodge of the capitalist classes to use the ratepayers' money for their own ends and the rewarding of blacklegs'[171] and because it was 'a bribe to destroy and disunite the trade union organisations'.[172] This complaint, of course, overlooked the disunity of the tramway unions in Liverpool. The proposal was, however, overwhelmingly accepted and the tramwaymen got their money.

VIII

This paper has not been concerned with the *national* aspects of the General Strike and we would not be prepared to generalise our conclusions. Merseyside was only one centre of the strike, albeit a very important one given its industrial structure and previous experiences. Nevertheless, since the strike was not truly 'General' and since it was in the great cities and industrial areas that it was pursued with some determination, we hope the conclusions set out in the remaining paragraphs may be of more than local interest.

The response to the strike call and the degree of solidarity both during the strike itself and during the difficult reinstatement troubles were very strong. However, the problem of reinstatement was severe, because the bulk of the volunteers had previously been unemployed. For the majority of the non-striking public the day-to-day inconvenience caused by the strike was not great. The unions were unable to achieve a total traffic standstill as they had done in 1911. Individual firms and the Emergency Services were important in maintaining supplies, but without the motor vehicle their efforts would have been unsuccessful, and they would have had to call in the army. Even the private car which could pick up pedestrians was a weapon against the strike.

In general, and again contrary to previous experience on Merseyside, the amount of violence and disorder in the area was minimal,[173] despite inflamatory speeches and writings from both sides. Three factors are of paramount importance. Firstly, the Liverpool police remained on duty and it was not necessary to bring in an outside force, or even worse, troops. Secondly, the local union leaders (wisely) were at great pains to maintain discipline and order. Thirdly, the failure to shut down much local transport, particularly the ferries and the Liverpool trams, not only had an obvious practical effect but also meant the city did not *look* as though it might be undergoing a civil war. Strikers at one point were asked to refrain from using the trams in view of their 'demoralising effect'.[174]

Perhaps the very solidarity of the unions during the strike meant there was a considerable amount of co-operation with the authorities by non-unionists.[175] Certainly, the willingness of the men to come out was matched on the other side by aid to the established authority whether given willingly or through force of circumstances. Faced with the organisation of the authorities—who for once were well prepared—the local unions had little freedom of manoeuvre. This does not mean, however, that the unions were not fully committed to the contest. Indeed, local officials and rank-and-file members were usually more in favour of the strike than the T.U.C. itself. Also, there was very little inter-union dispute and, more important in the Merseyside context, remarkably little religious dispute within the labour movement. This was not altogether new during a time of crisis but it was a harbinger of the defeat of religious bigotry in Merseyside politics, though most observers would not regard that defeat as complete until the 1964 General Election. The Council of Action did have problems, but they were in the main administrative.

The effect of the strike on the industries of the area was minimal. Those industries whose product could not be stored—such as transport undertakings—lost some marginal revenue[176] but many of the others were already plagued by excess capacity and it is doubtful if their performance for the whole of the year 1926 was substantially altered, particularly if they were able to operate nearer to capacity in the days immediately following the strike.[177] Many of the subsequent difficulties of local industry, such as the shortage of steel at Cammell Laird, were caused by the continuing coal dispute and not by the General Strike itself.[178]

There is evidence that a major local consequence of the failure of the strike, followed by the introduction of anti-union legislation the following year, was a move away from pressure on the industrial front towards pressure on the political. In the forthcoming local elections of November 1926 Labour was to make substantial headway on Merseyside, as elsewhere in the country. Labour gained six seats in Liverpool (three from Conservatives, two from the Catholics and one from the Protestants), two in Bootle and two in Birkenhead, where it regained control of the Council. All these gains occurred despite the efforts of the Conservatives to make political capital out of the strike. According to them, Labour had made an 'outrageous attempt to destroy Constitutional Government during the strike',[179] but in Liverpool such Labour gains were common after mass strikes. It was almost thirty years, however, before Labour was to gain control of the Liverpool Council.

(1) We are much indebted for criticism of the text to our colleagues in the University of Liverpool and at the London School of Economics. For any remaining errors the authors acknowledge responsibility and blame each other.

(2) Allan Bullock, *The Life and Times of Ernest Bevin* (1960), Vol. I, p. 345.

(3) For a more sceptical view of the long-term effects of the strike see H. A. Clegg, 'Some Consequences of the General Strike', *Transactions of the Manchester Statistical Society* (1954), pp. 1–28.

(4) W. Ashworth, *An Economic History of England 1870–1939* (1960), p. 374.

(5) Julian Symons, *The General Strike* (1957), p. 43.

(6) See R. Page Arnot, *The General Strike* (1926), p. 4.

(7) G. D. H. Cole, *British Trade Unionism Today* (1939), p. 73.

(8) V. L. Allen, *Trade Unions and the Government* (1960), p. 198.

(9) J. Symons, *op. cit.*, p. 143.

(10) For the purposes of this paper 'Merseyside' is taken to include the areas of present-day Liverpool, Bootle, Birkenhead and Wallasey. Also, for certain purposes notice has to be taken of the peripheral surburban areas such as West Kirby and Crosby and the neighbouring industrial communities of Ellesmere Port, Widnes, Runcorn and St. Helens, although none of these are included in our definition.

(11) William Hamling, *A Short History of The Liverpool Trades Council, 1848–1948* (Liverpool Trades Council and Labour Party, 1948), p. 8.

(12) D. Caradog Jones, ed., *The Social Survey of Merseyside* (1934), pp. 21–22.

(13) R. Lawton, 'Genesis of Population' in W. Smith, ed., *A Scientific Survey of Merseyside* (1953), pp. 123–25.

(14) 'There are two mimic armies in Liverpool who treat elections as a miniature Holy War', B. Whittingham-Jones, *The Pedigree of Liverpool Politics: White, Orange and Green* (privately printed Liverpool, 1936), p. 29. See also S. Maddock, *The Liverpool Trades Council and Politics, 1878–1918* (M.A. thesis, University of Liverpool, 1959), pp. 13–16.

(15) Sir James Sexton, *Sir James Sexton, Agitator* (1936), p. 109.

(16) Stanley Salvidge, *Salvidge of Liverpool* (1934), p. 79. It was said that during the 1890s the working class electorate of Liverpool were roused 'to heights of passionate feeling . . . not with any demands regarding housing, or wages, or conditions of labour, but with the correct procedure for the conduct of divine service in the Church of England' (*ibid.*).

(17) The Liberal victory at these elections was a freak result in that it came about largely from a lack of adjustment in municipal boundaries. The outward movement of the population to the suburbs meant that the poor tended to remain in the older, central parts of the town whereas the outer Tory wards had a steadily increasing population, yet with no increased representation on the council. The boundaries were altered in 1895 and the Liberals lost control. See B. D. White, *A History of the Corporation of Liverpool, 1835–1914* (1951), pp. 101–02.

(18 D. Caradog Jones, *op. cit.*, p. 45.

(19) B. Whittingham-Jones, *op. cit.*, p. 6.

(20) Early recorded strikes among Liverpool journeymen date from the mid-eighteenth century and include the tailors' strike in 1758 against the 'poor, mean and artful stratagems' of the master tailors in employing unskilled labour, and that of the cabinet makers who 'quit [their] shops' in 1760 to force a reduction in hours equivalent to those in the London trade. *Williamson's Liverpool Advertiser*, 23 June 1758, 13 June 1760.

(21) S. Maddock, *op. cit.*, pp. 66–68.

(22) The first attempt to organise the dockers had been made some years before

but it was a weak affair and the first strike in 1885, lasting only one day, was a complete failure.

(23) *Liverpool Daily Post*, 8 March 1890.

(24) W. Hamling, *op. cit.*, p. 23.

(25) For an analysis of comparative wage, price and employment statistics in this period see H. A. Clegg, Alan Fox and A. F. Thompson, *A History of British Trade Unions since 1889*, Vol. I, 1889–1910 (1964), pp. 479–83.

(26) The 1911 *Census of England and Wales* lists relative proportions per 10,000 males aged ten years and upwards engaged in certain groups of occupations as follows:

	City of Liverpool C.B.	England and Wales
Dock Labourers	768	99
General Labourers	266	222
Conveyance on Roads	565	345
Conveyance on Seas, Rivers and Canals	495	97
Conveyance on Railways	358	291
General Engineering, and Machine Making	386	491

In the 1921 *Census* a total occupied workforce of almost 250,000 males included 75,000 transport workers (of which more than 17,000 were dock labourers), 22,000 general labourers and 22,000 metal workers.

(27) Liverpool Trades and Labour Council, *Annual Report*, 1909–10. Some support for this statement (for the employment of dock and riverside labour in particular), can be found in the monthly employment reports of *The Board of Trade Labour Gazette*. In the latter half of 1908 and the last four months of 1909, for instance, employment appears to have been significantly worse in Liverpool than in the other principal ports, where the position was improving.

(28) Quoted in S. Maddock, *op. cit.*, p. 166.

(29) See H. R. Hikins, 'The Liverpool General Transport Strike, 1911', *Transactions of the Historic Society of Lancashire and Cheshire*, Vol. 113 (1961), p. 171.

(30) *Ibid.*, p. 175. The Carters' Union was not affiliated to the Trades Council and had strong associations with the local Workingmen's Conservative Association.

(31) H. R. Hikins, *op. cit.*, p. 178. See also Millie Toole, *Mrs. Bessie Braddock, M.P.* (1957), p. 28.

(32) The Plateau is the open area in the centre of the city surrounding St. George's Hall. It can hold a crowd of several hundred thousands.

(33) *Birkenhead Advertiser*, 13 August 1919.

(34) Fred Bower, *Rolling Stonemason* (1936), p. 195.

(35) *Liverpool Daily Post*, 14 August 1911.

(36) Millie Toole, *op. cit.*, p. 29.

(37) T. L. Drinkwater, *A History of the Trade Unions and Labour Party in Liverpool, 1911 to the Great Strike* (B. A. thesis, University of Liverpool, 1940), pp. 22–23.

(38) See *Liverpool Echo*, 15 August 1919. The Police and Prison Officers' Union had been granted affiliation to the Trades Council in 1918, in spite of opposition as a result of the crimes alleged against them in 1911. It was felt that they were equally entitled to labour representation and that it was safer to have them inside the council than remain outside it. S. Maddock, *op. cit.*, p. 70.

(39) *Liverpool Echo*, 13 September 1921.

(40) E. G. Hemmerde, Recorder of Liverpool 1909–48 and sometime Liberal, and later Labour, Member of Parliament.

(41) *Liverpool Post and Mercury*, 3 August 1934. The correspondence which continued in this paper for many days after the publication of these allegations gives ample confirmation that this boycott did exist.

(42) These two unions seceded from the Trades Council because of, respectively, its alleged pacifist and socialist tendencies, S. Maddock, *op. cit.*, p. 224.

(43) See T. L. Drinkwater, *op. cit.*, p. 39. Nevertheless, Labour did not contest Everton in the 1918 General Election where 'they were still blaming the Pope for causing the war'.

(44) Taken from Maddock, *op. cit.*, pp. 62–64, and Drinkwater, *op. cit.*, pp. 11, 20.

(45) City of Liverpool Health Department, *Report*, 1911, pp. 48–52.

(46) E. H. Phelps Brown, *The Growth of British Industrial Relations* (1959), p. 348.

(47) See below for the attitudes of local trades unions to the strike itself.

(48) Tom Mann was also present at this conference to support a resolution calling for unity between miners, metal, rail and transport workers and for 'no sectional settlements'. See *Minutes of the Liverpool Trades Council and Labour Party Executive Committee*, 31 July 1925 (MS in Liverpool Record Office).

(49) *Liverpool Daily Post*, 19 August 1920.

(50) J. H. Hayes (Edge Hill), J. Gibbins (West Toxteth) and J. Sexton (St. Helens).

(51) The 100,000 called out on Merseyside included 20,000 dockers, 20,000 railwaymen and 20,000 warehousemen and similar occupations. See also above (footnote 26). Postgate concluded that the dockers were the backbone of the strike in Liverpool. See R. W. Postgate *et al.*, *A Worker's History of the Great Strike* (1927).

(52) Liverpool Trades Council, 'Collection of Documents Relating to the General Strike, 1926' (in Liverpool Record Office), hereafter referred to as 'General Strike Documents'.

(53) R. W. Postgate *et al.*, *op. cit.*, p. 27.

(54) Liverpool Trades Council, 'General Strike Documents'.

(55) The Reports of the *British Gazette* (when compared with local publications) invariably exaggerated the degree of normality. For example, on 7 May it reported 'a good train service' when not 10 per cent of the normal service was running and that 'thousands of young men from shipping offices' were in the docks when it is doubtful if the number approached 2,000.

(56) *Echo and Express Bulletin*, 4 May 1926 and 8 May 1926. The Municipal Tramways Association reported that 50 per cent of the men were back by 6 May.

(57) In Liverpool a notice stated 'Those employees who have not turned in for duty, and are not prepared to help carry on the tramway service, can receive their wage cheques—subject to their handing in their Corporation uniforms'. *Liverpool Official News Bulletin 1*, 5 May 1926. Similar notices were posted at the docks, and at Pilkingtons in St. Helens, but in the former case the 'semi casual' nature of the employment and the needs of the industry would hardly give such notices much force. See V. H. Jensen, *The Hiring of Dock Labour* (1964) for details of the dock hiring procedure at this time.

(58) Indeed, the unions considered conditions on the Birkenhead tramways better than in Liverpool and compared them favourably with any in the country. *Liverpool Post and Mercury*, 15 May 1926.

(59) Communication from Secretary of Liverpool Trades Council to T.U.C. in 'Collection of documents relating to the General Strike', in T.U.C. Library.

(60) Maddock, *op. cit.*, pp. 171–72.

(61) *Liverpool Official News Bulletin*, 6 May 1926.

(62) Towards the end of the strike the police were also stopping private cars in

Aintree and making the drivers fill them up with passengers. *Walton Times*, 14 May 1926.

(63) *Post and Courier Bulletin*, 5 May 1926.

(64) T.U.C. statement, 1 May 1926. This was also true locally, 'Permits for Dr. Musson (the M.O.H.) would be honoured for anything he needed' it was reported in the *Liverpool Post and Mercury*, 3 May 1926.

(65) Statement by Captain of the Ferries, *ibid.*, 3 May 1926.

(66) A firm at Old Swan, for instance, was said to be carrying toys and metal polish labelled 'food'. Liverpool Trades Council, 'General Strike Documents'.

(67) The Transport Workers were already engaged in a dispute since they were attempting to fight the single-manning of lorries in excess of three tons. Pickets of the Liverpool Carters and Motormen's Union tried to stop single-manned lorries entering the docks once their ultimatum to the employers ran out on 1 May 1926. This in fact affected only the smaller firms since the larger ones had separate agreements with the union and in any case the Carters' individual picketing was soon forgotten in the general shut down and the difficulties of trying to maintain the permit system at the dock gates. *Journal of Commerce*, 1 May 1926. *Liverpool Echo*, 1 May 1926.

(68) *Echo and Express Bulletin*, 10 May 1926.

(69) See M.C.A. *Strike Bulletin*, No. 2 and No. 4.

(70) Between 400 and 500 ship repairers at Cammell Lairds had come out almost immediately, but the shipwrights were at work 'as usual' on 5 May. The 5,000 remaining ceased work at 5 o'clock on 11 May. A difficulty of this situation for the unions was that Cammell Lairds were able to transfer shipwrights to repair work. *Birkenhead News Strike Bulletin*, 5 May 1926; *Birkenhead News*, 12 May 1926.

(71) *Liverpool Post and Mercury*, 3 May 1926.

(72) *Post and Courier Bulletin* and *Liverpool Official News Bulletin*, 5 May 1926 and 6 May 1926. No trains at all entered Liverpool on 5 May.

(73) *Birkenhead News*, 5 May 1926. Partial loading was also caused by non-availability of cargoes because of transport difficulties.

(74) Shipping movements were estimated by comparing the list of ships in the various Merseyside docks given in the local *Journal of Commerce* on its last day of publication before the strike and its first after. These were then compared with a similar period previous to the strike. It is, of course, true that some of the ships leaving in the period 23 April 1926 to 4 May 1926 did so earlier than they intended, to beat the stoppage.

(75) *Birkenhead Advertiser*, 15 May 1926. See *Journal of Commerce*, 3 May 1926; *Birkenhead News*, 8 May 1926; and *Liverpool Echo* and *Liverpool Post and Mercury*, 21 July 1926 for details of the dispute.

(76) H. Pelling, *A Short History of the Labour Party* (1961), p. 61.

(77) See below p. 258.

(78) *Liverpool Post and Mercury*, 3 May 1926. *Garston News*, 14 May 1926.

(79) *Birkenhead Advertiser*, 8 May 1926.

(80) *Liverpool Official News Bulletin*, 7 May 1926.

(81) St. Helens Plate and Sheet Glass Industrial Council, *Minutes*, 29 April and 4 May 1926. He claimed that the local leaders were exceeding their authority.

(82) *Post and Courier Bulletin*, 12 May 1926 and *Liverpool Official News Bulletin*, 8 May 1926. See also T. & G.W.U. 'Report of a Joint Meeting of Officials, Area Committee, Group and Branch Committees', Clifton House, Liverpool, 10 June 1926.

(83) T.U.C. General Council, 'Report of Intelligence Committee'; in T.U.C. Library, (typewritten).

(84) Confirmation of the authorities' preparations was given by the Chief Con-

stable. He let it be known before the strike that there was no need for alarm 'as the whole thing has been carefully schemed out to meet any extraordinary emergency' and that the police would be ready to convoy goods should the need arise. *Liverpool Echo*, 1 May 1926. *Daily Courier*, 1 May 1926.

(85) Under the Emergency Powers Act (1920).

(86) G. C. Allen *et al.*, *The Import Trade of the Port of Liverpool* (Department of Social Science, Liverpool University, 1946), p. 22.

(87) Bootle was effectively amalgamated with Liverpool for emergency purposes since all public utility services and administration were dealt with centrally. *Liverpool Post and Mercury*, 3 May 1926.

(88) *British Gazette*, 8 May 1926.

(89) *Journal of Commerce*, 3 May 1926; *Birkenhead News*, 5 May 1926; *Garston News*, 7 May 1926; *Echo and Express Bulletin*, 6 May 1926.

(90)   LIVERPOOL ENROLMENTS BY 11 MAY 1926

Jobs to which allocated

Petrol lorry and steam waggon drivers	1402
Motor drivers	1404
Shipping	1230
Docks and cold storage	3733
Warehousemen and carters	1113
Labourers	2635

Out of a total (excluding 'specials' and Bootle area) of 17,176. (*Echo and Express Bulletin*, 11 May 1926.)

The estimates of the numbers of volunteers come unfortunately from either the Government-controlled publications or from the Town Hall. Since there was no complaint of their exaggeration at the time, we have assumed their reasonable accuracy. To the 20,000 would have to be added volunteers in other parts of Merseyside (possibly another 25 per cent), special constables, etc., and, as mentioned in the text, employees changing jobs in their own firms. The grand total of volunteers for the country was about 500,000. *British Gazette* 7 May 1926 and 12 May 1926; *Birkenhead News* 5 May 1926, 8 May 1926; *Birkenhead Advertiser* 12 May 1926.

(91) Some 100 of the headquarters staff of Elder, Dempster volunteered for work in the Liverpool docks. *Elder, Dempster Magazine*, June 1926, p. 45. The Corn Trades Association made special arrangements for an accident policy 'for those on national work'. Full salaries appear to have been paid to volunteers by their employers and, in the case of shop assistants, the average of their commission. *Echo and Express Bulletin*, 11 May 1926.

(92) Robert Gladstone in *Liverpool Echo*, 22 June 1926. See also *Liverpool Echo*, 11 May 1926 and 19 May 1926. The bureau opened on 24 May 1926 for one month.

(93) See letter to M.C.A., 6 May 1926 from N.U.W.C.M. and also its own broadsheet *The Unemployed Worker* 8 May 1926 ('General Strike Documents').

(94) MERSEYSIDE UNEMPLOYMENT (INSURED WORKERS)

Liverpool	22,879 men and 3,921 women
Birkenhead	5,088 persons
Wallasey	1,286 persons
Bootle	(not available).

Liverpool Echo, 3 September 1926. These figures and others in this newspaper are almost certainly understated. The Ministry of Labour reported 63,000 unemployed for mid-1926. *Social Survey of Merseyside*, Vol. II, p. 5.

(95) *Birkenhead Advertiser*, 15 May 1926, and *Birkenhead News*, 13 May 1926.

(96) Alderman Salvidge (Conservative Leader of the Council and for many years the 'unsalaried Bourgomaster of Liverpool') in the *Daily Courier*, 29 March 1926.

(97) Report of Mrs. Hock, Chairman of the West Derby Union, *Liverpool Echo* 26 May 1926. £7,500 in 'special' (as distinct from 'ordinary') relief was paid out during a period of 2 weeks. This was supposed to have relieved nearly 50,000 persons. The docker's strike pay at this time was 3/4d. per day with extra for dependants. *Echo and Express Bulletin*, 8 May 1926.

(98) For example in Southampton. See *Birkenhead News*, 5 May 1926.

(99) See *T.U.C. Intelligence Report*, 10 May 1926 (and M.C.A. Bulletin in 'General Strike Documents').

(100) *George Broomhall's Corn Trade News*, 6 May 1926.

(101) *Birkenhead News*, 5 May 1926.

(102) English beef had risen from 8d. to 1/10d. per lb., frozen beef from 4d. to 1/2d., English mutton from 10d. to 1/4d., frozen mutton from 4d. to 10d., Cheshire cheese from 10d. to 1/6d., potatoes from 2d. to 5d. (for 5 lb.), apples from 2d. to 6d., etc. (Some of these prices—for example that of potatoes—partially reflected genuine local shortages in Birkenhead as opposed to Liverpool, but most were the result of excess demand.) *Birkenhead News*, 5 May 1926.

(103) *Daily Courier*, 3 May 1926. Refers to New Brighton.

(104) Suggested in *Birkenhead Advertiser*, 19 May 1926.

(105) *Birkenhead News*, 12 May 1926. No advance in the wholesale prices of bacon, hams, butter, lard or cheese. These were mainly items that had been given priority treatment by the Emergency Committee. *Post and Courier Bulletin*, 10 May 1926.

(106) Where there was no gas stove in the house or where the inhabitants were sick or old, additional fuel could be obtained by permit. *Birkenhead News*, 29 May 1926 and 2 June 1926.

(107) *Monthly Journal of the Liverpool Chamber of Commerce*, June 1926, p. 109.

(108) Soon after the formation of the O.M.S., the Merseyside Branch of the British Fascists, estimated at some 2,000–3,000 strong, applied to the Liverpool Chief Constable to have its members enrolled as special constables! Initially their services were accepted, but the next day the Chief Constable withdrew his acceptance after criticism in the press and from local trade unions. *Liverpool Post and Mercury*, 5 October 1925 and 6 October 1925.

(109) There was even an emergency scheme in the north-west for the transfer of films by private vehicle. The scheme was headed, 'Keep this pinned to the wall. Whenever there is a rail strike you'll need it urgently.' *The Trade Show Critic*, May 1926.

(100) See below, Section VIII.

(111) The Birkenhead Gas Company for example claimed that with care their stock at 1 May would last 3 months. *Liverpool Post and Mercury*, 1 May 1926.

(112) *Ibid.*

(113) *Journal of Commerce*, 3 May 1926.

(114) Henry Tyrer & Co. The briquettes were probably German. We are indebted to Dr. P. N. Davies of Liverpool University for this information.

(115) Summary of Liverpool and District Grain Stocks; in quarters (including Birkenhead) *Journal of Commerce*, 3 May 1926, p. 291:—

	1 May 1926	24 April 1926	1 May 1925
Wheat	192,150	215,306	236,548
Maize	147,663	161,761	191,567
Oats	8,106	16,226	10,654
Barley	182,322	31,796	19,564

(116) *Ibid.*, 4 May 1926 and 5 May 1926.

(117) See *Liverpool Cotton Association, Weekly Circular*, 14 May 1926. Also *Daily Courier*, 4 May 1926.

(118) Liverpool Stock Exchange Committee, *Minutes*. (We are indebted to Mr. W. A. Thomas of Liverpool University for information concerning the Stock Exchange.) One of the members did offer to bring his wireless set so that the members could have the benefit of the Government's bulletins. This offer was accepted.

(119) *Monthly Journal of Liverpool Incorporated Chamber of Commerce*, June 1926.

(120) *Express and Echo Bulletin*, 8 May 1926.

(121) See *Birkenhead Advertiser*, 15 May 1926; *Post and Courier Bulletin*, 12 May 1926; *Liverpool Post and Mercury*, 15 May 1926. Buses were wire-netted in Wallasey. There was also trouble at the Bootle tram depot on 4 May 1926. *Walton Times*, 7 May 1926.

(122) Liverpool Chief Constable in *Liverpool Post and Mercury*, 15 May 1926. He may have been underestimating the total but there are no more references in the press.

(123) *Liverpool Echo*, 15 May 1926. The Government had in fact asked the brewers to cease deliveries. *British Gazette*, 11 May 1926.

(124) *Post and Courier Bulletin*, 12 May 1926.

(125) Report of the Liverpool Council of Action to the T.U.C., 10 May 1926 (T.U.C. Library).

(126) 'Whilst we are fighting for our very existence and liberty, we can still conduct ourselves like gentlemen.' McLeod, Secretary of Bootle Branch T. & G.W.U., reported in *Bootle Times*, 14 May 1926.

(127) See Watch Committee for the City of Liverpool, *Report of the Police Establishment and State of Crime for 1926*, p. 12, for the similar conclusions of the Chief Constable.

(128) There were exceptions to this. It was reported that the Wallasey tram-waymen were not enthusiastic. *Liverpool Post and Mercury*, 3 May 1926. Also the N.U.G.M.W. in Liverpool had refused to nominate representatives for the original Provisional Council of action.

(129) T. L. Drinkwater, *op. cit.*, p. 63.

(130) *Walton Times* 7 May 1926.

(131) *Liverpool Post and Mercury*, 3 May 1926.

(132) *Ibid.*

(133) *Ibid.*

(134) Liverpool Council of Action, *Strike Bulletin* No. 1, 5 May 1926.

(135) 'General Strike Documents.'

(136) *Ibid.*

(137) In response to this the Labour leader rejoined 'I can only say "God save the miners" '. See *Liverpool Official News Bulletin* and *Liverpool Echo*, 5 May 1926.

(138) *Liverpool Official News Bulletin*, 6 May 1926.

(139) See, for example, early April issues of the *Liverpool Post and Mercury*.

(140) *Daily Courier*, 30 April 1926.

(141) *Liverpool Post and Mercury*, 3 May 1926.

(142) *Birkenhead News*, 12 May 1926. This leader was headed 'England Expects'.

(143) *Journal of Commerce*, 3 May 1926. The choice offered the people was, apparently, between 'organised and stable' Britain and the 'chaos and misrule' of Russia.

(144) *Birkenhead Advertiser*, 1 May 1926.

(145) *Ibid.*, 5 May 1926.

(146) See *Parishioner*, June 1926, and *Catholic Times and Catholic Opinion*,

2 April 1926. The liberal Catholics were further hampered by Cardinal Bourne and others of their leaders who placed God securely on the side of the Government.

(147) *Birkenhead News*, 15 May 1926.

(148) In Birkenhead the first official statement that the strike had ended was displayed in a local shop surrounded by bottles of 'Tizer'. It was, not unnaturally, thought a hoax. *Birkenhead Advertiser*, 19 May 1926.

(149) At a public meeting 'The speakers claimed a victory for Trade Unionism'. *Post and Courier Bulletin*, 13 May 1926.

(150) Councillor Egan had warned the Mayor on 10 May that the running of an emergency bus service could mean the stopping of the ferries, the blackout of the town and violence, 'human nature being what it is'. See report of Birkenhead Council Meeting, 27 May (*Birkenhead Advertiser*, 29 May 1926). There was in fact a fracas at the bus depot on the first evening of volunteer operation. See *Birkenhead Advertiser*, 26 May 1926.

(151) *Echo and Express Bulletin*, 13 May 1926.

(152) See (undated) telegram from Secretary of M.C.A. to T.U.C. General Council, 'Collection of Documents Relating to General Strike' (T.U.C. Library).

(153) The feeling of uncertainty had some curious results. A service of intercession had been arranged in Wallasey for 16 May to be attended by all the civic dignitaries. At the last moment this was altered to one of thanksgiving, but when it was clear that the major strikers of the town were still out the official visit was abandoned.

(154) Reinstatement (subject to jobs being available) was to be based on seniority in each grade; there were to be no more strikes without negotiations; persons could be moved to other positions and the railway did not surrender the right to claim damages. Nor did the settlement apply to anyone 'guilty of violence or intimidation'. See, for example, *Birkenhead Advertiser*, 15 May 1926.

(155) *Birkenhead News*, 15 May 1926.

(156) The Garston docks were owned by the L.M. & S.R. See *Garston News*, 21 May 1926.

(157) T.&G.W.U. (Waterways Group) in *Annual Report and Balance Sheet*, 1926, p. 25.

(158) T.&G.W.U. 'Report of a Joint Meeting of Officials, Area Committee, Group and Branch Committees, Clifton House, Liverpool, June 10 1926' (duplicated). This meeting was addressed by Ernest Bevin. The situation was further complicated because many of the jobs had been taken by union men.

(159) *Wallasey and Wirral Chronicle*, 15 May 1926.

(160) *Liverpool Post and Mercury*, 17 January 1927.

(161) See Birkenhead Council Meeting, 27 May 1926. Reported in *Birkenhead News*, 29 May 1926. Also Report of Birkenhead Tramway Committee in *Birkenhead News*, 26 May 1926.

(162) *Liverpool Echo*, 23 June 1926.

(163) See *Liverpool Weekly Post*, 15 May 1926. The decision was 'hailed as a signal act of magnanimity'.

(164) 'Flour Milling' in M. P. Fogarty, *Further Studies in Industrial Organisation*, (1948), p. 64.

(165) *Liverpool Echo*, 18 May 1926.

(166) T. & G. W.U. 'Report of a Joint Meeting of Officials, Area Committee, Group and Branch Committees, Clifton House, Liverpool, June 10 1926'.

(167) *200 H.C. Debates* 5s., p. 391, 24 November 1926. James Sexton to Minister of Labour.

(168) *Post and Courier Bulletin*, 10 May 1926.

(169) *Liverpool Echo*, 19 May 1926.

(170) *Birkenhead Advertiser*, 19 May 1926.

(171) W. Smith at monthly meeting of Liverpool City Council, 2 June 1926. See *The Liverpool Official Red Book*, 1927.

(172) L. Hogan. *ibid.*

(173) See *Diocese of Liverpool Review*, Vol. 1, No. 2, June 1926, pp. 47–48 for an interesting summary of the reasons for the quietness of the dispute.

(174) *Garston Strike Bulletin* (undated) in 'General Strike Documents'.

(175) According to Jack Hayes, M.P., there was a large amount of co-operation between the authorities, the strike leaders and the strikers themselves. See *The Home Library Liverpool Bulletin*, 10 May 1926.

(176) The takings on the Liverpool trams for the first two weeks of May were 71 per cent of the takings in the last week of April and the third week in May. See Liverpool Corporation Tramways *Report* for 1927. The most serious losses were probably felt by those shipping firms whose vessels sailed partially loaded in order to clear the port before the strike.

(177) A contrary view was given in the *Monthly Journal of the Liverpool Incorporated Chamber of Commerce*, May 1926. The General Strike 'has prejudiced our markets, swept away the good that was just beginning to show for months of patient endurance and effort to revive our home and overseas trade, jeopardised the future of all industries, rendered the burden imposed by the Budget more discouraging, and has made that essential easing of taxation, even next year certainly more remote'. If this were the case it is difficult to see why the Stock Exchange was so unconcerned.

(178) Local rationing of coal continued and the Birkenhead Council was forced to alter (for the better) its contracting arrangements. *Birkenhead Advertiser*, 15 May 1926.

(179) Conservative advertisement in *Liverpool Echo*, 28 October 1926.

T

Index